Rand Smith
1110 Madison St.
Evanston, IL 60202

Italian Literature and Thought Series

The Italian Literature and Thought Series makes available in English some of the representative works of Italian culture. Although it focuses on the modern and contemporary periods, it does not neglect the humanistic roots of Italian thought. The series will include new scholarly monographs, anthologies, and critically updated republications of canonical works, as well as works of general interest.

ADVISORY BOARD

BEYOND
RIGHT AND LEFT

Democratic Elitism in Mosca and Gramsci

* * *

MAURICE A. FINOCCHIARO

YALE UNIVERSITY PRESS

NEW HAVEN & LONDON

Designed by James J. Johnson and set in Stemple Garamond type by Tseng Information
Systems, Inc. Durham, North Carolina.
Printed in the United States of America.

Library of Congress Cataloging-in-Publication Data

Finocchiaro, Maurice A., 1942–
Beyond right and left: democratic elitism in Mosca and Gramsci /
Maurice A. Finocchiaro.
p.   cm. — (Italian literature and thought series)
Includes bibliographical references and index.
ISBN 0-300-07535-9

1. Mosca, Gaetano, 1858–1941—Contributions in political science.
2. Gramsci, Antonio, 1891–1937—Contributions in political science.
3. Democracy.   4. Elite (Social sciences)   5. Right and left
(Political science)   I. Title.   II. Series.
JC265.M65F56   1999
320.5'0945—dc21   98-8642

A catalogue record for this book is available from the British Library.

The paper in this book meets the guidelines for permanence and durability of the Committee
on Production Guidelines for Book Longevity of the Council on Library Resources.

10 9 8 7 6 5 4 3 2 1

CONTENTS

PREFACE

Antonio Gramsci (1891-1937) is the controversial founding father of Italian Communism. His imprisonment by the Fascists during the last ten years of his tragic life had the paradoxical effect of sparing him from Stalinism; it also turned him into a bona fide social and political theorist. His theoretical legacy is found in his Prison Notebooks, despite their unedited and fragmentary character. He is widely regarded as "the patron saint of the Left" (Clark 1975), as well as the originator of a cultural version of Marxism (sometimes labeled Gramscism) immune to the intellectual criticism and economic failures that have rendered other versions obsolete. However, the scholarly accuracy of this interpretation is a matter of controversy, and Gramsci's real thought remains to be uncovered.

Gaetano Mosca (1858-1941) is best known as the author of a treatise originally published in 1896 under the title *Elements of Political Science,* and then translated into English as *The Ruling Class* (1939); he is a classic source for the so-called theory of elites, or for the elitist school in political sociology, as well as a founder of the discipline of political science. There is also a scholarly consensus that his "political science" had practical and ideological implications, which he tried to actualize in his own activity as a columnist and as a government official in the executive and legislative branches. These implications are widely regarded as conservative in character; indeed, many regard him as a classic exponent of the Right.

Against such traditional portrayals, this work offers an interpretation of Mosca's and Gramsci's doctrines as both belonging to the same tradition of political theory. The tradition in question is that of democratic elitism. By "elitism" is here meant a theoretical orientation which takes the most fundamental principle to be the distinction between elites and masses or leaders and led; all political phenomena are accordingly interpreted in terms of various relationships between the two groups. By "democracy" is here meant the special relationship between elites and masses such that elites are open to renewal through the influx of elements from the masses; and this definition is the basis for an original and distinctive theory of democracy. The democratic elitism of Mosca and Gramsci also includes a conception of political liberty as a relationship such that authority flows from the masses to the elites; and this is a feature of their approach which may also be called democratic in the ordinary sense of the term, though not in the technical elitist sense.

One implication of this interpretation is that Gramsci is much less of a radical revolutionary, Mosca much less of a reactionary conservative, and both thinkers much closer to the political center and to each other than commonly supposed. On the other hand, this interpretation also implies that theoretically, intellectually, and conceptually they are much more radical than is ordinarily believed because democratic elitism represents an extremely distinctive orientation in political theory. Hence, the interpretation also undermines the viability of the dichotomy between the Left and the Right.

This interpretation of their thought is documented and elaborated primarily by means of an analysis of Mosca's most important works (including *The Ruling Class*) and of Gramsci's Prison Notebooks. Further, I present an emblematic case study or critical comparison, which focuses on some significant similarities between the speeches that both Gramsci and Mosca made in the Italian Parliament in 1925 opposing the Fascist law against Freemasonry.

Although the emphasis is on textual analysis and interpretation and conceptual reconstruction, the discussion contains enough criticism and evaluation to suggest that democratic elitism of the kind being attributed to Mosca and Gramsci is an interesting, viable, and important alternative in political theory.

This project was originally conceived in 1984 at the end of a line of research which then resulted in my book *Gramsci and the History of Dialectical Thought* (Cambridge University Press, 1988). In relation to that earlier work, the following should be noted. Like that book, the present work consists largely of textual analysis, interpretive reconstruction, and critical evaluation; but whereas in that earlier book the focus was on Gramsci as a philosopher, the focus of the present one is on Gramsci as a political theorist. Whereas the earlier book was in part a critical comparison of Gramsci and Benedetto Croce, the present one contains a critical comparison of Gramsci and Mosca. Whereas the conceptual focus of the earlier book was the interrelated pair of dialectic and criticism, the conceptual focus now is democracy and elitism. It also turns out that the dialectical-critical interpretation and evaluation advanced earlier correspond to the democratic-elitist interpretation and evaluation now advanced, in the sense that the democratic-elitist orientation is what one would expect as a result of the dialectical-critical manner of thinking, and vice versa.

All quotations from Gramsci have been translated by the present author from the Italian critical editions of his works. Thus, to facilitate cross-referencing, the Appendix gives a concordance table indicating the page-by-page correspondence between passages in the critical edition of the Prison Notebooks (Gramsci 1975b) and the various volumes of English translations, edited by Marks (1957), Hoare and Nowell-Smith (1971), Forgacs and Nowell-Smith (1985), Forgacs (1988), Buttigieg (1992, 1996), and Boothman (1995).

Acknowledgments

In creating this work, I have received valuable assistance from many persons and institutions, and here I should like to express my acknowledgment of them.

Beginning with my own institution, the University of Nevada, Las Vegas, I have been fortunate to enjoy the freedom of research necessary to pursue investigations which, because of their very broad interdisciplinary ramifications (not to mention the geopolitical ones), might have encountered obstacles in a different academic environment. In particular, I have benefited from the following: appointment as Distinguished Professor since 1991; a research leave in the year 1991-1992; a reduction in teaching load in spring 1993; the Nevada State Board of Regents' Researcher Award in 1993; and a sabbatical leave in fall 1994.

I also gratefully acknowledge the support of the following institutions: first and foremost, the American Council of Learned Societies, for a one-year fellowship in 1991–1992, during which this book was re-searched and partly written and without which it would not have come into being; the Hoover Institution at Stanford, for the privilege of being a visiting scholar there in the summer of 1984, when this work was first conceived; the Library of the Chamber of Deputies of the Republic of Italy, for the privilege of using its collections and for photocopying assis-tance during my seven-month stay in Rome in 1991–1992; the Department of Political Science at the University of Rome and the editorial offices of the magazine *Mondoperaio* and of the journal *Physis* in Rome, for clerical and other practical assistance during the same period; the Departments of Political Science at the University of Genoa and at the University of Bologna for the opportunity to lecture there in 1992; and the University of Cagliari and the Istituto Gramsci della Sardegna for their invitation, hospitality, inspiration, and opportunity for a lecture there in 1996.

Many individuals provided encouragement, support, comments, or criticism at various stages of this lengthy process. I am indebted espe-cially to Walter Adamson (Emory University), Norberto Bobbio (Uni-versity of Turin), Luigi Bonanate (University of Turin), Joseph Buttigieg (University of Notre Dame), James Colbert (Fitchburg State College), Mario D'Addio (University of Rome), Joseph Femia (Liverpool Uni-versity), Benedetto Fontana (Baruch College), Dante Germino (Univer-sity of Virginia), Valentino Gerratana (Istituto Gramsci, Rome), Tullio Gregory (University of Rome), Renate Holub (University of California, Berkeley), Emilia Lamaro (Rome), Domenico Losurdo (University of Urbino), Rita Medici (University of Bologna), Carlo Mongardini (Uni-versity of Rome), Giancarlo Nonnoi (University of Cagliari), Eugenio Orrù (Cagliari), Luciano Pellicani (LUISS, Rome), Mauro Pesce (Uni-versity of Bologna), Gianfranco Poggi (University of Virginia), Antonio Santucci (Istituto Gramsci, Rome), Giorgio Sola (University of Genoa), Claudio Torneo (Rome), Paolo Valesio (Yale University) and my institu-tional colleagues: James Malek, Cyrill Pasterk, and John Unrue.

Finally, acknowledgments are due to the appropriate publishers and editors, on account of the fact that a few parts of this work have appeared in different form in print, as follows: portions of section 3 of the Intro-duction appeared in my entry on "Gramsci," in *The Cambridge Dic-tionary of Philosophy*, ed. R. Audi (Cambridge University Press, 1995), p. 304; the bulk of Chapter 1, in Italian translation, in my "Gramsci e Gae-tano Mosca," in *Gramsci e l'Italia*, ed. R. Giacomini *et al.* (Naples: Edi-zioni La Città del Sole, 1994), pp. 115–64; parts of section 4 of Chapter 5 in

"Democracy, Philosophy, and Gramsci," *The Philosophical Forum*, vol. 29 (1997-1998); the bulk of Chapter 7, in Italian translation, in "Gramsci, Mosca, e la Massoneria," *Teoria politica* (Turin), 1993, 9(2):135–61; and portions of the Appendix in the appendix to my *Gramsci and the History of Dialectical Thought* (Cambridge University Press, 1988), pp. 249–53.

INTRODUCTION

RIGHT, LEFT, AND CLASSIC APPROACHES TO GRAMSCI

ANTONIO GRAMSCI (1891-1937) represents a unique case in modern political and intellectual history because his life and writings can appeal to the Left and to the Right, as well as to political theorists who shun practical involvement and to common people who seek political enlightenment or inspiration. Thus, on the one hand, he has been hailed as the "Patron Saint of the Left"[1] by such a cultural icon as the London *Times Literary Supplement.* On the other hand, recently he has become something of an anti-hero of the Right, where he has attracted the attention of no less than Rush Limbaugh.[2] And anyone can examine Gramsci's life and writings and end up agreeing with British historian James Joll's judgment that he is a "true intellectual hero of our time."[3] Of course, the respective reasons for such appeal are different and will be seen presently. However, the possibility of such diversity of appeal suggests to me that we are faced with a modern classic.

1. Rush Limbaugh's Gramsci: Anti-Hero of the Right

The geopolitical collapse of communism, together with the end of the Cold War, must surely be ranked as one of the most significant events of our time. Applying Socrates' dictum that the unexamined life is not worth living, one could say that no one can lead an intelligent life in the contemporary world without some critical examination of the demise of that political system.

One of the first questions that come to mind is, Who won the Cold War? Many would answer that the United States won. It would be difficult to disagree with that interpretation, which leads to another question: If the United States and the West won the Cold War against communism and socialism, why are so many ideas on which these philosophies were based still so popular in the West?

One explanation for the apparent discrepancy has been advanced by Rush Limbaugh,[4] among others. In his book *See, I Told You So,* he claims that, while the United States was winning the economic and geopolitical Cold War, leftist ideas were winning the cultural war. In turn, the reason the Left has been winning this war is that leftist thinkers have a better understanding of the importance of culture and have articulated a theory about cultural struggle and its role in social change.

Limbaugh then names Gramsci as the principal author of this theory of cultural struggle. Limbaugh formulates the problem and summarizes Gramsci's ideas as follows:

We have lost control of our cultural institutions. Liberalism long ago captured the arts, the press, the entertainment industry, the universities, the schools, the libraries, the foundations, etc. This was no accident.

In the early 1900s, an obscure Italian communist by the name of Antonio Gramsci theorized that it would take a "long march through the institutions" before socialism and relativism would be victorious. Up until then, most of the radical left still believed that they would take power only when they convinced enough people in the working class to take up arms in their cause. But Gramsci theorized that by capturing these key institutions and using their power, cultural values would be changed, traditional morals would be broken down, and the stage would be set for the political and economic power of the West to fall.

The key, according to Gramsci, was to change the way the whole society thinks about its problems. . . .

Gramsci succeeded in defining a strategy for waging cultural warfare—a tactic that has been adopted by the modern left, and which remains the last great hope for chronic America-bashers.[5]

Now, it would be easy to criticize many of the details of Limbaugh's account, such as his apparent conflation of liberalism, socialism, relativism, radicalism, and the Left; his apparent attribution to Gramsci of such attitudes as rejection of "traditional morals"; and his apparent unawareness that the cultural theory of socialist revolution is an *interpreta-*

tion of Gramsci's thought. However, such criticism of Limbaugh would distract us from our main point here. For the fact is that Limbaugh is *essentially* correct in claiming that left-wing ideas tend to dominate U.S. cultural institutions, that a key reason for this is the Left's greater appreciation of the cultural theory of social change, and that Gramsci is the classic source for such a theory.

The more important point in this context is to draw the proper consequences from these essential facts. One conclusion is explicitly drawn by Limbaugh himself. That is, conservatives and the Right should become involved in the cultural struggle: "The Culture War is a bilateral conflict, my friends. There's no reason on earth we should be content to sit back and watch our values and our cultural heritage slip away. Why don't we simply get in the game and start competing for control of those key cultural institutions? In other words, why not fight back?" [6]

Although Limbaugh does not say so, this conclusion is actually another Gramscian thesis. For Gramsci also theorized that knowledge of one's opponents is essential in any struggle, and that if an imbalance exists between two opponents in this regard, the side which understands the opponent usually has a decisive advantage over the side which does not.

Moreover, I want to stress another conclusion, which Limbaugh does not draw explicitly but which seems to be clearly implied. That is, given that Gramsci's cultural theory accounts for the success achieved by the Left at the level of cultural institutions, and given that conservatism and the Right must join the cultural struggle, it follows that conservatives and right-wingers should seriously study Gramsci in order to learn better what to do and how to do it.

Thus, Gramsci's works can and should become the object of study by both sides in the cultural struggle. If this prescription is feasible, its feasibility in turn becomes a clue of the correctness of Gramsci's theory. For, as he also theorized, a clue to the objectivity and scientific validity of a social theory is the fact that it can be used by both sides.

Limbaugh is not the only conservative writer to regard Gramsci as some kind of anti-hero. In Italy, there is a long tradition of conservative Catholics who study Gramsci in order to fight his ideas more effectively.[7] The example most relevant here is that of Michael Novak because his argument is very similar to that of Limbaugh and also takes into account the economic failure of Marxism.

The March 20, 1989, issue of *Forbes* magazine published a column by Novak revealingly entitled "The Gramscists Are Coming." It was meant as a warning to the effect that, now that the West had proved the superiority of its economic system over socialism, it was going to have to deal with the cultural version of Marxism—Gramscism.

Novak is certainly right to contrast Gramscism with ordinary Marxism, which tries to bring about the socialist dream by economic means, such as central planning and the nationalization of industrial production. It is also important to realize, as Novak does, that the means employed by Gramscism are peaceful and cultural—for example, education, communication, and persuasion. And it is perceptive of him to note that Gramscism has a special attraction for a segment of American academia.

There is some irony, however, when Novak advises die-hard academics to "take into account the rambling wrecks of actual Marxist societies"[8] and to study the American system. The irony is that this advice corresponds in large part to what Gramsci himself ended up doing in the last ten years of his life, from 1926 to 1937: a key background concern was his attempt to learn from the general failure of socialist revolutions in Western Europe in the decade 1917–1926, as well as from the problematic evolution of the Bolshevik Revolution in Russia; and a central focus of his Prison Notebooks was the phenomenon of what he called "Americanism and Fordism."[9]

Even in his moments of youthful and high revolutionary zeal, Gramsci's ideal bears an astounding resemblance to the one which Novak quotes from one of the American founding fathers, James Madison. Novak makes an eloquent plea for realism and anti-utopianism; in the process he quotes Madison as saying that a "cool and candid people will at once reflect, that the purest of human blessings must have a portion of alloy in them, that the choice must always be made, if not of the lesser evil, at least of the greater, not the perfect good."[10] In fact, we find Gramsci in 1917 asserting that "we conceive life as always revolutionary, and thus tomorrow we shall not declare the world we have built to be final, but rather we shall always leave open the road toward betterment, toward better harmonies."[11]

I am not saying that the conclusions reached by Gramsci then are the same as the ones Novak thinks one should reach now. Rather, I would argue that, if by Gramscism one means the pursuit of the usual Marxist ends by cultural, peaceful means, then Gramsci was no more of a Gramscist than Marx was a Marxist. The main difference is that Marx lived long enough to feel the need to clarify, "Moi, je ne suis pas marxiste," whereas

Gramsci's premature death gave him no opportunity to oppose, and indeed actually triggered, the construction of the myth of Gramscism. The myth was largely contrived by Palmiro Togliatti, the leader of the Italian Communist Party for about forty years from 1926 to 1964, about which more presently.[12]

However, like all myths that achieve a certain level of popularity, Gramscism must have had a basis in fact. And there is no question that Gramsci's life, his death, and its aftermath lent themselves very easily to the construction of the myth. To begin to explain both why the myth of Gramscism became possible and why it is no longer acceptable, it will be useful to give a sketch of Gramsci's life from the generally "heroic" point of view suggested by Joll.[13]

Who was this "obscure Italian communist" of whom Limbaugh speaks and whose theory will allegedly remedy the disadvantage conservatives have suffered in their culture war with liberals? Joll has formulated the memorable description that Gramsci is "a true intellectual hero of our time,"[14] not only because of the depth, originality, and influence of his ideas but also because he is "one of the greatest examples of the independence of the human spirit from its material limitations."[15]

2. Sardinian, Hunchback, Outcast: "True Intellectual Hero"

Gramsci was born in 1891 on the Italian island of Sardinia. He grew up and lived there for about twenty years until he began attending the University of Turin in northern Italy in 1911. His birthplace and geographical background are the first significant biographical detail that needs to be mentioned in any account of Gramsci's life. In fact, Sardinia is the second-largest island in the Mediterranean, with an area slightly larger than the state of Massachusetts. It was then (and remains today) one of the most backward and isolated regions of the country. Moreover, Sardinians speak a dialect that is incomprehensible to other Italians; indeed some would regard Sardinian as a distinct Romance language. A convergence of geographical, historical, economic, cultural, and linguistic factors have thus made the island a very different place from the rest of Italy. It is not surprising, therefore, that ever since the unification of Italy in 1861 a separatist movement has been under way to make the island independent; although this movement has never gained great popularity, it has never completely disappeared. Gramsci was always keenly aware of being a Sardinian; in the Italian context this meant that he saw himself as a member of an ethnic minority which had suffered and continued to suffer many disadvantages.

At the age of three or four, Gramsci was the victim of an accident that left him permanently handicapped. Falling from the arms of a baby-sitter, he incurred injuries that never properly healed. The injuries are believed to have been the cause of his humpback and less-than-average height. Besides the initial physical pain and the later clearly visible physical deformity, Gramsci also suffered from various indignities during the initial attempts to cure him. For example, during one period soon after the accident he was hung from the ceiling with his hands stretched above his head and tied to strings; the hope was that this procedure would straighten his back. Indeed, his overall health was never good. A sickly constitution, malnutrition, and imprisonment subjected him to a host of ailments, ranging from nervous breakdowns, hernias, bad teeth, and uricacidemia to high blood pressure, arteriosclerosis, Pott's disease (tuberculosis of the spine), and tuberculosis of the lungs.

As if the ethnic disadvantage and the physical handicap were not enough, Gramsci endured a socially and psychologically traumatic experience in his childhood. His family can be regarded as middle class, for his father was a minor government employee working in the office of voter registration in a small town. When Gramsci was seven years old, his father was charged with bureaucratic crimes and lost his job, and two years after that he was tried and imprisoned for about five years. Though the charges and the condemnation stemmed from local political power struggles, one can imagine the impression that the incident must have made on the child and the effects it had on the family. There were six other children; the mother's moral strength and hard work kept the family from starving. As soon as Gramsci finished elementary school at age twelve, he had to halt his formal education and for two years worked full-time in a government office that kept real estate registration records. Working ten hours a day, and half a day on Sunday, he earned enough to enable the family to buy one kilogram of bread a day.[16] When his father got out of prison two years later, Gramsci (then fifteen) was able to resume his studies.

Despite all these adversities, Gramsci's intelligence and superior academic achievements were evident, and so his parents encouraged him to pursue his studies. On completing high school in 1911 at age twenty, he applied for and received a scholarship to attend the University of Turin.

For the next four years he studied linguistics, literature, history, and philosophy. His intention had been to major in linguistics, but he discontinued formal course work in 1915 and never did complete his degree. Instead, he became increasingly interested in social, political, and cultural problems, and increasingly involved in writing articles and columns for various socialist newspapers and magazines.

The new environment in Turin acted as a catalyst for the social, political, and cultural awareness he had acquired growing up as a hunchback in a depressed area and under the stigma of his father's criminal record. In fact, the contrast between Sardinia and Turin could hardly have been greater. Turin was a big city, a world-class center of modern industry (the home of the Fiat automobile works), and the seat of a first-rate university which had attracted an unusually large number of prominent scientists and scholars. The city was also the former capital of the small state of Piedmont, which had led the struggle for Italian unification and whose king had thus become the first monarch of the Kingdom of Italy in 1861.

Moreover, geopolitical developments naturally made great demands on the attention and thinking of someone like Gramsci. In 1915, a year after World War I broke out, Italy entered the alliance with England, France, and Russia against Germany and the Austrian-Hungarian Empire. Like all wars, this one had an element of struggle for existence. But it also had epoch-making social repercussions. In fact, large numbers of common people were engaged in the military struggle; for example, 600,000 Italians lost their lives during the war. Therefore, large numbers of people were compelled to play an active part (however small) in events of worldwide significance. When the war ended in 1918, these masses could not simply go back to life as they had known it before. Further, the economic restructuring caused by the end of hostilities produced great economic dislocations.

In addition, even before the world war ended in 1918, the Bolshevik Revolution of November 1917 had broken out. The international political struggle between communism and capitalism had begun. It would last about seventy years, until Gorbachev's perestroika and the dissolution of the Soviet Union put an end to the Cold War. Early on, the Bolshevik Revolution was followed not only by civil war in the Soviet Union and an international attempt by other countries to contain the new menace, but also by attempts to duplicate the proletarian revolution in other parts of the world. Therefore, in many European countries, including Italy, outright civil war was narrowly averted. A significant party in this quasi-civil war was Fascism, which constituted one response to both the world war and the Russian Revolution.

It is not surprising, therefore, that in the five years from 1915 to 1920 Gramsci wrote hundreds of articles discussing current events. His emphasis was on the cultural, intellectual, and philosophical aspects of political and economic developments. His orientation was generally socialist, though his was undoubtedly an original version of socialism, and he engaged in polemics against other socialists as well as against non-socialists. He also became increasingly active in organizing laborers in the many factories in Turin. In the years 1919–1920 he was a strong advocate of the factory council movement, which was dedicated to the advancement of both democratic ideals and labor interests through the organization of workers into groups based in the workplace and centering on the actual process of production. Those two years witnessed so many demonstrations, strikes, occupations of factories, and other unrest that they came to be know as the Red Biennium.

The failure of the factory council movement and Gramsci's disenchantment with the policies and behavior of the Italian Socialist Party led him to support the creation of a separate communist party in January 1921. Thus, for the next six years, until his arrest in November 1926, Gramsci was primarily a politician and political organizer. To be sure, he continued his journalistic writing, but actual politics increasingly took up his time.

For the first year of the new communist party's existence, Gramsci was merely a member of its central committee and the leader of the Turin communists known as the *Ordine Nuovo* group. *Ordine Nuovo* (new order) was the title of a weekly journal which had begun publication on May 1, 1919, with Gramsci as the chief editor. It became a daily newspaper on January 1, 1921. The reason for Gramsci's initially limited involvement in party activities was that the dominant group was led by a Neapolitan engineer named Amadeo Bordiga, who conceived the party in an excessively intellectualist, elitist, sectarian, and avant-gardist fashion, and Gramsci disagreed with this conception.

At the second party congress in March 1922 in Rome, Gramsci was selected to represent the party in the executive committee of the Third International, the so-called Comintern, in Moscow. In May 1922, then, he left for Russia, where he remained for about a year. The trip saved him from arrest when, as a result of the March on Rome in the fall, the Fascists gained control of the Italian government and arrested most of the communist leaders. While in Russia Gramsci also married the Russian woman who would bear him two sons.

In November 1923, the Third International sent Gramsci to Vienna to be closer to Italy and thus more effective in helping to run the Italian party, whose persecution by the Fascists continued. During the six months he remained in Vienna, he took the leading role, through correspondence, in a reorganization of the Italian Communist Party along more democratic lines. He favored an expansion of the party's power base to include peasants as well as industrial workers, a greater responsiveness by the party leaders to influence from the general membership, greater openness and more freedom of discussion in running the party, and more tolerance toward dissident factions. It so happened that Gramsci's approach also corresponded to the one favored at that particular juncture by the Third International in Moscow.

In April 1924 general elections were held in Italy, the Communist Party took part in them, and Gramsci was elected to the Chamber of Deputies of the Italian Parliament. Because members of Parliament enjoyed parliamentary immunity from arrest, this post enabled him to return to Italy, even though the Fascists had won a majority and therefore still controlled the government. Soon after, in August, Gramsci became the general secretary of his party. For the next two years he thus lived in Rome, with two jobs on his hands.

As party leader, he was responsible for its democratic reorganization along the lines just mentioned, and for the planning of a general party congress which would ratify the reorganization. The convention was held in the French city of Lyons because in Italy the Fascist persecution was (if anything) intensifying. At the congress the platform and policies proposed by Gramsci received the endorsement of 91 percent of the delegates. The losing opponent was the party's previous leader, Bordiga.

As a member of Parliament, Gramsci had to decide what attitude to adopt toward the government as well as toward the other opposition parties. Taking a stand became especially critical because soon after the new legislative session began in 1924, a socialist member of Parliament named Giacomo Matteotti was murdered by Fascist sympathizers who were widely believed to have been instigated by the top Fascist officials, and perhaps by the Prime Minister Mussolini himself. As a result, all non-Fascist parties left Parliament and tried to organize an effective counterassembly. At first the Communist Party joined this antiparliamentary move and tried to convince the other opposition parties to organize mass demonstrations to bring the Fascist government down. This plan was rejected by the other parties, which tended to favor a more legalistic approach involving the king, who was after all still the head of the state. Partly because of this disagreement, the Communist Party, led by Gramsci, was the only opposition party to go back into Parliament when the chamber of deputies reopened in the fall of 1924. Thus, it seems that Gramsci played the role of more or less loyal opposition for the next two years. Unfortunately, the return to Parliament helped the Fascists overcome the Matteotti crisis and consolidate their power.

The events that put an end to Gramsci's political career were as follows. In the fall of 1926, as a result of a failed attempt to assassinate Mussolini, the Fascists convinced the king to endorse a decree expelling from Parliament all deputies who were not attending. In fact, with the exception of the Communists, the opposition parties were still boycotting official legislative activity. In an obvious abuse of power, it was decided to include the Communists in the expulsion, even though they had gone back to the chamber long before. Then some special laws were passed, and a Special Tribunal for the Defense of the State was created to deal with transgressions of these laws. This development led to the arrest of Gramsci and other Communist leaders who had not yet gone into exile. For a number of reasons, he had chosen not to leave the country, even though his life had become increasingly difficult and he could have predicted that sooner or later he would be arrested. From November of 1926 until the end of his life, he would endure various states of imprisonment in about half a dozen different locations.

For four years, ever since the March on Rome in the fall of 1922, the Fascist government had conducted "legal" persecution of the Italian Communist Party and of opposition parties in general. The legal persecution was, of course, in addition to the illegal terrorism it inspired or secretly supported. Opposition politicians were arrested and prosecuted on such charges as conspiracy, membership in a seditious organization, or incitement to insurrection and to class hatred. However, in almost every case, the judicial branch, which was still autonomous, refused to cooperate and acquitted the defendants. The measures taken in the fall of 1926 were meant to bypass the courts and the regular judicial process.

For about one week Gramsci was held without charges (and even without being booked) at the main prison in Rome. Then the Roman chief of police filed a complaint requesting that Gramsci be held in police confinement because of his subversive ideas and activities. This allowed the application of the new laws, and so after another week Gramsci was confined on the small island of Ustica, off the north coast of Sicily. While imprisoned in Rome, Gramsci wrote a letter to his landlady asking for three books from his apartment: a German grammar, a linguistics text-book, and Dante's *Divine Comedy.*

After about a month, the Fascists decided to hold a trial for Gramsci and other communist leaders. The Special Tribunal for the Defense of the State issued an arrest warrant, mentioning the usual charges. Gramsci was taken to a prison in Milan, where for about a year he underwent as-sorted pretrial interrogations and depositions; the authorities were also trying to gather or produce new incriminating evidence by planting pris-oners who would inform on Gramsci.

It was during his Milan imprisonment that Gramsci wrote a famous letter to his sister-in-law in which he stated that he planned to start work on a research project dealing with historical, philosophical, and political questions. He added that, given his situation, he wanted to undertake the project "from the point of view of eternity."[17] His wife had returned to Russia, and he had begun a relationship with her sister, who was living in Italy. In fact, Gramsci's sister-in-law (Tatiana Schucht), who remained in Italy until his death, was his main interlocutor and source of comfort during those years. She would often move to towns where he happened to be held, and would stay there for months. She is also the person who gained possession of the manuscripts of the notebooks when Gramsci died in 1937, and she managed to send them to Italian communist leaders who were in exile in Russia. They began publishing the notebooks after World War II.

In May 1928, Gramsci was moved to Rome to stand trial together with other communists. Since the trial was being held by the Special Tri-bunal, the result was a foregone conclusion. The only witnesses against Gramsci were the chiefs of police of different cities. He was found guilty and sentenced to twenty years.

Because of his ill health, he was sent a special prison in the town of Turi, in the region of Puglie of southern Italy. He arrived in July 1928 and stayed there for about four years. Soon he was able to get a single cell, number 1 of section number 1, closest to the guards. Having received permission to read and write, he was also furnished with pen, pencil, and paper. The paper consisted of single notebooks, which he had to fill with writing one by one before he could obtain another. He began jotting down his first notes in February 1929. Eventually, he used a total of thirty-three notebooks.

In November 1932, on the occasion of the anniversary of the Fascist March on Rome, his prison term was reduced by eight years, to twelve. During his Turi imprisonment there was some talk of an exchange of prisoners with the Soviet Union, but nothing came of this plan. Instead, his health began to deteriorate, and in March 1933 he collapsed and was unable to get up. The sister-in-law finally succeeded in arranging a visit by a private doctor, who reported that Gramsci was so ill that he should be moved to a regular hospital or clinic. As a result, international support for his release was voiced by such people as Romain Rolland in France,[18] the Archbishop of Canterbury in Britain, and Mahatma Gandhi in India.[19] Gramsci himself refused to apply for a pardon, which would have necessitated some admission of wrongdoing. In December 1933, he was moved to a private clinic in the town of Formia, in central Italy.

Gramsci's health did not improve in Formia, and he filed an application for parole on grounds of ill health. The parole was granted in October 1934. It took another year, until August 1935, before he was allowed to move to another clinic, this one in Rome. He would remain there for two years. However, by then he was so sick that he even stopped writing in his notebooks. His parole officially ended on April 25, 1937, but he died two days later, attended by his faithful sister-in-law. The immediate cause of death was cerebral hemorrhage. Gramsci is now buried in the English Cemetery in Rome.

3. The Gramsci Myth: "Patron Saint of the Left"

The most widespread interpretation of Gramsci's life and thought was popularized by Palmiro Togliatti, Gramsci's college classmate, his successor as leader of the Italian Communist Party, and an important figure in his own right. After the fall of Fascism and the end of World War II, Togliatti supervised the edition of Gramsci's writings and read into them what came to be known as the "Italian road to socialism": a strategy for bringing about the traditional Marxist goals of the classless society and the nationalization of the means of production by cultural means, such as education and persuasion; the idea was that social and cultural institutions had to be conquered first; control of these would then yield the desired changes in economic and political institutions. This approach contrasted with Bolshevism, whose advocates had first seized political power and then used it to change culture and society. An essential part of the rationale for the divergent Italian Communist approach was, in Gramsci's words, that "in the East the state was everything, but civil society was primordial and gelatinous; in the West there was a proper relation between state and civil society, and when the state trembled, a sturdy structure of civil society was immediately revealed."[20]

This strategy was extremely successful for about thirty years, during which the party experienced constant growth. The popularity of Gramsci's writings grew accordingly, and gradually but steadily spread outside Italy.

However, beginning in the late seventies, Gramscism went into a continuing decline in Italy. (I use the term to apply to Togliatti's interpretation of Gramsci as just sketched.) The decline had several causes, not the least of which were Gorbachev's leadership of the Soviet Union in the late 1980s, the dissolution of the Soviet Union, and the end of the Cold War. One of the causes was cultural: in 1975 a critical edition of the Notebooks was published, and since then Togliatti's interpretation has come to be seen as less and less defensible. No new consensus has emerged yet, nor is one likely to emerge anytime soon, because it would have to be based on interpretive and analytical spadework of a sort that has barely begun. The present inquiry is in part a contribution to that effort.

My interpretation is along the following lines. I would begin by stressing Gramsci's famous article of 1917, in which he welcomed the Bolshevik Revolution as a "revolution against *Capital.*"[21] He meant that, rather than being the overthrow of capitalism, the revolution was a refutation of the deterministic interpretation of Marx's *Capital,* according to which socialism could come into being only through the gradual evolution of capitalism; the revolution was also a confirmation that the willful radical transformation of social institutions was possible. Partly in light of these conclusions, in the next few years Gramsci took a leading role in the unrest which followed the end of World War I in Italy; the Red Biennium of the years 1919–1920 included the workers' occupation of the factories but climaxed in the essential defeat of the workers.

I would then stress that, being of a historical and empirical turn of mind, Gramsci always tried to learn from experience. So he concluded that a major cause of this defeat was inadequate *political* leadership by the Italian socialist party. Thus, in 1921 he favored the creation of a new political party to provide the proper leadership; this was the beginning of the Italian Communist Party. However, the new party was no more successful than the old one; in fact, in the following year the Fascists staged the March on Rome, gained control of the government, and arrested the party leaders. As mentioned earlier, Gramsci was one of the few who escaped arrest, because he was then in the Soviet Union as the party's representative to the Communist International. Nevertheless, the latest defeat called for a new diagnosis, and so Gramsci located a major source of the problem in the undemocratic and sectarian character of the just-founded party.

He soon had the opportunity to begin acting on this new lesson. After the 1924 parliamentary elections that allowed him to return to Italy as leader of the party, Gramsci tried to give it more mass appeal, especially among peasants. The task was a difficult one, partly because the Fascists were consolidating their rule, and so the Communist Party had to operate in a semi-clandestine manner. There were other reasons for this difficulty, but Gramsci did not perceive them until later, after another setback—his own arrest—forced him to do further rethinking.

I would add that it was to be expected that while in prison Gramsci would reflect on the causes of his latest setback and on the nature of communism in general. There is general agreement that he did just that. And, as we have seen, he filled more than a thousand pages in thirty-three notebooks with notes varying in length from a few lines to chapter-length essays but left essentially unedited by him. Therefore, the Notebooks have always posed a major interpretive challenge.

One key issue in this wider type of investigation is to explore whether in that most sustained revision of his thinking, Gramsci, rather than limiting himself to revising the means, was not inevitably led to question the ends he had previously taken for granted. Exploration of this question will require us to appreciate the democratic implications of Gramsci's emphasis on the "educator who must be educated." [22] My hunch is that he revised or abandoned typically Marxist aims once his tragic imprisonment had the ironic result of giving him the intellectual freedom and leisure to examine the issues in a more objective manner, or, in his words, "from the point of view of eternity." [23]

ONE

GRAMSCI AS A POLITICAL THEORIST: BACK TO MOSCA

MOST WORKS ON Gramsci tend to reverse the relative weight and importance which ought to be given to his practical life and to his sustained thought; that is, they discuss at great length the details of his life before prison, and then they give a small amount of space to his thinking as recorded in the prison writings.[1] One reason for this stems from the difficulty of interpreting the Prison Notebooks. Another reason is the interpretation of Gramsci in terms ranging from communist revolutionary to socialist radical and left-wing ideologue (in short, the Gramsci myth); for this interpretation requires that one should first be exposed to him in the context of such activities, and then one can read the Notebooks as the continuation of those activities.

However, I have always felt that it was Gramsci's theoretical legacy from prison that made him of some general relevance, and thus of potential interest to those of us far removed from him in time and space; and conversely that, without his prison experience, Gramsci would be of interest only to the few erudite specialists studying the history of Marxism, communism, and socialism, and to the few social and political activists committed to pursuing such aims. If this was a controversial judgment before the geopolitical dissolution of communism, nowadays it should be much easier to accept. As a consequence, those interested in Gramsci should spend the bulk of their time and effort becoming acquainted with the Prison Notebooks; his life can then be viewed as a groping toward the views expressed there.

Now, the most striking thing about the Notebooks is the presence of a keen, inquiring mind, desirous of improving the plight of the underprivileged, the disadvantaged, and the oppressed. The terminology, conceptual structure, methodology, and doctrines Gramsci employs transcend the usual categories of communism, socialism, and Marxism.

In particular, in this book I plan to test and explore the hypothesis that Gramsci's political theory is in large measure a constructive critique or critical development of that of Gaetano Mosca (1858–1941); that the key element common to both theories is what I shall call democratic elitism; and that a critical comparison reveals that democratic elitism is an interesting, important, and viable idea. The first thing that needs to be done about this hypothesis is to make a number of preliminary clarifications.

1. Interpreting Gramsci's Political Theory

This democratic-elitist interpretation is in part a new approach to the study of Gramsci. All novelty is of course relative, and so relative novelty is all I am claiming here, if for no other reason than that this carries further my previous work on Gramsci;[2] in that earlier work I focused on the more philosophical aspects of his Prison Notebooks, whereas here I plan to stress their more scientific content (scientific in the sense of political and social science and political and social theory). Moreover, this interpretive hypothesis is obviously in accordance with the classic approach to Gramsci discussed in the Introduction; thus, it may be said to follow that emerging tradition.

Additionally, the treatment of Gramsci as a political theorist is by no means unprecedented, as the works of Joseph V. Femia[3] amply demonstrate; in fact, I would have no hesitation in admitting that the present work may also be viewed as a continuation of his; the main difference is that while he concentrated on the phenomena of hegemony and revolution, my focus is on those of elites and democracy. Another good example of such a political-theoretical orientation is Sue Golding's *Gramsci's Democratic Theory: Contributions to Post-Liberal Democracy*,[4] which also shares my emphasis on democracy and advances some analogous interpretations of Gramsci's concept; however, Golding's conclusions are embedded in a theoretical and terminological framework which I find strikingly obscure and too Marxist-oriented, and which in any case ignores the crucial connection with Mosca and elitism. Finally, I do not mean to exclude other novel approaches.[5]

Second, we must be clear that the Moschian political theory to which the Gramscian one would be connected is not the theory many scholars have attributed to Mosca. For example, the Mosca I plan to elaborate is not a member of the Mosca-Pareto pair, for I agree with scholars[6] who maintain that the association of those two thinkers has been unfortunate, especially for Mosca. Nor do I believe that Mosca is a representative of the "proto-fascist" sociological tradition, as others have claimed.[7] Similarly, I do not find convincing the interpretation[8] of Mosca as an uncritical follower of the antidemocratic collective psychology of such writers as Gabriel Tarde, Gustave LeBon, and Scipio Sighele, who viewed the masses as passive, irrational, and inferior. And I do not think that Mosca is the hypocritical reactionary portrayed by some.[9] Generally speaking, I think Mosca should be placed in the tradition of democratic elitism, as suggested by many authors,[10] although this point has not been sufficiently elaborated or correctly evaluated by anyone. In other words, in the context of this investigation, I shall reinterpret Mosca's political theory as well as Gramsci's.

Third, it should be noted that I have stated my hypothesis by using the qualification "in large measure," and that this does not mean "entirely." That is, I do not think it would be correct to claim that *all* of Gramsci's political theory derives *exclusively* from Mosca's. In fact, it is undeniable that it derives in part from the views of Croce and Marx.[11]

Fourth, when I speak of political theory I am not referring to the whole of Gramsci's thought, but to that part which deals with topics and questions that are directly and explicitly political and social, such as classes, forces, crises, revolutions, governments, parties, states, elites, hegemony, and democracy. I am *not* referring primarily to the Gramscian views on the nature of the *concepts* philosophy, dialectic, religion, science, the nexus between theory and practice, and the like, whose articulation may be taken to belong to the domain of philosophy; nor am I referring to his historical interpretations of the Italian Risorgimento, the French Revolution, the medieval city-states, and so on. Naturally, this distinction between the political-theoretical, philosophical, and historical aspects of his thought is not meant to be a separation, since there are important relationships among them; however, the distinction is meant to avoid confusion or conflation of different things. To quote Gramsci, qualifying his thesis that in one sense everything reduces to politics, "If everything is 'political,' then one must, in order not to fall into tautological and boring phraseology, distinguish by means of new concepts the politics corresponding to that branch of scholarship traditionally called 'philosophy' from the politics called political science in a strict sense" (Q 1766).[12] I would only add that one must also distinguish the politics which is political theory from the politics which is practical activity and action. And this brings me to the next clarification.

Fifth, it would be an error of excessive intellectualism to claim that Gramsci's thought derives only from other thought, be it Moschian, Crocean, or Marxian. There can be no doubt that it also derives from Gramsci's practical political involvements, in the sense that it is also a reflection on his life as a labor union, socialist party, and communist party organizer and leader.

Moreover, aside from the question of the origins of Gramsci's thought, it would be an error of one-sidedness to claim that the study of his thought exhausts the interest in his personality and its relevance. Obviously, his life was a drama in which thought and action entered into dynamic interplay, and it must be studied and understood in relation to the history of his time.

In the case of Gramsci, the history of his time has a triple aspect: not only the period preceding and contemporaneous with his lifespan (1891–1937), but also the developments following his death. The reason for this third historical relevance is that, after his death, his life and thought were mythologized by his old fellow party members. As a result, after his physical death Gramsci acquired a new spiritual life and became the subject of a left-wing mythology.[13] Whatever one may think of the original justification for such a myth and of its current validity (anno Domini 1997), it originated in a natural and understandable manner and constitutes an integral part of the entire Gramsci affair.

Having explained that thought and action ought to be distinguished but not separated, and connected but not confused, I also think it would be reductionist and prejudicial to privilege his active political life or a part of it (namely, the period 1921-1926) and then interpret his political thought on that basis, as is often done. Such interpretations promote to the status of sustained thought items written by Gramsci at a time (before his imprisonment) when he did not have the time to undertake serious, calm, or coherent reflection,[14] or written in prison, when he had the time, but whose content merely echoes the earlier involvements. Here we can adopt Gramsci's own words that "the identification of theory and practice is a critical act such that either practice is shown to be rational and necessary or theory is shown to be realistic and rational" (Q 1780). I believe this means that the relationship between theory and practice is a reciprocal one, and that there is no logical or epistemological priority of practice over theory.

Finally, even the creator of the traditional myth of Gramsci on one occasion managed to suggest that perhaps Gramsci should be interpreted in such a way as to transcend the history of communism. On the eve of his death, Palmiro Togliatti wrote, "Today . . . it seemed to me that the very person of Antonio Gramsci should be placed in a more living light that transcends the historical vicissitudes of our party."[15] But this is easier said than done. How can Gramsci "be placed in a more living light that transcends" communism? A critical comparison between the thought of Mosca and that of Gramsci may be viewed as one way of doing this.

In summary, the interpretation I plan to explore is that an important part of Gramsci's thought (his political theory) is intellectually traceable in a significant though not exclusive manner to Mosca's political theory, at least when the latter is interpreted as an example of the political science paradigm of democratic elitism.

2. The Mosca-Gramsci Connection

The relation between Mosca and Gramsci has been generally neglected. Of the more than ten thousand entries making up the Gramscian bibliography,[16] I think that only about ten discuss this topic.[17] However, none of these few articles provides a systematic analysis, and almost all deal with the relation between Gramsci and the elitist school in general, which also includes Pareto and Michels. On the other hand, Mosca scholars usually do not even bother to discuss the issue explicitly in the body of their analyses but do so only incidentally, parenthetically, or in footnotes;[18] however, they typically admit the correctness and inclusiveness of Gramsci's criticism of Mosca's concept of political class.[19] In other words, it seems that no one has studied in a direct, explicit, and special manner the connection between Gramsci and Mosca.[20]

In a sense it is not surprising that the Mosca-Gramsci connection has been generally neglected, given that Mosca seems to have been a conservative, anti-Marxist, antisocialist, and anticommunist, whereas Gramsci seems tied to the history of revolutionism, Marxism, socialism, and communism. However, these interpretations are correct at best as a first ap-

GRAMSCI AS A POLITICAL THEORIST

proximation, whereas the obligation of a scholar is to try to penetrate beneath the surface of phenomena and to deepen the analysis of superficial appearances.

In other words, Mosca is often viewed as a classic exponent of the Right.[21] We could almost speak of him as a patron saint of the Right, were it not that his life does not exhibit the tragedy and high drama that Gramsci had to endure, and so Mosca does not lend himself to being mythologized as readily as Gramsci. Thus, given the traditional associations with Mosca, and the prima facie associations with Gramsci, it easy to understand that few would even think of associating the two of them. However, this situation merely explains, but does not justify, the neglect of the Mosca-Gramsci connection. In fact, I am convinced that this neglect is unjustified, and in the present investigation I aim to demonstrate the promise and fruitfulness of the connection.

On the other hand, the connection or at least the critical comparison between Gramsci and Mosca has an initial plausibility, which could be articulated as follows. Mosca was undoubtedly the most relevant, well-known, and influential political theorist in Italy during Gramsci's life. As the author of the *Elements of Political Science,* Mosca was in fact the founder of political science in Italy. Now, it can be asserted with certainty that the Prison Notebooks contain a project for a science of politics. Therefore, the critical examination of Mosca's doctrines by Gramsci would have been a normal and natural undertaking. This critical examination would have been especially likely for the prisoner who, in a letter to his sister-in-law, made the following confession: "All my intellectual development has been of a polemical sort. . . . Ordinarily it is necessary to place myself from a dialectical or dialogical point of view; otherwise, I do not feel any intellectual stimulus."[22]

To this preliminary argument one could object that the Prison Notebooks contain other important projects and elements. However, I readily admit this, for I do not plan to follow a simplistic and reductionist approach. In fact, it is obvious that another key Gramscian involvement is what he calls the art of politics. But this point strengthens the initial plausibility of the Gramsci-Mosca connection since the same is true for Mosca. In fact, although Mosca was not fond of the phrase "art of politics" (as Gramsci was), Mosca's work can be easily seen to contain an aspect which is usually labeled ideological. For example, to quote only the most eloquent descriptions, Norberto Bobbio has attributed to Mosca "the mirage of a science of antirevolution";[23] Paolo Frascani has attributed to him a mythology of the middle class;[24] and Eugenio Ripepe speaks of Mosca's "apology for the intelligentsia."[25] Speaking less ideologically, one could say that Mosca's political doctrines have a practical function and a normative dimension and are not a purely theoretical abstraction. Gramsci himself recognized this in a number of places, so he was perfectly aware that Mosca's political theory was not a "value-free" science of politics, any more than his own was. Both thinkers are therefore engaged in that two-dimensional activity which combines interpretive analysis and normative evaluation, and which may rightfully be called political theory.[26]

My conclusion is that the idea of a critical comparison between Gramsci and Mosca is not hopeless but more promising than it may seem at first sight.

TWO

MOSCA'S POLITICAL SCIENCE: DEMOCRATIC ELITISM AND BALANCED PLURALISM

THE TERMS "elitism" and "democracy" are commonly regarded as antonyms, and yet there exists a tradition of political thought which treats the two notions as distinct but not opposite, and indeed as mutually interdependent. Gaetano Mosca is one of the earliest and most eloquent exponents of such a tradition, and I believe that this alone would justify the serious study of his thought. However, this does not begin to do justice to this thinker because his elitism turns out to be democratic not only in his own special sense of democracy, which he defines in terms of open elites, but also in senses that pertain to other concepts, which he labels liberalism, meritocracy, and pluralism. Indeed, the last is especially important, and in Mosca's theoretical system pluralism tends to rival elitism in importance and overshadow it; a balance of sorts can perhaps be forged between these two essentially by regarding elitism as an analytical explanatory principle and pluralism as a normative evaluative one.

1. The Fundamental Elitist Principle

In 1884 Mosca published a book entitled *On the Theory of Governments and on Parliamentary Government: Historical and Social Studies.*[1] As the title suggests, the book has two parts: the first advances a number of basic principles for the study of political phenomena in general and governmental institutions in particular, while the second part is an analysis and criticism of that type of government called parliamentary, especially as it existed in Italy at the time. The most fundamental principle of Mosca's theory was formulated as follows: In all societies which have a government, those who control and exercise public power (the governors) are always a minority, whereas the majority (the governed) never really participate in the government but are merely subject to it.[2]

This was to be a constant theme in Mosca's thought, and so in later writings we find the principle restated, applied, and elaborated. For example, in the first volume of the *Elements of Political Science* (1896), Mosca speaks of the governors and the governed as "two classes" such that "the first, which is always less numerous, performs all political functions, monopolizes power, and enjoys its advantages; whereas the second, more numerous one is led and regulated by the first by more or less legal means, namely more or less arbitrary and violent, and supplies it (at least apparently) with the material means of subsistence."[3] Mosca adds that this claim amounts also to a denial of egalitarianism, in the sense that "we almost could not imagine the real existence of a world differently organized, in which everyone equally and without a hierarchy was subject to a single person, or where all equally would manage political affairs."[4]

A third useful and interesting statement of the idea appeared in the preface to the second edition of *Theory of Governments*, published in 1925. There Mosca asserts that he still regards as unassailable the principle advanced four decades earlier, but he now expresses it in these words: "In the study of the political organizations of different human societies, the main differences which we find in them at various times and places are those relating to the formation and the functioning of the classes of their leaders."[5] He contrasts this approach to that of emphasizing great and exceptional men on the one hand, or the people and masses on the other.

Mosca himself liked to call the class of governors or leaders the political class, and to speak of the "theory of the political class" to refer either to this particular principle or to his whole system of theoretical principles. Although some scholars[6] keep rather close to Mosca's own terminology of political class, others speak of it as the "ruling class."[7] The literature also abounds with other terms whose meanings partially overlap, such as "governing," "directing," "leading," and "dominant class." Sometimes attempts are made to clarify and systematize this cluster of notions,[8] but no scholarly consensus has been reached.

Moreover, many scholars like to speak of "elitism" in this connection, and so this can be called Mosca's fundamental elitist principle, at least when one wants to draw attention to what is common to his many statements of it. In so doing, one is adopting a term popularized by Pareto, who studied analogous and overlapping phenomena and advanced partly similar ideas; indeed the similarity engendered a famous dispute between the two thinkers, in which Mosca claimed priority of discovery.[9] Of course, there is no agreement on the many meanings of elitism, and though a clarification would be useful,[10] it would be premature at the moment.

It may also be helpful to refer to the above-mentioned principles in a more specific and descriptive way, especially if we want to emphasize the differences between Mosca's various expressions. Thus, the 1884 formulation in his first book may be called the principle of minority rule; the 1896 formulation in the first volume of his major work may be called the principle of unequal power; and the 1925 statement in the preface to the second edition of his first book may be labeled the methodological principle of leadership.

To acquire a better understanding of Mosca's principle, it will be useful to examine some of its functions and uses. One of its most important functions was to provide the fundamental law of the science of politics. In other words, one of Mosca's aims was to establish the study of politics on a scientific footing by means of a universal generalization confirmable by all available evidence.[11] I am not attributing to Mosca the simplistic and positivist view that knowledge is scientific if and only if it consists of immutable and eternal laws like the laws of nature. However, there is no question that he regarded invariant regularities as a key criterion of scientificity. Applying this epistemological metacriterion to the principle of minority rule, we would have one of the key "elements of political science."

At a more substantive, less formal level, Mosca's principle was meant to offer a better solution to the problem of the classification of governments than the two classic ones attributable to Aristotle and Montesquieu. Aristotle[12] had classified governments into monarchical, aristocratic, and democratic, according to whether the supreme power is held by one person, a small group, or the majority. On the other hand, Montesquieu[13] classified them into despotic, monarchical, and republican: despotic if there exists a hereditary ruler with absolute power, monarchical if the hereditary ruler has limited power, and republican if the ruler or rulers are not hereditary but elected by a part or all of the citizens.

Mosca's main objection to these classifications is that they are insufficiently realistic. That is, for example, by Aristotle's own definition, we would have to say that the class of democracies known to him was an empty one because even in Pericles' Athens most of the inhabitants were slaves or foreigners who had no rights of citizenship, and so it was really an aristocracy rather than a democracy. Similarly, by Montesquieu's definition, at the end of the nineteenth century, Belgium and Britain were (constitutional) monarchies, while France and the United States were republics; and yet Belgium and France resembled each other more closely than did either Belgium and Britain or France and the United States;[14] in other words, Montesquieu's classification allows for significant intraclass differences and significant interclass similarities, and so it is based on superficial criteria, namely criteria that do not cover the reality lying under the surface.

It should be added that this criticism of the traditional classification of governments is incomplete: besides saying what they all have in common, Mosca needs to delineate how they differ and what the deeper features are in regard to which they fall into different kinds. We shall discuss this topic later. For the moment, let us note simply that the Moschian realism just described is a constant feature of his way of thinking, and here we have merely an example.

Mosca's principle was also meant to be a refutation of the populist theory of democracy stemming from Rousseau.[15] According to this view, democracy is government by the people, and the only legitimate government is that which derives from the will of the majority of the people. Clearly, if the principle of minority rule is correct, then democracy in this sense has never existed; Mosca would also argue that there is no reason to believe it could ever exist in the future. Here we have another element of Mosca's realistic approach, namely an emphasis on the real vis-à-vis the ideal. This is not to say the he advocated a "value-free" social science, but rather that he thought that values and ideals, while they are distinct from facts, should be based on facts; they should not be mere utopian dreams and wishful thinking.

It should also be noted that at this juncture and in this context Mosca's primary objection is to a *theory* of democracy, a way of conceiving democracy, and not to particular democratic institutions and practices; the real nature of democratic institutions and their acceptability would require separate argument. Nevertheless, Mosca's principle was, and continues to be, widely perceived as antidemocratic, an issue to which we shall return.

In this initial sketch of Mosca's position, we also need to compare and contrast it with two other doctrines, Marxism and social Darwinism.

It is obvious that Mosca's fundamental principle is reminiscent of Marx's theory of the state and of class struggle, namely the view that governments are instruments whereby the upper classes dominate and exploit the lower classes, and the view that the struggle between these classes is the moving force of history.[16] However, Mosca rejects Marxist economism, both in the causation of historical events and in the definition of classes: rather than the economic structure's determining all other aspects of society, a mutual causal interaction exists, whereby political or intellectual phenomena sometimes determine economic ones; similarly, classes are to be defined not only by means of economic criteria, but also with the help of several other factors. More relevantly, class struggle, for Mosca, does not take place primarily between the ruling class and the masses, but between a ruling elite and a subaltern elite claiming to represent the interests of the masses; that is, for him, the action of the masses can take place only through the agency of a select group of leaders. Finally, the Marxian prediction of a classless society appears as wishful thinking to Mosca, who could confidently counter that the fundamental elitist principle would guarantee the re-emergence of class distinctions, thus making the classless society impossible.[17]

Social Darwinism is the attempt to extend to the social sphere and human affairs Darwin's biological theories of the struggle for existence, natural selection, and survival of the fittest. On more than one occasion, Mosca argued that the elitist principle neither implies nor is implied by social Darwinism.[18] The belief in a connection between the two was for Mosca the result of a confusion between the struggle for *existence* and the struggle for *pre-eminence*. He held the latter to be indeed an important fact of human life, and to be connected with the elitist idea.

2. Scientific and Methodological Merits of the Elitist Principle

One way of judging the worth of a scientific idea is to examine its fruitfulness—namely, to examine the quantity, quality, and variety of research and insights it inspires or generates.[19] From this point of view,

Mosca's fundamental elitist principle is of very high merit. Its fruitfulness may be illustrated by summarizing three striking developments: Michels's so-called iron law of oligarchy; C. Wright Mills's doctrine of the power elite; and the empirical study of elites. I am not saying, of course, that Mosca's influence was the only factor involved, nor would I deny that such work has other significant dimensions and deserves attention in its own right; I am claiming only that Mosca's principle was an important antecedent to an aspect of such work. However, I do not count Pareto—primarily because his work was essentially independent of Mosca's, but also because I feel that his system is largely incommensurable with Mosca's, both substantively and methodologically.[20]

In 1911 Robert Michels published in German a book whose title speaks of the sociology of political parties in modern democracies, and whose subtitle refers to the oligarchic tendencies of political aggregates. A year later the work appeared in Italian, and in 1915 in English.[21] At the time, the author was a junior faculty member at the University of Turin, Italy, the same institution where Mosca had held a chair in constitutional law since 1896; the two were in fact well acquainted with each other. Whatever their personal and biographical ties may have been, Michels's book leaves no doubt that it is a confirmation of Mosca's fundamental principle. Indeed it is much more than a confirmation, in the sense that it really is a severe test of the principle by applying it to a phenomenon—political parties—which was novel compared to those examined by Mosca himself and was such that one would not expect it to hold true there (the German Social Democratic Party). Michels's version of Mosca's principle is now known as the iron law of oligarchy, and it may be stated as follows: Every political organization has the more or less irresistible tendency to become an oligarchy—namely, to end up being dominated by a restricted and relatively closed minority group. The crucial factor causing the tendency is the organizational element present in a political grouping such as a party. In fact, Michels argued that even in democratic parties minorities dominate majorities for the following reasons: majority direction is technically impossible; the better elements of the masses get constantly re-elected; the first leaders have an advantage over newcomers; the leaders control party machinery, such as the party press; and leaders undergo psychological change owing to the salary they receive, the power they exercise, their age, and their attachment to their own accomplishments.

An analogous confirming test is provided by the work of C. Wright

Mills on what he liked to call the power elite in the United States. That is, American society could be claimed, with some justice, to be the most open, egalitarian, and democratic in the world, and so it could be expected to be the last place where Mosca's elitist principle would hold. Although Mills personally did not like to see himself as belonging to the Moschian tradition, and although there are undeniable differences, he can be easily fitted into it.[22] Mills argued that there exists a power elite in the United States which decides on national affairs and consists of those who occupy the higher positions in the country's political, economic, and military institutions; he claims that this elite is neither conspiratorial nor cohesive, but rather uses socialization and co-optation to perpetuate itself and accomplish its goals.

A third example of the scientific fruitfulness of Mosca's principle is the emergence of the field of elite studies as a branch of political sociology.[23] The empirical side of this field typically tests whether a political elite is present in a given society, or (if its presence can be assumed) what its characteristics are. The conceptual dimension of this branch of scholarship primarily attempts to give clear and viable definitions of the general notion of elite and of its subtypes. Another aspect of the field is perhaps more interpretive and more genuinely theoretical: it formulates and tests hypotheses about the structure, origin, accountability, mobility, and openness of elites. Thus, for example, while Lasswell and his collaborators admit that "in all large-scale societies the decisions at any given time are typically in the hands of a small number of people,"[24] they also argue that "this fact does not settle the question of the degree of democracy,"[25] because *"the key question turns on accountability"*;[26] now, what they call accountability is really the relationship between the elite and the masses or body politic. This means that while elite studies begin with the study of elites as such, they can also become an approach to sociology and political science in general, insofar as they investigate the relation between elites and other things.

We shall see presently that Mosca himself also pioneered this type of interpretive theorizing, but for the moment I want to emphasize that he also explicitly recognized the scientific advisability of this kind of research. In fact, elite studies as just described correspond clearly, exactly, and explicitly to what I earlier called Mosca's methodological principle of leadership. He also gave similar indications elsewhere—for example, in the first volume of the *Elements of Political Science* (immediately after stating his fundamental elitist principle): "The reason for the true superiority of the political class as a basis for scientific research is the preponderant importance which its varying constitution has in determining the political character and the degree of civilization of different peoples."[27] And at the beginning of the second volume of the *Elements*, he declares: "We intend to continue and to develop the analytical study of the political class."[28]

Besides theoretical fruitfulness, the ability to make (correct) predictions is another principle for the evaluation of a scientific idea. To be sure, predictive power is more problematic than theoretical fertility. For one thing, it is less general, in the sense that in many fields prediction is either impossible, practically unattainable, or unrealistic; and certainly political science, sociology, and history are some of the best candidates for fields where prediction is largely beside the point. Moreover, even when prediction is attainable, it carries perhaps less weight than fruitfulness. Nevertheless, even in the essentially apredictive fields, if and when predictions are made, their success or failure may be used as a gauge of scientific worth.

Now, Mosca was not at all prone to make predictions and was very much aware of the problematic nature of that activity in his own discipline. In fact, he even formulated an interesting principle suggesting that there is an asymmetry between negative and positive predictions in the social sciences: that while it is impossible to predict what will happen in the future, especially if remote, it is easy to predict what will never happen.[29] I am not sure such a thesis is acceptable, or that Mosca's supporting argument is valid, but at least they both illustrate his sensitivity to the issue.

With these qualifications, it can be said that as early as the 1890s, in the first volume of the *Elements*, Mosca was confident in predicting that a communist or socialist abolition of private property not only would *not* result in greater wealth, but would not even bring about greater social justice, more mutual love and understanding, better protection of the weak, or fewer abuses by the strong. He also offered a vision of such a future society which is sufficiently eloquent and quaint to deserve extended quotation:

In his *Progress and Poverty* Henry George many times quotes an ancient Hindu document which held that splendid elephants and parasols embroidered in gold were the fruits of the private ownership of land. In our day civilization is much more sophisticated than that, and life more many-sided. Wealth is producing a great deal besides elephants and parasols. But, after all, the privileges that wealth confers on those who possess it come down to the fact that wealth makes the pursuit of intellectual pleasures easier and the enjoyment of material pleasures more abundant. It provides satisfaction for vanity and pride and, especially, power to manipulate the will of others while leaving one's own independence intact. The heads of a communist or collectivist republic would control the will of others more tyrannically than ever; and since they would be able to distribute privations or favors as they chose, they would have the means to enjoy, perhaps more hypocritically but in no less abundance, all the material pleasures, all the triumphs of vanity, which are now perquisites of the powerful and the wealthy. Like these, and even more than these, they would be in a position to degrade the dignity of other men and to corrupt the virtue of women.[30]

This prediction was made before the Bolshevik Revolution. After communism had taken root in Russia, in the second volume of the *Elements* (1923) Mosca could note the confirmation of his earlier prediction.[31] Soon thereafter, in 1926, he made the uncanny remark that "it is probable that by the year 2000 . . . Russia itself will have completely re-established private property in land and in capital."[32]

The telling point regarding these predictions about communism is not only that they were correct, but that they were derived from his principles. In other words, these were not offhand remarks, casually made and unrelated to Mosca's theory; rather, they are a sign of the predictive power of his theory.[33] Strictly speaking, the fundamental elitist principle alone is insufficient to yield such predictions: others are needed to complete the derivation. The primary additional principle is one I shall be calling the principle of the separation of powers (between church and state, politics and economics, and so forth). Separation of powers will be discussed in due course, but since the elitist principle does play a fundamental role in these predictions, it too gets confirmed and its cognitive worth enhanced.

3. Objections to the Elitist Principle

If the fundamental elitist principle can be seen to possess great merit from the points of view of its theoretical fruitfulness and predictive power, the same cannot be said in regard to direct empirical support for it. That is, one may well ask what evidence there is that the real world corresponds to the principle. In a sense, this is the first and most important question one may want to ask about it. I am not sure I would want to assign such a prominent role to the methodological principle of direct empirical support, but there is no question that it is an important criterion. So let us see how the elitist idea compares to the facts.

How does one determine whether every society is ruled by a minority? Robert Dahl deserves credit for having pursued this question the most systematically, persistently, and insightfully.[34] In accordance with his suggestions, we can say that the empirical test must check two main things, corresponding to the two senses in which the elitist principle is a generalization. First, the principle is partly a generalization about societies, and so one investigation would be to look for possible counterexamples, which would refute it. Here Dahl's work has shown that democratic societies are not ruled by a single minority, but by several minority groups, and so are best described as "polyarchies"; in other words, democracies seem to be an (important) exception to the elitist principle. Second, if a given minority is the ruling one, then according to Mosca's fundamental principle, that group's decisions should generally prevail over those of others, at least in cases of disagreement; moreover, the links in the chain of domination binding ruler to ruled must be specifiable and identifiable. Here, I am inclined to agree with Dahl that direct empirical specification and identification are so problematic that no convincing confirmation or disconfirmation has been produced.

Another way of looking at the problem of direct empirical support is to draw on the distinction between a mathematical or statistical and an empirical or real class.[35] That is, one may accept as true in a sense the claim that every society is governed by a minority political class, but the crucial distinction becomes whether this political class is merely a statistical epiphenomenon or has empirical reality. What would give it empirical reality? Meisel has plausibly suggested that this would derive from the "three C's: group consciousness, coherence, and conspiracy."[36] This means that if the minority group is to have more robustness than a simple statistical class, then its members must be aware of belonging to it, must have enough connections among themselves to be relatively monolithic, and must engage in explicit discussion, planning, and action to pursue their common interests. Now, with this definition of a political or ruling class, empirical research reveals only that some societies are sometimes ruled by such a political class, but that not all of them are, and so the fundamental elitist principle is empirically falsified.

In conclusion, I would say that, on the one hand, empirical investigation has established that many societies are polyarchal and pluralist—that is, characterized by a diffusion of power among several groups; moreover, these are important characteristics of those societies which are ordinarily regarded as democratic. On the other hand, whether these empirical facts refute the fundamental elitist principle depends on how it is formulated and what one means by certain crucial terms, with the result that it is refuted under some interpretations but not under others. It is not refuted if one states the principle in terms of inequality of power, as we have seen that Mosca occasionally did; this formulation would run that in all societies minorities rule over majorities but would leave it open whether there is only one, or more than one, ruling minority, and how cohesive and monolithic a ruling minority must be. What this implies is that the fundamental elitist principle cannot really be tested empirically in a direct manner, by comparing it alone with the empirical facts; rather, its empirical evaluation must be conducted in the context of other principles with which it is combined in such a way that the whole system can be compared with the empirical facts. In short, the empirical evaluation of the elitist principle should be holistic rather than atomistic. Therefore, we shall shortly examine what some of the other important principles in Mosca's theoretical system are,[37] principles that are interesting and important in their own right.

The need suggested by this empirical criticism for a more contextual or holistic evaluation involves an issue analogous to an aspect of the development of the field of elite studies discussed earlier in connection with theoretical fruitfulness. That aspect was the study of how elites relate to other aspects of society, especially the masses, or the nonelite element; for example, the "accountability" of elites obviously involves principles different from those which govern the nature and internal structure of elites as such, and the study of such accountability is a natural development in elite studies. It would be quite artificial to separate these additional principles from the fundamental one. A move toward a more contextual evaluation is also suggested by a number of other objections that have been raised against Mosca's basic principle.

In fact, this principle has sometimes been criticized as being tautological and empty of content.[38] The reason lies in the statement that in every society with a government a minority of governors rule over the majority of governed: we notice that the distinction between governors and governed is really part of the definition of a government, and so perhaps the principle says nothing beyond the triviality that governors govern and the governed are governed. This judgment is reinforced when we examine some of the justifications Mosca gives for his principle; sometimes[39] these come close to giving an analysis of the meaning of government or political power, which would then yield a tautologically true proposition.

Actually this criticism must be slightly modified if it to be more effective. It is usually expanded into the judgment that, insofar as the principle is true, it is tautologically and trivially true, and insofar as it has content and is not trivial and tautological, it is empirically false; in other words, either the principle contains no information, or it contains false information. (The empirical falsification would be along the lines mentioned above.)

One answer to this criticism is that definitionally true statements are not always cognitively and scientifically worthless. To claim that they always are would be to presuppose a questionable conception of what a definition is, an arbitrary definition of definition, as it were; there are good and there are bad definitions, and a good one must reflect reality in significant ways.[40] Moreover, a definition might be worthless if considered by itself, but not if considered together with other principles in such a way that the whole collection sheds light on some domain of phenomena, is theoretically fruitful, or has explanatory power, predictive power, and empirical content.

For example, it would be easy to make it look as if the law of inertia (also called the first law of motion) is devoid of content: we could begin by paraphrasing Isaac Newton's own statement of it, to the effect that every body persists in its state of rest or uniform motion in a straight line unless compelled by an external force to change that state; the analyticity of this statement would be a consequence of the definition of a force as ultimately being nothing but that which changes a body's state of rest or uniform motion in a straight line; from this point of view the law would be saying simply that every body persists in its state of rest or uniform and rectilinear motion unless a change in this state occurs. Now, an answer to this classic puzzle in the foundations of physics[41] is to say that the law of inertia calls attention to the physical importance of changes in a body's state of rest or uniform rectilinear motion, and then to add that the law's informational content must be sought only when it is applied in conjunction with other laws and principles; these are, for example, the law that force equals mass times acceleration, the law that for every action there is an equal and opposite reaction, the law of universal gravitation, and Hook's law that the force exerted by a spring is proportional to its displacement.

The situation is exactly analogous in our case. Moreover, though Mosca did not mention the analogy to physics, he seems to have had the right epistemological intuitions about it. These are expressed when, as mentioned earlier, Mosca proposes that his fundamental principle be used as a basis for the "analytical study of the political class."[42] In other words, insofar as his fundamental principle is tautologically true, it serves the function of calling attention to the importance of the distinction and the interaction between rulers and ruled; this is largely a piece of methodological advice; if one wants informational content, then one must consider this principle in combination with others.

Before we do that, it will be useful to examine other objections. The next criticism to be considered here is formally analogous to the previous one but conflicts with it in substance. In fact, it charges that, although Mosca's elitist principle is descriptively and empirically true, it is not prescriptively and normatively desirable and acceptable. While the previous criticism presupposed a simplistic and unacceptable dichotomy between tautological definitions and empirical descriptions (that is, between analytic and synthetic judgments), the present one assumes an equally oversimplified dichotomy between facts and values or, specifically, between factual descriptions and normative prescriptions, between the "is" and the "ought"; but while the former claimed that Mosca's principle is false if empirically interpreted, the present criticism claims that it is descriptively true from the empirical point of view. In other words, the present objection begins by distinguishing between two kinds of elitism, descriptive or analytical, and prescriptive or normative; the first is declared to be essentially correct; and the second is deemed not to be justifiable by the truth of the first, but to be independently objectionable (by means of arguments one can easily surmise).[43]

In answer to this I would like to point out that Mosca is not, as a matter of fact, a normative elitist, in the sense of being someone who holds that it is a good thing that in every society minorities rule over majorities. I am not saying that he believed and practiced what some like to call "value-free" social science; indeed we shall soon examine some of the main normative principles he preached and practiced. I am rather saying that, with respect to this particular state of affairs, he does not seem to have felt the need or desire to express an evaluation; and I would add that there is nothing wrong with this attitude, which seems to reflect a kind of selectiveness in the activity of evaluation.

On the other hand, suppose one had forced Mosca to come to an evaluation; or suppose one asks whether a related normative principle is implicitly suggested by his words and deeds concerning this and other matters. I believe that, if pressed, Mosca would have asserted that human societies ought to be organized in such a way that minorities rule over majorities. If challenged for an argument to support this preference, he would, I believe, have produced something in accordance with his "realism." However, this realism does not imply a conflation of facts and values; hence the distinction, as a conceptual distinction, would remain. Nor does his realism depend on a pretension that normative evaluations are formally deducible from factual descriptions; hence the formal logical gap would remain. Rather, his realism involves a distinction between two kinds of "values," utopian dreams and realistic ideals: utopian dreams are values which are either groundless or supported only by flimsy arguments and sophistries; whereas realistic ideals are those which can be justified by strong and plausible arguments based on facts, though admittedly not formally valid or completely conclusive arguments. Now, given this distinction, and assuming that the context is such that one is forced to make an evaluation, I believe Mosca would begin by pointing out that one has two alternatives: either that minorities ought to rule over majorities or that minorities ought not to rule over majorities. This second alternative would then have to be declared a utopian dream, insofar as it presumably contradicts all available historical evidence. This, in turn, would leave the former evaluation as the only viable one.[44]

A related objection turns on the explicability of Mosca's principle. For example, Sidney Hook is willing to grant that the study of history does reveal that "all historical change, whether reform or revolution, consists of the substitution of one ruling minority for another."[45] However, he goes on to point out that the explanation for why this is so is a more difficult question. He attributes to Mosca an explanation in terms of human nature, and then claims that this explanation need not be accepted. But if human nature is not the cause, the possibility exists that matters might happen otherwise, and thus that, in the future, elitist social division will not necessarily persist. The connection with the evaluation objection is that this one provides elements for a potentially plausible argument in support of some alternative realistic ideal. This argument would depend on the alternative explanation for the agreed-upon generalization.

The distinction between an empirical fact and a theoretical explanation is an important and interesting one, and I am far from denying it. Thus one of Hook's points is acceptable. However, one problem with his criticism is that Mosca's explanation of his own "law" does not rely simply on an appeal to human nature. I believe his explanation, in the precise sense in which it is distinguished from the fact-to-be-explained, would be essentially the one put forward by Michels, which we have already summarized.[46] As we have seen, Michels argues that the oligarchic tendency is inevitable in a political organization. A key element in these considerations is the nature of organization. Thus it is not so much the nature of human beings in some abstract or abstruse sense which is the crucial factor, but rather the nature of organization. At any rate, another problem for someone (like Hook) who accepts the empirical accuracy of Mosca's principle but not his explanation is that he can fairly be challenged to provide an alternative explanation; and here I do not see that this critic provides one.

I do not wish to give the impression that Mosca's principle is unobjectionable, so let me mention for the record one of the most cogent objections: to wit, that Mosca's notion of political class is unclear and ambiguous. In fact, with this phrase he refers rather indiscriminately to politicians in general, elected officials, civil service bureaucrats, intellectuals, property owners, and the whole middle class. Anticipating somewhat, let me point out that Gramsci is one of those who was most bothered by this feature of Mosca's concept, and that there is a broad consensus that the Gramscian criticism is largely correct.[47]

The objection on grounds of explicability is not the only one closely related to the normative objection. Actually, the normative criticism discussed earlier is only one of a family of evaluation-oriented objections. That is, besides being charged with normative elitism, Mosca has also been accused of advancing, under the guise of a science, what some call a "myth" and others regard as an ideology.

The criticism that Mosca's principle promotes a myth has been put forth in Meisel's *The Myth of the Ruling Class*,[48] which is the most significant critical study of Mosca available in English. Meisel makes the point that a profound analogy can be drawn between Mosca and Machiavelli, whose *Prince* is full of dispassionate, objective, detached, and scientific analysis of the effective means whereby a ruler gains and retains power, but whose last chapter departs from this style and attitude and makes a passionate plea and a call to action for an absolute ruler to create a unified Italy out of the anarchy of city-states and principalities that covered the peninsula at the time. In fact, in the last section of the last chapter of the last volume of the *Elements of Political Science,* which was published in 1923, Mosca turns moralist and addresses the ruling classes of European representative democracies in general, and of his own country in particular. Like Machiavelli's, Mosca's appeal does not lack a certain eloquence:

> If the present crisis that is threatening our political systems and the social structure itself is to be surmounted, the ruling class must rid itself of many of its prejudices and change its psychological attitude. It must become aware that it is a ruling class, and so gain a clear conception of its rights and its duties. It will never be able to do that unless it can raise the level of its political competence and understanding, which have so far been woefully defective in the most highly civilized countries in Europe, and in some countries altogether lacking. [The reason is that] only then will it learn how to appraise the conduct of its leaders soundly; will it gradually regain in the eyes of the masses the prestige that it has in large part lost; and will it be able to see a little beyond its immediate interests and no longer squander most of its energies in the pursuit of objectives that are of advantage to certain individuals only, or to the little cliques that are grouped about certain individuals.[49]

Meisel correctly points out that this is really an appeal to the ruling class, an "elitist" appeal grounded on a concern for the people or masses, a "populist" or popular concern, if you will. To him, this means that "the doctrine of the ruling class is a myth, in the sense that it directs attention to a single aspect of the social process which is slated to epitomize and symbolize the working of the whole. It is however not the whole but a mere part, although perhaps the most intelligible and enticing part. But taken by itself, the ruling elite is not an 'intelligible field of study'; since it does not function in a void, we must be careful not to lose sight of the total context."[50]

I agree with Meisel on the substance of his observation, but I would question the critical, "mythological" tenor of his analysis. That is, the principle of the ruling class, the fundamental elitist principle, is in Mosca part of a theoretical system of ideas and principles, and so it must be examined contextually and holistically; this requirement has already emerged more than once in the present discussion, and now we hear Meisel expressing the same view. But we must also ask, Who is responsible for the myth—that is, for the one-sided interpretation of Mosca's principle?

Part of the explanation lies in that Mosca is usually paired with Pareto, whose views come closer to a one-sided emphasis on elites.[51] In an English-speaking context, one reason is that Mosca's *Elements of Political Science* was translated and published under the title *The Ruling Class.* Another reason is probably the initial impression made by Mosca with his first book (1884), whose critique of parliamentary government can easily appear to be one-sidedly elitist. But these are issues in the sociology of knowledge and in intellectual history, which have a fascination in their own right, but which do not relate centrally to the present, more interpretive, analytical, and critical investigation. For the moment let me say simply that, for me, Mosca's ultimate "moralistic" appeal is evidence for not regarding him as a mere elitist, and it leads me to see his fundamental elitist principle as only one element in his political philosophy.

Meisel is not the only scholar who has criticized Mosca as a mythmaker. Other scholars attribute to him the "myth of the middle class."[52] But they refer less to mythology than to ideology, in the sense of some kind of questionable evaluative commitment. Mosca was presumably committed to the middle class, as the class deserving to be the ruling class. This commitment gives at least an initial semblance of plausibility to the remark, otherwise quite puzzling, to the effect that Mosca's "political class" is an unclear concept which subsumes all sorts of things, the middle class among them. The objectionable thing here is that this commitment introduces a partisan or subjective element into a theory which claims to be scientific and objective.

An analogous, but distinct, point is being advanced by scholars who claim that Mosca's political science is an "apology for the intelligentsia."[53] That is, he presumably thought intellectuals should be the ruling class.

Similarly, it is very common to attribute to Mosca some kind of conservatism. The shade of conservatism attributed to him ranges from reactionary to moderate to liberal. In the last case, "liberal" conservatism,[54] the label is not supposed to be oxymoronic, partly because the term "liberal" is not being used in the American but in the European sense, according to which "liberal" and "conservative" are largely overlapping. From the point of view of the ruling class, conservatism in general is essentially the unwillingness to replace the ruling class: the will to re-empower some past ruling class which has already lost its power can be regarded as reactionary conservatism; merely to maintain the existing ruling class—as conservatism pure and simple; to retain the existing ruling class, but with allowance for some change (as long as it is not too rapid or too radical)—as moderate conservatism.

Although these three criticisms are obviously similar, I am not sure they are substantively consistent in content: the middle class, the intellectuals, and the existing ruling class do not necessarily coincide unless the terms are defined in some special way, and unless appropriate qualifications are made regarding time and space. Another thing these three criticisms have in common is that they are often made in contexts where merely to advance the given interpretation is *ipso facto* a condemnation; thus the middle-class interpretation is obviously an implicit criticism from the point of view of someone committed to proletarianism or most versions of Marxism; the intellectual interpretation would constitute a negative comment from the point of view of most capitalists; and the conservative interpretation would speak for itself in a circle of progressivists. Third, as already suggested, to the extent that these value judgments are present in Mosca, his political science can be considered tainted if one is looking for value-free social science.

Now, beginning with the last point, the advocacy of a value-free social science is itself a value judgment and an ideology. Moreover, it presupposes that it is possible to avoid making value judgments in scientific inquiry, which I would deny, arguing instead that scientific thought is always *to some extent* value-laden. By this I do not mean, however, that all value judgments are equally valid, or that any particular value judgment is appropriate; rather, value judgments have a role to play, more in some discipline than others, and they themselves need to be rationally evaluated; in short, what one must avoid is value judgments that are inappropriate, arbitrary, unjustified, and so on. Finally, I would add that the ideology that touts value-free analysis also presupposes a questionable view of the epistemological status of descriptive, analytical, and explanatory principles in science; that is, it tends to regard them as conclusively demonstrable and fails to appreciate their fallible, probable, and hypothetical elements; my point is that descriptive, theoretical hypotheses of the most fundamental importance in science are not conclusively demonstrable in any simple or uncontroversial way; once we admit this, the contrast between facts and values in science evaporates, and we get instead a continuum of rational justification, applicable in principle to both descriptive and normative principles.[55]

Thus Mosca was not at fault for merely having made the evaluative commitments just mentioned, to the extent that he did make them. Nor was he at fault for having made value judgments different from those made by others.

It is useful at this point to give a sketch of Mosca's justification of these judgments. For in a certain sense he did indeed advance all three. However, it is also important to understand what he means by "middle class," "intellectuals," and "conservatism." Now, not only is there an intimate connection between this justification and this elucidation, but it turns out that all three derive from or reflect the same fundamental principle. And this will be another avenue by which we shall, again, be led to examine the other elements of Mosca's political science, besides the fundamental elitist principle.

In regard to the middle class, it can be said at the outset that at a time and in a place where the middle class constitutes the majority of the population, Mosca's commitment to the middle class ought to be no cause for alarm. But that perhaps is not a very Moschian proposition. A more pertinent point is that, as his thinking developed, Mosca found it necessary to postulate a distinction within the ruling class between a small upper stratum and a larger stratum, and that the latter is what he means by the middle class.[56] Moreover, it should be repeated that Mosca also envisaged a reverse distinction within the ruled class—namely, the emergence of elites and leaders who aim to replace the existing ruling class for the governance of society. Thus we do not have simply a minority elite ruling over the majority, but rather one group, with the help of a second larger group, ruling over a third still larger group, which presumably would like to be ruled over by a fourth small group. So it seems that Mosca is grappling with the nature and intricacies of self-government. Moreover, Mosca's preference for the middle class is, I believe, a consequence of what is perhaps his most fundamental normative principle, which I call balanced pluralism and which, as we shall see presently, also leads Mosca to several other normative evaluations, such as the balance of social forces, checks and balances among branches of government, the ideal of mixed government, and the separation of powers.

In regard to intellectuals, it should be pointed out first that what Mosca has in mind is, in general, the "class that makes a living from mental labor"[57] as distinct from manual labor, and not merely or primarily high-powered, professional, or technical intellectuals. When so defined, they correspond in large measure to the middle class. In any case, Mosca's idea of the approach of the professional intellectual is, as Eugenio Ripepe has argued, to follow a "way which is neither that of politics as partisanship nor that of science as apoliticism and indifference—neither dirty hands nor ivory tower—but that of commitment understood essentially as intellectual commitment."[58] This, too, seems to be a special case of the Moschian ideal of balanced pluralism.

In regard to conservatism, we shall soon see that he advocated a constant renewal of the ruling class by the injection of elements of the ruled class, though he felt the change should not be too rapid. Notable here is his awareness of the pitfalls of stagnation. We might even accept Norberto Bobbio's characterization of Mosca's views as a "science of counterrevolution,"[59] but only if we agree with what Meisel says about the proper meaning of the term: that counterrevolution can "be viewed as another form of revolution—one leading in a direction opposite to that of the temporarily successful current."[60] Mosca himself stated this counterrevolutionary principle very clearly:

> The soundness of political institutions depends upon an appropriate fusing and balancing of the differing but constant principles and tendencies which are at work in all political organisms. It would be premature in the present state of political science to attempt to formulate a law, but some such hypothesis as the following might be ventured: That violent political upheavals . . . arise primarily from the virtually absolute predominance of one of the two principles, or one of the two tendencies, that we have been studying; whereas the stability of states, the infrequency of such catastrophes, depends on a proper balancing of the two principles, the two tendencies. . . . One practical method has occurred to us for helping well-meaning persons, whose exclusive aim is the general welfare and prosperity quite apart from any personal interest, or any systematic preconception. . . . To put the matter in two words, it is just a question of following a rule that is the opposite of the one that climbers have consciously or unconsciously followed at all times in all countries.[61]

Thus, from many quarters we have been led to the conclusion that the proper interpretation and evaluation of Mosca's fundamental elitist principle require that it be examined in relation with other principles, both analytical and normative. To these we now turn.

4. The Principle of Balanced Pluralism

Besides the fundamental elitist principle, one of Mosca's most important concepts is his doctrine of democracy, which itself comprises more
than one principle. Such a doctrine is needed by Mosca in part to complete his classification of governments, by providing alternate constructive criteria to the traditional classifications once these have been denied
by the sweeping elitist principle. Moreover, the phenomenon of democracy is obviously too important to be entirely neglected in a systematic
study of politics. Finally, his elitist principle struck many people as being
antidemocratic, and so it is not surprising that sooner or later he would
have had to clarify how his fundamental principle relates to democracy.
To understand these functions and these relationships, it is best to focus
on Mosca's mature view in the second volume of the *Elements*, disregarding whatever evolution his thinking may have undergone and whatever
minor incoherences may be present in the entire corpus of his writings.

We thus come first to Mosca's conception of democracy, which he
both defines in terms of the ruling class mentioned in the fundamental
principle and distinguishes from another type of government, opposite
to it and labeled aristocracy. In fact, the definition is best analyzed by
considering the parts together, as in the following: "The term 'democratic' seems more suitable for the tendency which aims to replenish the
ruling class with elements deriving from the lower classes, and which is
always at work, openly or latently and with greater or lesser intensity,
in all political organisms. 'Aristocratic' we would call the opposite tendency, which also is constant and varies in intensity, and which aims to
stabilize social control and political power in the descendants of the class
that happens to hold possession of it at the given historical moment."[62]
This is indeed a peculiar, but not an arbitrary, conception of democracy.
It defines democracy in terms of a relationship between the ruling class
and the ruled, and the relationship seems to me that of social mobility
from the latter to the former, or renewal of the ruling class through the
infusion of members of the ruled class. The definition makes democracy
a matter of degree, rather that an all-or-none affair. When so conceived,
democracy is (to some extent) always present in any given society; only
the extent to which it is present varies. However, the opposite of democracy (aristocracy) is also always present (to some extent).

Implicit in this quotation is the suggestion that the interaction or
struggle between the two opposite tendencies is one of the most impor-

tant moving forces in history. Elsewhere Mosca is very explicit about this principle, which can be called the principle of the interaction between democracy and aristocracy.[63]

Besides this conceptual definition and the principle of interaction, Mosca also advances a normative principle about the desirability of democracy so conceived: "It is undeniable that the democratic tendency, especially if restricted within moderate limits, is in a way indispensable for what is called, and often really is, the progress of human societies."[64] Here Mosca clarifies one sense in which democracy is a good thing—namely, that it is indispensable to progress. But there is a second reason for Mosca's positive evaluation of this kind of democracy: its conservative role. This sounds paradoxical, but it is difficult to find fault with Mosca's logic: "When its action does not become excessive and exclusive, the democratic tendency represents what in common language would be called a conservative force. For it enables the ruling classes to continuously acquire fresh blood through the admission of new elements who innately and spontaneously possess inclinations toward leadership and the willingness to lead, and so it prevents that exhaustion of aristocracies of birth which usually paves the way for the great social cataclysms."[65]

Mosca's endorsement of democracy so understood is unequivocal, but it is not unqualified; the democratic tendency must be kept moderate and must not be excessive or exclusive. If it were given free reign and allowed to annihilate the aristocratic tendency completely, the elimination of any accidental birth privilege would ensue; this in turn would mean that the struggle to enter the ruling class, the struggle for pre-eminence, would be "intensified to the point of frenzy. This would entail an enormous expenditure of energy for strictly personal ends, with no corresponding benefit to the social organism, at least in the majority of cases."[66]

When, in the definition quoted above, Mosca says that he thinks it is "more suitable" to define democracy the way he does, he has in mind that his is preferable to alternative definitions. One of these, which he attributes to Plato,[67] depicts democracy as a political organization in which authority flows from the bottom up. However, Mosca believes it is more appropriate to label the latter a liberal system, for he seems to be elaborating a definition of political liberty traceable to Guicciardini,[68] according to which political liberty exists when both rulers and ruled are subject to the laws and both participate in their creation. At any rate, Mosca has a systemic reason for wanting to call attention to this feature—that "in all forms of political organization, either authority is transmitted from the top toward the bottom of the political and social spectrum . . . or it is delegated from the bottom to those who are at the top, from the governed to the governors."[69] He labels the former polity autocratic and the latter liberal.

Like his conception of democracy, this definition of liberalism is also a distinction between it and its opposite. It is likewise formulated in terms of a relationship between rulers and ruled, and the relationship here can be defined according to the direction of the flow of power.[70] Mosca does not explicitly assert that liberalism too is a matter of degree, but I believe this conclusion to be an immediate consequence of three things: (1) his elaboration of upward power flow in terms of the consent given by the governed to the governors; (2) his discussion of the relation of representation between them; and (3) his analysis of the limitations on government power due to civil liberties.[71] Now, each of these three characteristics is a matter of degree.

Analogously, Mosca believes in the interaction between autocracy and liberty, though in the form of a perennial historical succession of periods in which one prevails over the other. Moreover, he thinks that liberalism is better than autocracy, though he also seems to think that the autocratic element has a necessary role to play. That is,

> It would seem, therefore, as though the liberal principle were likely to prevail at those exceptional periods in the lives of the peoples when some of the noblest faculties of men are able to show themselves in all their intensity and energy, and when seeds are ripening that will shortly produce considerable increases in political power and economic prosperity. But it would seem as though those periods, which mark some of the most important milestones on the road of civilization, were followed by other periods during which human societies feel, as it were, an overpowering need for a long sleep. This they find in the political field by slowing down to an autocracy that is more or less masked and more or less well-adapted to the level of development and culture that they have attained.[72]

Besides these two distinctions, between democracy and aristocracy and between liberty and autocracy, Mosca advances a third which is less explicit but obvious enough to leave no doubt about his intent. It is the distinction between feudalism and bureaucracy. Once again, the distinction is exhaustive in the sense that all political organisms can be classified as belonging to one of these two types.[73] The criterion of distinction is something which prima facie looks like merely a property of the ruling class pertaining to its internal structure, namely the degree of overlap or specialization in the exercise of executive functions: "By 'feudal state' we mean that type of political organization in which all the executive functions of society—the economic, the judicial, the administrative, the military—are exercised simultaneously by the same individuals, while at the same time the state is made up of small social aggregates, each of which possesses all the organs that are required for self-sufficiency. . . . In a bureaucratic state there is always a greater specialization in the functions of government than in a feudal state. The first and most elementary division of capacities is the withdrawal of administrative and judiciary powers from the military element."[74] This internal characteristic of the ruling class has an effect on its relationship with the ruled class; for with the development of the division of labor, there arises a need for the financial support of state administrators and military troops through the taxation of the ruled class. We thus get what Mosca calls the principal characteristic of a bureaucratic state: "Wherever it exists, the central power conscripts a considerable portion of the social wealth by taxation and uses it first to maintain a military establishment and then to support a more or less extensive number of public services."[75]

Like previous types, it is clear that feudalism and bureaucracy are a matter of degree: "The greater the number of officials who perform public duties and receive their salaries from the central government or from its local agencies, the more bureaucratic a society becomes."[76] Analogous is also the relationship or interaction between feudalism and bureaucracy: neither is ever completely absent; the two are opposites, in the sense that movement toward one is simultaneously movement away from the other; and there is no absolute unidirectional trend in history, although modern times have brought about an obvious increase in bureaucratization. In Mosca's own words:

This classification, it should be noted, is not based upon essential, unchanging criteria. It is not our view that there is any psychological law peculiar to either one of the two types and therefore alien to the other. It seems to us, rather, that the two types are just different manifestations, different phases, of a single constant tendency whereby human societies become less simple, or, if one will, more complicated in political organization, as they grow in size and are perfected in civilization. Level of civilization is, on the whole, more important in this regard than size, since, in actual fact, a literally huge state may once have been feudally organized. At bottom, therefore, a bureaucratic state is just a feudal state that has advanced and developed in organization and so grown more complex; and a feudal state may derive from a once bureaucratized society that has decayed in civilization and reverted to a simpler, more primitive form of political organization, perhaps falling to pieces in the process.[77]

The principal value judgment about feudalism and bureaucracy can be described as a certain skepticism about excessive bureaucratization, especially about the bureaucratization of economic activity. I speak of skepticism rather than opposition, because we have just seen that in a sense the degree of bureaucratization is an indication of the level of civilization. The point is that "history shows no instance of a great society in which all human activities have been completely bureaucratized. This, perhaps, is one of the many indications of the great complexity of social laws, for a type of political organization may produce good results when applied up to a certain point, but become impracticable and harmful when it is generalized and systematized. . . . What is more, we have fairly strong evidence that the extension of bureaucratic control to the production and distribution of wealth as a whole would be fatal."[78]

These three pairs of six types may be said to constitute Mosca's classification of governments, to substitute for the traditional ones stemming from Aristotle and Montesquieu. These six definitions may also be regarded as a set of ideal types in Max Weber's sense; that is, we have six abstractly defined types of government whose relation to empirical reality is that actual past or existing governments approximate the types to a greater or lesser extent; so I make no pretension to finding perfect illustrations of these types. Also, the three distinctions crisscross each other in such a way that the six pure cases generate eight mixed types; the mixed types are still ideal types in Weber's sense. That is, although an opposition exists between the members of each pair, no opposition is supposed to exist, but only a difference between the members of one pair and those of another. For example, it may perhaps be true that some correlation exists between democracy and liberalism, but there is no inconsistency between democracy and autocracy (the opposite of liberalism); an autocratic democracy would be a society or organization with a relatively open ruling class, but where authority flows from top to bottom; here the Catholic Church would be the paradigm.[79] Nor is there any inconsistency between liberalism and aristocracy (the opposite of democracy), Mosca's examples being the Republic of Venice and Poland in the eighteenth century.

The mixed types just considered involve relatively analytical and descriptive considerations, in the sense that they prescind from normative evaluations. But they do bring us to the topic of the ideal of mixed government, which is one of Mosca's most fundamental and overarching normative principles.[80] We have already seen that he expresses a preference for democracy and for liberalism, and some skepticism about bureaucratization. The common and striking element about these value judgments is his judiciousness—that is to say, his concern with avoiding one-sidedness and extremes, and with achieving a balance; for in each case his commitment is a moderate one: he is careful not to go too far in the preferred direction, and sensitive about not entirely neglecting the other side. Mosca not only assumes this attitude in discussing the individual types, but he explicitly formulates it when he takes up the classic question of what the best form of government is. His answer is that "the soundness of political institutions depends upon an appropriate fusing and balancing of the differing but constant principles and tendencies which are at work in all political organisms."[81] He admits that this is only the latest version of "the old doctrine of the golden mean, which judged mixed governments [to be] best."[82] The novelty here is only that the mixture is based on newly conceptualized types, which in turn are the result of "the more exact and profound knowledge that our times have attained as to the natural laws that influence and control the political organization of society."[83]

Thus, Mosca's ideal of mixed government is a more general normative principle vis-à-vis his democratic, liberal, and anti-bureaucratic ideals, which may be regarded as special cases. Now, mixed government is itself only a particular case of an even more basic principle; it is in a sense an application of this deeper principle to forms of government. In fact, besides forms of government, another important domain of application is what might be called structural elements of society, such as politics, economics, and religion. It is in connection with these that Mosca advanced what can be called the principle of the separation of powers; it has two main parts, one dealing with church and state, the other with politics and economics: "The first, and indeed the most essential, element for a political organism to be able to progress, in the sense of acquiring an increasingly better juridical defense, is the separation of secular and ecclesiastical powers; or, to be more exact, the principle in the name of which temporal power is exercised must have nothing sacred and immutable about it."[84] Secondly, there is no use either in cherishing illusions as to the practical consequences of a system in which political power and control of economic production and distribution are irrevocably delegated to, or conferred upon, the same persons. . . . A society is best placed to develop a relatively perfect political organization when it contains a large class of people whose economic position is virtually independent of those who hold supreme power and who have sufficient means to be able to devote a portion of their time to perfecting their culture and acquiring their interest in the public weal—that aristocratic spirit, we are almost tempted to say—which alone can induce people to serve their country with no other satisfactions than those that come from individual pride and self-respect.[85]

Now, separation (of powers) sounds like the opposite of mixture (of forms of government). However, the point is that those who hold political power should not also have religious or economic power; that is, religious and economic power should be independent of political power. And this independence is intended to prevent any one power or group of people from becoming too powerful, from acquiring excessive power. This is the same objective which one is trying to accomplish by combining types of government. In one case one is trying to prevent any of the main tendencies from becoming so strong that it destroys the others, in the other case one is trying to prevent any of the main components of society from overpowering the others. All of this may be said to reflect a commitment not only to balance but also to pluralism. What may thus be called the principle of balanced pluralism was stated by Mosca as follows: "The absolute preponderance of a single political force, the predominance of any over-simplified concept in the organization of a state, the strictly logical application of any single principle in all public law are the essential elements in any type of despotism, whether it be a despotism based upon divine right or a despotism based ostensibly on popular sovereignty."[86]

Mosca applied this very general normative principle in another area, or rather, there is another, more particular normative commitment whose plausibility led him to formulate the more general one. The more particular concern is the question of checks and balances in regard to branches of government, specifically the executive, the legislative, and the judicial. He explicitly credits Montesquieu with having formulated the principle that these three main functions of government should be entrusted to distinct institutions independent of one another.[87] Mosca criticizes Montesquieu's followers, however, for being excessively formalistic about this principle, in the sense that they focused on having such checks and balances explicitly spelled out in the written constitution; Mosca found it more important that such checks and balances should actually operate in the political practice of a given society, which in turn relates to whether there are checks and balances between social and political forces, along the lines mentioned earlier in the discussion of Mosca's other principles. Nevertheless, in Mosca's own career as a political critic and reformer, he applied the principle on various occasions. For example, his famous critique of parliamentarism was largely based on this principle, insofar as one of his key objections was that parliament had acquired too much power vis-à-vis the executive branch and the king;[88] another example would be his attempt to define a fourth branch of government, involving a moderating function, and exercised by the king together with a privy council in a constitutional monarchy or by the president in a parliamentary republic;[89] a third example would be his suggestions for ensuring and strengthening the independence of the judiciary in Italy.[90] Thus I believe we can conclude that, although the principle of checks and balances (between government branches or functions) is related to the general principle of balanced pluralism, it is a distinct normative commitment on Mosca's part.

The cases of balanced pluralism examined so far can be systematized as follows. They involve relationships between rulers and ruled (democracy, liberty, and bureaucracy, and their opposite tendencies) and relationships among various segments of the ruling classes (the political, religious, and economic elites; and officials of the legislative, executive, and judicial branches of government). Symmetry would now suggest that Mosca would devote attention to elements of the ruled classes, or subaltern classes.

This expectation is fulfilled, in the sense that Mosca also advocates a balanced pluralism among what he frequently calls social forces. In fact, he believes that "as civilization grows, the number of the moral and material influences which are capable of becoming social forces increases."[91] However,

history teaches us that whenever, in the course of the ages, a social organization has exerted an influence in a beneficial way, it has done so because the individual and collective will of the men who have held power in their hands has been curbed and balanced by other men, who have occupied positions of absolute independence and have had no common interests with those whom they have had to curb and balance. It has been necessary, nay indispensable, that there should be a multiplicity of social forces, that there should be many different roads by which social importance could be acquired, and that the various political forces should each be represented in the government and the administration of the state.[92]

As usual, Mosca did not merely state this principle in the abstract but also showed his commitment to it in practice. For example, in 1910 he defended the appropriateness of an upper chamber of parliament (a senate) with membership criteria different from those of the lower house; he did so on the grounds that the differently constituted upper chamber offers an opportunity for active participation to forces and talents not easily or properly represented in the lower chamber.[93] And in 1912, while arguing *against* the extension of suffrage, he was willing to give some weight to one argument in favor; this was the argument that near-universal suffrage would reduce and counterbalance the power of the unions of public employees.[94] I am not saying, of course, that these arguments are unobjectionable, but rather that they illustrate his commitment to the principle of balanced pluralism in regard to social forces in general.

His recurring concern with abuse of power on the part of public employees, in the civil service or the bureaucracy, eventually led Mosca to an heightened and interesting appreciation of modern representative government. On the one hand, in the concluding chapter of the second edition of the *Elements* (1923) he wrote one of the most eloquent celebrations of this regime; for example, he went to so far as to assert that "if, therefore, the nations of European civilization have succeeded in maintaining their primacy in the world during the age that is now closing, the fact has been due in large part to the beneficent effects of their political system."[95] Now, the essential feature to which he thought this success should be credited was the separation and mutual control of elected officials and the career civil service: "This development, it should be noted, has divided the political class into two distinct branches, one issuing from popular suffrage, and the other from bureaucratic appointment. This has not only permitted a better utilization of individual capacities; it has also made it possible to distribute the sovereign functions, or powers, of the state, and that distribution, whenever social conditions are such as to make it effective, constitutes the chief virtue of the representative regimes. It is the chief reason why they have given better results than any of the many others that have so far been applied to great political organizations."[96]

As a final special case of Mosca's balanced pluralism, we should mention his counterrevolutionary principle. As we saw above, this is the principle which advises us to oppose whatever trend has become predominant.[97] The connection with balanced pluralism should now be obvious: engaging in such opposition is an attempt to re-establish the balance with respect to the various elements we have examined—namely, tendencies affecting the relationship between rulers and ruled (the types or forms of government), elements of the power structure, branches of government, social forces, and classes of government officials.

5. The Ideal of Meritocracy

The principle of balanced pluralism is, then, very pervasive and wide-ranging; there can be no question of its fundamental, central, and crucial importance. However, it is not immediately obvious that it can encompass one other important normative evaluation made by Mosca, which I shall call the meritocratic principle.

At the end of his *Theory of Governments* (1884), Mosca appears to give as much importance to this principle as to balanced pluralism. In fact, he regards both as the principal legacies of modern civilization, which he proposes as the bases for a radical reform of that complex of abuses which he labeled parliamentarism. The reform "should aim at a true and real renewal of the entire political class, and at the actualization of the two great objectives which may be politically regarded as the synthesis of all modern civilization: the formation of this class on the basis of personal merit and technical capacity; and the reciprocal control of all its members in such a way as to avoid, as much as humanly possible, arbitrary and irresponsible actions by any single individual or group of individuals."[98] However, it turns out that his commitment to meritocracy is qualified by a number of considerations; this qualification means that, once again, we have a re-assertion of the primacy of balanced pluralism, at least as a mental attitude, manner of thinking, or methodological orientation.[99]

In fact, the first qualification that must be noted is that "personal merit is one of those things that the passions and interests of men best manage to counterfeit."[100] For example, in an autocratic system the counterfeiting is largely accomplished by intrigue; and in liberal systems, and especially in democratic ones, it is accomplished largely by charlatanry.[101]

To this difficulty from the side of the person judged, we must add another from the side of the judge. In fact, Mosca believes judgments of personal merit to be irreducibly subjective, in the sense that "each judge will, entirely in good faith, appreciate more those intellectual and moral qualities of candidates which he possesses himself."[102]

Unfortunately these difficulties cannot be easily circumvented. The attempt to do so is likely to produce worse side effects. Such would be the case, for example, for the institution of automatic advancement based on seniority in a bureaucratic system. Mosca's words leave no doubt about where his commitment lies:

> Suppose, then, that in our distrust of human impartiality we try to re-place choice and appointment by superiors with automatic rules of ad-vancement. Such rules can be based only upon the principle of seniority. In this case, unfailingly, the lazy and the diligent, the intelligent and the stupid, get along equally well. The public employee knows perfectly well that it will not help him to do any more or any better than others. He will therefore do the minimum that is indispensable if he is not to lose his position or his promotion. In such circumstances the bureaucratic career tends to become the refuge of the talentless, or of people who absolutely need to have salaried positions in order to provide for their daily wants. If an intelligent man does happen to stray into the bureaucracy, he de-votes only a part of his activity and his talent to his office, and often it is not the best part.[103]

Another proposal, which Mosca thinks to have been first devised by Saint-Simon, is to define personal merit in terms of the service one has rendered or is rendering to society, and then to establish an exact, complete, perfect, and almost mathematical correspondence between this service and the place one occupies in the social hierarchy.[104] Mosca plau-sibly argues[105] that for the Saint-Simonian formula to work, the abolition of private property and of the family would be required, along with un-bridled competition to the point of frenzy; and such concomitants and consequences are certainly undesirable.

A third difficulty with meritocracy is more specifically political. In the quotation in which Mosca regards meritocracy as one of the two key legacies of modern civilization, he is speaking about using personal merit as a basis for membership in the *political* class; so he is presumably talk-ing about the desirability of a correlation between personal political merit and one's place in the political hierarchy. The political hierarchy may be related to the social, intellectual, and moral hierarchies, but they are not the same, so personal merit is similarly distinct. Mosca discusses this explicitly when he takes up the issues of government by the best and who the best are.[106]

He distinguishes between personal merit in an absolute sense, and personal merit in a political sense. In an absolute sense, personal merit means moral goodness, which Mosca tends to equate with altruism and a sense of justice in one's relations to others. He gives two reasons political merit cannot be equated with these two virtues. One is that moral merit may be fine in a static society in which all is already perfect as it is or in which all are satisfied with their status. However, real societies are not static, and "to rise in the social scale, even in calm and normal times, the prime requisite, beyond any question, is a capacity for hard work; but the requisite next in importance is ambition, a firm resolve to get on in the world, to excel over one's fellows. Now those traits hardly go with extreme sensitiveness or, to be quite frank, with 'goodness' either."[107] Nor is the capacity to work, or the quantity and quality of work accomplished, statically a given; rather, "work always has to be reinforced to a certain extent by 'ability,' that is to say, by the art of winning recognition."[108]

Mosca's second reason is that political merit for him is simply the aptitude to govern one's fellows. But "if one is to govern men, more useful than a sense of justice—and much more useful than altruism, or even than extent of knowledge or broadness of view—are perspicacity, a ready intuition of individual and mass psychology, strength of will and, especially, confidence in oneself."[109] In making this distinction, Mosca is, of course, pursuing a tradition going back at least to Machiavelli, from whose work he quotes approvingly here and elsewhere the aphorism that "states are not governed with prayer books."[110]

Political merit must also be distinguished from intellectual merit, according to Mosca, who thus rejects the traditional Platonic ideal of the philosopher-king.[111] If we interpret intellectual merit in the sense of philosophical, scientific, theoretical, and conceptual understanding, Mosca's argument is that "first of all, very often true wisdom does not excite but smothers ambition; and then, lofty qualities of character and intellect bring them [philosophers] not closer to but farther from the highest offices."[112]

Finally, determination of political merit is complicated by the existence of two distinct subtypes, which do not always come together—namely, statesmanship and the quality of being a politician: "The statesman is a man who, by the breadth of his knowledge and the depth of his insight, acquires a clear and accurate awareness of the needs of the society in which he lives, and who knows how to find the best means for leading that society with the least possible shock and suffering to the goal which it should, or at least can, attain. . . . . The politician, on the other hand, is a man who has the qualifications that are required for reaching the highest posts in the governmental system and knows how to stay there."[113]

It would seem, therefore, that Mosca's ideal of meritocracy is largely an application of balanced pluralism to the problem of defining political merit, observing its operation in the real world, and formulating normative principles of evaluation. To justify this conclusion, it will be useful to analyze in more detail the relevant oppositions and distinctions.

His normative principle of meritocracy is meant to be partly a denial of the birth privilege in its pure form, according to which membership in the ruling class is determined solely by birth. In this regard, meritocracy is in accordance with democracy as understood by Mosca, insofar as it contributes to the renewal of the ruling class and to the social mobility of the ruled class; however, it is distinct from Moschian democracy in the sense that it has a different conceptual content. Moreover, he also rejects extreme meritocracy and would not want to do away altogether with the accidental advantages of birth.

Mosca's meritocracy is also opposed to the seniority principle in its pure form, which would make advancement in a hierarchy dependent solely on length of service. From this point of view, meritocracy is opposed to egalitarianism and in accordance with the elitist principle; but, again, it is not identical to elitism. And presumably, though he does not say so explicitly, he would not want to extirpate considerations of seniority altogether.

He is also critical of the Saint-Simonian principle of absolute justice, which would establish a perfect correlation between service to society and position in the hierarchy. Here Mosca is denying the absolutism and simplism embodied in this principle, in regard to which it should be noted that whenever he formulates it he always attributes to the Saint-Simonians the desire for a perfect, complete, mathematical, and exact correlation between service and position; this suggests that he would favor some degree of correlation.

Finally, meritocracy has an element of individualism, as opposed to collectivism, because the personal merit in question refers to individual merit; from this point of view, Mosca's arguments against extreme versions of meritocracy mean that he can show some appreciation for the interests of society as a whole.

So Mosca seems to advocate neither that personal merit should be irrelevant nor that it should be the only criterion, but that is should be the primary criterion for advancement in the social hierarchy. His pluralism emerges from his willingness to allow for other factors; his balance from his concern with the avoidance of excesses. However, this regards meritocracy in general. In regard to political merit, or personal merit in politics as such, he has given us a definition of the concept.

He defines political merit in terms of such qualities as willpower, psychological perspicacity, social wisdom, and skill in acquiring and holding on to power. Willpower involves such things as ambition, resoluteness, aggressiveness or assertiveness, and self-confidence. Perspicacity pertains primarily to perceptiveness in regard to human needs, desires, and behavior, at both the individual and the collective level. Social wisdom is the intuitive understanding of society's proper ends and means; it is what the statesman possesses. And skill in acquiring and holding on to power is the politician's forte.

When political merit is so conceived, it is obviously distinct from both moral goodness and intellectual merit. It might also seem that Mosca is exaggerating the distinction into an opposition, but the rest of his account reinforces, once again, his typically judicious attitude. In fact, in regard to moral goodness, he does not hesitate to require of those who govern "that they should not fall below the average moral level of the society they govern, that they should harmonize their interests *to a certain extent* with the public interest, and that they should not do anything that is too base, too cheap, too repulsive—anything, in short, that would disqualify the man who does it in the environment in which he lives." [114] Moreover, after quoting the Machiavellian dictum about prayer books, Mosca adds the qualification that "if a man, however wicked he might be, tried to rule a state strictly on blasphemy, that is by relying exclusively on material interests and the baser sentiments, he would be just as ingenuous as the man who tried to govern with prayer books alone." [115]

The situation is analogous in regard to the distinction between intellectual and political merit. That is, Mosca requires that the intellectual level of rulers should not fall below the general intellectual level of the ruled. Moreover, he envisages that as political science and political philosophy develop, they will exercise an increasingly healthy influence on rulers; in other words, that it is not necessary for rulers to be philosophers, as long as they take the advice of philosophers; and this advice will be increasingly inescapable as public opinion becomes increasingly better educated.[116]

Our conclusion must be that Mosca's commitment to meritocracy, while real, is not on a par with his commitment to balanced pluralism but can be regarded as yet another special case of the latter.

6. The Problem of Elitism Versus Pluralism

Can the same analysis that has been made of Mosca's doctrine of meritocracy be given for his fundamental elitist principle? That is, would a closer examination of the status of the latter show that his attitude toward it is really another special case of his balanced pluralism? At any rate, what exactly is the relationship between elitism and balanced pluralism in Mosca?

We have already seen that Mosca's "elitism" cannot be equated with closed aristocracies, autocracy, bureaucratic excess, or special privileges, since he uses the elitist distinction between rulers and ruled to formulate his definition of and his commitment to the opposites of these entities, namely democracy, liberty, bureaucratic moderation, and meritocracy. So there is no justification for interpreting or criticizing his fundamental elitist principle as something it is not. Still, so far, Mosca's commitment to it seems absolute and unqualified. Is this really so?

A major clue that this is not so is his attributing to this principle the status of a "tendency." Although in his first book, *Theory of Governments* (1884), he calls minority rule a fact or law, at least beginning with the first edition of *Elements* (1896) he usually speaks of minority rule as a fact or tendency, or as a law or tendency.[117] "Tendency" is the same concept which Mosca uses explicitly in regard to the distinction between democracy and aristocracy and between feudalism and bureaucracy, and implicitly in regard to liberty and autocracy, and personal merit and birth privilege. In other words, elitism is not a brute fact, but merely one of a number of tendencies which have to be properly combined to yield the facts, for a tendency becomes a fact only when no countervailing tendencies are present. Now, in a way we have already examined the combination of the elitist principle with the other important tendencies, but this has been a combination of things that are distinct and different without being opposite and incompatible. However, if the elitist principle is to be analyzed in terms of the notion of a tendency, we must identify the two poles of the spectrum along which the principle operates; that is, we must identify the two opposite tendencies whose clash helps to generate socio-political reality. Thus the question becomes whether there is a tendency which is opposite to (not merely distinct from) the elitist tendency; if so, what it is; and whether it is really true that the elitist tendency always predominates over its opposite.

The difficulty in examining this question is that Mosca's own state-ment of his fundamental principle contains several elements, which would generate distinct opposites. One of these elements is certainly the *mi-nority* point of view, which Mosca himself explicitly contrasts with the *majority* point of view. I believe that the best way to generate opposite tendencies here it to contrast minority rule with majority consent. That is, while it is always minorities who rule, they always do so with the consent of the majority; this consent may be somewhat indirect, passive, and tacit, and its extent may vary, but without it the state could not subsist. I be-lieve this is recognized by Mosca in his doctrine of the political formula:

> In fairly populous societies that have attained a certain level of civili-zation, ruling classes do not justify their power exclusively by de facto possession of it, but try to find a moral and legal basis for it, represent-ing it as the logical and necessary consequence of doctrines and beliefs that are generally recognized and accepted. . . . The various political for-mulas may be based either upon supernatural beliefs or upon concepts which, if they do not correspond to positive realities, at least appear to be rational. We shall not say that they correspond in either case to sci-entific truths. . . . And yet that does not mean that political formulas are mere quackeries aptly invented to trick the masses into obedience. Any-one who viewed them in that light would fall into grave error. The truth is that they answer a real need in man's social nature, and this need, so universally felt, of governing and knowing that one is governed not on the basis of mere material or intellectual force, but on the basis of a moral principle, has beyond any doubt a real and practical importance.[118]

Thus my conclusion is that Mosca supplements the idea of minority rule, governance, or direction with the idea of majority consent, acquiescence, or acceptance.

Another important element of the fundamental elitist principle is the inequality of power. From this point of view, political power in any society is not distributed equally, but rather concentrated in the hands of a small (ruling) class. We also saw earlier that Mosca himself explicitly mentioned this feature when he stated the principle at the beginning of *Elements;*[119] many scholars have called also attention to this aspect.[120] Now, this aspect of the elitist principle can easily be interpreted as a tendency—namely, a tendency toward inequality of power. When so interpreted, the opposite tendency is also easy to identify as the tendency toward equality.

Next, despite Mosca's talk of elites in what is really a tendential and bipolar principle, Mosca was far from denying either the existence or the importance of the clash between these two opposite tendencies in human history. For example, in his important essay on "The Aristocratic and the Democratic Principles," which was the inaugural lecture for the academic year 1902-1903 at the University of Turin, he suggested that much of the history of ancient Greek city-states was the result of a struggle between these two tendencies. To be more exact, he held that it was the result of the tension between the apparent political equality of the citizens and their social, economic, and psychological inequalities.[121] And in regard to the modern world, Mosca interprets as tendencies toward equality much of the democratic movement stemming from Rousseau and much of the socialist movement stemming from Marx; he himself had first-hand experience of the reality of this clash in his own lost battle against universal suffrage, a development one can construe as egalitarian.[122]

Finally, there is evidence that Mosca was not one-sidedly or totally in favor of elitist inequality. At the end of his first book, he expressed a commitment to reducing the inequality he saw around him in the modern world in Italy and the rest of Europe. His formulation there includes an explicit qualification of the elitist principle:

> The truth is that equality of wealth cannot be established in the world, just as political equality cannot. Ultimately, both run up against the same difficulty, the natural inequality of men. The existence of rich and poor is the consequence of the same natural fact whereby there are, have been, and always will be in the world those who command and those who obey. However, while always keeping to our comparison, we must say that the problem has another aspect, which serves to clarify the first of the two hypotheses we are discussing. For, if it is most true that the few have always been in command, it is also true that the criteria by which they are recruited have not been always the same, nor has the domination been always equally harsh and arbitrary. Analogously, it remains to be seen

whether, while there must always be rich and poor, one can hope for an economic arrangement such that the most severe and degrading poverty is avoided, . . . whether it can happen that wealth itself should be less often the effect of birth and fortune, and more frequently the just reward for meritorious efforts and intelligent activity. We believe the accomplishment of these aspirations not to be easy, but to be perfectly possible.[123]

Here, Mosca's hope that better criteria can be employed in the recruitment of the ruling class is an expression of his commitment to democracy in the sense in which he was later to conceptualize it. His hope for a less harsh and arbitrary domination expresses his liberalism, again in his own technical sense of domination deriving its legitimacy and character from below. He obviously also advocates an increased meritocracy. But all these value judgments accord with our previous analysis. What especially interests us here is the explicit connection with political equality. He seems to be saying that, while some degree of inequality is inevitable, it may be possible and desirable to reduce certain inequalities.

So, I conclude that if Mosca's fundamental elitist principle is interpreted in anti-egalitarian terms, then we have a case of balanced pluralism, insofar as we are dealing with two tendencies which are opposite, perennial, and historically interacting; moreover, while Mosca does feel obliged to oppose the egalitarian tendency, his opposition is critical, moderate, and perhaps in the spirit of his counterrevolutionary principle.

However, there is a third way of interpreting Mosca's fundamental principle. As we have seen, he himself sometimes stated it in methodological terms, as advice to people conducting political studies and research.[124] His advice was to emphasize the class of leaders and study their behavior and origin and structure, in order to understand the most important features of political organizations. Here, the connection with balanced pluralism is clear and immediate, for emphasis on the class of leaders is meant to be, and can arguably be regarded as, an intermediate position between the emphasis on great and exceptional individuals and the emphasis on the people and the masses.

Finally, a fourth significant way of interpreting the fundamental elitist principle is in terms of organization. From this point of view, Mosca says, power is always in the hands of those who are organized. This formulation is very explicit in Michels's elaboration of the principle, but Mosca too is aware of its centrality.[125]

So interpreted, the elitist principle could become largely equivalent to Mosca's distinction between feudalism and bureaucracy, since organization is the essential point of bureaucratization. Thus, much of what we said before in connection with that distinction could be repeated with regard to the elitist principle. In particular its compatibility with balanced pluralism would become obvious. The only new point I would wish to discuss is the following.

As Eugenio Ripepe has argued,[126] the organizational tendency is monistic and antipluralist. From this he attempts to conclude that there is a deep inconsistency in Mosca between his undeniable pluralism and his elitist principle. I believe that the lesson is different: pluralism itself should not be carried too far. If the multiplicity of social forces, social structures, tendencies, governmental functions and branches, sub-elements of the ruling class and of the ruled class, etc., is excessive and lacks a unifying principle, then what we have is anarchy and not balanced pluralism. This lesson is obviously in accordance with Mosca's discussion of the connection between organization and minorities, where he asserts that "the minority is organized for the very reason that it is a minority." [127] Therefore, balanced pluralism must be itself balanced by a monistic, unifying tendency. I believe that the organizational element of the elitist principle is such a tendency. So, while there is indeed an opposition between Mosca's elitism and his pluralism, this very opposition is a sign of a deeper balance in his thinking. In this case, however, the conceptual and epistemological status of the elitist principle is enhanced in that it would constitute an irreducible element of the theoretical system and become more or less coequal with the principle of balanced pluralism.

7. Epilogue

In this chapter I have undertaken a reinterpretation and a re-evaluation of Mosca's political theory. We began with an examination of the principle which he regarded as a universally true generalization capable of providing the key foundational law of political science: that in every society political power is not equally distributed but rather concentrated in the hands of elites which rule over the masses.

I then evaluated this fundamental principle from the points of view of theoretical fruitfulness and predictive power, suggesting that it has considerable scientific and methodological merit, according to these criteria. Next, a number of objections to Mosca's law were discussed, such as whether it has any empirical content, whether it is empirically accurate, whether it is normatively desirable, whether it is causally explicable, whether it will be forever valid, whether it is essentially a myth, whether it is sufficiently free of ideological or class bias, and whether the concept of elite is sufficiently clear; the main result of this investigation was that Mosca's law needs to be understood and evaluated in the context of other analytical and normative principles which make up his theoretical system.

The other principles of his system are as follows: his conception of democracy in terms of open elites, his conception of liberty in terms of authority flowing from the bottom up, his distinction between feudalistic and bureaucratic tendencies, his ideal of mixed government, his ideal of the separation of powers, his ideal of checks and balances in government, his ideal of the balance of different social forces, his counterrevolutionary principle, and his ideal of meritocracy; the systemic thrust of this cluster of principles was revealed by relating them all to the basic principle of balanced pluralism. Finally, I discussed the tension between, and relative importance of, Mosca's fundamental elitist principle and his principle of balanced pluralism.

THREE

GRAMSCI ON MOSCA: METHODOLOGICAL AND THEORETICAL CRITICISM

THE PRISON NOTEBOOKS contain three layers of evidence in regard to Gramsci's acquaintance with Mosca and Mosca's influence on Gramsci. The most extensive layer is also the deepest, both in the sense that it involves the conceptual structure of Gramsci's political theory and in the sense that it is most deeply buried in the Notebooks, because it consists of discussions and analyses in which no *explicit* mention is made of Mosca and his ideas; this layer will be examined in later chapters. The second layer consists of a number of explicit comments, which will be analyzed presently. The third layer comprises three passages providing documentary evidence of Gramsci's direct acquaintance with Mosca's major works. Let us begin with the last group.

1. Gramsci's Direct Acquaintance with Mosca's Works

One of the passages proving Gramsci's direct acquaintance with Mosca's works is found in the notes on the Italian Risorgimento. Gramsci is attempting to give a systematic classification of the secondary literature on the subject. One group of works to which Gramsci pays special attention consists of nine books and several articles which he describes as consequences of the fall of the Historical Right in 1876. Besides these and other descriptions and analyses, Gramsci also gives some bibliographical information about the works. These bibliographical references are somewhat abbreviated and inaccurate. Curiously, it happens that the identity

of these works, as well as these abbreviations and inaccuracies, corre-
spond almost exactly to those contained in two footnotes in Mosca's
Theory of Governments. It is impossible to avoid the conclusion that
Gramsci had the second edition of this book (1925) in his hands when
he first wrote the paragraph of his notes on the Risorgimento. I am not
claiming to have made this discovery, which instead must be attributed to
Valentino Gerratana, the editor of the critical edition of the Notebooks;
I am merely focusing on this fact in order to use it together with other
facts to shed new light on the connection between these two thinkers.[1]

The second Gramscian passage involves a completely different matter, and the Moschian work in question is the second edition of *Elements
of Political Science* (1923); but the conclusion is analogous. Gramsci is
discussing the general phenomenon of transformism, which here may be
taken to refer to the assimilation of leaders of popular or left-wing parties
by more moderate or establishment institutions. In particular, he is referring to some aspects of the behavior of Italian socialist intellectuals in
the 1890s. The bulk of this note consists of a very long quotation from
an 1895 book on reactionary politics by Guglielmo Ferrero, but Gramsci
himself tells us that he is copying the passage from Mosca's *Elements*,
where it is indeed quoted. Ferrero's words are extremely interesting and
provocative:

> There have always been a certain number of individuals who need to be-
> come emotionally involved with something which is neither immediate
> nor personal and comes from afar; for them the business of their own af-
> fairs, of science, and of art is not enough to use up all their psychic energy.
> What was left to them in Italy but the socialist idea? It came from afar,
> which is always seductive; it was sufficiently complex and sufficiently
> vague, at least in part, to satisfy the so widely different moral needs of its
> many converts; on the one hand, it brought with it a broad spirit of fra-
> ternity and internationalism, which corresponds to a real modern need;
> on the other hand, it was oriented toward a scientific method which was
> reassuring to those educated in the experimental schools. Given this, it
> was not surprising that a large number of young people should have be-
> come members of such a party; that is, a party such that, if there was the
> risk of meeting some unimportant person who had come out of prison
> or some petty second-offender, at least there was no chance of meeting
> any exploiter of the Panama situation, any political speculator, any pro-
> fessional dealer in patriotism, any member of that band of adventurers
> without conscience or shame who, after creating modern Italy, devoured

it. The most superficial observation shows that almost nowhere in Italy do we have the economic and social conditions for the formation of a true and significant socialist party; moreover, a socialist party should logically find the bulk of its recruits in the working classes, not in the bourgeoisie as happened in Italy. Now, if a socialist party was developing in Italy under such unfavorable conditions and in such an illogical manner, it must have been because it corresponded primarily to a moral need on the part of a certain number of young people who were fed up by so much corruption, baseness, and vileness, and who would have sold themselves to the devil in order to escape the old parties rotten to the bone.[2]

It is unclear why Gramsci should have wanted to copy such a long quotation, though it is undoubtedly provocative. However, that need not concern us here. Suffice it to say that this quotation does establish that sometime while in prison Gramsci did read Mosca's *Elements*.

Finally, Gramsci may have been acquainted with Mosca's book entitled *Notes on Constitutional Law;* it was first published in 1908 and contains an account of the genesis of modern European constitutions and an account of the details of the Italian constitution. The evidence is as follows. Occasionally Gramsci used some pages in his Notebooks to write down things of a practical nature, such as drafts of letters to officials with specific requests or complaints about the prison situation; lists of books and journals received from, sent to, or requested from various relatives or bookstores; and accountings and calculations of a financial nature. All these things are duly noted and reported in a separate section of the critical edition of the Notebooks, rather than interspersed with the scholarly and philosophical discussions. Now, on the last three pages of one of his earliest notebooks, compiled in 1929, there are four lists of books. One of them is a list of books which had not been included in a particular shipment to him in prison, as he mentions to his sister-in-law in a letter dated 11 March 1929. Two are lists of books which he had in Rome at the time of his arrest in November 1926; on 25 March 1929 he wrote to his sister-in-law, who was living in Rome at the time, asking her to send him these books. The fourth list seems to be a group of books which he wanted to read, because in the same letter (25 March) he describes several of them as books he would like sent to him. Now, Mosca's book on constitutional law is not mentioned in the letter, but it is included in this fourth list. In fact, in this list Gramsci also speaks of "other books by Mosca,"[3] without giving their titles.

My conclusion is that, in regard to Mosca's book on constitutional law, we cannot be as certain that Gramsci read it in prison as we can be in regard to the other two. Nevertheless, just as he did eventually obtain these two, he probably also obtained that one. Later, in our discussion of the implicit connections between the two thinkers, we will see that access to this book would explain how Gramsci could say some things on the topic of the relation between the concepts of state and of civil society which seem to be taken right out of Mosca's book on constitutional law.[4]

Gramsci must have done more than consult or merely read Mosca's major works; he must have given considerable thought to them and the issues they raise, because the Notebooks contain a number of explicit remarks on Mosca. To be sure, these are not as frequent, lengthy, polished, and systematized as Gramsci's comments on some other thinkers, such as Croce, Bukharin, and Machiavelli.[5] In fact, only nine passages contain direct and explicit discussions of Mosca, but, as will be shown in later chapters, these discussions are but the tip of an iceberg which easily rivals the splendor and depth of the better-known and more polished critiques. Moreover, of the nine explicitly Moschian passages, three are early notes which were later expanded and revised; we are left with only six distinct passages. However, most of these raise several points, some of which overlap. So it is best to follow a systematic approach, rather than simply examine the notes one by one.[6]

These points may be systematized into three clusters, dealing with general methodological issues, with general substantive issues, and with *Theory of Governments.* We will see that Gramsci's comments will often tell us more about Gramsci than about Mosca, but this should not be surprising; this normally happens with original thinkers, who examine the views of others primarily with a theoretical, evaluative, and problem-oriented interest rather than a historical, interpretive, and text-oriented interest.[7]

2. Scientific Objectivity, Philosophical Sophistication, Historical Awareness

It is best to begin with Gramsci's general methodological critique. His most significant charge is that "Mosca's focus wavers between a position which is 'objective' and disinterested like that of a scientist and a position which is impassioned like that of a directly involved partisan who is witnessing events which he dislikes and against which he would like to react" (Q 1565). It is tempting to interpret this comment as a charge of unscientific bias, but that would not do justice to either Mosca or Gramsci; not to Gramsci because then one would have to go on and criticize him for having advanced an unjustified and misleading charge; and not to Mosca because it would give an inaccurate, one-sided, and unfair portrayal of his thinking. Moreover, this temptation ought to be resisted because to succumb to it would mean taking half of the sentence just quoted out of context.

Gramsci's essential difficulty seems to be that Mosca is "wavering" between the two points of view. Now, it is true that "wavering" sounds negative and suggests an illegitimate mixing of the two components; but since Gramsci does not elaborate how exactly the mixing is accomplished and what is illegitimate about it, it is not clear how seriously the negative aspect of the charge should be taken. So, Gramsci's remark is best interpreted as indicating, first, that there are two aspects to Mosca's work, a descriptive, analytical, and explanatory dimension and a normative, evaluative, and practical component; and second, that there are problems in the way in which these two parts interrelate. When so interpreted, Gramsci's comment is essentially correct and in fact corresponds to my own account of Mosca, outlined earlier (Chapter 2); this includes the point about the problematic character of the relationship between fact and value in Mosca, for I have not meant to deny that there are problems, but only that they are insurmountable.

A similar contextual interpretation must be given for a comment along the same lines that Gramsci makes elsewhere. Referring to *Elements,* he comments, "Mosca's book is a huge miscellany possessing a sociological and positivistic character, together with the added tendentiousness of immediate politics, which makes it less indigestible and from a literary point of view more lively" (Q 956). Here, Gramsci is not saying merely that Mosca's work is politically tendentious, but that this tendentiousness is one of two main features. The other feature has to do with sociologism and positivism.[8] By "positivism," Gramsci means the attempt to follow the alleged methods of the natural sciences in the disciplines which study society and politics; these methods allegedly consist of such procedures as the search for universal laws or regularities, the prediction of events, and the adoption of a value-free attitude. By "sociology," or a sociological approach, Gramsci means the positivistic study of society, including political institutions, which among other things would entail treating society as a static and unchanging entity whose history is of no importance; such an orientation may be called an ahistorical attitude, and it is obviously connected with some of the natural-scientific methods just mentioned, especially the search for universal laws. So, Gramsci is saying that Mosca's work is partly value-neutral (in the way that positivists and sociologists allegedly operate) and partly full of value judgments (like those common in practical politics) or, in other words, that it contains descriptive and analytical accounts as well as normative prescriptions and evaluations.

However, this is, as it were, merely the descriptive and analytical content of Gramsci's remark, for it cannot be denied that it also conveys something of a negative and unfavorable evaluation; in fact, the term "tendentious" is pejorative in any context, while "positivism" and "sociology" are pejorative in Gramsci's own lexicon. In short, here, again, Gramsci seems primarily to call attention to the twofold aim of Mosca's work (analytical and normative), and secondarily to suggest he is not entirely satisfied with either aspect; but the specific objections require separate discussion.

Just as Gramsci is not saying simply that Mosca's work is politically tendentious, he is not saying simply that it is methodologically positivist. As before, to take such an attribution out of context would be unfair to both authors. Therefore, although many scholars[9] have claimed that Mosca is a positivist, I do not think Gramsci should be included as one of the proponents of such a claim. And I believe this is to Gramsci's credit because I do not think that in fact Mosca is a positivist. For my interpretation (Chapter 2) provides the basis of a demonstration that this is not so.

In fact, the strong normative component of Mosca's work obviously conflicts with the positivist goal of a value-free social science; but this is not the only contradiction. We also saw that, although Mosca does aim at the formulation of general regularities, his own interpretation of these is a "tendential" one; the implication is that regularities in the social sciences are not like the laws of physical nature, and so his interpretation deviates from the key positivist tenet about the unity of science. In regard to prediction, the complexity of Mosca's outlook was illustrated by his skepticism about this activity in the social sciences, and by his suggestion of a possible asymmetry between positive and negative predictions; and this conflicts with the epistemological importance which positivism attaches to prediction. As regards history, Mosca's own approach is historical in the sense that he uses historical data and evidence to support his theoretical generalizations, although admittedly not in the historicist sense that he sees human nature and society as intrinsically evolving over the course of history; nevertheless, such a historical, nonhistoricist method is non-positivistic insofar as particular historical data and evidence are neither experimentally arranged nor directly observable, and hence they are unlike the data and evidence in the natural sciences which positivism takes as the models to emulate. Finally, we will see later (Chapter 7) that Mosca dismisses the doctrine advocated by Freemasons, and this dismissal is essentially an antipositivistic stance because their doctrine is essentially positivistic.

The two-sidedness of these two Gramscian general methodological comments helps us to understand better a pair of judgments advanced by Gramsci about Mosca's first book (published in 1884). In this case, Gramsci himself makes the two comments in two different notes, and so the separation does encourage scholars to focus on one to the exclusion of the other. As it happens, they have focused almost exclusively on the negative remark in this pair. The judgment in question is that Mosca's first book belongs to a group of works and type of literature which is "pseudohistorical and pseudocritical" (Q 1976). What Gramsci has in mind is that "this literature is a consequence of the fall of the Historical Right, of the coming to power of the so-called Left, and of the de facto innovations introduced. . . . They are in large measure complaints, recriminations, and pessimistic and catastrophic judgments of the national situation . . . furious over the fall of the Right and of the Consorteria (that is, over the diminished importance in the life of the state of certain groups of large landowners and of the aristocracy, for one cannot speak of the replacement of one class by another)" (Q 1976). The literature in question is exemplified by the list of works mentioned earlier, which was copied out of Mosca's footnotes. Moreover, in Gramsci's list, Mosca's own book is added to head the list, an addition which suggests that it too is being labeled pseudohistorical and pseudocritical.

However, Gramsci must not intend this criticism to apply to Mosca's book because, in another long and important note dealing with the nature of organic crises, he states that in the book Mosca "understood better in 1883 the techniques of the politics of subaltern classes than the representatives of these subaltern classes understood them even many decades afterwards" (Q 1607). This is very high praise from the point of view of theoretical analysis and cognitive worth.

Although Gramsci does not intend to dismiss Mosca's book as pseudoscholarly, he does maintain that Mosca and his first book were expressions of the middle and small rural bourgeoisie, a claim made quite explicit in the other note where Gramsci offers this appreciation. Finally, if the book can contain such a superior theoretical analysis while being an expression of a conservative class interest, then it follows that for Gramsci there is no contradiction between these two things; in short, a committed work is not necessarily cognitively flawed. This is a point very well worth emphasizing because I intend to apply it to Gramsci's own work. That is, while in some obvious sense Gramsci is taking the side of "subaltern classes," that does not necessarily deprive the Notebooks of scientific and philosophical merit. I am thus rejecting the common practice of criticizing or dismissing their doctrines on the basis of Gramsci's (alleged) practical commitments.[10]

Another general methodological objection advanced by Gramsci calls into question Mosca's philosophical sophistication. The charge is that "his philosophical preparation is nonexistent (and such it has remained for Mosca's entire literary career)" (Q 1978). This is essentially true, but its relevance is unclear, for it seems to me one must first distinguish between different branches of philosophy: in this context branches like methodology, epistemology, and ethics are highly relevant, whereas branches like metaphysics and aesthetics are largely irrelevant. Then I would distinguish between concrete and abstract analyses, and I would argue that the former are much more important than the latter. Finally, I would point out that, while Mosca does indeed stay away from abstract analyses, his particular methodological and ethical arguments are extremely sophisticated and insightful. For example, it is much more important for Mosca to have and express the right intuitions about particular predictions in his field than to be able to state and justify a general formulation of some maxim for prediction or to give an adequate account of the meaning of the concept of prediction;[11] similarly, it is more important to be able to argue the particular pros and cons of some ethical issue like the question of the correlation between service to society and personal merit than to be able to give some general definition of what justice is.[12]

This is ironic in two ways. First, this defense of Mosca from Gramsci's charge of philosophical naivete is Gramscian in character, insofar as it is an application to the case at hand of ideas Gramsci advances in various places in the Notebooks and applies primarily to the case of the relations between professional philosophy and popular common sense and between intellectuals and the masses.[13] One of his central points is that the popular masses have their own worldview according to which they live through their actions, and professional intellectuals, far from dismissing it, ought to learn from it in building their own theories, by making explicit what is implicit. The same holds in the domain of scientific practice and inquiry; a working scientist like Mosca is to the ethical or epistemological theorist as the man in the street is to the Gramscian intellectual. The second irony is that it has now become fashionable to question Gramsci's own philosophical sophistication and preparation;[14] and I believe that to defend Gramsci effectively and properly, it is necessary to call on the argument sketched here in regard to Mosca.

The objection just discussed raises the issue of the role of philosophical awareness in scientific investigation and scholarly inquiry in general. I do not mean to convey the impression that, in denying its relative importance vis-à-vis scientific and scholarly practice and intuition, I seek to deprive it of any importance. On the contrary, I would argue that, other things being equal, epistemological and methodological self-awareness is good; but we have to make sure that the other things are equal. In other words, although philosophical awareness is no substitute for good concrete scientific theorizing, and although it is not as important as other criteria for the evaluation of a scientific theory, it is not completely unimportant or irrelevant. And, in fairness to Gramsci, it must be said that he himself only mentions the present objection in a cursory and somewhat peripheral manner, without undue emphasis; moreover, in a more explicit methodological discussion, in the context of a critique of Bukharin's sociology, he discusses methodological awareness explicitly as only one of several criteria.[15] So what I have outlined here as my position may not be far from Gramsci's own.

Similar considerations apply to historical awareness—that is, to the question of the role and importance of knowing the relation between one's own theory and previous theories. In regard to this, Gramsci also objects that Mosca has not explored adequately the relations between his theory of the political class and historical materialism:

> Mosca unconsciously reflects the discussions generated by historical materialism, but he reflects them like someone from the provinces who feels in the air the discussions taking place in the capital but does not have the means to acquire the documents and the fundamental texts. In Mosca's case, not to have the means for acquiring the texts and the documents of the problem, which he nevertheless treats, means that Mosca belongs to the group of academics who think it is their duty to show all the care of the historical method when they are studying the insignificant ideas of a third-rate medieval popularizer, but do not think or did not think

worthy of the method the doctrines of historical materialism, did not think it necessary to go to the original sources, and were satisfied with rummaging through the popular press. [Q 1565]

Now, we already saw in my discussion of Mosca's political theory (Chapter 2) that, upon becoming acquainted with his basic elitist principle, it is only natural to wonder about how it relates to the Marxist theory of class struggle; indeed, many writers have noted the fact, and some of them have explored it to a greater or lesser extent. Gramsci's point is analogous, but much more critical. He seems to be saying that Mosca was methodologically obliged to undertake this inquiry himself.

Moreover, this type of objection is very common in the social sciences and in the humanities, in numerous versions. Sometimes one is told that one's own theory is stillborn, as it were, because some precursor advanced it before and it has already been refuted. At other times the theory is presumably correct, but one is told that the credit for it must go to someone else who advanced it before. Still other times one's own theory is slightly different, but the problem arises that what is new is not true and what is true is not new.

Finally, this kind of issue has acquired some relevance even for the natural sciences, at least at the level of the metascientific analysis of scientific method.[16] That is, there is a broad consensus among historians, sociologists, and philosophers of science that the history of an idea has some relevance to its validity; that evaluation of a physical-scientific theory is conducted and ought to be conducted in part on the basis of how the theory has developed, of its track record in providing solutions to old problems and in dealing with new ones. However, although this consensus has to do in part with the factual, historical claim that this is one way in which scientific theories are and have been evaluated, it cannot be reported that scientists have internalized the process to such an extent that they make explicit use of this criterion, or for that matter that even in the course of history scientists can be said to have explicitly acknowledged such a historical criterion. Therefore, the gap between science and history seems to remain.[17]

In any case, even if and to the extent that the history of a theory is relevant to its scientific validity, this does not mean that any kind of historical investigation about it would have this relevance. Presumably, one might want to know all sorts of things from the point of view of historical erudition or scholarship which are perfectly legitimate from such a point of view and which, in fact, define the nature of the enterprise of historiography, but which would have no relevance from the scientific and theoretical point of view.

So, my conclusion is that Gramsci's historical-methodological objection is not improper and cannot be dismissed as being either irrelevant or unfair. Nevertheless, I am not sure it hits the mark for the following reason. The fact is that Mosca did do a certain amount of historical investigation. His first book (1884) did contain in the preface a brief acknowledgment to a number of precursors, especially Taine.[18] In the second edition of *Elements*, the second volume begins with a longer historical discussion of the theory, and credits primarily Henri de Saint-Simon and Ludwig Gumplowicz, but also mentions Marx and Engels.[19] And at the same time that Gramsci was writing this criticism in prison, Mosca was, unbeknownst to him, teaching and researching the history of political doctrines; the resulting book was first published in 1933, and contains an even lengthier account of Marx and historical materialism.[20]

Therefore, I believe that the situation is as follows. Mosca did examine historical materialism but concluded that the differences between it and his own doctrine were greater than the similarities; in particular, he must have felt that the differences consisted precisely of the weak and false aspects of historical materialism. Hence, in his works, he emphasized the differences and focused on negative, destructive criticism. Presumably Gramsci would not agree with those conclusions and decisions of Mosca's. But that is another story. Gramsci would then have had to advance his specific disagreements about the relation between Mosca's theory and historical materialism. He could not merely advance the present historical-methodological objection. In short, while the objection is generally valid, it is specifically incorrect and misdirected.

In conclusion, Gramsci seems to impugn Mosca's scientific objectivity, philosophical sophistication, and historical awareness. On closer inspection, the first objection turns out to be less of a negative criticism and more of an analytical interpretation accompanied by a slightly negative warning; the interpretation is that Mosca's work contains both scientific analyses and value judgments, and the warning is that the relation between these two elements is problematic. On the other hand, the other two objections are meant to be essentially negative; however, they involve equivocations such that if the charges are true, the sense in which they are true makes them irrelevant; whereas if the charges are interpreted in a sense which gives them relevance, then they are materially false.

3. Relations of Force, Intellectuals, and the Political Party

Gramsci also makes several general substantive comments about Mosca's work. These suggest a number of theoretical connections between the work of the two authors and shed light on the sense in which Gramsci can be said to be pursuing the Moschian research program.

The most important connection is perhaps the one at the beginning of the special notebook on Machiavelli. There Gramsci sketches not one but two research projects. The better-known project is the one relating more directly to Machiavelli, as well as the political party as the "modern prince" and the question of revolution; this need not concern us here.[21] However, we also find the outline of another project, which Gramsci regards as an elementary exposition of the science and art of politics. Though introduced by Gramsci with less inspirational zeal than the first-mentioned project, this one is equally explicit as regards the theoretical effort and the importance of the research program: "The study of how 'situations' should be analyzed, in other words how to establish the various levels of the relations of force, offers an opportunity for an elementary exposition of the science and art of politics—understood as a body of practical rules for research and of detailed observations useful for awakening an interest in effective reality and for stimulating more rigorous and more vigorous political insight. This should be accompanied by the explanation of what is meant in politics by strategy and tactics, by strategic 'plan,' by propaganda and agitation, by [the organics] or science of political organization and administration."[22]

What is more striking is that in this particular notebook Gramsci actually goes on to elaborate on these topics.[23] Thus we find a distinction between "organic" and "conjunctural" developments, namely between deep-seated, long-range forces and superficial, short-range ones; a classification of forces into four types: international, material or productive or economic, political, and military; a subdivision of political forces into corporative-political, class-political, party-political, and state-political; a subdivision of military forces into political-military and technical-military; and the notion of "hegemony" as referring to a certain relationship of forces characterized by a stable equilibrium resulting from the primacy of one over the other with the consent of the other. Then in terms of such a conceptual framework, we find the analysis of such phenomena as social crises, great powers (in international affairs), caesarism, and dictatorship; a criticism of various forms of economism, including one species of liberalism, theoretical syndicalism, electoral abstention-ism, Rosa Luxemburg's theory of the war of maneuver, and the attitude of uncompromising intransigence; and the criticism of various forms of ideologism, including Croce's notion of ethico-political history and Trotsky's theory of permanent revolution.

The important consideration here is that Gramsci continues the passage just quoted by explaining how he thinks this project is an improvement on Mosca's own political science: "The elements of empirical observation which are habitually included higgledy-piggledy in works of political science (G. Mosca's *Elementi di scienza politica* may be taken as typical) ought, insofar as they are not abstract and illusory, to be inserted into the context of the relations of force, on one level or another."[24] The suggestion here seems to be that, insofar as they are descriptively accurate, the empirical generalizations in a work like Mosca's could be given a deeper interpretation through their incorporation into the doctrine of relations of force. Viewed from another angle, one might say that the principles of this doctrine would be improvements on or extensions of Mosca's generalizations.

Of course, what we have here is a mere suggestion, which could turn out to be wrong. Nevertheless, it is obvious that for Gramsci there is a relationship. I should add that, in the light of my analysis of Mosca's political theory (Chapter 2), the relationship mentioned by Gramsci makes more sense, insofar as the balance of social forces is a key theme in Mosca's work.

An analogous connection is supported by Gramsci's remarks on the notion of political class. The difference is that he is more forceful in his criticism but also more specific and helpful in his constructive suggestion. In my account of Mosca's political theory (Chapter 2), I paraphrased Gramsci's criticism and suggested that it is essentially correct. Now it is worth quoting his words: "The question of the political class, as presented in the works of Gaetano Mosca, has become a puzzle. The notion is so elastic and wavering that one cannot clearly understand what exactly Mosca means by political class. It seems that sometimes he means the middle class; at other times the collection of the property-owning classes; at still other times what is called the 'educated part' of society, or the 'political personnel' (the parliamentary class) of the state. Sometimes it seems that the bureaucracy, even the upper layer, is excluded from the political class, insofar as it must be controlled and guided by the political class" (Q 1565). As I have said before, it seems to me that Mosca's concept is full of such ambiguities.

However, the important thing to stress in this context is that Gramsci also thinks it is possible to find a way out of these ambiguities and difficulties. The answer lies in the direction of his own doctrine about intellectuals: *"History of Intellectuals.* Mosca's *Elements of Political Science* (new augmented edition of 1923) should be examined under this heading. Mosca's so-called political class is nothing but the intellectual class of the dominant social group. Mosca's concept of 'political class' should be compared to Pareto's concept of 'elite,' which is another attempt to interpret the historical phenomenon of intellectuals and their function in political and social life" (Q 1956).[25] Now, the doctrine of intellectuals is unquestionably one of the central topics in the Notebooks. Gramsci devotes a special notebook to it (Q 12), but the topic is much more pervasive than even that would suggest. For example, much of what he has to say about philosophers in general (in Q 11,12), and about Croce (in Q 10), involves intellectuals.

Therefore, what we have here is that Gramsci sees a flaw in Mosca's system, he thinks he has a remedy for it, and he engages in a considerable effort to elaborate on this replacement.[26]

In his comment on relations of force, Gramsci's constructive suggestion is very obvious, while the negative criticism of Mosca is very mild. In regard to the political class and intellectuals, as mentioned, Gramsci seems to give equal emphasis to destructive criticism and to constructive elaboration. In his next point the destructive criticism is the only explicit element, while the constructive element is more hidden.

The criticism is that "the deficiency of Mosca's treatment lies in the fact that he does not face in its complexity the problem of the political party" (Q 1565). This criticism is fair because it is indeed true that Mosca does not pay much attention to this theoretical problem, although of course he does not completely ignore it; for example, the first volume of *Elements* does have a chapter on "churches, parties, and sects."[27]

Gramsci had a practical reason for regarding the problem of the political party as an important one: in the middle part of his life he had been actively involved in founding, organizing, and leading a political party, and so a theory of the party would be an attempt to gain an adequate understanding of such activities, and perhaps to improve upon them. However, he also has a more theoretical reason—namely, that the problem of the party is an immediate consequence of the fundamental elitist principle: "Given the principle that there are those who are led and those who lead, those who are governed and those who govern, it is true that so far parties are the most adequate means for the formation of leaders and the ability to lead. ('Parties' can present themselves under the most diverse names, even that of 'anti-party' or 'negation of parties'; in reality, even so-called individualists are party men, only that they would like to be 'party chiefs' by the grace of God or of the stupidity of those who follow them" (Q 1753–54).

At any rate, the nature of political parties is one of the most frequent topics of discussion in the Notebooks.[28] Therefore, it appears that Gramsci was in part trying to fill a significant lacuna in Mosca's political science. To that extent, his thinking was a critical elaboration of Mosca's.

In conclusion, the theory of the relations of force, the theory of intellectuals, and the theory of the political party are three of the most important themes in the Notebooks. I have no intention of denying that these three doctrines have many sources, some of them practical and some intellectual. Among the practical sources, Gramsci's own political career played an obvious part, in the sense of at least leading him to think about these topics. And among the intellectual sources, Croce, Machiavelli, Bukharin, Marx, and Lenin played some part. However, the evidence presented here shows that it is equally undeniable that Mosca was an important source. The same documentation suggests something more precise in regard to the connection with this source. That is, these three Gramscian theoretical efforts are, at least in Gramsci's own view, attempts to improve on Mosca's political science. Gramsci's theory of the relations of force is supposedly an attempt to systematize and render more practical and concrete many of the generalizations and principles in Mosca's *Elements,* whose empirical correctness Gramsci admits. Gramsci's doctrine of intellectuals is presumably an attempt to clarify the ambiguities in Mosca's notion of political class, and more generally to do better the work this notion was intended to accomplish. And Gramsci's theory of the party is partly an attempt to solve a theoretical problem which immediately arises in Mosca's political science but which he neglected.

4. Political Irresponsibility, Extremism, and Legalism

The depth, wealth, and judiciousness of Gramsci's view of Mosca, and the significance of what is revealed about Gramsci's own general outlook, are well illustrated by his commentary on Mosca's *Theory of Governments*, first published in 1884 and reprinted in 1925. Gramsci's paragraph on this score also happens to be the single longest Gramscian note on Mosca, but it has never been translated into English, perhaps because it occurs in the context of a critical review of the literature in the special notebook on the Risorgimento (and that notebook has received little attention outside Italy). Let us examine Gramsci's words:

> The books in the Mosca-Turiello group began to become fashionable once again in the years preceding the war (one can see the constant references to Turiello in the *Voce*); Mosca's youthful book was reprinted in 1925 with a note by the author to indicate that these ideas go back to 1883 and that in 1925 the author no longer agrees with the twenty-four-year-old writer of 1883.[29] The reprinting of Mosca's book is one of the many instances of the unconscionableness and the political dilettantism of the liberals during the first as well as the second period after the war. After all, the book is crude, unseasoned, and hastily written by a young man who wants to "distinguish" himself in his own time by means of an extremist attitude and big words, which are often trivial and reactionary-oriented. Mosca's political concepts are vague and wavering; his philosophical preparation is nonexistent (and such it has remained for Mosca's entire literary career); his principles for the technicalities of politics are also vague and abstract and have a somewhat juridical character. The concept of 'political class,' which was to become the center of all of Mosca's writings in political science, is extremely thin and is neither derived nor justified theoretically. However, Mosca's book is useful as a document. The author wants to be open-minded as a matter of principle, and outspoken, and so he manages to bring to light many aspects of the Italian life of the time which would otherwise not have been documented. On such topics as the civilian and military bureaucracy, the police, etc., Mosca provides portrayals which are sometimes trendy but substantially true (for example, on noncommissioned officers in the army, on police officers, etc.). His observations are especially valuable for the case of Sicily, because of Mosca's direct acquaintance with that environment. In 1925 Mosca changed his point of view and his attitude, and his material was superseded; however, he reprinted the book out of literary vanity, thinking he could neutralize it with a few notes of retraction. [Q 1978–79]

The "balanced pluralism" of this comment should be obvious: Gramsci is saying both negative or unfavorable and positive or favorable things about Mosca; and he is expressing judgments on several aspects of

Mosca's work: political, scientific-theoretical, scientific-methodological, and historical. This feature gives a general Moschian flavor to the passage, in the sense that Gramsci is displaying balanced pluralism in the context of textual interpretation and critical practice. Certain more specific Moschian features touch on some new matters not previously discussed.

One is the political criticism that the 1925 reprinting of Mosca's first book was politically irresponsible. What Gramsci has in mind, of course, is that in 1925 in Italy Fascism was in the process of consolidating the power it had come to control ever since the March on Rome in 1922. The problem was that, since the book was in some respects a theoretical criticism of parliamentary government, it reinforced the Fascists' practical criticism of that institution, whereas Mosca had become increasingly favorable to it after the publication of his first book (1884). Indeed, before the end of the year (1925), Mosca himself came explicitly to the defense of parliamentary government, but by then it was too late.[30]

It is difficult to disagree with Gramsci in this assessment, just as it is difficult to explain this political error on the part of Mosca. It can only be mentioned in his justification that it is easy to speak with wisdom after the event, but at the time Mosca and other liberals (like Croce) felt for a while that Fascism was the least of several evils (such as anarchy, civil war, and Bolshevism) and that they would soon be able to tame it.

This having been said, another aspect calls for analysis. Gramsci's political criticism obviously pertains to the second edition of the book, not to its original publication in 1884. In fact, Gramsci's remark about the work's usefulness as a document gives a clue that his judgment on the earlier situation would be different, and probably favorable. This conclusion emerges explicitly in the paragraph which immediately precedes the one just quoted. In the earlier paragraph, Gramsci clarifies the value of that earlier literature:

> The whole of this literature collectively has a "documentary" importance in regard to the times when it appeared. The books of the "right-wingers" portray the political and moral corruption of the period when the Left was in power, whereas the publications of the epigones of the Action Party present as no better the period when the Right controlled the government. The result is that there has been no essential change with the transition from the Right to the Left: the morass in which the country has found itself is not due to the parliamentary regime (which renders public and known what earlier remained hidden or elicited clandestine

publications of a libelous nature) but to the weakness and the organic incoherence of the ruling [*dirigente*] class and to the great poverty and backwardness of the country. [Q 1977-78]

This judgment is extremely important because it shows that Gramsci is here being in a sense more Moschian than Mosca himself. Two principles are involved. The more obvious one is some version of the elitist principle: Gramsci is focusing on the elite and attributing to it more importance than he attributes to the institutions of parliamentary government in the determination of events. Hence, Gramsci's judgment about the 1884 situation exhibits a significant commitment to Mosca's fundamental principle.

The second is that having differential judgments about the same work in the context of the two respective historical periods is more than merely plausible and commonsensical. It is reminiscent of what I have called Mosca's "counterrevolutionary principle" (discussed in Chapter 2, section 3). In fact, the earlier period was one when the prevailing trend was to sing the praises of parliamentary institutions, and in this context, this principle suggests that one do precisely what Mosca did. However, the early 1920s were a period when those same institutions were generally coming under attack, and so to advance the same criticism then was to join a prevailing trend rather than oppose it; and this is precisely the reverse of what the same principle advises. Therefore, Gramsci seems to be implicitly committed to this Moschian principle.

A second revealing remark relates to Gramsci's judgment that the book is crude, unseasoned, and extremist. It reveals that Gramsci values moderation, balance, and judiciousness. Now, this attitude contradicts the traditional interpretations of Gramsci, according to which he was first and foremost a radical and a revolutionary, and which equate radicalism and revolution with extremism and one-sidedness.[31] However, my interpretation does correspond to the account I have elaborated elsewhere in connection with other aspects of the Notebooks and other theoretical problems; in that account I argue that an essential feature of the Notebooks is the so-called dialectical manner of thinking and that, when properly analyzed, an essential feature of dialectic is the avoidance of one-sidedness and of extremes.[32] An any rate, we certainly have an instance of that approach in this Gramscian judgment on Mosca's first book.

Despite the formal merit of Gramsci's judgment, I would question its accuracy. That is, he fails to recognize the book's true character, and his charge of crude extremism must be regarded as misdirected. In fact, aside from the scientific, theoretical, and generalizing part of the book, the historical and "documentary" part is a critique of parliamentarism. Now, his primary criticism is that parliamentarism is an abuse of power in a representative government in which the system of checks and balances is not functioning and excessive power is concentrated in one institution, the chamber of deputies elected by popular suffrage; and in which the abuse takes place at the expense of traditional institutions like the executive branch, the king, the senate, and the judiciary, and without thought to new institutions which might be able to reduce the abuses. Thus I believe De Mattei is right when he asserts that the book "aimed only at moderating the prevailing blind faith in the magical virtues of the parliamentary regimes. . . . Mosca did not intend to propose hasty recipes and panaceas: 'To find the remedies is, to be frank, less easy.' "[33]

And this brings us to Gramsci's criticism of Mosca's principles regarding the technicalities of politics as vague, abstract, and juridical. He is referring to Mosca's proposed reforms. I believe that the main feature he is attributing to them is what is usually labeled formalism, so that the objection reflects an attitude of realism or antiformalism. That is, Gramsci is charging Mosca with proposing reforms which are concerned more with abstract and formal legal and constitutional mechanisms than with the social conditions and actual political processes.

The most striking thing about such a charge is that it reflects a Gramscian commitment to an approach pioneered, pursued, and advocated by Mosca himself. We have, as it were, a Moschian charge against Mosca, an indication that Gramsci is implicitly trying to be more Moschian than Mosca himself. So the charge is serious and important: methodologically, because it helps us to understand Gramsci's own approach; historically, because it strengthens the connection between him and Mosca; and evaluatively, because, if accurate, the charge does indicate an internal inconsistency in Mosca's thought.

From the last chapter, we are already familiar with Mosca's realism or antiformalism in general. For example, it emerges in his criticism of Montesquieu's theory of checks and balances, which Mosca feels must be either reinterpreted as, or supplemented by a principle of, the balance of social forces. More generally, Mosca's realism is apparent in his fundamental elitist principle, insofar as it is presented as a superior alternative to traditional classifications of government; these are criticized as being based on criteria which are formalistic, as well as superficial and abstract;

whereas the character and origin of the "political class" can serve as more realistic criteria. We might add that one of Mosca's constant concerns was to distinguish what he wanted to call political science from what is variously called legal theory, constitutional law, or public law; and he found the main difference to lie in the contrast between social forces and interests on the one hand and legal institutions on the other.[34] We will see later (in Chapter 7) that in regard to the Fascist law against Freemasonry, Mosca showed great concern for its social and practical consequences.

Despite such antilegalistic realism in general, it might have happened that Mosca's first book deviated from that somewhat or had not developed sufficiently in that direction. So, the accuracy of this specific Gramscian charge is a separate issue. Now, it is indeed true that some of the reforms of the parliamentary government (especially in Italy) proposed in that book are juridical; as we saw in the last chapter, Mosca had specific proposals for new laws and constitutional changes, involving such matters as the interrelationship of the legislative, executive, and judicial branches of governments, and a possible fourth branch with the explicit function of serving as a moderator and guarantor of a proper balance of power. However, his emphasis lies elsewhere, namely in the social conditions. The following quotations both typify and summarize his central point:

> Although legally all our institutions are organized in such a way that positions and promotions must be granted always for personal merit, yet in practice this principle is constantly violated, not only by the usual weaknesses of human character (which are common in all places and at all times) but also by a constant and general influence: that is, by the power (not legal, but effective power) which [elected] deputies and the elements tied to them exert on all our administration and especially on its highest officials.[35] . . .

> If we want checks on the power of the so-called representatives of the people and we mean checks which are really effective, it is necessary not only that our written constitution should mention the existence of a king and of a senate but also that these should really be centers of real and independent political values. It would be necessary for the king really to be the head of all regular bureaucratic hierarchy, and for his ministers who surround him to be the most distinguished leaders of this hierarchy and not merely those who are recommended for royal selection by the majority of the deputies. For example, it would be necessary that the senate should be selected from a class of officials who are independent of both the governmental hierarchy and of popular elections, and that it should

include the best-educated and most independent elements of the country; at the same time this class should be entrusted with the whole of provincial administration and with wide participation in the work of the provincial bureaucracy. King and senate would then have great prestige and great power, and the chamber of deputies would be not only balanced but also effectively checked; but these and similar reforms, which correspond not only to our opinions but also to our aspirations, cannot be advocated or still less actualized unless one leaves entirely the conceptual framework and the point of view which characterize the parliamentary system.[36]

Gramsci's charge of formalism does, therefore, have a basis in the Moschian text, but it is largely a one-sided exaggeration. This in turn implies that, while the charge does reflect Moschian antiformalistic realism on the part of Gramsci, it also happens to represent an atypical divergence from balanced pluralism on his part.

5. Epilogue

We have seen evidence that while in prison (if not before) Gramsci read Mosca's major works. Thus, it is not surprising to find a number of explicit comments on Mosca in the Prison Notebooks. There are three main strands.

The general methodological criticism seems to impugn Mosca's scientific objectivity, philosophical sophistication, and historical awareness. However, the reality underlying this appearance is that Gramsci is underscoring the important fact that Mosca's work has a normative or evaluative component besides a descriptive or analytical one. Moreover, while Gramsci is right that some kind of philosophical and of historical sensitivity is important in scholarly research, Mosca did in fact possess the relevant kind, though admittedly not the irrelevant kind, of each. In regard to the relation between Gramsci and Mosca, one important consequence is that they seem to share some important methodological characteristics: that is, sensitivity to and interest in certain specific kinds of normative, philosophical, and historical considerations in the course of scientific inquiry.

With regard to the general substantive or theoretical critique, Gramsci seems to criticize Mosca's systematization of empirical generalizations, his concept of the political class, and his failure to treat the problem of the political party. However, in each of these cases the alleged flaw is to be remedied by a specific Gramscian substitute, the theory of relations of force, the theory of intellectuals, and the theory of the political party, respectively. These doctrines, which constitute important themes in the Prison Notebooks, may then be viewed as critical elaborations or constructive criticisms of Mosca's work. To that extent, the two thinkers may be said to be working within the same political-scientific research program or tradition of political theory.

Finally, in his focused critique of Mosca's first book, *Theory of Governments* (1884), Gramsci seems to charge Mosca with political irresponsibility for having the book reprinted in 1925, and seems to object to its content as exhibiting extremism and legalism. However, Gramsci balances his charge of Mosca's irresponsibility in 1925 with an appreciation for his original contribution in 1884; and this balanced view demonstrates Gramsci's commitment to a number of Moschian ideas and practices—specifically, the principle of elitism, balanced pluralism, and the counterrevolutionary principle. On the other hand, the charges of extremism and legalism, while inaccurate, do betray Gramsci's own commitment to moderation and to realism; to the extent that these are also typical Moschian traits, the methodological ties between the two men are further strengthened.

Therefore, Gramsci's critique of Mosca begins to substantiate the extent and depth of their similarities and ties. These include the methodological or formal practices of normative (in addition to analytical) interest, proper philosophical and historical awareness, balanced pluralism, moderation, and antilegalist realism; and, substantively and theoretically, they include the fundamental elitist principle, along with the problems of relations of force, intellectuals or political class, and the political party.

FOUR

GRAMSCI'S ELITISM: AN EXTENSION OF MOSCA'S LAW

THERE ARE MANY PASSAGES in the Prison Notebooks which have an implicitly Moschian character, in the sense that the particular ideas advanced by Gramsci are reminiscent of Mosca, although the latter is not mentioned explicitly. The most significant of these passages cluster around the notions of elitism, democracy, liberty, the relation between Gramsci's "hegemony" and Mosca's "political formula," the relation between state and civil society, the balancing function in a government, and parliamentarism. I shall begin with the elitist cluster, not only because *Mosca* believes the elitist principle to be the most fundamental principle of political science, but also because *Gramsci* shares that judgment about the status of the elitist principle. Thus, in this chapter I shall examine Gramsci's elitism and how it compares and contrasts with Mosca's.[1]

1. From Domination to Leadership

One of the most revealing notes in all of the Prison Notebooks is the fourth one in notebook 15 (Q 15,4). Notebook 15 deals with miscellaneous subjects, and so this note bears a title and a subtitle, "Machiavelli: Elements of Politics" (Q 1752). The title aims to tells us that this note is part of the series on Machiavelli, who is the subject of two special notebooks and whose name is used by Gramsci as a convenient label for his own systematic reflections on explicitly political topics.[2] The subtitle is reminiscent of Mosca's *Elements of Political Science,* and the initial paragraph leaves little doubt of the allusion, for it contains a statement of the fundamental elitist principle very similar to that found at the beginning of that work, and it expresses a very Moschian judgment about the role and status of this principle in the scientific study of politics:

> *Machiavelli: Elements of Politics.* It must really be said that the first things to be forgotten are precisely the first elements, the most elementary things; on the other hand, if they are repeated countless times, they become the pillars of politics and of any collective action whatever. The first element is that there really exist the governed and the governors, the leaders and the led. All political art and science are based on this primordial and (under certain general conditions) irreducible fact. The origins of this fact are a separate problem, which must be studied separately . . ., but the fact remains that there exist leaders and led, governors and governed. Given this fact, one must see how one can lead in the most effective manner (given certain aims), and therefore how best to prepare the leaders (and here precisely lies the first chapter of political science and art); one must also see, on the other hand, what are the lines of least resistance, namely the rational means, to gain the obedience of the led or governed. [Q 1752]

It is clear that Gramsci's emphasis is not on minority rule, that is, on the fact that the governors are always the few and the governed are always the many, but rather on the distinction (and the relationship, as we shall see) between the two groups. However, as we saw earlier, in my account of Mosca's political theory (Chapter 2, section 1), Mosca's own emphasis was the same in the formulation he gave at the beginning of *Elements,* although in his earlier *Theory of Governments* he had indeed stated the principle by stressing minority rule. That is, in *Elements* Mosca stresses the distinction (the inequality of power, as it were), and minority rule is just one of several aspects of the distinction: "Among the constant tendencies and facts which are found in all political organisms, there is one which is easily and clearly evident to all: in every society . . . there exist two classes of persons: that of the governors and the other one of the governed. The first, which is always less numerous, takes care of all political functions, monopolizes power, and enjoys all the advantages it brings; while the other, which is more numerous, is led and ruled by the first in a more or less legal manner (namely, in a more or less arbitrary and violent manner) and supplies to the first (at least apparently) the material means of subsistence and the means necessary to the vitality of the political organism."[3]

I do not mean to deny that there are differences between Mosca's and Gramsci's formulations and elaborations, but the differences can be best understood in the context of an essential initial agreement. The two essentially agree in regard to the empirical truth and scientific importance of the elitist distinction—namely, the differences in the power held by different groups and individuals. At any rate, one apparent disagreement may turn out to be more apparent than real; it regards the evaluation of the desirability of the fact, for Gramsci makes a number of statements suggesting that it may not be unchangeable, and so the ideal to strive for is the elimination of the distinction and the equalization of power; this issue will be examined later in this chapter. The other main difference, which will be examined first, is that Gramsci is more elitist than Mosca, in the sense that he indicates on several occasions that he thinks the elitist distinction is more deeply true, more scientifically important, and more general in scope than Mosca thought.

One way in which Gramsci generalizes Mosca's principle is to argue that the elitist distinction applies not only when one social class dominates a different social class, but also when the context is one homogeneous class; inevitably, in the latter case, one part leads another. There are certainly traces of this idea in Mosca, for example, in the second edition of *Elements* where he elaborates a distinction within the "political class" between an upper and a lower stratum.[4] However, Gramsci's explicitness, clarity, and immediate recognition of this intraclass character of the distinction are such as to justify our saying that we have here an illustration of his generalization of Mosca's principle. In fact, in the same fourth section of the fifteenth notebook, soon after stating the fundamental elitist principle quoted above, Gramsci adds, "One must be clear that, although the division between governed and governors in the final analysis stems from a division of social groups, nevertheless, given things as they are, it exists within the interior of the same group, even when it is socially homogeneous; in a sense, one may say that this division is a consequence of the division of labor, is a technical fact" (Q 1752).

Gramsci's generalization is made in other, complementary ways. One of the most important and explicit of these is that he distinguishes two basic kinds of relationships between classes or groups, which he calls domination and leadership. Moreover, he feels this point is so important that he gives it the status of a methodological criterion:

> The methodological criterion on which one must base one's examination is this: The supremacy of a social group is manifested in two ways, as "domination" and as "intellectual and moral leadership." A social group is "dominant" over opposed groups, which it tends to "liquidate" and subjugate even with the force of arms; and it is "leading" in regard to kindred and allied groups. A social group can and indeed must be leading before acquiring governmental power (this is one of the principal conditions for the very acquisition of power); thereafter, when it exercises power and even if it holds this power firmly in hand, it becomes "dominant" but must continue to be also "leading." [Q 2010–11].

This passage occurs in the context of a discussion of nineteenth-century Italian history, and Gramsci immediately gives the example of the Moderate Party leading the more populist Action Party both before and after Italian unification, at which time the moderates also became dominant. However, there is no question about the generality of Gramsci's intention and expression. By labeling it a methodological criterion, he means that it is a general principle to be used as a guide in the interpretation of historical and political developments. There are two aspects to what Gramsci is saying. On the one hand, not all supremacy is domination, which involves the use of force; some has the character of leadership, which involves kinder and gentler means such as moral principles and intellectual arguments. On the other hand, even among allies that have things in common—and not just among enemies—actual equality or complete mutuality may be unrealistic, and it is inevitable that one group will lead the other(s).

This distinction between domination and leadership enables us to grasp the significance of some of Gramsci's language in his statement of the elitist principle. In fact, in that statement, and on many other occasions where he discusses the elitist distinction, he speaks of the division between the governors and the governed, the leaders and the led. At first, the two pairs of terms may seem to be synonymous, but we can now see that they are not. The relationship between leaders and led is a specific one between allied groups or segments of the same group, whereas the relationship between the governors and the governed is equivalent either to the domination relation or to the more inclusive one of supremacy; that the latter is probably the case is shown by the fact that when Gramsci discusses the technical necessity of the elitist distinction (in the earlier passage), he says that the division of governors and governed exists within a homogeneous social group. So we can now say that Gramsci's generalization of Mosca's principle consists of extending the elitist distinction from cases of domination to cases of leadership. In other words, in Gramsci's conception, the elitist principle is not just or primarily a principle for the classification of governments and political systems (as it largely is for Mosca); it has a much wider scope.

Further evidence is provided by some of Gramsci's remarks about the analogies between state and party. For example, in the same note discussed more than once already (Q 15,4), he argues that there is an important correlation between what he calls the state spirit and the party spirit. On the one hand, he asks, and answers affirmatively, the question "Does there exist something similar to what is called state spirit in every serious movement?" (Q 1754). A key element of such state spirit, Gramsci claims, is a judicious historical attitude which avoids both the excess of the cult of the past and the arrogance of belief in a completely new future.[5] On the other hand, Gramsci also declares that "the party spirit is the fundamental element of the state spirit" (Q 1755). In this context, for Gramsci the party spirit is not at all what it sounds like—namely, partisanship; in fact, he dismisses sectarianism as a form of "apoliticism" (Q 1755) and suggests that selfish individualism is another form of the same; and so he seems to be saying that what he calls party spirit is a judiciously social awareness which avoids both egoism and sectarianism. This suggestion, which barely emerges in this passage, is explicitly elaborated elsewhere, in the context of a discussion of spontaneity versus discipline, where he argues that "what is really difficult and hard is to place an emphasis on discipline and sociality, while at the same time insisting on sincerity, spontaneity, originality, and personality" (Q 1720); I will also discuss this sort of issue at great length in my examination of liberalism (Chapter 7).

However, this analogy between state and party provides only an indirect connection to my present point, which is that the elitist distinction applies to both institutions; and the connection is simply that, insofar as the workings of both are similar, if a given principle applies to one, it also applies to the other. A more direct connection is provided by another example, where Gramsci explicitly extends an aspect of the elitist distinction from state to party. The aspect in question is the prestige which the authority of a given institution confers on the class from which that institution emanates, and the topic is examined in two notes (Q 15,2 and Q 15,18) occurring near the place where the crucial one (Q 15,4) does: "The fact that a state or government (conceived as an autonomous force) sheds its prestige on the class which is its foundation, is one of the most important facts both practically and theoretically, and it deserves to be analyzed in all its scope if one wants to have a more realistic concept of the state itself. On the other hand, one is not dealing here with something which is exceptional or characteristic of only one type of state; it seems that it can be encompassed within the function of elites or vanguards, and hence of parties, in regard to the class which they represent" (Q 1775). Gramsci seems to be formulating a general principle of the propagation of prestige from representing institutions to represented classes, and he is applying it both to a state and to a party—that is, both in the context of the distinction between rulers and ruled and in that between leaders and led.

2. The Importance of Elites

Besides widening the scope of the elitist phenomenon, Gramsci seems to attach greater importance to it even within the domain of Mosca's key concern, the domain of state and governmental institutions. One indication of this emphasis is the Gramscian judgment that the rise of bureaucracies has primordial importance in political science. The term "primordial" here is the same one Gramsci uses to describe the importance of the basic elitist distinction; so what he seems to be saying is that the rise of a particular type of elite (career bureaucrats) is about as fundamental a fact as the perennial division. Mosca does not go that far in his discussion of the bureaucratic state; as we have seen, he does indeed define it as one of the basic types, but regards it as always potentially counterbalanced by the opposite feudal tendency, and as in need of being combined with other distinct (but not opposite) tendencies, such as the democratic and the liberal. In Gramsci's own words, "The fact that in the historical development of political and economic forms we have seen the coming into being of the type of career public servants technically trained for bureaucratic work (both civilian and military) has a primordial significance in political science and the history of state formations" (Q 1632). After such a judgment, it should come as no surprise to see Gramsci add that "the problem of public servants coincides in part with the problem of intellectuals" (Q 1632), if we also recall that the problem of intellectuals is a key theme of his political theory and that his own theory of intellectuals is supposed to represent an improvement on Mosca's theory of the political class.

Another way in which Gramsci's emphasis on elites emerges is through his formulation and application of a corollary principle, which may be called the principle of the primacy of the responsibility of leaders. Although this is a relatively obvious consequence, I do not think we find any such formulation or application in Mosca's works. This principle is one of the first things elaborated by Gramsci in the note subtitled "Elements of Politics" (Q 15,4) discussed earlier. The principle states simply that "after any setback, one must always look, first of all, for the responsibility of the leaders, and do this in a strict sense. For example, a front consists of many sections, and every section has its leaders; it is possible that the leaders of one section are more responsible for a defeat than those of another, but we are dealing with more or less, and not—never—with the exclusion of anyone from responsibility" (Q 1753). The qualification in the last sentence typifies, of course, Gramsci's judiciousness, or balanced pluralism, at is were. Nevertheless, his emphasis on elitist responsibility is equally clear.

Nor is this emphasis on elitist responsibility purely abstract and only at the level of general principle. In fact, on many occasions Gramsci uses this principle, or to be more exact, he carries out concrete critical analyses of historical developments which are in accordance with the principle. To take an example, he blames the defeat of the Piedmontese by the Austrians at Novara in 1849 on the conservative politicians who ruled Piedmont at the time and on their allegedly undemocratic policy of seeking an expansion of Piedmont rather than a popular national Italian revolution; since this defeat concluded the first of several wars of national independence, Gramsci also thinks that the same political class was responsible for delaying the unification of Italy by more than a decade.[6] Another intriguing example regards Gramsci's admission that a kind of apolitical individualism is a national trait of Italians; but then he adds that it "has remote historical origins, and that the national leading group is responsible for the continuation of such a situation" (Q 815).

One of his most frequent examples involves the great defeat suffered by the Italians at Caporetto during World War I (in 1917).[7] The explanation of this defeat has been something of a cause célèbre in Italian historiography and political and popular culture: some regard it as a military accident, others as a crime perpetrated by defeatist and treason-able elements, still others as a military strike by the mass of soldiers, and others attribute it to the incompetence of the commander-in-chief, Gen-eral Luigi Cadorna. Gramsci rejects all these explanations as one-sided or unbalanced; instead, he offers the following analysis, which strikes me as a model of both elitism and balanced pluralism:

> 1. Was Caporetto a purely military fact? . . . Every military fact is also a political and social fact. . . . Even if it were demonstrated . . . that Capo-retto was a "military strike," . . . historically, namely from the highest political viewpoint, the responsibility would always belong to the gover-nors and their inability to predict that certain particular facts might have led to a military strike. . . . It is understandable that the military masses should wage the war and bear the burden of all kinds of sacrifices; but it is characteristic of simpletons—namely, of incompetent politicians—to believe that this will always happen without taking into account the social conditions of the military masses and without trying to meet the needs inherent in these conditions.
>
> 2. Thus, if we relieve the military masses of the responsibility, neither can it belong to the commander-in-chief, namely Cadorna, except up to a certain point. . . . Cadorna . . . is certainly responsible, but not as much as the government and the leading class in general. . . . The fact that there has not been an objective analysis of the factors which determined Capo-retto and a concrete action to eliminate them, is a "historical" proof of the extent of this responsibility.
>
> . . . The absence of self-criticism means unwillingness to eliminate the causes of the evil and hence is a symptom of serious political weakness. [Q 740–42]

The character of this Gramscian elitism should not be misunderstood. I have already pointed out that it seems to be combined with a gen-eral attitude of judiciousness and balanced pluralism; and it is also obvi-ous that this Gramscian emphasis on elitist responsibility aims to avoid placing the blame on both of the two relevant poles, namely the popular masses and a particular individual. In both regards, of course, Gramsci shares these traits with Mosca. However, it is equally important to point out what is probably a difference. That is, Gramsci is focusing on the re-sponsibility of the ruling class, but in the process he is criticizing it for pursuing antipopulist or undemocratic policies. This means that while he is being elitist in the sense of emphasizing elitist responsibility, he is being antielitist in another sense of "elitism"—favoring the (given) elite vis-à-vis the people. He is emphasizing the responsibility of the ruling class, for the sake of exonerating or defending the ruled class. He is being elitist at the level of historical and theoretical interpretation, in order to be antielitist at the practical, critical, and evaluative level.

At this point one final example and one controversial question are in order. In Gramsci's own practical political career, as we saw earlier in our account of his life (in the Introduction), Gramsci did seem to act in accordance with this principle. That is, he held the leadership of the Italian Socialist Party responsible for the defeat of the factory council movement in 1920, and this belief motivated him to help found a new proletarian party in 1921, the Italian Communist Party. Then again, when the new party itself suffered a serious setback in 1922–1923, due to the Fascist acquisition of governmental power, Gramsci led the reconstitution of the Communist Party in 1924–1926 along more democratic lines. The controversial question regards the explanation of the defeat of the newly reconstituted party in the fall of 1926, which caused his own imprisonment together with the imprisonment of other communist leaders and the exile of all others. Would it not be a consequence of the principle of elitist responsibility that Gramsci's earlier party and views needed some radical revision and correction? And does it not stand to reason that this is what he is doing in prison? And would it be sufficient for a radical revision to revise merely the means for accomplishing the same old ends sought before, or would it be necessary to revise those ends?

Be that as it may, the problem of responsibility is not the only case where Gramsci stresses an aspect of elitism for the sake of a popular, democratic purpose. Another case involves what can be called the principle of the elitist origin and diffusion of ideas. This principle states that "ideas and opinions are not 'born' spontaneously in the brain of each single person; they have a center of formation, irradiation, diffusion, and persuasion; there is a group of men or even a single individual who elaborates and presents them in a relevant political form" (Q 1625). In the context in which this principle is explicitly stated (Q 13,30), Gramsci's purpose is to defend universal suffrage from the objection that it presupposes that quantity is more important than quality and that all opinions have the same value; the point would be that, where everyone (or at least every adult) can vote and has one vote, all opinions are being given the same weight and no qualitative distinctions are being made. Gramsci's replies as follows:

However, the fact is that it is not at all true that numbers are the "supreme criterion," nor that the weight of each voter's opinion is "exactly" equal. As usual, numbers have merely an instrumental value and yield a measure and a relationship, nothing more. What, then, is one measuring? One is really measuring the effectiveness and the expansive and persuasive power of the opinions of the few, the active minorities, the elites, the vanguards, etc., namely, their concrete rationality, historicity, or functionality. . . . The counting of votes is the final manifestation of a long process in which the greatest influence belongs precisely to those who "dedicate to the state and the nation their best efforts." . . . "Unfortunately," everyone is inclined to confuse his own "particular" interest with the national one, and hence to regard as "horrible," etc., the fact that the numerical criterion decides; indeed, it would be easier to become elite by decree. However, the issue is not that someone who has much to offer intellectually is reduced to the level of an illiterate, but rather that there are some who claim to have much and want to take away from a common person even that infinitesimal fraction of power which he has in deciding on the course of state life. [Q 1625]

In short, Gramsci answers the objection by arguing that, because of the principle of the elitist origin of ideas, universal suffrage does not really regard all opinions as equal, but rather it measures the concrete rationality of various ideas; therefore, when someone does dedicate himself to public service, his ideas do count more than those of someone who is politically inactive.

Gramsci's elitism here also emerges in two other ways. One is that he labels this objection to universal suffrage a "criticism of oligarchic rather than elitist origin" (Q 1625). Such a label presupposes that he is distinguishing between oligarchy and elitism; it is also clear that he opposes the former and favors the latter. However, since he does not elaborate, we cannot be sure of what else he has in mind. For example, what does he mean by an oligarchy-oriented point of view and by an elite-oriented point of view? By oligarchy he probably means the same thing which Mosca means by aristocracy—namely, a situation where the class of rulers or leaders is relatively closed to the influx of individuals from the ruled or led class. On the other hand, the elitist viewpoint would be probably defined in terms of the acceptance of the basic elitist distinction. Then, as in the Moschian system, it is easy to see that the two viewpoints are not identical.

The other indication of Gramsci's elitism has to do with the way he formulates the problem. He does not really speak of universal suffrage as the target of this "oligarchic" objection. Instead, he refers to it as an objection "against the electoral system for the formation of the state organs" (Q 1624). This betrays his elitism, in the sense that he seems to be presupposing the elitist distinction, and to be reflecting on various methods for the formation of the ruling class, focusing on the method of general election.

It should be pointed out that there is also a sense in which this Gramscian analysis is directed against Mosca. Not that Gramsci took Mosca as his explicit target. Instead, this note was occasioned by his reading an article by Da Silva in a Fascist journal published in 1932,[8] containing the objection he criticizes. On the other hand, Mosca was an opponent of universal suffrage; not only did he vote against it in parliament in 1912, but he advanced a number of arguments against it.[9] Although this stance has contributed to Mosca's antidemocratic reputation, if we examine his arguments, a central concern they reveal is a desire to avoid the lowering of the moral and intellectual level of discussion and to encourage its being raised to a higher level, which is a democratic concern, in one sense of democracy. So the situation seems to be that, on the one hand, Gramsci's defense of universal suffrage reveals a deeper elitist commitment little appreciated by Mosca himself, and on the other hand, Mosca's criticism of universal suffrage reveals a deeper democratic commitment analogously underappreciated by Gramsci.[10]

Both of the Gramscian principles about the responsibility for failures and about the origin of ideas emphasize elitism, but they do so for the sake of a popular cause. One difference between the two, however, is that the former is primarily an evaluative principle for apportioning blame, while the latter is primarily an explanatory principle for tracing out factors which influence development; on the other hand, such evaluations and explanations are related, and so in a secondary way each principle also possesses the primary function of the other. The next Gramscian principle to be discussed also emphasizes elitism in a popular context, but it does not emphasize either evaluation or explanation more than the other. It can be called the principle of the dynamic interaction, or of the analytic interdependence, of elites and masses. There can be no doubt of the generality of Gramsci's intent, since one of the most explicit statements of this principle is given in a context where he labels it a methodological criterion (Q 2283).

The principle states that "subaltern groups always undergo the initiative of dominant groups, even when they rebel and rise up; only a 'permanent' victory breaks the subordination, although not immediately" (Q 2283). This opinion is given in a discussion of the history of subaltern social groups, which will be discussed presently. A more elaborate statement is given in a discussion of Italian history, where Gramsci also applies the principle concretely to the many popular uprisings against the French which took place in Italy at the end of the eighteenth century. In that discussion, Gramsci's ulterior motive is, I suppose, to defend such popular behavior, which may appear antiprogressive, given that at that time the ideas of the French Revolution represented a progressive force. However, what interests us more is the generalization Gramsci advances: "The question of the attitude of the popular masses cannot be posed independently of the question of the leading classes, because popular masses can rise up against 'foreign' invaders for immediate and contingent reasons, only insofar as no one has taught them to understand and follow a political outlook different from the narrow local one. The spontaneous reactions of the popular masses (insofar as they are spontaneous) can only serve to indicate the 'strength' of leadership of the higher classes" (Q 1972–73).

The content of this principle should not be misunderstood. I do not think Gramsci is saying that the masses are helpless and incompetent and can do nothing without the elites, or that the elites manipulate the masses to make them believe and do whatever serves elitist interests and desires. This caution is needed because some scholars understand elitism to refer to this kind of popular helplessness and elitist manipulation. Moreover, this kind of pejorative elitism is what is often attributed to Mosca.[11] Therefore, especially in the context of the present investigation, it might be thought that I am trying to articulate another similarity between these two thinkers and maintain that they shared such pejorative elitism.

My aim is actually the reverse. Rather than seeing Gramsci's thought through the spectacles of Mosca's elitism and the latter through the spectacles of the manipulatory conception, I endeavor in my investigation to look at elitism from the viewpoint of Mosca's elitism and at the latter from the viewpoint of Gramsci's thought. Then, when Gramsci's thought is examined with an open mind, it is almost impossible to find any trace of manipulatory elitism. Finally, this approach paves the way for a more adequate understanding of Mosca as well.

Now, after the earlier discussion of Gramsci's distinction between dominance and leadership, there would be no excuse in the interpretation of the last Gramscian quotation for ignoring that he speaks of "leadership" and of "teaching"; and such language should leave no doubt that Gramsci is very far removed from manipulatory pseudoelitism. Admittedly, the first statement of this principle quoted above does mention "dominant groups," which in Gramsci's formal and official lexicon refers to relationships among enemies, together with the use of force if necessary. However, two clarifications must be made. First, manipulation suggests something worse than even the use of force since it implies a deceptiveness which the latter does not. Second, Gramsci's allowance for "dominant" relationships reflects his realism, for the principle in question is one for the interpretation of the history of subaltern classes; and such realism can be violated only at the risk of utopian dreaming.

Thus, this latest Gramscian principle is in part another instance of his emphasis on elites; and the special interest here is that elites are important not merely when we take them as our subject matter but also when we are studying something apparently different, namely subaltern classes. The principle is also a statement of the dynamic interaction and the analytic interdependence of subaltern classes or popular masses with elites, both in the sense of external dominant classes and internal leading strata. All this becomes clearer in another, more explicit discussion which in many ways summarizes Gramsci's elitism in all its complexity; to this discussion we now turn.

3. The History of Subaltern Classes

That Gramsci should choose to formulate the fundamental principle of political science (and art) in terms of the elitist distinction is not surprising, for after all, he had an important precedent for this formulation, namely Mosca. That Gramsci should have widened the scope of this principle from relationships of dominance and the domain of states and governments to relationships of intellectual and moral leadership and the domain of parties and homogeneous classes ought not to be surprising either, in view of his practical life as a social activist and party leader whose power consisted primarily of superior intellectual analysis and moral argument. That he should want to subsume under the scope of the principle the epoch-making growth of career bureaucrats and public servants is a sign of his emphasis on the elitist phenomenon. That he should want to emphasize the leaders' responsibility for failures is understandable in someone who is committed to the cause of the powerless masses.

That he should want to emphasize the elitist origin and diffusion of ideas is perhaps to be expected in an intellectual. That he should emphasize the dynamic interdependence of elites and masses is also to be expected, since that is also the version of elitism prevalent in Mosca. What is relatively surprising, or rather, a sign of the depth (but also of the character) of Gramsci's elitism is that elites should crop up in a significant way in the context of the history of subaltern classes. That this was a topic very dear to his heart is clear; that he should approach the topic the way he did is more revealing.

What is his approach to the study of the development of subaltern classes? He explicitly formulates a number of methodological principles in a note bearing the title "methodic criteria" (Q 25,5) in a "special" notebook on the general topic. He begins by elaborating the familiar point about the interdependence of ruling and subaltern classes; he does so by arguing that, though the history of subaltern classes pertains primarily to civil society, while the history of ruling classes pertains primarily to political society, each really involves an interaction with the other, and so that is what largely matters. In his own words:

> The historical unity of leading classes takes place in the state, and their history is essentially the history of states or of groups of states. But one must not think that such a unity is purely legal and political. . . . The fundamental historical unity, in its concreteness, is the result of the organic relations between the state or political society and the "civil society." Subaltern classes, . . . their history, . . . is interwoven with that of the civil society, is a disconnected and discontinuous aspect of the history of civil society and, by this avenue, of the history of states or groups of states. [Q 2287–88]

Then the analysis gets rather complicated insofar as Gramsci goes on to exploit the elitist distinction in three ways, or to emphasize it on three levels: (1) the distinction between ruling and subaltern classes, (2) the distinction between parties and masses within the subaltern classes, and (3) the distinction between a leading party of a subaltern class and a led party of a subaltern class. In his own words:

> The history of the parties of subaltern groups is also very complex, insofar as it must include all the repercussions of party activities . . . on the attitudes of the dominant groups and insofar as it must include the repercussions of the much more effective activities . . . of dominant groups on subaltern groups and on their parties. Among the subaltern groups one

will exercise or will tend to exercise a certain hegemony by means of a party; this must be determined by studying also the developments of all the other parties insofar as they include elements of the hegemonic group or of the other subaltern groups which are subject to such hegemony. [Q 2289]

Finally, Gramsci sketches an application of these principles to Italian history, especially the period of the medieval city-states and the nineteenth-century movement for national unification and independence:

Many canons for historical research can be constructed from the examination of the innovative forces in Italy which guided the national Risorgimento. These forces gained power and were unified into the modern Italian state by struggling against other specific forces and by receiving assistance from particular auxiliary or allied forces; in order to become a state they had to subjugate or eliminate the former and had to have the active or passive consent of the latter. The study of the development of these innovative forces from subaltern groups into leading and dominant groups must therefore search for and identify the phases through which they acquired (a) autonomy vis-à-vis the enemies which had to be destroyed and (b) the agreement of the groups which helped them actively or passively; this whole process was historically necessary for their unification into a state. The degree of political-historical consciousness to which these innovative forces gradually came during the various phases is measured precisely with these two criteria and not only with that of the separation from the previously dominant forces. One usually applies only the latter criterion, and thus we have a one-sided history; sometimes one does not understand anything, as in the case of the history of the peninsula since the era of the city-states. [Q 2289]

The conclusion is that, for Gramsci, it is impossible to understand the history of subaltern classes without understanding the history of elites, and without realizing that elites may be (1) dominant, and/or (2) leading vis-à-vis the masses, and/or (3) leading vis-à-vis allied elites. For him the history of subaltern classes is not merely the study of the past development of such classes but includes what might be called the political theory or the social theory of subaltern classes. I believe the reason he speaks of "history" here is analogous to the reason he does so in the context of the history of intellectuals; that is, he wants to contrast his approach to the "sociological" one as he understands it—namely, to the positivist orientation in sociology.[12] In other words, like his history of intellectuals, his history of subaltern classes is really a historically oriented approach to what *we* (in contrast to Gramsci) might want to call the political sociology of subaltern classes. Therefore, the Gramscian conclusion being advanced here in turn means that, at the analytical and scientific level, an adequate populism is impossible without an adequate elitism.

4. The Problem of the Withering Away of the Elites

It is necessary now to discuss a problem which I have so far ignored merely for expository reasons. The issue is raised by Gramsci himself immediately after he formulates the fundamental elitist principle in the key note mentioned at the beginning of this chapter (Q 15,4). That is, no sooner does he finish claiming that the distinction between governors or leaders and governed or led has always existed than he goes on to ask whether this must continue forever into the future. Moreover, on many occasions he speaks of such possibilities as the "absorption of political by civil society," the coming into being of an "ethical state," and the emergence of a "regulated society";[13] these notions and his statements in such contexts seem to suggest that Gramsci's "elitism" is limited to the past, in the sense that it is merely an instrument for the interpretation of past history, but that it does not have the character of an immutable and eternal principle of human nature. Finally, this skepticism is supported in a general way by Gramsci's historicism, which, despite being liable to different interpretations,[14] would seem to have to include the idea that there is no immutable human nature.

My procedure here will be to review the most important passages where Gramsci appears to make such a qualification of his elitist principle, in order to determine whether such an appearance corresponds to reality and to analyze exactly what kind of limitations he is placing on the fundamental principle. This critical analysis will also deepen our historical and critical comparison and contrast between his elitism and Mosca's, because it is clear that the latter does not raise this problem and does not envisage any such restriction.

In the key passage with which we began this chapter, after stating that the elitist distinction is a "primordial and (under certain general conditions) irreducible fact" (Q 1752), Gramsci goes on to formulate a number of research problems. One of these is the question of the origin of this primordial fact; he notes parenthetically that "at least one could and should study how to attenuate and extinguish the fact, by changing certain conditions identifiable as instrumental in this regard" (Q 1752). Then he becomes more explicit and elaborates as follows: "In the formation of leaders, this question is fundamental: does one wish that there should always be governed and governors, or does one want to create the conditions in which the necessity for the existence of this division would disappear? That is, does one start from the premise of the perpetual division of humankind, or does one believe that it is only a historical fact, corresponding to certain conditions?" (Q 1752). Finally, Gramsci goes on to suggest that the elitist distinction is partly a result of a division along the lines of social class and partly a consequence of the division of labor and hence a technical necessity; and then he opines that "this coexistence of causes is exploited by those who see everywhere only 'technicalities,' 'technical' necessity, etc., in order not to face the fundamental problem" (Q 1752).

We can certainly agree with Gramsci that whether the "primordial" elitist fact is changeable depends on whether its cause or causes is or are changeable; that one of its causes is the technical division of labor; and that another cause is division by social class. However, it is not clear that he is reaching any definite conclusion about the changeability of the primordial fact. His willingness to ask the fundamental question is indeed an indication that he is not convinced that the primordial fact is also irreducible and unchangeable, but this is not to say that he convinced that it is changeable. Still, his not being convinced that the primordial fact is unchangeable seems to indicate that he rejects the argument that, since it has always been that way so far, it will always be that way in the future. Now, the rejection of this argument is in accordance with his historicism, but it would seem to conflict with his realism. I believe that realism, rather than positivism or scientism, is all that such an argument reflects. Therefore, while I am firmly convinced on other grounds that Gramsci is indeed a realist, I admit that here we have one piece of evidence against the realist interpretation.

In short, in regard to the eternal validity of the fundamental elitist principle, Gramsci is exhibiting an attitude of tentativeness, rather than rejection; his tentative acceptance is contingent on an adequate investigation of whether it can be explained on the basis of more fundamental principles or facts. Such an attitude is not only not objectionable but methodologically sophisticated. Therefore, this passage is better interpreted as evidence against Gramsci's realism than as evidence against his elitism. We shall soon see, however, that his realism reasserts itself in the other relevant passages which raise the possibility of the disappearance of the elitist distinction.

We will also see something which first emerges clearly in the present passage: namely, what I have called his generalization of the elitist distinction from relationships of domination between different classes to relationships of leadership within the same class. In fact, after briefly discussing the possibility of doing away with the distinction, he goes to great lengths to elaborate the nature of leadership:

> Since the division between governors and governed also exists within the same group, it is necessary to establish some principles to be strictly observed; indeed it is in this field that the most serious errors occur— namely, that we see the manifestation of the most criminal incompetence, most difficult to correct. One thinks that, since the rule is demanded by the same group, obedience must be automatic and must occur without a demonstration of necessity and rationality. . . . Given the principle that there exist led and leaders, governed and governors, it is true that so far parties are the most adequate means to form leaders and the skill of leadership ('parties' may appear under the most diverse names, even that of 'antiparty' or 'negation of parties'; indeed, even so-called individualists are party men, except that they would like to be 'party heads' by the grace of God or of the stupidity of their followers). [Q 1753–54]

The implication is clear: there is really no way of eliminating the elitist distinction once it has been extended to leadership relations. Therefore, besides being inconsistent with his usual realism, Gramsci's suggestion about the disappearance of the elitist distinction is inconsistent with the more general version of elitism which he undoubtedly holds.

This implication applies to the many statements where Gramsci seems to advocate the withering away of the elitist distinction by way of the absorption of political society by civil society. One of the most explicit of these statements comes at the end of a discussion of the nature and function of a head of state, where Gramsci proposes the creation of a "system of principles affirming that the purpose of the state is its own ending, its own disappearance, that is, the reabsorption of political society into civil society" (Q 662). However, according to Gramsci himself, the distinction between leaders and led would have to exist in civil society because (1) "political parties" operate in civil society and they cannot do without the technical distinction, and (2) civil society is the domain of persuasion (as contrasted to coercion) and persuasion also presupposes the distinction. In other words, what Gramsci is really advocating by such a statement is the replacement of coercion by persuasion, rather than the abolition of the distinction between elites and masses.

An analogous point applies in regard to what Gramsci says about the development of a universal class: "A class which regards itself as capable of assimilating the whole society, and which at the same time is really able to express this process, brings to perfection this conception of the state and of law; it conceives the end of the state and of law as useless insofar as they have accomplished their task and have been absorbed by civil society" (Q 937). Again, for Gramsci, the distinction between leaders and led is a phenomenon which occurs within the confines of the same homogeneous group, and therefore it would not disappear even if the whole human race were to be homogenized into the same class.

In regard to realism, we may begin to see its reassertion in Gramsci in his claim that some kind of coercion or hierarchy is inevitable, which would make some kind of elitist distinction inevitable. This reassertion occurs in an extremely revealing discussion where he criticizes the answer Antonio Labriola is reported to have given to a question from one of his students; the question was how he would go about imparting moral education to a savage. Labriola is supposed to have answered that he would start by making the savage temporarily a slave. Gramsci finds this preposterous but harbors no illusions about the existence of shortcuts to progress. In a good example of his typical balanced pluralism, he is on the one hand willing to discuss what he calls the "historical necessity" (Q 1367) of slavery, but, on the other, he distinguishes it from absolute necessity and is very sensitive to the issue of accelerating the progressive development of earlier stages by utilizing the experience and knowledge available at more developed stages. However, his most telling claim is that "there is a coercion of the military type which extends even to work, which can be applied even to the dominant class, and which is not 'slavery' but rather the adequate expression of modern pedagogy aimed at the education of an immature element" (Q 1368). Notice that to recognize that even work and education require *some* coercion is to recognize the necessity of the elitist distinction.

Let us now examine other relevant passages. The disappearance of the elitist distinction is reminiscent of the Marxian transition from the kingdom of necessity to the kingdom of freedom, and Gramsci explicitly draws the comparison; but he is also aware that that disappearance shares the utopian character of this transition. On the one hand, he raises the issue when he says that "intellectually, Marx begins a historical epoch which will probably last for centuries—namely, until the disappearance of political society and the advent of the regulated society. Only then will his worldview be superseded (notion of necessity superseded by notion of freedom)" (Q 882). In this context, by "regulated society," Gramsci means a self-regulated society, self-regulated in the sense that it would not need to be regulated by a government and other *political* institutions. On the other hand, Gramsci is clear that "the proposition of the transition from the kingdom of necessity to that of freedom must be analyzed and elaborated with great subtlety and acumen" (Q 1489). His reasoning is equally clear:

That the philosophy of praxis conceives itself in a historicist fashion, namely as a transitory phase of philosophical thought, emerges not only implicitly from its whole system but also explicitly from the well-known thesis that at a certain point historical development will be characterized by the transition from the kingdom of necessity to the kingdom of freedom. . . . However, if the philosophy of praxis is also an expression of historical contradictions (indeed it is the fullest expression of them, on account of its awareness), this means that it is tied to "necessity" and not to "freedom," which does not and cannot yet exist historically. Therefore, if one proves that the contradictions will disappear, one implicitly proves that the philosophy of praxis will also disappear: namely, it will be superseded; in the kingdom of "freedom," thoughts and ideas can no longer be born in the domain of contradictions and of the necessary struggle. For the present, the philosopher (of praxis) can only make this general assertion without going any further; for he cannot escape from the present domain of contradictions, and he cannot talk (except generally) about a world without contradictions, on pain of immediately creating a utopia.

This does not mean that the utopia cannot have philosophical value, for it has political value, and every political commitment is implicitly a philosophy, however disconnected and sketchy it may be. [Q 1487–88]

In this context, "philosophical" means "scientific" or, more exactly, cognitive. So, I take Gramsci's point to be that, like the disappearance of the Marxian kingdom of necessity, the disappearance of the elitist distinction is utopian; utopias are not completely worthless, for they have a political function; but they are scientifically questionable.

The anti-utopian theme is elaborated further in a contrast Gramsci draws elsewhere between what he calls the night-watchman state and the ethical state:

> In a doctrine of the state which conceives it as having the tendency toward and being liable to withering away and to being reduced to a regulated society . . . the element of state coercion can be imagined as withering away gradually, while we see an increasing assertion of constantly stronger elements of regulated society (or ethical state or civil society). The expressions "ethical state" or "civil society" would mean that this "image" of a state without a state was present to the greatest political scientists and legal theorists, insofar as they took the point of view of pure science (which equals pure utopia, inasmuch as it is based on the presupposition that all men are really equal and hence equally reasonable and moral—namely, liable to accept the law spontaneously and freely, and not because of coercion and as something imposed by another class and external to their conscience). . . . In the doctrine of the state's transition to a regulated society, between a phase in which state equals government and one in which the state will be identified with the civil society, we will have to go through the phase of the night-watchman state, that is, a coercive organization which will safeguard the development of the continuously growing elements of regulated society and thus gradually reduce its authoritative and coercive interventions.[15]

Here we have a definition of the night-watchman state as a state whose key function is to guarantee the development of individual freedom vis-à-vis coercive governmental institutions, and of moral and rational relationships among individuals. The ethical state seems to be defined as a state without a state, as it were—that is, as a society where state and political institutions have been completely replaced by ethical, moral, and rational relationships and considerations. Gramsci regards the night-watchman state as viable but the ethical state as utopian because it is based on a false egalitarian assumption. However, this claim about the night-watchman state implies that the distinction between governed and governors is here to stay. In other words, the night-watchman state is in a sense a means to an end, the end being the ethical state; but the latter is really an unreachable goal and can only be approached. Therefore, Gramsci may also be interpreted as saying that the night-watchman state is a sensible and realistic version of the ethical state, and that the ethical state is a utopian dream except in the form of the night-watchman state.

He comes close to stating this conclusion in another note, where he compares and contrasts three conceptions of the ethical state: the one which he calls "the most sensible and concrete" (Q 1049), another that he attributes to Hegel, and a third defined in terms of the abolition of the elitist distinction. The obvious implication is that the last—the antielitist conception of the ethical state—is not the most sensible and realistic one, but rather a utopian dream. In Gramsci's own words:

> It seems to me that the most sensible and concrete thing one can say in regard to the ethical state or cultural state is this: every state is ethical insofar as one of its most important functions is to lift the great mass of the population to a particular cultural and moral level, which corresponds to what is required for the development of the productive forces and hence for the interests of the dominant classes. . . . Hegel's conception is typical of a time when the extensive development of the bourgeoisie could seem boundless, and so its ethical and universalistic character could be reduced to the claim, All of humankind will be bourgeois. However, in reality only a social group which proposes the disappearance of the state and of itself as an end to reach can create an ethical state tending to put an end to the internal divisions between those who are dominated, etc., and create a unified and technical-moral social organism.[16]

Although Gramsci does not explicitly say so here, the contrast he does draw between "the most sensible and concrete" conception of the ethical state and the antielitist definition suggests that the latter has a utopian aspect. Moreover, there is indeed something obviously unrealistic (perhaps even self-contradictory) in the idea of a social group which would aim at its own dissolution.[17] On the other hand, there is nothing essentially wrong with the general idea of a group's arguing that membership in it is open to all human beings, and this general idea is not invalidated even if Gramsci is right that the so-called Hegelian bourgeoisie did not really turn out to be such an all-inclusive group. Yet from a "sensible and realistic" point of view, even the Hegelian conception is problematic because of the absolutist, pretentious, and teleological tendencies associated with the claim to being such a universalistic group. By contrast with this assertion as well, Gramsci's "most sensible and concrete" conception reflects a tentativeness and a pluralism reminiscent of Mosca.

The key passage on the night-watchman state contains, as we have seen, an anti-utopian argument grounded on a criticism of a certain version of egalitarianism. At about the same time that he wrote that key passage (March to August 1931),[18] Gramsci penned a pair of notes (Q 6, 12 and 82) in which he discusses the same problem of the possibility of the emergence of a regulated society or ethical state and advances an analogous argument which is both anti-utopian and critical of egalitarianism. The occasions were very different, since in connection with the night-watchman state he is referring primarily to the German labor and political leader Ferdinand Lassalle, whereas in these two notes Gramsci is explicitly criticizing primarily the views of Italian philosopher Ugo Spirito;[19] I believe that the difference makes the similarities all the more revealing and significant.

It is, of course, beyond the scope of this investigation to determine the accuracy of Gramsci's interpretation of Spirito. However, it is important to know the content of the view that Gramsci is criticizing as utopian, in order to understand better the content of his objections. He thinks that "Spirito and Volpicelli's utopia consists in a conflation of the state and the regulated society. . . . The characteristic which differentiates this 'utopia' from traditional utopias and from the general inquiries concerning the 'best government' is that Spirito and Volpicelli take as already existing this 'imaginary' entity of theirs" (Q 755). Three objections are raised against this.

The first is that this is merely a metaphorical manner of speaking; that is, "as long as the class state exists, the regulated society cannot exist, except metaphorically—that is, only in the sense that even the class state is a regulated society" (Q 693). A class state is presumably a state with economic class divisions and hence economic inequalities. By "regulated society" Gramsci seems to understand a society with a *special type* of regulation, namely, with complete and economic equality, which can be taken to involve self-regulation. This first objection is instructive primarily in regard to what he means by "regulated society." The second objection is more telling: "Spirito and Volpicelli's conception is a logical derivation of the silliest and most 'rational' democratic theories. It is still tied to the conception of 'human nature' as being always the same and without development, as it was conceived before Marx: according to it all men are fundamentally equal in the domain of the spirit."[20] The implications of this passage for the Gramscian conception of democracy will be discussed in the next chapter; for now we should note that the ahistorical view of human nature and human equality is pseudorational and pseudoegalitarian. But what is really wrong with it? Here we come to Gramsci's third and most significant point:

In the kinds of societies portrayed by the various utopias, they introduce economic equality as the necessary basis for the projected reform; now, in this regard the utopians were not utopians but concrete scientists of politics and coherent critics. The utopian character of some of them was due to the fact that they thought economic equality could be introduced by means of arbitrary laws, willpower, etc. However, the idea is correct: that no complete and perfect political equality can exist without economic equality, as other political writers have held (even right-wingers, namely critics of democracy). [Q 693]

The real issue, then, would seem to be whether and how to establish economic equality. In summary, Gramsci's point is that the regulated society (with the abolition of the elitist distinction that it implies) cannot be based on mechanical equality, but must take into account the historicity of human nature and must include economic equality; and the latter cannot be introduced by fiat.

5. A Democratic Regulated Society

Many of the points mentioned are combined in a very brief but dense and rich passage, not previously available in English translation. Gramsci is reacting to a book review he has just read about the prison years of Louis-Napoleon. What captures his interest is Louis-Napoleon's idea of a government newspaper and his justification for it:

The idea of a state newspaper is logically tied to illiberal governmental institutions (namely, those in which civil society is confused with political society), whether they are despotic or democratic (namely, such that the oligarchic minority claims to be the whole society, or such that the undifferentiated people claims and believes to really be the state). If there is state schooling, why should there not be state journalism, which is the school for adults?

Napoleon argued by starting from the premise that if we accept the truth of the legal axiom that the ignorance of laws is no excuse for being liable, then the state must keep citizens informed about all its activities—that is, it must educate them; this is a democratic argument which is transformed into a justification for oligarchic activity. However, the argument is not without merit; it can be "democratic" only in a society where the historical unity of civil society and political society is understood dialectically (in accordance with real and not merely conceptual dialectic) and where the state is conceived as liable to be superseded by "regulated society": in such a society the dominant party is not organically confused with the government, but it is an instrument for the transition from the civil-political society to the "regulated society," which absorbs both within itself in order to supersede them (rather than perpetuating their opposition), etc. [Q 734]

Here we have a distinction between elitism and oligarchism similar to the one we saw before in Gramsci's elitist analysis of universal suffrage, and a distinction between the utopian regulated society and the realistic society that can only approach it, a distinction which is similar to the Gramscian notion of the night-watchman state. We also have a distinction between the illiberal conflation of civil and political society and their dialectical union which characterizes this realistic "transitional" society of the night-watchman state, as if to ward off a Moschian objection involving the principle of the separation of powers. Finally, we have a distinction between liberalism and democracy which is reminiscent of Mosca's, as well as a distinction between two or more concepts of democracy (one of which would correspond to Mosca's).

In this passage Gramsci is considering two arguments in favor of a state newspaper, which we can call the illiberal and the pseudodemocratic arguments. The illiberal justification is that since everyone favors state schools and a newspaper is like a school for adults, everyone should favor a state newspaper. Gramsci's implicit criticism of this argument is an objection precisely to its illiberalism; that is, the argument presupposes that there is no essential difference between the schooling of children and the schooling of adults; on the other hand, presumably one big difference concerning children is that it is possible to reach agreement about the essentials of their education, whereas in the case of adults it is not possible. In other words, a newspaper is an institution of and operates in the domain of civil society, but a government belongs to political society; thus a government newspaper would be a case of a political institution operating outside its proper domain. Thus a government newspaper would represent a violation of a basic principle of "liberalism," namely the separation of powers.

Gramsci's elitism emerges in the qualification he makes to this criticism. He discerns at least two kinds of illiberalism, despotic and democratic. By despotic illiberalism, he means a situation where the "oligarchic minority" claims to coincide with the whole society; "democratic illiberalism" refers to a situation where the "undifferentiated people" makes the same claim. It seems clear that Gramsci finds both objectionable. The despotism of the former lies in the attempt by a minority to impose its will and interests on the rest of society without seriously questioning whether the rest may have distinct desires and interests. The difficulty with the democratic illiberalism, which might be better labeled populism, seems to lie with the undifferentiated character of the situation; this lack of differentiation may refer to the idea that the people is a monolithic entity with a single will and interest or to the lack of effective leadership among the people. Both definitions of illiberalism seem to presuppose the elitist distinction in order to define possible abuses at opposite ends of the spectrum: despotic or oligarchic illiberalism is an abuse perpetrated by the elite at the expense of the people or masses, whereas democratic or populist illiberalism is an abuse perpetrated by the people or masses at the expense of the elites. Therefore, here the elitist distinction is the analytical instrument enabling Gramsci to conceive these two undesirable extremes.

What I have labeled Louis-Napoleon's pseudodemocratic argument claims that, since ignorance of the law is no excuse for acting to violate it, citizens should be kept informed about what the laws are; this would be the key function of a state or government newspaper. Gramsci expressed both a negative criticism and a positive evaluation of this argument. The criticism is that democratic considerations are being used to justify an instance of oligarchism; that is, starting with democratic premises, the argument reaches an oligarchic conclusion. The conclusion is oligarchic in the sense clarified earlier—that is, in the sense of despotic or oligarchic illiberalism. However, the premises are not democratic in the populist sense. Instead, the conception of democracy inherent in this argument relates to the ideal of keeping citizens informed and educating them. This is the Moschian conception insofar as this ideal presupposes the elitist distinction and then defines democracy as a relationship between rulers and ruled where the members of the ruled class have the possibility of rising to the level of the ruling class. This possibility is *apparently* being encouraged when the argument alludes to educating and informing the people, since this education and information would give them the means for the social mobility envisaged by Moschian democracy. However, according to Gramsci's criticism here, the appearance does not correspond to reality, because the democratic aspect of the argument is frustrated once it reaches a conclusion which is oligarchic (or aristocratic or antidemocratic in the Moschian sense). This explains the reason for my own choice of the label "pseudodemocratic," while it also makes clear that the

Gramscian criticism is elitist according to the fundamental elitist principle. And this brings us to his favorable evaluation.

Gramsci finds something right about the argument as long as political and civil society are understood as being dialectically united; that is, they ought to be distinguished without being separated, and related without being conflated, and their relation is regarded as subject to historical development.[21] The key development he seems to envisage here is the transition from the state as we know it—and the just-mentioned relation between political and civil society—to a "regulated society." Now, if the regulated society is to transcend this distinction, and if one is to avoid the illiberal conflation of the two, the only possibility would seem to be the absorption of political society into civil society, something which Gramsci after all explicitly mentions elsewhere. However, here this absorption acquires new meaning because it is being contrasted with illiberalism, which may be regarded as the reverse—namely, the absorption of civil society into political society. In fact, the existence of a state newspaper would involve the interference of a political institution into civil society. However, as mentioned above, once Gramsci has generalized the elitist distinction into civil society and the relationship of leadership, the regulated society in the sense just clarified retains an elitist character.

Another indication of Gramsci's elitism here is that he regards as "democratic" the appropriately modified Napoleonic argument and the society described by the stipulations embodying this modification. How and why would there be democracy in either the (perhaps eternally) transitional society in which existing society would be induced to move in the direction of the regulated society or in this regulated society once it had been brought about (naturally, we are speaking in a utopian mode and disregarding realistic considerations)? It seems to me that the only answer is that the absorption of political by civil society would mean the regular[22] flow of individuals from the ruled or led class to the ruling or leading class; here the elitist distinction would not disappear but remain at least as a technical necessity. Note that, if Gramsci is setting aside the populist notion of democracy, and if he is adopting the Moschian notion, as he seems to be, then to describe the ideal society as a democracy is to presuppose the elitist distinction in that ideal society, for the simple reason that Mosca's concept of democracy presupposes the fundamental elitist principle. This inference brings new urgency to the task of examining Gramsci's notion of democracy and its relation to Mosca's, a topic which is also important in its own right. The examination will be undertaken in the next chapter.

6. Epilogue

We have conducted a systematic examination of a series of related and relevant passages in the Prison Notebooks, with the aim of determining both the character of Gramsci's elitism as a theoretical orientation in political science and its historical relation to Mosca's (historical in the sense of the history of social and political science and philosophy). It has emerged that, like Mosca, Gramsci adopts the fundamental elitist principle as the most basic principle in the scientific study of politics. However, in many ways, Gramsci's elitist disposition goes further and deeper than Mosca's.

For one thing, Gramsci extends the scope of the elitist distinction to relationships of moral, intellectual, and civil leadership, besides relationships of governmental, military, and political domination. He also generalizes the principle from the domain of external interclass relationships to the domain of internal intraclass relationships. And he widens the scope of the principle to apply to questions about the nature and behavior of parties as well as about the state.

The greater depth of Gramsci's theoretical elitism (vis-à-vis Mosca's) emerges from the fact that Gramsci formulates and applies a number of corollary principles which seem to have little or no counterpart in Mosca (though, of course, they not only are consistent with the latter but also can be seen to be articulations of basic Moschian insights). In the theory of governments, Gramsci takes more seriously than Mosca the rise of career bureaucrats as a fundamental phenomenon for the political scientist to come to grips with. He also explicitly formulates the principle that the responsibility of groups of leaders (especially for failures) is primary, vis-à-vis the responsibility of both the masses and an individual supreme head or commander. Another corollary is the principle that ideas do not originate from all persons equally and do not spread uniformly in all directions, but rather have particular points of origin and particular trajectories of diffusion; and this intellectual discontinuity and anisotropy in a sense involve the extension of the essential elitist idea to the intellectual domain. Gramsci also explicitly formulates and applies a corollary about the dynamic interaction and analytic interdependence of elites and masses, according to which the two groups are inextricably interwoven; now, while this corollary does imply that popular behavior depends essentially on elite leadership, the reverse is also true, and hence we do not have here the manipulatory and much-disparaged system of ideas which some understand as elitism.

Few topics reveal Gramsci's elitism as clearly and authentically as the history of subaltern classes, a topic which was very dear to Gramsci's heart. In describing the methodological criteria he used in this connection, Gramsci affirmed that to study the history of subaltern classes, one must also study the history of elites. That is, the real protagonists of the story become (1) the relationship between ruling and subaltern classes; (2) the relationship, within subaltern classes, between intellectuals and leaders on the one hand and masses and the people on the other; and (3) the relationship between leading or primary parties and led or secondary parties of the subaltern classes. This yields a three-dimensional elitism, as it were.

Although Gramsci occasionally suggests and apparently believes that elites should and eventually will wither away, the reality behind the appearance seems tenuous: Gramsci's commitment to elitism emerges unscathed from our analysis of his remarks on the topic.

One reason is that one of Gramsci's most pertinent notions is that of the absorption of political into civil society; but this absorption does not eliminate the fundamental elitist distinction, least of all in Gramsci's own thinking, because the distinction operates in the domain of civil as well as political society; in fact, the leadership relation and civil society essentially overlap, as do the domination relation and political society. Hence, Gramsci himself speaks of the technical necessity of the elitist distinction.

Moreover, Gramsci's talk of the withering away of elites is undermined by his realism and anti-utopianism. His realism reasserts itself in his remarks on and attitude toward Labriola's problem of the enslaved savage, Marx's notion of the transition to the kingdom of freedom, the concept of the night-watchman state, the idea of the ethical state, and the concept of the regulated society. Gramsci's central point is that, whether one is speaking of the kingdom of freedom or the ethical state or the regulated society, each is a utopia impossible to actualize or reach. What is permanently real is the process of trying to move toward these goals by a constant effort to bring about the elements of freedom, moral autonomy, and self-regulation mentioned in these utopias. One meaning he attaches to the "night-watchman state" is that of a government which encourages this process; this meaning is his own preferred version of the notion, as the most sensible and concrete.

Finally, in a key discussion of the regulated society, he speaks of the likelihood and desirability of its being democratic. Now, since this turns out to be a Moschian kind of democracy, and since the Moschian concept presupposes the elitist distinction (and is in fact defined in its terms), Gramsci's discussion of the democratic regulated society brings home that even were (*per impossibile*) a regulated society to be actualized, if democracy were to take hold in it, the elitist distinction would have to constitute a technical feature of that society.

FIVE

GRAMSCI'S DEMOCRACY: AN APPLICATION OF MOSCA'S CONCEPT

THE WORD "democracy" has many meanings in ordinary language and everyday life as well as in practical politics and among scholarly experts. One of the most common definitions is in terms of majority rule, although the inadequacy of such a definition is also commonly recognized by admitting the possibility of a tyranny of the majority. Until recently, when the world was divided into communist and capitalist camps waging a cold war against each other, that geopolitical struggle was also reflected in a disagreement over the conception of democracy; the one side backed a version of democracy variously called proletarian, socialist, Marxist, or economic, and the other a brand labeled liberal, individualist, or political. Scholars hardly alleviate the situation or help achieve consensus and unanimity, since, once the phenomenon of democracy became the subject of scientific investigation and the theory of democracy emerged as a branch of scholarship, the result was the proliferation of theories. It is unclear whether one can in all sincerity bemoan this result, for to do so would be to presuppose a majoritarian and consensus-oriented view of scientific progress, and hence perhaps to beg the issue by assuming as given a particular theory of democracy—the very matter which is in question.[1] We have seen that Mosca had his own preferred conception of democracy as a relationship between rulers and ruled such that the ruling class is open to the influx of individuals from the ruled class; however, he did not deny the existence of other conceptions, and occasionally he even succumbed to them in his own usage of the term.[2] It would therefore be unrealistic

[114]

to expect to find in Gramsci's Prison Notebooks a single conception of democracy and a single meaning attributed to the term.[3] Nevertheless, it is surprising that the most significant notion of democracy in Gramsci, and the one that he calls on most frequently, is the Moschian conception; Gramsci's concern seems to be primarily to apply it rather than to articulate it theoretically. We now undertake the demonstration of this point.

1. The Most Realistic and Concrete Meaning of Democracy

One of the most striking and neglected[4] passages ever written by Gramsci is a note entitled "Hegemony and Democracy," in which he formulates a definition of what he calls the most realistic and concrete meaning of democracy:

> *Hegemony and Democracy.* Among the many meanings of democracy, the most realistic and concrete one seems to me to be that which connects with the concept of hegemony. In an hegemonic system, there is democracy between the leading group and the led groups to the extent that (the development of the economy and thus) the legislation (that expresses this development) favors the (molecular) transition from the led groups to the leading group. In the Roman Empire there existed an imperial-territorial democracy through the granting of citizenship to conquered peoples, etc. There could not be democracy in feudalism on account of the existence of closed groups, etc. [Q 8,191/Q 1056][5]

Aside from the terminology of "hegemony," which here seems to be synonymous with "leadership," the most striking thing in this passage is a definition of democracy. Five things stand out about the meaning he attaches to the concept. First, democracy is a relationship between leaders and led, or governors and governed, or rulers and ruled, or elites and masses. Second, the relationship in question is that of social mobility from a lower to a higher class, or openness of the ruling class to the influx of members from the ruled class, or renewal of the former with members from the latter. Third, democracy is a quantitative phenomenon or notion, in the sense of being susceptible of realization to a greater or lesser degree; this claim contrasts with its being seen as a discrete, all-or-none affair. Fourth, democracy is an essentially individualist phenomenon, in the sense that it hinges primarily on the social mobility of individuals or persons; this is the meaning of Gramsci's molecular metaphor, according to which the individual persons are the molecules of society.[6] Fifth, the definition presupposes the fundamental elitist principle, since social mobility from led to leader is explicitly a formulation in terms of the elitist distinction.

This definition is so peculiar that it immediately raises the question whether it is Gramsci's original formulation, or whether he adopted it from some other author. It is, in fact, essentially identical to Mosca's mature view, that is, the conception that emerges clearly in the second edition (1923) of *Elements of Political Science;* for all five features just discussed are also present there. As we saw earlier (Chapter 2), Mosca states that "the term 'democratic' seems more suitable for the tendency which aims to replenish the ruling class with elements deriving from the lower classes, and which is always at work, openly or latently and with greater or lesser intensity, in all political organisms."[7] Mosca *contrasts* the democratic with the "aristocratic" tendency, "which aims to stabilize social control and political power in the descendants of the class that happens to hold possession of it at the given historical moment."[8] And he *distinguishes* the democratic tendency from the liberal principle, according to which authority is transmitted from the ruled to the rulers, and which is in turn contrasted with the autocratic principle that transmits authority from the rulers to the ruled.[9]

I believe that the conceptual similarities between the two definitions are sufficiently striking to leave no doubt about the Moschian origin of Gramsci's definition. However, another coincidence can be noted, which is more linguistic or semantical in character. It pertains to the molecular metaphor: it had been used by Mosca in the elaboration of his definition, which contains the following point: "The democratic tendency is more likely to prevail in unsettled times. . . . In general, changes in religion, new movements in philosophy and political thinking, inventions of new weapons or new instruments of warfare, applications of new discoveries to economic production, and corresponding increases in economic production, are all elements that favor rapid translations and interchanges of the *molecules* that make up the various social strata."[10]

One other commonality between the two concepts regards the "tendential" character of democracy. We have seen that this formulation is an extremely important epistemological feature of Mosca's conception and stems from his belief in the existence of an "aristocratic" tendency opposite to democracy, as well as the existence of other distinct tendencies along other dimensions; this understanding, in turn, provided an illustration of Mosca's balanced pluralism. As for Gramsci, we find him revealing his adoption of this additional Moschian feature in the context of an application of the notion of democracy to education. This is also an extremely important context in its own right from a substantive, political, and pedagogical point of view;[11] however, here I shall focus on the methodological, epistemological, conceptual, and historical issues.

Gramsci is criticizing a number of recent pedagogical developments in Italy, such as the Gentile reform, the rise of adult-oriented so-called popular universities, and the proliferation of many different types of vocational schools; he is groping toward the articulation of a concept of a unified general education school not meant to satisfy immediate practical interests. The greatest difficulty he finds with the new schools is their pseudodemocratic character: "The greatest paradox is that this new type of school appears and is described as democratic, whereas it is destined instead not only to perpetuate social differences but to crystallize them" (Q 1547). This feature makes the situation pseudodemocratic for a reason stemming from the definition of democracy: "Intrinsically, the democratic tendency cannot mean only that a manual laborer becomes skilled, but that every 'citizen' can become a 'governor' and that society puts him, even if only 'abstractly,' in the general conditions to become that; political democracy tends to make governors and governed coincide (in the sense of government with the consent of the governed), guaranteeing to each subject the free development of the general capacity and technical preparation necessary to that end" (Q 1547–48).[12] That is, when a large increase has taken place in the number and types of professional schools, the new situation allows individuals originating from the class of unskilled laborers to become skilled, and children of peasants to become agricultural experts. Their education in turn creates the impression of social mobility and advancement, and of the openness of social groups to influx from below. And that is how the new schools appear and claim to be democratic. However, this is not true democracy, which brings with it mobility across the divide from governed to governors. Instead, we have a growing compartmentalization and stratification of society. Now, "if we want to break this trend, we must not, therefore, multiply and graduate the types of professional schools, but create a unified type of (elementary and middle) preparatory school which would lead a youth to the threshold of the choice of a profession, while at the same time forming him as a person capable of thinking, studying, leading, or holding those who lead in check" (Q 1547).

Conversely, the old type of school being replaced by such recent developments was undemocratic not in its teaching method, which Gramsci defends, but on account of its closed character: "The traditional school was 'oligarchic' because it was attended only by the children of the upper class destined to become leaders; but it was not 'oligarchic' in its teaching method" (Q 501). It is obvious that by "oligarchic," Gramsci means the opposite of democratic (in the Moschian sense just defined), which Mosca labeled aristocratic; it is equally obvious that Gramsci does not refer to oligarchy in the etymological sense of rule by the few, which corresponds to the fundamental elitist principle. Here, Gramsci's notion of oligarchy, his opposition to it, his nonopposition to the elitist distinction, and his consequent distinction between oligarchy and elitism, are all analogous to what we saw before in his elitist defense of universal suffrage.[13] What this means is that to the previously discussed seven affinities we can add another, consisting of conceiving democracy as the opposite of something else—in such a way that it is only one of two sides of or directions along a spectrum, or to be more exact, along one spectrum among many.

And this brings us to one final affinity. The dichotomy between democracy and antidemocracy (whether it is labeled oligarchy or aristocracy) is only one of several. Another important one is the dichotomy between liberalism and autocracy, to use Mosca's terminology. This in turn means, in relation to liberalism, that democracy is neither the same nor the opposite, but merely distinct; that is, democracy as such is compatible with both liberalism and autocracy. We have already seen Gramsci concede this when he admitted the possibility of an illiberal democracy, in connection with his criticism of Louis-Napoleon's idea of a state newspaper.[14] Here is a much more explicit and concrete example: "From this point of view, the Church is a perfectly democratic organism (in a paternalistic sense): the son of a peasant or of an artisan can, theoretically, become cardinal or pope, if he is intelligent and talented, and if he is sufficiently malleable to let himself be assimilated by the ecclesiastical structure and to feel the appropriate esprit de corps and conservative attitude and the importance of present and future interests" (Q 1869). The Catholic Church has long been recognized by Moschian scholars[15] as constituting a perfect example of both Moschian democracy and Moschian autocracy. The reason for its democratic character is directly expressed by Gramsci, whereas its autocracy lies in the fact that in Catholicism authority flows from the top (ultimately from God) down. Gramsci is here drawing a logical consequence from Mosca's conceptual framework and from well-known facts about Catholicism. The only difference is terminological: Gramsci speaks of paternalism rather than autocracy, and this is certainly justified, since the traditional family is another good example of an autocratic institution.

In summary, in the Prison Notebooks, Gramsci does have a concept of democracy. Moreover, like Mosca, Gramsci conceives democracy in terms of social mobility or open elites; as compatible with, indeed as a special case of, elitism; as a tendency which exists in the context of other tendencies; as distinguishable and distinct from liberalism, and logically compatible with autocracy or paternalism; as opposed to aristocracy or oligarchy; as a quantitative phenomenon whose presence is a matter of degree; as having an ontological basis in individualism, despite its superficial collectivist appearance at the macroscopic level; and as being relational in several senses, starting with an empirical relationship between elites and masses, and proceeding to logical relations with other concepts (such as aristocracy and autocracy). And like Mosca, Gramsci uses the molecular metaphor.

Any one of these nine features provides a clue to the Moschian character of Gramsci's concept of democracy. Some of them are so characteristic of Mosca's theory as to be individually emblematic. Here I have in mind primarily the criterion of social mobility or open elites, the tendential conception, and the example of the Catholic Church as an autocratic democracy. The passages containing these three emblematic coincidences should give pause to any open-minded reader of Gramsci acquainted with Mosca. Taken collectively, the nine affinities leave no doubt about the Mosca-Gramsci connection in this regard. That is, the concept of democracy which Gramsci regards as "the most realistic and concrete" is unquestionably the one embedded in Mosca's theory of democracy.

2. Democratic Centralism

The preceding demonstration is important not only historically, through the articulation of the connection between the two thinkers, but also theoretically, in the sense that it shows that Gramsci does have a theory of democracy. However, so far we have seen only a relatively abstract aspect of his theory. But Gramsci is nothing if not realistic and concrete. And so it is equally significant that he did not merely pay lip service to such an idea but also applied it in a number of areas.

The applications touch primarily on three areas: administration or management, intellectuals in general and philosophy in particular, and literature. The last category relates to his otherwise widely discussed notion of "national-popular" literature.[16] Gramsci's idea of a democratic philosophy is related to his slogan-like dictum that "all men are 'philosophers'" (Q 1375), although, needless to say, this principle must be properly understood; and the same applies to his theory of intellectuals, according to which "all men are intellectuals" (Q 1516). And his reflections on democratic administration or management are found in his discussion of what he calls democratic centralism. Let us begin with the last.

The issue which Gramsci discusses under the rubric of democratic centralism is one which affects the manner of operation of organizations at many levels and in many contexts, such as national affairs, international relations, political parties, labor unions, churches, and cultural associations. The first thing Gramsci clarifies is that democratic centralism "has nothing to do with abstract democracy, as shown by the fact that the French Revolution and the Third Republic have developed forms of organic centralism which did not exist under either the absolute monarchy or Napoleon I" (Q 1632–33). I believe Gramsci is saying that the example of the French Revolution shows that abstract democracy is compatible with forms of tyranny and absolutism which are obviously incompatible with democratic centralism, and so democratic centralism should not be equated with abstract democracy. By "abstract democracy," he probably means an excessive and inappropriate emphasis on some of the ideals of the French Revolution, namely equality and fraternity. This would be a situation in which one would try to tamper with the elitist distinction as such. Adapting a formulation from a context in which Gramsci was alluding to a sense of democracy of which he was skeptical, we might say that abstract democracy is a situation in which "the undifferentiated people claims and believes to really be the state" (Q 734). Thus, with his clarification Gramsci is implicitly rejecting other theories or conceptions of democracy.[17]

If this is a relatively indirect statement of what democratic centralism is not, Gramsci is fortunately more explicit in regard to what he does understand by the phrase: "Democratic centralism . . . is a 'centralism' in motion, so to speak, namely a constant adaptation of the organization to the real movement, a matching of thrusts from below with orders from above, a constant insertion of elements stemming from the depths of the popular masses into the solid framework of the leadership apparatus; this ensures continuity and the regular accumulation of experience"

(Q 1634). Obviously the "insertion of elements" mentioned here corresponds to the "molecular transition" in the earlier fundamental note, and they are both equivalent to the movement from lower to upper class in Mosca's conception. Here, too, the Moschian content of Gramsci's concept of democracy is accompanied by at least one other important clue. It appears in the last clause of the passage where Gramsci recognizes and stipulates that such a democratic transition should ensure continuity and the preservation of accumulated knowledge. This is a characteristic Moschian point of the emblematic category, so to speak. For, as we saw earlier (Chapter 2, section 4)[18] Mosca expresses a very original and plausible point about the conservative nature of democracy, or at least of democratic change when it is not too rapid.

Besides defining democratic centralism in terms of an open elite and contrasting it to a nonelitist (abstract) democracy, Gramsci contrasts democratic centralism with a closed elite, a comparison analogous to Mosca's contrast between democracy and aristocracy. In the same note (Q 13,36), Gramsci contrasts democratic centralism to what he calls bureaucratic centralism, in regard to which he asserts that "the prevalence of bureaucratic centralism in a state indicates that the leading group is saturated and has become a narrow clique which tends to perpetuate its petty privileges by regulating and even strangling the emergence of contrasting forces, even when these forces are in harmony with the main fundamental interests" (Q 1634). Here, we see once again Gramsci's opposition to what he elsewhere calls oligarchy. Nevertheless, variation in terminology within his writings is no more significant than the terminological differences with Mosca. The important point is that, with regard to both the term and the concept of democracy, the content of the contrast with bureaucratic centralism reinforces the essential Moschian character of Gramsci's theory of democracy.

At the higher level of analysis and ratiocination, Gramsci also gives a more puzzling characterization of democratic elitism:

Democratic centralism offers an elastic formula which lends itself to many incarnations, and which lives insofar as it is continuously interpreted and adapted to different necessities. It consists of the critical search for what is equal in the apparent diversity, and distinct and even opposite in the apparent uniformity, in order to render organic and to connect closely what is similar, but in such a way that the organic process and the connection appear as a practical and 'inductive' experimental necessity, and not as the result of a rationalistic, deductivist, and abstractionist process, characteristic of pure intellectuals. [Q 1635]

What is puzzling about this passage [19] is that it is not clear how any of this relates to democracy conceived in terms of open elites and contrasted both with the nonexistence of elites and with closed elites, which we have seen to be the conception Gramsci elaborates in the rest of this note.

In the passage, democratic centralism is being related to two things: the critical search for equality within diversity and diversity within equality; and a practical, inductive, and experimental approach, as contrasted with a rationalistic, deductivist, abstractionist, and intellectualist approach. Beginning with the first, such a critical search by Gramsci is obviously an attempt to avoid one-sidedness and extremes with respect to the notions of equality and diversity; he rejects both equality without diversity and diversity without equality. Now, if we think of equality without diversity as abstract equality, then we begin to see the connection with the other way Gramsci defines democratic centralism, for, as we saw, the abstract democracy he rejects is essentially equivalent to abstract equality. This clarifies how his rejection here of mere equality without diversity corresponds to his rejection of abstract democracy mentioned earlier. Therefore, presumably, his acceptance here of both equality and diversity should correspond to his earlier acceptance both of the distinction between the masses and the leadership and of the individual transition from the former to the latter. Does it and how? I believe the equality would lie in the fact that each individual would have the opportunity to become a leader; that is, the equality in question is equality of opportunity. On the other hand, the diversity would lie in the fact that at any given time there would exist leaders and led, and that the respective conditions, positions, functions, duties, and prerogatives of the two would remain distinct and not identical. In short, Moschian and Gramscian elitist democracy is a special case of equality within diversity and diversity within equality; thus, the two apparently different definitions of democratic centralism advanced by Gramsci coalesce.

Or at least they coalesce to this extent, that the two key elements are contained in each. However, Gramsci's second formulation contains another key element, involving the distinction between an inductive and a deductive approach; that is, he is also saying that democratic centralism is an inductive rather than deductive style or method of administration or management or government. What are we to make of this? First, let us note that the things Gramsci is rejecting are "isms," as it were; he is objecting to excesses, abuses, misuses, and perversions of rationality, deduction, abstraction, and intellectuality, and not necessarily to the activities as such. Second, and conversely, he is advocating an inductive, not an inductivist, approach, and the fact that he has quotation marks around the word "inductive" is a sign that he may be aware of some of the controversies about the nature of induction;[20] it follows that there is no good reason for equating his inductive approach with simple induction by enumeration, that is, the process of drawing a general conclusion merely from the knowledge of the truth of particular instances of the generalization. Third, in also speaking of an experimental approach, he suggests a comparison between theories and speculation on the one hand and experience and observation on the other, the comparison being such as to avoid giving priority to either one of the two elements being compared and contrasted. Fourth, Gramsci does not seem to want to make any fine discrimination between inductive and experimental, and so we may take the two as largely coterminous.

If we now take Gramsci's essential point to be about the comparison and contrast between theories or ideas and observations or experience, then that immediately establishes a connection with what he says in the earlier passage. In fact, another element of that other characterization which I have not discussed so far refers to "a constant adaptation of the organization to the real movement, a matching of thrusts from below with orders from above" (Q 1634); so we really have an analogy between the situation in experimental science and the situation in administration, management, and government. Experimental science exists in a domain where it has to deal with the distinction between theories and observations; but a sound experimental method does not dichotomize them by drawing an absolute separation between them, as if the two were qualitatively different things; nor does it confuse them by mistaking the researcher's own imagined ideas as real facts in the world, or by claiming that the ascertained facts carry their own meanings and interpretations with them and have no need of the creative contribution of the mind. Analogously, administration, management, and government operate in the domain of the distinction between elites and masses, the elites being the analogue of theories, and the masses the analogue of observations; democratic centralism neither denies their difference nor is satisfied with their separation but encourages appropriate interactions between the two, especially the slow, gradual, Moschian, and "conservative" influx of individuals from the masses into the elites. Just as one sometimes speaks of the experimental method as involving the combination of theory and observation, with the stipulation that the combination must be judicious, so one could speak (with the same stipulation) of the combination of elites and masses.

Gramsci does so explicitly a few sentences after the initially puzzling passage being analyzed here. He goes on to state that democratic centralism "requires an organic unity between theory and practice, between intellectual strata and popular masses, between governors and governed" (Q 1635). And it is clear that by "organic unity" he does not mean one which obliterates the distinction. It is equally clear that Gramsci's organic unity is not that which is present in bureaucratic centralism. We might say that such organic unity is of the same type as the dialectical unity of political and civil society of which Gramsci spoke in the context of the problem of the withering away of the state and of elites.[21]

To summarize, in his articulation and discussion of the notion of democratic centralism, Gramsci is applying the elitist, Moschian concept of democracy defined in terms of social mobility, open elites, and renewal of elites. Gramsci explicitly contrasts his view with egalitarianism, which he calls abstract democracy; and this contrast is in the Moschian tradition. There is an explicit contrast to oligarchy or closed elitism, which Gramsci labels bureaucratic centralism as well as organic centralism, in the bad, pejorative sense of "organic"; this contrast corresponds to Mosca's contrasting of democracy and aristocracy. Gramsci also advances an explicit analogy between the elite-masses relationship stipulated by democratic centralism and the judicious combination of speculation and observation in experimental science; this analogy is in the tradition of Mosca's balanced pluralism.

3. National-Popular Literature

It has already been mentioned that Gramsci also applied Mosca's concept of democracy to literature. Two preliminary cautions need to be expressed in this regard. First, Gramsci's application should not be taken in a mechanical sense—that is, as an indication that he first learned about and internalized the Moschian concept, later set out looking for domains on which to bring the concept to bear, and eventually found that the field of literature was a fruitful one to explore. Rather, I would say that he had always had a keen interest in literature, besides such other fields as politics, history, and philosophy; as he gradually became more and more attracted to this concept of democracy, his reflections on literature began more and more to bear the imprint of the concept. This strikes me as a natural development in scholarly and scientific investigation.

The second caveat is that Gramsci was very well aware that the analysis of the democratic elements in literature cannot pretend to be a substitute for aesthetic criticism—that is, the evaluation of the poetic or artistic value or merit of a literary work. He regards the democratic analysis as a type of historical and cultural interpretation and criticism; it is concerned with what might be called the moral, political, and philosophical presuppositions of literary works. Democratic analysis is even connected with artistic or aesthetic criticism, in the sense that such an analysis may discover that it is the writer himself who is explicitly advocating a moral, political, or philosophical view, and so to that extent weakening the aesthetic merit of his art. All this, of course, is what one would expect from someone who had been educated in the tradition of Benedetto Croce's aesthetics and literary criticism, had learned and digested the Crocean insights, and was struggling to move ahead in that direction.[22]

With these clarifications in mind, we can go on to examine a number of relevant passages in which Gramsci discusses the democratic or antidemocratic elements of such movements as Parnassianism and Romanticism, and such authors as Alessandro Manzoni, Leo Tolstoy, and William Shakespeare.[23] One of the most important of these passages is the note (Q 14,72) in which Gramsci discusses the nature and relationship of form and content in art, poetry, and literature, and the controversy between the Parnassians, formalists, or classicists on the one hand and the Romantics on the other. The former advocated and the latter opposed art for art's sake and an emphasis on form and pure beauty; or conversely, the former opposed while the latter favored the importance of emotional and imaginative content and material. Given his penchant for concreteness, it is perhaps not surprising that Gramsci tends to side with the antiformalists and Romantics. However, more important for our purpose here is that he expresses his judgment in terms of democracy: "One may also say that historically, so far, the so-called advocates of content have been 'more democratic' than their Parnassian opponents (for example); that is, they wanted a literature not aimed at 'intellectuals,' etc." (Q 1737). That is, the Parnassians wanted to restrict art and poetry to artists, poets, and intellectuals, whereas their opponents wanted to make it more generally accessible to common people; thus we can say that the issue was whether the class of artists should be closed or open, or rather how open or closed it should be; in other words, the question was whether the distinction between artists and masses should be a rigid separation or a grouping susceptible to regrouping due to individual mobility. The Moschian character of this concept of democracy is obvious.

The point is further elaborated when Gramsci takes up the nature of Romanticism as such: "Among other meanings, Romanticism has acquired that of a special relation or tie between the intellectuals and the people or nation; that is, it is a particular case of 'democracy' (in the wide sense) applied to literature (in the wide sense, such that even Catholicism may be 'democratic,' whereas it is possible that 'liberalism' is not)" (Q 1739). We have already seen that a special consequence of the Moschian concept of democracy is that the Catholic Church becomes a good example of it; for Mosca, if one wants to criticize Catholicism one must focus on its autocracy. Similarly, if we want to allow for the possibility of an undemocratic liberalism, we must follow Mosca and take liberalism to refer to the flow of authority from bottom up; then, as in the Republic of Venice, this may happen while the ruling class is relatively closed, and hence aristocratic or undemocratic. So, Gramsci is saying that Romanticism is an approach to, a type of, literature which advocates a close relationship between writers and masses, so that art is accessible to the masses and so that there can be movement of ideas, feelings, and persons across the elitist divide.

Finally, at the end of this note, Gramsci makes one additional clarification: "It has been said that the word 'democracy' ought to be taken to have not only a 'lay' or 'secular' meaning (as they say), but also a 'Catholic' meaning, and even a reactionary meaning, if you will; what is important is to strive for a tie with the people or nation, to admit the necessity of a unity which is not servile and due to passive obedience but active and alive, regardless of the content of one's life" (Q 1740). The reference to a reactionary meaning of democracy is puzzling, but the contrast between Catholicism and secularism seems relatively clear; it is the contrast between a religious orientation where all authority derives ultimately from God, and a humanist viewpoint in which authority flows upward from the people. This is the Moschian distinction between autocracy and liberalism, which crisscrosses the distinction between democracy and aristocracy to yield the possibility that democracy per se may be liberal (secular) as well as autocratic (Catholic). For democracy per se refers specifically and merely to a tie between elite and people which is characterized by the degree of mobility from the latter to the former. It is significant that besides democracy so defined and besides this kind of bond and movement, an active and free obedience rather than servile and passive obedience should be specified. Moschian liberalism may be taken to correspond in large measure to such active and free obedience.

This Moschian, democratic-elitist conceptual structure emerges in the context of a discussion which deals, as we have seen, with the problem of artistic content versus form and with the controversy between Parnassians and Romantics. In this crucial note (Q 14,72), Gramsci also discusses the issue of whether or not Italian literature has been Romantic, in the democratic sense just specified; and he expresses a general inclination to think that it has not. Elsewhere he is more specific about this and speaks of the "negative popular-national quality of Italian literature" (Q 402–5) and of the "absence of a national-popular quality in Italian literature" (Q 942–43). Gramsci does not deny that Italian literature has a tradition, going back at least to Manzoni in the nineteenth century and extending to the "verism" of Giovanni Verga in the twentieth, of depicting characters belonging to the lower classes and common people. However, Gramsci thinks that this is not sufficient, and that the writer's attitude toward the characters is more important (Q 896, 943). What is wrong, or rather, what is undemocratic, about their attitude?

The most relevant passages regard Manzoni, whose novel *The Betrothed* is widely regarded as second only to Dante's *Divine Comedy* among the masterpieces of Italian literature.[24] These passages are especially instructive because Gramsci contrasts Manzoni to Tolstoy, whose work he does regard as essentially democratic. Let us begin with some terminological elucidations: "*Popular* Literature. On the non-popular-national quality of Italian literature. The attitude toward the people in *The Betrothed*. The 'aristocratic' quality of Manzoni's Catholicism emerges from the jocular 'sympathy' toward characters who are common people (which does not emerge in Tolstoy). . . . This attitude is clearly reminiscent of castes, albeit in a religious Catholic form" (Q 895–96]). Here we see that Gramsci's "non-popular-national" is equivalent to "aristocratic," which in turn is equivalent to "reminiscent of castes." But the last is equivalent to "being characterized by a closed class," which is the same as Mosca's "aristocratic" or "antidemocratic." It follows that Gramsci's notion of popular-national (or national-popular) corresponds to Mosca's concept of democratic.

A main reason why Manzoni's novel is aristocratic is that "in *The Be-trothed* there are no popular characters who are not made fun of and ridi-culed. . . . They are portrayed as miserable and bigoted people, without any inner life. Only the upper classes have an inner life" (Q 2245). This contrasts with Tolstoy's characters, who give an indication of an oppo-site attitude on his part, a democratic attitude: "It is typical of Tolstoy that the authentic and instinctive wisdom of the people, expressed even with a casual word, enlightens and causes a crisis in an educated man. This is precisely the most relevant trait of the religion of Tolstoy, who understands the Gospel 'democratically': namely, in accordance with its original and novel spirit" (Q 2245). Now, this sounds as if Tolstoy depicts the masses favorably and Manzoni depicts them unfavorably; but such an assertion would be too vague and general. Gramsci is being more spe-cific: he is referring to one type of relationship or interchange between upper and lower classes, a relationship that might be called one of cul-tural, moral, or psychological influence. The popular wisdom to which Gramsci is referring is the occasional ability of common people to en-lighten upper-class persons or make them aware of some real problem. Therefore, we are dealing with the question whether or not the upper classes are open-minded, in the sense of whether their mind is open to experiences originating from the masses. We thus have an analogue of Mosca's open elites and upward mobility, and hence an application of his concept of democracy.

Gramsci ends his note on Manzoni and Tolstoy (Q 23,51) with a criticism of the criticism leveled at Shakespeare by Tolstoy and George Bernard Shaw.[25] Tolstoy had added his own twist from a Christian moral viewpoint to the objection of those who found fault with Shakespeare for showing no sympathy for the lower or even the middle classes, indeed for portraying them as contemptible, repulsive, and comical and for display-ing bias toward the upper classes. And Shaw had targeted Shakespeare's thought, rather than his art, and argued that primary importance should be given to writers who have transcended the morality of their own time and groped toward that of the future, which Shakespeare, he maintained, did not do. Gramsci does not want his own idea of a national-popular literature and of democratic analysis to be confused with either of these approaches:

> In these notes one must avoid any moralistic tendentiousness à la Tolstoy and also any tendentiousness stemming from "wisdom after the event"

à la Shaw. One is dealing with an inquiry into cultural history, and not with artistic criticism in the strict sense; one wants to show that it is the authors being examined who introduce an extrinsic moral content (namely, are engaged in propaganda and not in artistic activity), and that the worldview implicit in their works is narrow and biased—not national-popular, but characteristic of a closed caste. The search for the beauty of a work is subordinated to the search for why it is "read," is "popular," is "in demand," or on the other hand why it does not touch and interest the people—thus bringing to light the absence of unity in the national cultural life. [Q 2247]

This provides a good summary of Gramsci's reflections on national-popular literature. The mention of a closed caste is an implicit reference to Mosca's aristocracy, and what is labeled the national-popular viewpoint corresponds to Moschian democracy; thus, by advocating a national-popular literature, Gramsci is advocating a democratic literature, in the elitist sense of democracy. This Gramscian, national-popular, and democratic literature would promote the openness and renewal of elites through a greater interaction of elites with the people or masses, and this passage is a reminder that three levels of interaction are involved: one the level of the characters portrayed in the story, where there may or may not be democracy; the other the level of the interaction between the writer and the masses in his own society; and the third the level of the literary critic in the analysis of the two preceding levels. These distinctions help one avoid moralistic and progressivist tendentiousness, and Gramsci's concern with this issue should leave no doubt that his national-popular literature is not only an application of Mosca's concept of democracy, but also of the balanced pluralism we have encountered before and seen to characterize both thinkers.

4. The Democratic Conception of Philosophy

Gramsci's attitude toward philosophy is much more complex that his attitude toward literature. One main reason for this is that philosophy is something which he wants to and does practice, engage in, and produce, as well as theorize about; indeed, I would say he is concerned primarily with practicing philosophy and only secondarily with the theorizing about it, whereas in regard to literature he is interested principally if not exclusively in its analysis, appreciation, and criticism. Thus, for example, the Gramscian views on elites, democracy, and related topics which are being reconstructed in this investigation constitute also a political and social philosophy, from the point of view of any number of conceptions of philosophy. Therefore, it should not be surprising that Gramsci devoted to the topic of the nature of philosophy one of the longest, most polished, and most inspired essays (Q 11,12) to be found not only in the Prison Notebooks but in all his writings. That his view of philosophy is implicitly and explicitly democratic (in the Moschian, elitist sense) provides us with the essential reason for considering it in the context of this investigation.

The inspired tone of Gramsci's metaphilosophical reflections is obvious from the opening sentences of his essay: "One must destroy the very widespread prejudice that philosophy is something very difficult insofar as it is the characteristic intellectual activity of a determinate category of specialized scientists or professional and systematic philosophers. One must therefore demonstrate, as a preliminary, that all men are 'philosophers,' and define the limitations and properties of this 'spontaneous philosophy' characteristic of 'the whole world'" (Q 1374). Equally obvious is the anti-aristocratic content of the first sentence here, for the determinate category of which it speaks may be interpreted as the closed elite which defines the Moschian concept of aristocracy; Gramsci is expressing his opposition to defining philosophy only in terms of a closed group of specialists or professionals who talk exclusively to one another and insulate themselves from the rest of the world. The second sentence makes clear that he wants to define philosophy as an activity open, at least in principle, to everyone, which is a way of making philosophers an open class. Still, it would be easy to confuse such anti-aristocratic and inclusive pronouncements with antielitism and egalitarianism; that is, one may get the impression that Gramsci is saying that there is no difference between philosophers and nonphilosophers and that all philosophers are equally good. This is certainly not his meaning, and in fact we find him expressing the proper qualifications and giving a rather sophisticated and complicated account, which leaves little doubt about the concept of democracy he has in mind. So we need to analyze his account in more depth.

One of his most important and revealing clarifications has to do with his criticism of the traditional argument that philosophy is the most democratic of all disciplines, or intrinsically democratic, or the democratic discipline par excellence because it uses and studies the ratiocinative faculty, which is common to all human beings.[26] Gramsci leaves no doubt about what he thinks of this argument when he says that it presupposes "one of the silliest and most 'rational' democratic theories. It is still tied to the conception of 'human nature' as being always the same and without development, as it was conceived before Marx, according to which all men are fundamentally equal" (Q 756). That is, the argument presupposes the egalitarian theory of democracy, which is being labeled rational in the sense that human equality is seen as based on equal rationality. Gramsci's justification of his criticism is found in another extremely important note (Q 7,35). There he argues that human beings really have not a nature but a history, namely that human nature is not a static but a developing and historical entity. He does not regard human equality as being de facto true, even in regard to the faculty of reason; it is rather a desirable moral ideal to strive for and to be actualized in the more or less distant future. It is a point of arrival rather than a point of departure. Gramsci's words on this point are worth quoting at length:

> The oneness of mankind does not lie in the "biological" nature of man; the human differences which count in history are not biological ones. . . . Not even the faculty of "reasoning" or the "mind" has created oneness, nor can it be recognized as a unifying fact, because it is only a formal categorial concept. It is not "thinking" but what one really thinks which unifies or differentiates men.
>
> The most satisfactory answer is that "human nature" is the "network of social relations" because this includes the idea of becoming. . . . One can also say that human nature is "history" . . . if history is given the precise meaning of "becoming," in a *concordia discors* which does not start with oneness but embodies within itself the reasons for a possible oneness.
>
> . . . In the course of history, real "equality," that is, the degree of "rationality" reached by "human nature" in the historical process, lies in the system of "private and public" and explicit and implicit associations which are centered in the "state" and in the world political system; one is dealing with "equalities" felt to be such among the members of a given association and with "inequalities" felt among the various associations; these equalities and inequalities are real insofar as they are are perceived individually and collectively. [Q 884–86]

Thus, Gramsci rejects the traditional justification of the democratic nature of philosophy, but not because he intends to deny the conclusion that philosophy is essentially democratic: rather because that traditional justification presupposes the egalitarian theory of democracy and egalitarianism presupposes an unrealistic and static view of human nature.

[131]

His democratic conception of philosophy has for its basis what I shall call the pedagogical conception of philosophy, and the Moschian, elitist definition of democracy provides the connection between pedagogy and democracy. This emerges explicitly is a crucial note (Q 10,II,44) where Gramsci advocates "a new type of philosopher who may be called democratic philosopher, that is, a philosopher convinced that his personality is not limited to his physical individuality but involves an active social relationship aimed at the modification of the cultural environment" (Q 1332). To understand how he arrives at this conclusion, we must begin with his elucidation of the pedagogical conception of philosophy: "Philosophy is taken as a worldview, and philosophical activity is conceived no longer merely as an 'individual' elaboration of systematically coherent concepts, but also and especially as a cultural struggle to transform the popular 'mentality' and to disseminate philosophical innovations; these will be shown to be 'historically true' to the extent that they will become concretely (namely, historically and socially) universal" (Q 1330). That is, Gramsci conceives of philosophy primarily in terms of the teaching of a worldview to the people, in terms of philosophers teaching nonphilosophers, and in terms of the dissemination of philosophical ideas among the masses. It is clear that he is not limiting philosophy to this conception, for he explicitly allows a place for individual theorizing; he is saying that the social dissemination of philosophical ideas is at least as important as their individual creation.[27]

He is giving one reason for the importance of philosophical teaching here: namely, that the degree of diffusion of a philosophical idea is a clue to its validity. Now, this sounds as if Gramsci is subscribing to a consensus theory of truth, according to which a proposition is true if enough people believe or accept it as true; here we would have "democraticism" with a vengeance—that is, a "democratic" theory of truth: "democratic" in the sense of majority or mob rule. However, this very possibility ought to be a warning that this interpretation is far from what Gramsci has in mind. Instead, he tells us,

It is evident that a mass-oriented framework of this sort cannot come about "arbitrarily," around just any ideology, as a result of the formally assertive will of a person or group who might advocate it out of philosophical or religious fanaticism. The adherence or nonadherence of the masses to an ideology is the way in which the realistic criticism of the rationality and historicity of worldviews takes place. Arbitrary frameworks are more or less rapidly eliminated by the historical competition, even if occasionally (owing to a combination of favorable immediate circumstances) they are able to enjoy a certain popularity; on the other hand, frameworks which correspond to the needs of a complex and organic historical period always end up getting the upper hand and prevailing, even if they go through many intermediate phases in which they succeed only through more or less bizarre and anomalous combinations. [Q 1393]

I would add, in accordance with Gramsci's outlook, that here we are dealing with philosophical truth or the truth of philosophical ideas (rather than with historical or scientific truth), and so the ideas in questions are primarily principles of conduct and principles of reasoning; but the adequacy of such principles is not and cannot be independent of actual conduct and reasoning, on pain of irrelevance. In other words, when the domain of inquiry is human behavior, even the traditional correspondence theory of truth requires that a theory about such a phenomenon be tested in terms of the extent to which the phenomenon corresponds to it; but the phenomenon in this case is precisely human reasoning and conduct.[28]

Another reason for the importance of philosophical teaching is that, for Gramsci, such teaching is not a one-way affair but a reciprocal one. That is, the teacher learns or is supposed to learn in the process of teaching, so that the pedagogical context coincides to some extent with the context of discovery and creation. And here we approach the heart of the argument:

> This problem can and must be brought closer to the modern approach to pedagogical doctrine and practice, according to which the relationship between teacher and pupil is an active relationship of reciprocal interactions, so that every teacher is always a pupil and every pupil a teacher. However, the pedagogical relationship cannot be limited to specifically "scholastic" interactions; in these, the new generations come in contact with the old and absorb the historically necessary experiences and values, thus "maturing" and developing their own historically and culturally superior personality. This relationship exists in all of society as a whole and for every individual vis-à-vis other individuals, between intellectual and nonintellectual strata, between governors and governed, between elites and followers, between leaders and led, and between army officers and troops. [Q 1331]

It is clear that Gramsci is conceiving the teacher-pupil relationship in the open manner in which Mosca's concept of democracy defines the relationship between rulers and ruled; it is the pedagogical analogue of Mosca's political democracy, where the class of governors is open to renewal from the influx of members of the governed class; just as in the political context we have an exchange of persons across the divide between governors and governed, in the pedagogical situation we have an exchange of experiences and information across the teacher-pupil divide. It should therefore come as no surprise that Gramsci calls a philosopher who takes seriously the (reciprocity of) the pedagogical relationship a democratic philosopher; it is essentially an application to a new domain of the Moschian, elitist conception of democracy. Gramsci is here defining a democratic philosopher as someone who gives primary importance to the pedagogical mission of philosophy and who is aware of the importance of the reciprocal and interactive nature of the pedagogical relationship.[29]

But why should the pedagogical relationship be conceived in this manner? Here we can appreciate the relevance of the the idea that all men are philosophers. That is, the philosophical teacher, discoverer, or expert can learn from the layman because the latter is in a sense a philosopher. In what sense? In the spontaneous or implicit sense. That is, Gramsci is talking about the philosophy which is implicit in language, in common sense and common belief,[30] in religion, and in folklore (Q 1375). And he is also talking about the philosophy which is implicit in practical action, for "most men are philosophers insofar as they are practically engaged in action, and insofar as in their practical action (in the guiding lines of their conduct) is implicitly contained a worldview, a philosophy" (Q 1255). Indeed, he makes it a methodological duty for a professional philosopher to study such implicit philosophy: "From the point of view which concerns us, the study of the history and of the logic of the various philosophies of philosophers is not sufficient. One must call attention, at least as a methodological orientation, to the other parts of the history of philosophy, that is, to the worldviews of the great masses, to those of the less numerous leading (or intellectual) groups, and finally to the relations among these various cultural frameworks and the philosophy of philosophers" (Q 1255). It is entirely typical of Gramsci that while stressing the importance of popular, implicit philosophy, he does not do so one-sidedly, but judiciously, in accordance with what I have called his (and Mosca's) balanced pluralism. Gramsci is distinguishing three types of philosophy: the implicit philosophy of the popular masses, the philosophy of the cultural and intellectual elite, and the systematic philosophy of the professional philosophers. And he is also stressing the need for interrelating them. Nevertheless, given the common neglect of the implicit popular philosophy, his analysis exhibits a refreshing openness to the lower classes; this openness would be regarded as democratic from many points of view (many theories of democracy, as it were), and it is also democratic from the viewpoint of Moschian democracy when it is combined with recognition of the existence of philosophical elites and the concern to bridge the gap between them and the masses.

The same point emerges in two other ways. For example, after noting that everyone is implicitly a philosopher, Gramsci asks the rhetorical question: "Is it preferable 'to think' without a critical awareness of it, in an incoherent and occasional manner, ... or is it preferable to elaborate one's own worldview with awareness and critically?" (Q 1375–76). For him, critical thinking implies partly self-knowledge, in the sense of knowing what one's own worldview is; partly theoretical systematization, in the sense of increasing the logical coherence of one's own thoughts by eliminating contradictions and articulating unifying principles; and partly historical sensitivity, in the sense of knowing the various preceding views and present alternatives and being able to justify one's view vis-à-vis the others (Q 1376). But this is not all, for

> historically and politically, critical self-awareness means the creation of an intellectual elite: a human mass does not "distinguish" itself and does not become independent ("for itself") without organizing (in the broad sense), and there is no organization without intellectuals, namely without organizers and leaders—that is, without its happening that the theoretical element of the theory-practice nexus should distinguish itself as a stratum of persons "specializing" in conceptual and philosophical elaboration. However, this process of creating intellectuals is long, difficult, and full of contradictions, forward and backward steps, swervings and regroupings; in it the "loyalty" of the masses . . . is sometimes severely tested. The process of development is tied to a dialectic of intellectuals and masses; the stratum of intellectuals develops quantitatively and qualitatively, but every leap toward a new "breadth" and complexity of the stratum of intellectuals is tied to an analogous movement of the mass of simple people; the latter is raised toward higher levels of culture and simultaneously enlarges the extent of its influence, with more or less important instances of movement by individuals or even groups toward the stratum of specialized intellectuals. [Q 1386]

That is, the critical awareness required to improve the spontaneous, implicit, popular philosophy requires the elitist distinction *and* the democratic connection between philosophical specialists and laymen.

Gramsci is led to the same result by following the reverse path of starting from the technical point of view of metaphilosophy and working his way down to the philosophy of the masses. That is, having established the metaphilosophical claim that all men are philosophers, one cannot stop there; this claim is just the beginning of a proper analysis, a "preliminary" claim, in Gramsci's expression (Q 1375). After this, in order not to lapse into an empty and boring manner of speaking and a confused and confusing manner of thinking,[31] one needs to formulate by means of new criteria the differences among various kinds of philosophy; for example, one needs to give a reinterpretation of the difference between professional philosophers and lay philosophers:

> Let us take as established the principle that all men are "philosophers"—namely, that between professional or "technical" philosophers and other men there is not a "qualitative" difference but only a "quantitative" one; in this case "quantity" has a special meaning which cannot be confused with an arithmetical sum, because it indicates greater or lesser "homogeneity," "coherence," "logicalness," etc., namely a greater or lesser quantity of qualitative elements. Given this principle, one must nevertheless see wherein exactly lies the difference. Thus, it is not exact to call philosophy just any tendency of thought, any general orientation, etc., nor just any "view of the world and of life." A philosopher may be called a skilled worker in contrast to an unskilled laborer; but even this is not exact because in industry besides the unskilled laborer and the skilled worker there is the engineer, who knows the trade not only practically but also theoretically and historically. A professional or technical philosopher not only "thinks" with greater logical rigor, with greater coherence, and with greater systemic thrust than other men, but he knows the whole history of thought; that is, he can explain the development of thought until the present and is able to tackle problems at the point they have reached after having undergone the greatest efforts to solve them, etc. In the domain of thought philosophers have the same function which specialists have in the various scientific fields. [Q 1342]

So to claim that all men are philosophers is not to pretend that there is no difference between philosophers and nonphilosophers, or between professional and nonprofessional philosophers; the point is rather to stress that the difference between the two groups is a quantitative one involving matters of degree, rather than a qualitative one involving discrete and separate kinds. And the differences of degree involve such traits as a greater or lesser logical rigor, systemic coherence, and historical understanding. The democratic implications of such a quantitative criterion should be clear: it is possible for everyone to become a systematic philosopher; everyone is *potentially* a systematic philosopher. And it should not need much elaboration to explain why this presupposes the Moschian conception of democracy, and not some other one such as the egalitarian: since the systematic philosopher does not engage in activities which are intrinsically different from those of the layman, but only thinks better and more systematically, it then becomes possible and likely for the non-philosophical mass to move up to the philosophical elite, and for the latter to be liable to renewal, and to be open to influx, from below.

However, that is not all. Although the professional philosopher is a specialist, he is not like other specialists; his special connection with the masses emerges once more by the following route:

> However, there is a difference between the philosophical specialist and other specialists: the philosophical specialist comes closer to other men than is the case for other specialists. To have given to the philosophical specialist a portrayal similar to that of other scientific specialists is precisely what has generated the caricature of philosophers. In fact, one can imagine an entomological specialist without all other men being "entomologists," a trigonometrical specialist without most other men being involved with trigonometry, etc. (and there can be sciences which are extremely refined, extremely specialized, necessary, and hence not "common"); but one cannot think of a man who is not also a philosopher, who does not think, precisely because thinking is characteristic of man as such (unless one is a pathological idiot). [Q 1342–43]

The key point is that the philosophical specialist comes closer to other men than other specialists. That is, the gap between the philosophical elite and the philosophical masses is or should be more bridgeable than other gaps; the philosophical elite must be especially open to the influx of new members from the masses through the latter's enhancement of their critical awareness, as well as open to the experiences of the masses by means of a properly conceived relationship between teacher and pupil.

In conclusion, then, Gramsci's view of philosophy is similar to his view of literature and of administration or management. He advocates mutual contact, interaction, and exchange between the leaders and the led, whether the leaders be philosophers, writers, or administrators, and whether the led be laymen, readers, or rank-and-file subordinates. The Gramscian account is democratic partly in the sense that it implicitly presupposes the Moschian concept of democracy in the ways I have articulated. However, the Gramscian account seems also to be explicitly committed to it, insofar as he explicitly mentions the term "democracy" in all three of these areas, and insofar as his analysis is in accordance with his explicit claim that this concept is the most realistic and concrete definition of democracy (Q 1056); in this regard, we can say he is explicitly articulating a theory of democracy. Moreover, as we have seen, this theory is, historically speaking, Moschian, for it originates with Mosca; conceptually speaking, the theory is elitist, but neither oligarchic nor aristocratic; and it may be called an-egalitarian, but not antiegalitarian, because while it denies the empirical and historical truth of human equality, it admits and even advocates equality as a moral ideal to be actualized in the future. On the other hand, never for a moment does Gramsci forget the constraints imposed by reality on such a moral ideal, and so methodologically his theory remains realistic or anti-utopian. His methodological orientation is also characterized by a manner of thinking which I have occasionally labeled dialectical,[32] though in this context nothing depends on such a label; it could with equal justice be labeled the method of analysis and synthesis, but this would also generate misleading connotations.[33] Labels aside, what is important to remember about this manner of thinking is, to repeat a formulation quoted earlier, that "it consists of the critical search for what is equal in the apparent diversity, and distinct and even opposite in the apparent uniformity" (Q 1635).

5. The Problem of Transformism

At this point we need to face the following difficulty. Gramsci has a notion of "transformism" which appears prima facie to be similar to his concept of democracy, and yet his evaluation of transformism would appear to be unfavorable. In this context "transformism" refers to a phenomenon which is said to characterize Italian political history from the middle of the nineteenth century onward. With regard to party politics, the phenomenon involved the dissolution of traditional right-wing and left-wing political parties, and the practice of forming parliamentary majorities by working out deals with particular interest groups or influential individuals, irrespective of parties; and from an intellectual point of view, transformism involves the overcoming of differences, the amalgamation of dogmas, and the softening of consciences.[34] Ordinarily, the word "transformism" has a negative connotation. The aspect of the phenomenon on which Gramsci focuses is the following: "Indeed one may say that the whole of Italian state life from 1848 onward is characterized by transformism, namely by the elaboration of an increasingly larger leading class within the framework established by the Moderates after 1848 and the fall of neo-Guelph and federalist utopias, and by the gradual absorption of the active elements originating from allied groups and also from adversary groups which seemed irreconcilable enemies" (Q 2011). The difficulty is that such an enlargement of the ruling class by the absorption of elements from other classes sounds like democracy, in the precise Moschian sense accepted by Gramsci. If there is really no difference between transformism and democracy, and if Gramsci's evaluation of transformism is really unfavorable, then we would have one of the following two consequences: either there is a serious internal inconsistency in Gramsci, insofar as he advocates democracy but opposes its synonym "transformism"; or else his commitment to democracy is undermined and he is as opposed to it as he is to transformism.

To resolve this difficulty, I would begin by pointing out that Gramsci sees an important difference between democracy and transformism. The difference is that in transformism the elements absorbed into the ruling class are not just ordinary members of the ruled classes but the leaders of the ruled class: "So-called transformism is nothing but the parliamentary expression of the fact that the Action Party is incorporated in a molecular manner by the Moderates and the popular masses are decapitated rather than absorbed into the framework of the new state" (Q 2042).[35] It is the distinction between democracy and transformism which helps us to understand Gramsci's remarks on Giolitti, the Italian statesman widely regarded as a classic practitioner of transformism, a judgment with which Gramsci seems to agree (Q 387). For, on the one hand, Gramsci admits that Giolitti was able "to destroy the old and particularistic cliques (living like parasites with the support of the state police, which defended their privileges and their parasitism) and to establish a wider participation of 'some' masses in state life through the parliament" (Q 997). On the other hand, Gramsci judges that Giolitti "hindered the formation of a democratic Italy" (Q 997). It is perhaps questionable whether this interpretation and evaluation are historically correct, for after all it was Giolitti who, for example, managed to have universal male suffrage passed in the parliament. But such an issue is beyond the scope of this investigation.[36] The important point to remember is that the Gramscian judgment on Giolitti reinforces my interpretation that Gramsci does not identify transformism with democracy; there is a general difference between the two notions, as well as at least one particular case allegedly instantiating the former but not the latter.

Moreover, if we examine what exactly Gramsci finds objectionable about transformism, we see that his criticism is indeed in accordance with a democratic commitment. The major objection is that "the government has in fact acted like a 'party'; it has taken a position above the parties, not to harmonize their interests and activities in the permanent institutions of the life and interests of the state and the nation, but to erode the parties, to detach them from the great masses, and to have 'a force of partyless people tied to the government by paternalistic bonds of the Bonapartist or Caesarist type.' This is the way in which one must analyze the so-called *dictatorships* of Depretis, Crispi, and Giolitti, and the parliamentary phenomenon of *transformism*" (Q 387). That is, transformism gives the leaders of the ruled masses entrance into the ruling class, not in order to the bridge the gap between governors and governed (which would enhance democracy), but in order to deprive the masses of their leaders (which has the effect that the governors can better control and manipulate the governed in paternalistic and dictatorial ways). This feature implies that it is not transformism per se which is objectionable, but the context in which it occurs and the effects it produces. Or to be more exact, it is not the democratic element of social mobility which makes transformism objectionable, but the fact that such democratic movement is combined with other objectionable features. Now, the chief of these features seems to correspond to what Mosca calls autocracy, namely the flow of authority from the top down. Of course, if such an autocratic element is made part of the definition of transformism, then transformism would be an intrinsically objectionable phenomenon for Gramsci; but that would not change the fact that the undesirable element would be its autocracy and not its democracy.

Two related points elaborated by Gramsci reinforce this interpretation. The first regards the effect of transformism on the bureaucracy or public administration. The effect is simply to lead in the direction of what Mosca would call bureaucratic absolutism, which is a species of autocracy: "Thus the bureaucracy became estranged from the people and became a true political party by means of administrative positions; this was the worst of all parties because the bureaucratic hierarchy replaced the intellectual and political hierarchy; the bureaucracy became the state-Bonapartist party" (Q 388). The second point is that on more than one occasion Gramsci suggests that transformism ought to be interpreted as a form of "passive revolution" (Q 962, 1238). Now, without going into a full analysis of this important concept,[37] we can say that a passive revolution is an elite-led series of reforms benefiting the people but lacking popular initiative, and that what is wrong with it for Gramsci is obviously not the particular results but the manner of accomplishing them; and the top-down method used is precisely the autocratic approach.

However, now a new difficulty emerges. It is that given his elitism, Gramsci should believe that transformism is the only way of accomplishing democracy. In other words, his negative evaluation of transformism is inconsistent not with his doctrine of democracy but with his doctrine of elitism. That is why indications are that perhaps he is not completely opposed to transformism. This emerges in a discussion of what Gramsci himself calls the dynamics of passive revolutions and of transformism:

In the struggle between Cavour and Mazzini, in which Cavour is the exponent of passive revolution and war of position and Mazzini the exponent of popular initiative and war of maneuver, are they not both indispensable to the exact same extent? . . . Now, since similar situations occur in every historical event, one should see whether from this one could derive some general principle of the science and art of politics. One could apply to the concept of passive revolution (and one could use the Italian Risorgimento as documentation) the interpretive criterion of molecular modifications which in reality progressively modify the previous composition of forces and hence become the source of new modifications. Thus we have seen how in the Italian Risorgimento after 1848 the switching to Cavour's side of more and more elements of the Action Party has progressively modified the composition of the Moderate forces, by eliminating neo-Guelphism on the one hand, and by impoverishing Mazzini's movement on the other (Garibaldi's oscillations also belong to this process, etc.). This element is, however, the original phase of the phenomenon which later was called transformism and whose importance has not yet, it seems, been brought to light as a form of historical development. [Q 1767]

So Gramsci does attribute a certain historical necessity to transformism; that is, he attributes to it an important function in the historical process. Actually, his talk of progressiveness suggests that, besides being necessary, this function is positive and good. Gramsci's analysis of dynamics is, in fact, very much in line with Mosca's account of the conservative consequences of democratic mobility, openness, and renewal.[38] Gramsci even goes so far as to say (Q 1767) that in one sense the transformist Cavour was better than the populist Mazzini: insofar as the former had a greater philosophical and reflective awareness of the situation and of their respective positions. This comparative judgment is a reflection of Gramsci's penchant for philosophical politics, in the sense of politics based on principle. Indeed, ultimately his objection to transformism seems to reduce to an objection to the opportunism of many of its practitioners: "The weakness of Italian political parties in the entire period of their activity from the Risorgimento onward . . . has consisted in what one could call an imbalance between agitation and propaganda, and which in other terms is called lack of principles, opportunism, lack of organic continuity, imbalance between tactics and strategy" (Q 386). However, the democratic conception of philosophy which Gramsci holds (just to mention one thing) ought to be a warning to us that Gramsci's anti-opportunism cannot be interpreted as dogmatism, which would be the other extreme. Here, again, Gramsci's attitude of balanced pluralism emerges as the most fundamental position he seems to hold.

Thus we have a solution to the apparent problem of the relation between the Gramscian notions of democracy and transformism. The apparent problem is that both democracy and transformism seem to refer to the transition of individuals from the ruled to the ruling class, and yet Gramsci seems to approve the former and disapprove the latter process. My account has shown a difference between the two notions, since transformism refers to a situation where the transition is made by the leaders of the ruled class and not by its rank and file; moreover, Gramsci's negative evaluation of transformism is grounded not on its democratic component, but on its autocratic element and on its opportunistic aspect; finally, his evaluation is not entirely negative, for transformism seems to be a consequence of the elitist distinction and to have an indispensable function in historical development.

6. Epilogue

In this chapter I have carried out a systematic examination of Gramsci's remarks on democracy in the Notebooks. The first point to emerge is that Gramsci claims clearly and explicitly that the most realistic and concrete definition is that democracy is a relationship between elites and masses such that the elites are open to renewal by the influx of elements from the masses; though he does not mention Mosca, the Moschian origin and character of the definition is unmistakable.

Other relevant passages are those embodying the Gramscian notions of national-popular literature, democratic philosophy, and democratic centralism (namely, democratic administration or management). In each case, Gramsci advocates mutual contact, interaction, and exchange between the leaders and the led, whether the leaders be philosophers, writers, or administrators, and whether the led be laymen, readers, or rank-and-file subordinates in a hierarchy or bureaucracy. These Gramscian claims are shown to involve an application of the Moschian conception of democracy, insofar as these connections between leaders and led are instances of democracy as defined by Mosca.

In the course of the discussion, Gramsci's critique of alternative theories of democracy is also analyzed, especially the egalitarian one, so that the elitist character of Gramsci's democracy acquires reinforcement. Finally, a resolution is offered to the problem that Gramsci also has a notion of "transformism" such that both democracy and transformism seem to refer to the transition of individuals from the ruled to the ruling class, and yet Gramsci seems to approve democracy but disapprove transformism.

SIX

LIBERALISM AND ANTI-LIBERALISM IN MOSCA AND GRAMSCI

IN AN ELITIST POLITICAL THEORY, the distinction between elites and masses is taken as fundamental, and then the main problems are discussed in terms of the diverse relationships between them. One of the most important and basic relationships is, as we have seen, the influx of members of the masses into the elites, or the openness of the latter to individuals from the former, or the renewal of the latter with elements from the former; this relationship provides the special content and meaning for the special concept of democracy which both Mosca and Gramsci accept, and which they contrast with aristocracy. However, we also saw that the democratic relationship so defined is not the only important one; another is what Mosca called the liberal relationship, in the special sense according to which authority flows from the bottom up—that is, originates in the masses; this is the opposite of what he calls autocracy, where authority flows in the opposite direction—from the top down.

1. Varieties of Liberty and Liberalism in Mosca

The anti-autocratic principle is not, however, the only thing Mosca has in mind when he speaks of liberty and liberalism. Thus, it is important at this point to examine more exactly what he means and to catalogue his meanings. His most mature view is the following one, found in the second volume of *Elements of Political Science:*

Looking for the essential characteristic of the system which we call 'liberal,' one may say that in such systems the law is based upon the consent of the majority of citizens, though only a small fraction of the inhabitants may be citizens; and then that the officials who apply the law are named directly or indirectly by their subordinates, that their posts are temporary and that they are personally responsible for the lawfulness of their acts. In the great liberal states, in general, citizens do not exercise legislative power personally. They delegate it to assemblies which are directly or indirectly named by them, and the work of the elective officials is supplemented and coordinated by the work of a bureaucracy proper. Furthermore, in cases where the liberal principle prevails, the state customarily recognizes certain limits to its powers in its relations to individual citizens and to associations of citizens. Such limits were not entirely unknown to classical Greece and ancient Rome. They are almost always recognized in modern constitutions. They relate to such things as freedom of worship, of the press, of education, of assembly and of speech. They guarantee personal liberty, private property and the inviolability of domicile.[1]

That is, a liberal system is one where authority flows from the ruled to the rulers, in the following senses. First, the law is based on the consent of the citizens, although (as Mosca points out) the citizens may not be identical with the entire body of the ruled, and although (as we might add) "consent" means subsequent approval and not prior origination; this claim amounts to a doctrine of popular sovereignty insofar as the popular mass of citizens is the supreme authority for validating the law; however, such a concept of popular sovereignty is obviously different from the idea that the law is an expression of the will of the people, since according to Mosca there is no such thing as popular will, for the simple reason that the people are not a unified or organized body. Moreover, both the officials who apply the law and those who make it are chosen directly or indirectly by the ruled; in short, the rulers represent the ruled; this can be called the representative system. Finally, the law guarantees individual citizens a number of civil liberties, which neither governors nor legislators (nor bureaucrats) are allowed to violate; this can be called the doctrine of civil liberties.

It should be noted that universal suffrage in not one of these essential characteristics; but note also that it is not necessarily excluded. Moreover, although all three of the mentioned characteristics may be essential, I am not sure they all have the exact same status. I believe that popular sovereignty is the defining characteristic, and that representation and civil liberties are what can be called practically necessary concomitants. Nevertheless, strictly speaking, the three elements seem to be conceptually and logically distinct.

Mosca believes that this idea of political liberty originated in ancient Greece and Rome, was elaborated later by Guicciardini, and was practiced and developed in the English parliamentary system. He also believes that this is the etymological connotation of the phrase "free people," namely a people which governs itself.[2]

Mosca further believes that political liberty so defined derives from and depends on the separation of powers, and that the latter in turn derives from a balanced pluralism of social forces and of elites or directing groups.[3] This claim introduces into the discussion two other elements, which are for Mosca the grounds for political liberty; the separation of powers could be called the intermediate ground, and pluralism the ultimate ground, for political liberty.

The result is the possibility of terminological confusion in regard to the meaning of liberalism. For by "liberalism" one means sometimes the separation of powers, and sometimes the balanced pluralism of social and political forces. Occasionally, Mosca himself uses the term with these distinct (though related) meanings,[4] although usually the different usages are obvious, and the careful reader need not be led astray. The best example of a case where Mosca uses "liberalism" in the sense of pluralism is the famous 1904 interview where he defined himself as "antidemocratic because liberal":

> I can certainly call myself an antidemocrat, but I am not an anti-liberal; indeed I am opposed to pure democracy precisely because I am a liberal. I believe that the ruling class ought not to be monolithic and homogeneous but ought to consist of elements which are diverse in regard to origin and interests; when, instead, political power originates from a single source, even if this be elections with universal suffrage, I regard it as dangerous and liable to become oppressive. Democratic Jacobinism is an illiberal doctrine precisely because it subordinates everything to a single force, that of the so-called majority, on which it does not set any limits. There exist extremely important political forces which do not have the means to prevail in a popular election, and it is not useful that because of this they should be suppressed and be unable to exercise any effective political action.[5]

Mosca is saying that he is against pure democracy because of his liberalism; by pure democracy he means the attempt to restrict the method of selecting the rulers to the single one of popular election; whereas by liberalism he means allowing a plurality of such methods and a plurality of the forces which can emerge through these methods. When so defined, the two are clearly inconsistent.

Sometimes by "liberalism" a writer means specifically the doctrine of civil liberties, perhaps in the sense of a special stress on the importance and value of one or more of the civil liberties. Again, even Mosca occasionally uses the term in this sense, without causing any real harm to the reader. A beautiful example occurs in his 1917 essay discussing the pros and cons of rationing and of price increases for foodstuffs.[6] He argues that, while rationing is more egalitarian because it aims to impose equal privations on everybody, price increases are more liberal because they give individuals and families a greater choice of privations; this part of his argument is, I suppose, primarily an objective analysis of the situation. Then he exhibits his liberalism when he also argues that, from a utilitarian point of view, rationing distributes sacrifices equally, but a price increase produces a smaller sum total of sacrifices.

While this theory of political liberty is inconsistent with some conceptions of democracy (for example, the Jacobinist pure democracy just mentioned) and consistent with but distinct from others (such as the Moschian conception), it is obvious that it in any case overlaps with other conceptions of democracy; this is especially true in regard to popular sovereignty and representation. In elaborating his own conceptual framework, Mosca explicitly recognizes the existence of such an alternative definition of democracy and attributes it originally to Plato;[7] but he goes on to state and defend his own terminological preference. Now, this means that, while on the one hand the "democratic" character of Mosca's political theory is enhanced, on the other hand the overlap between non-Moschian, Platonic democracy and Moschian liberalism introduces another possible source of confusion. However, since such terminological ambiguities are part of the situation, it would be self-defeating to ignore them.

In short, Mosca's liberalism has perhaps six parts: the general anti-autocratic conception of authority flowing from the bottom up, the principle of popular sovereignty (in the sense specified), the representative system, the doctrine of civil liberties, the separation of powers, and balanced pluralism.[8] If such variety exists within Mosca, who is a relatively systematic writer, it should not be surprising that on this topic the Prison Notebooks contain a variety of meanings and conceptions. Therefore, if we want to explore the connection between Gramsci and Mosca in regard to this topic, we cannot do it the way we have in regard to elitism and democracy; these two ideas have a relatively univocal meaning in Mosca, and so Gramsci's involvement with them turned out to be definable in terms of the fairly simple relationships of generalization and application, respectively. In regard to liberty, on the other hand, the situation is more complex. What we shall do, therefore, is examine whether Gramsci reveals an analogous type of complexity, and what the character of his attitude toward these things is (whether it is favorable or unfavorable).

2. Liberty Versus Discipline in Gramsci

We saw earlier (Chapter 4, section 1) that Gramsci thinks the elitist distinction is the most fundamental principle of the science and art of politics.[9] The note (Q 15,4) where he expresses this judgment begins with a statement of the principle, a judgment about its fundamental importance, an extension of its scope from domination to leadership relations, and a formulation of the fundamental problem of the formation of governors and leaders. These observations are offered within the space of one page, after which Gramsci devotes another page to the formulation of a second problem and a final page to the problem of the role and function of political parties and their connection with individualism. What I have called the second fundamental problem is the following:

> Given that the division between governors and governed exists within the same group, one must lay down some principles to be strictly observed. Indeed, it is in this domain that the most serious errors occur; that is, it is here where we witness incompetence of the most criminal sort and of a type which is most difficult to correct. One believes that, since we are dealing with the same group, obedience should be automatic; not only that it should come about without the need to demonstrate its necessity and rationality, but also that it is unquestionable. (Some think and, what is worse, act in accordance with the thought that obedience will come without being asked for, without an indication of the way to follow.) Thus, it is difficult to extirpate from leaders the so-called Cadornism, namely the belief that a thing will be done because the leader thinks it is

right and rational that it be done, and that if it is not done, the blame falls on whoever should have done it, etc. [Q 1752–53]

It is obvious that Gramsci is raising a problem having to do with the relationship between leaders and led, since he is talking about the elitist distinction within the same class. At issue is the problem of obedience. He thinks we need to formulate some inexorable principles about it, and in this passage he does so indirectly by mentioning some examples of errors and evils to avoid. Gramsci is saying that the led should not obey the leaders automatically or unquestioningly; that they should not do something merely because the leaders think it should be done; that leaders should ask for obedience from their followers, should justify its need to them, and should make suggestions about how the led can proceed. Although Gramsci does not use the word "liberty" here, the concept is implicitly present because what he is really saying is that obedience should take place in an atmosphere of liberty; that is, obedience should be free, in the sense of freely given, which in turn does not mean arbitrarily or whimsically granted, but rather as the result of individual autonomy or self-determination. The implicit sense of liberty would seem to be the civil-libertarian one.

The connection between the problems and notions of obedience and of liberty is addressed explicitly by Gramsci in other notes. Perhaps the best discussion occurs in a note on discipline, which is especially remarkable because Gramsci introduces the problem in so many words as one involving the elitist distinction and relationship:

> How should we conceive of discipline, if this word is taken to mean a permanent and continued relationship between governors and governed which brings about the collective will? Certainly not as a passive and submissive acceptance of orders, as a mechanical execution of instructions (although this will be necessary on particular occasions—for example, in the midst of an action already decided upon and initiated); rather we should conceive it as a conscious and clear assimilation of the directive to be put into practice. Therefore, discipline does not organically annihilate one's personality, but only limits arbitrariness and irresponsible impulsiveness, not to mention the fatuous and vain inclination to stand out. . . . Therefore, discipline does not annihilate personality and liberty. [Q 1706]

What Gramsci calls discipline here may be taken as equivalent to what he was calling obedience in the earlier passage. His talk of personality here is a reference to individuality. He is now explicitly saying that obedience or discipline is compatible with individual liberty; indeed, he advocates a type of discipline which allows freedom.

Here, the notion of responsibility is indirectly introduced, but its crucial importance may be seen in the fact that "the concept of liberty should be accompanied by that of the responsibility which generates discipline, and not directly by that of discipline, which in this case is regarded as imposed from the outside and as a forced limitation of liberty. Responsibility is opposed to individual arbitrariness; liberty must be 'responsible,' namely 'universal,' insofar as it presents itself as an individual aspect of collective, or group, 'liberty' or as an individual expression of a law" (Q 692). That is, liberty must be responsible, and responsibility implies discipline; so Gramsci is led to discipline by starting from liberty. This is the reverse of, but analogous to, his earlier procedure when he was led to liberty after starting from discipline, by way of the idea and the ideal of rational justification: discipline or obedience must be rationally justified, and when it is, we have the possibility of self-motivation, autonomy, and liberty.

The aim is not to conflate or confuse liberty and discipline but to interrelate and combine them. This intention emerges more clearly in another note (Q 14,61), where Gramsci argues that there is good and bad sincerity, spontaneity, or originality; that there is good and bad discipline, conformism, or sociality; but that the real challenge is to combine good originality with good conformism, proper liberty with proper discipline:

> Is sincerity (or spontaneity) always a worthwhile and valuable thing? It is a worthwhile and valuable thing only if disciplined. Sincerity (or spontaneity) means the maximum of individualism, even in the sense of idiosyncrasy (in this case originality is equivalent to idiotism). The individual is historically original when he gives the most emphasis and vital energy to "sociality," without which he would be an "idiot" (in the etymological sense, which however is not far from the popular and common meaning). There is a Romantic meaning of the notions of originality, personality, and sincerity, and this meaning is historically justified insofar as it originated in opposition to a certain conformism which was essentially "Jesuitical"; that is, an artificial and fictitious conformism, created superficially for the interests of a small group or clique and not of a vanguard. However, there is a conformism which is "rational"—namely, corresponding to what is necessary, to the smallest effort needed to obtain a useful result; the discipline related to such conformism should be

exalted and promoted and should be induced to become "spontaneity" or "sincerity." In this case, conformism means nothing but "sociality," although one likes to use the word "conformism" precisely to upset idiots. This does not preclude the possibility of forming one's own personality and of being original, but the task is rendered harder. It is too easy to be original by doing the opposite of what all are doing; that is a mechanical thing. It is too easy to speak differently from others, to be neologistic; the difficulty is to distinguish oneself from others without being an acrobat in the process. Nowadays people are in search of a cheap originality and personality. Prisons and insane asylums are full of men who are original and have a strong personality. What is truly hard and difficult is the following: to place an emphasis on discipline and sociality, and yet to demand sincerity, spontaneity, originality, and personality. Nor can one say that conformism is too easy and reduces the world to a convent. The question is: What is "true conformism"; that is, what is the conduct which is "rationally" most useful and which is most free insofar as it obeys "necessity"? That is, what is "necessary"? Everyone has a tendency to make himself into an archetype of "fashion" and "sociality," and to regard himself as an "exemplar." Therefore, sociality or conformism is the result of a cultural struggle (though not merely cultural); it is an "objective" or universal given, just as objective and universal as the "necessity" on which stands the framework of liberty. [Q 1719-20]

The most striking thing here is Gramsci's judiciousness; certainly there is no one-sided advocacy of either liberty or discipline, but rather an appreciation of both and an attempt to combine them appropriately.

In this passage, he also introduces the notion of necessity, and so this discussion can be regarded as his own version of the traditional Hegelian conception of liberty as the awareness of necessity, to which he refers more explicitly elsewhere (Q 968, 1394). However, because of the autocratic, authoritarian, and totalitarian connotations of this Hegelian idea, it may be useful to discuss a number of explicit disclaimers offered by Gramsci. For example, in a discussion of the concept of the natural, at one point he explains that, in a perfectly good sense, education is obligatory, but that this need not imply any loss of proper liberty. That is, on the one hand, "the fact that education is obligatory does not mean that it should be rejected, nor that one cannot justify a new form of obligation by means of new arguments. One must turn into 'liberty' that which is 'necessary'; but, for this, one must acknowledge an 'objective' necessity—namely, a necessity which is objective mainly for the group in question. One must therefore refer to the technical relations of productions, to a particular type of economic civilization which, in order to be developed, requires a particular way of life, particular rules of conduct, particular customs" (Q 1875–76). On the other hand, "there is the problem of who will decide that a particular form of moral conduct is the one most in accordance with a particular stage of development of productive forces. Certainly, one cannot speak of creating a special 'pope' or a special office in charge. The leading forces will emerge through the very fact that the way of thinking will be oriented in this realistic direction, and they will emerge from the very clash of conflicting opinions, without 'conventionality' and 'artifice' but 'naturally'" (Q 1878–79). This thought is repeated elsewhere, in a discussion of the proper relationship between the intellectual elites and the popular masses. Gramsci feels that the problem will inevitably arise whether and how some limits should be set to freedom of discussion:

> One is dealing with establishing limits to freedom of discussion and of propaganda; these must not be construed in the administrative and police sense, but in the sense of a self-limitation which leaders place on their own activity, or, to be exact, in the sense of the establishment of a direction for cultural policy. In other words, who will establish the "rights of science" and the limits on scientific research, and can these rights and these limits be properly established? It seems necessary that the labor of searching for new and better truths and for clearer and more coherent formulations of old truths ought to be left to the free initiative of individual scientists, even if they constantly question, again and again, those principles which seem the most essential. After all, it will not be difficult to clarify when such questioning initiatives have a biased motivation and a nonscientific character; it is not impossible to think that individual initiatives should be disciplined and coordinated in such a way that they go through the screening of various kinds of academies and cultural institutions and then become public only after they have been selected, etc. [Q 1393]

Once again, Gramsci's commitment to civil liberties is clear, but it is equally clear that he thinks they need to be subject to judicious controls; such controls take the form of self-regulation (especially on the part of the leaders) and institutionalized peer review.

3. Liberty Versus Liberalism in Gramsci

As we have seen, Gramsci's appreciation of civil liberties is liable to be misunderstood because of his simultaneous appreciation of discipline and necessity; but this is not the only source of potential misunderstanding. Another source is his distinction between liberty and liberalism, which goes together with his appreciation of the former and criticism of the latter. The way to avoid this second potential misunderstanding is to attend carefully to what he means in the contexts where he makes such a distinction. It will emerge that by liberty he means mostly the Moschian anti-autocratic principle (namely, "Platonic" democracy), and by liberalism he means Moschian aristocracy (namely, *undemocratic* elitism). Thus, while Gramsci's distinction and criticism appear at first to be anti-Moschian, they do not really imply an anti-Moschian stance but rather provide further confirmation of a democratic-elitist orientation.

One of these distinctions occurs in the note (Q 6,88) on the night-watchman state. We saw earlier (Chapter 4, section 4) that to Gramsci this notion means a state whose central purpose is the protection and the promotion of individual liberty, and that the night-watchman state so conceived is for him the most realistic conception of the "regulated" society; on the other hand, strictly speaking, by "regulated society" he understands a completely self-regulated society where all human behavior is self-motivated or based on ethical considerations and rational discussions, an eventuality which he regards as a utopian situation susceptible of being only approached, not reached. The note ends as follows: "In the doctrine of the state's transition to a regulated society, between a phase in which state equals government and one in which the state will be identified with the civil society, we will have to go through the phase of the night-watchman state, that is, a coercive organization which will safeguard the development of the continuously growing elements of regulated society and thus gradually reduce its authoritative and coercive interventions. Nor can this make one think of a new 'liberalism,' although it is the beginning of an era of organic liberty" (Q 764).[10] That is, Gramsci's "night-watchman state" promotes "liberty" in the civil-libertarian sense, but does not promote "liberalism." What is this liberalism thus contrasted to liberty?

Before tackling this question, let us look at another such contrast. This occurs in a discussion (Q 6,162) of what Gramsci regards as one of the national characteristics of Italians, their individualism. Gramsci understands this traditional Italian individualism as a form of "apoliti-cism," rooted partly in the inadequate satisfaction of material needs and partly in the character of the Italian ruling class. For him, the solution of this problem cannot be brought about "with the methods of state cen-tralization (schooling, legislation, courts, and police) which would tend to standardize life according to a single national type—that is, by means of resolute and energetic action from above" (Q 815). Instead the solu-tion lies in "the method of liberty, but not understood in a 'liberal' sense; the new framework can only emerge from below, insofar as the whole nation, including the economically and culturally lowest layer, would participate in a radical historical development which affects the whole life of the people and brutally places everyone in front of his inexorable responsibilities" (Q 816). This nonliberal "method of liberty" obviously corresponds to Mosca's anti-autocratic principle, or to what Mosca calls the liberal principle. Therefore, it is equally obvious that what Gramsci here calls liberalism does not correspond to Mosca calls liberalism, but to something else. Gramsci here is endorsing Moschian liberty in the sense of the anti-autocratic principle. That Gramsci does this should not be surprising; it is, however, surprising that he should use such terminology and such a conceptual framework. That is, we certainly would expect Gramsci to endorse the principle of authority and power flowing from the bottom up (Platonic democracy, as it were); but that he should regard that direction of flow as the method of liberty is a sign of Moschian influence.

This Moschian trace is even more striking in the note (Q 14,48) on discipline, the first part of which was discussed earlier in this chapter. In that same note, Gramsci also raises the following issue:

> The question of "personality and liberty" arises not in connection with the fact of discipline, but with the "origin of the power which orders the discipline." If this origin is "democratic," namely if authority is a special-ized technical function and not something arbitrary or an extrinsic and external injunction, then discipline is a necessary element of a democratic arrangement, of liberty. Authority can be called a specialized technical function when it is exercised within a socially or nationally homoge-neous group; when it is exercised from one group toward another group, discipline will be autonomous and free within the first but not within the second. [Q 1706–7]

That is, Gramsci calls liberty a "democratic" arrangement when the ori-gin of power is the people. Thus, while he is employing the notion of liberty in the Moschian anti-autocratic sense, he is also deviating from the notion of Moschian democracy, which he normally prefers, and lapsing into the Platonic understanding of democracy.

Nevertheless, Gramsci's contrast between liberty and liberalism remains problematic. The clearest and most sustained articulation of what he means by liberalism is found in his criticism of Croce's liberalism.[11] In this context there also emerges a new meaning of liberty, not discussed so far because it plays no significant role in either Mosca's or Gramsci's thought, though it is important in Croce's. In fact, Gramsci's key criticism here is directed at two of Croce's views:[12] his philosophy of history, which adapted and added new twists to Hegel's idea on the role of liberty in the development of human society, and his account of nineteenth-century Europe, which stressed the emergence and development of what he called the religion of liberty. Gramsci objects that "the equivocation inherent in Croce's most recent historical works is based precisely on this confusion between history as the story of liberty and history as an apology for liberalism" (Q 1007). That is, Croce is alleged to perpetrate an equivocation between a notion of liberty which could be called philosophical and liberalism as a particular ideology. The problem is not that philosophical liberty is illegitimate or unreal, but that it ought not to be confused with liberal ideology and that Gramsci finds the latter objectionable.

Gramsci's elucidation of the meaning of what he calls the (Crocean) philosophical concept of liberty is a model of clarity:

> If history is the story of liberty (in accordance with Hegel's assertion), the formula is valid for the history of all mankind at all times and places; even the history of Oriental satrapies is one of liberty. Then liberty means "movement," development, dialectic. The history of Oriental satrapies is also one of liberty because it has consisted of movement and development, so much so that those satrapies have fallen. Again: history is liberty insofar as it is a struggle between liberty and authority, between revolution and conservation, which is a struggle in which liberty and revolution constantly prevail over authority and conservation. But then, are not every faction and every party expressions of liberty, dialectical aspects of the process of liberty? [Q 1229]

It seems also clear to me that Gramsci is endorsing this notion of liberty in the sense that he regards it as *a* legitimate meaning. This notion of liberty is admittedly of dubious practical applicability, but I do not think that that objection makes either the notion itself or Gramsci's acceptance of it empty. All it means is that this idea of liberty is primarily a principle for the interpretation of past historical events, and not a recipe for action and the creation of new history; in regard to practical action, the idea can still have an indirect function and provide nondetermining guidance.

If, then, the liberalism to which Gramsci objects is not Crocean philosophical liberty nor Moschian political liberty nor the civil-libertarian notion of liberty, all of which he indeed accepts, what is it? Referring to the nineteenth century, Gramsci explains: "A trend or party was formed which was specifically called liberal; out of Hegel's speculative and contemplative philosophy, it created an immediate political ideology, a practical instrument of domination and of social hegemony, a means for the conservation of particular political and economic institutions founded in the course of the French Revolution and of the repercussions which the French Revolution had in Europe" (Q 1230).

One feature of this liberalism is that it did not promote liberty among the peasant masses, any more than any other party did: "The fact that no party coordinated the aspirations of the great peasant masses for an agrarian reform had the precise effect of preventing these masses from becoming believers in the religion of liberty; instead, for them liberty meant the freedom and the right to preserve their barbaric superstitions, their primitivism" (Q 1230).

A second feature is that liberty was restricted to the elites, whereas among the masses it was seen in terms of nationalism and consequently authoritarianism:

> For Croce a religion is any worldview which presents itself as an ethics. But did this happen to "liberty"? It has been a religion for a small number of intellectuals; in the masses it appeared as an ideological mixture or compound, one of whose constituent parts was the old Catholic religion; another important element, perhaps crucial from a lay viewpoint, was that of "fatherland." Nor can one say that the concept of "fatherland" was a synonym for "liberty"; it was indeed synonymous with something, but this synonym was the state, namely authority and not "liberty"; it was an element of "conservation," a source of persecution and of a new Inquisition. [Q 1231]

Third, Gramsci refers to the fact that in the early 1920s Croce served as minister of public instruction and that, after some initial setbacks, the reforms he inspired were approved; one of these reforms was the introduction of the teaching of Catholic religious doctrine in Italian public schools: "Croce should explain why the liberal worldview cannot become a pedagogical element of instruction in elementary schools, and why as a cabinet minister he introduced the teaching of confessional religion in elementary schools. This absence of expansive power among the great masses bears witness to the restricted and immediately practical character of the philosophy of liberty" (Q 1231–32).

So by "liberalism" (in the pejorative sense) Gramsci means an ideology which had historical roots in the ideal of liberty of the French Revolution but which did not open itself to the peasant masses or the Catholic masses; instead, it remained restricted to small circles of intellectuals, and by way of nationalism it even came close to betraying its original civil-libertarian inspiration. For those acquainted with Mosca's notions of aristocracy and democracy, it should be obvious that Gramsci is objecting to the aristocratic, oligarchic, and undemocratic tendencies and practices of liberal ideology, which are undemocratic in the Moschian sense of closed elites.[13] We can now also make sense of Gramsci's frequent contrasting of liberty and liberalism; he is drawing the contrast between democratic and undemocratic elitism (using the terms in the proper Moschian sense).[14]

4. Laissez-Faire Versus Statism in Gramsci

Undemocratic elitism is not, however, the only "liberalism" to which Gramsci objects. Another is liberalism in the sense of the separation of powers, a common meaning of the term and one which not infrequently finds its way even into the Moschian lexicon. Thus it is neither surprising nor particularly significant that this is one of Gramsci's conceptions of liberalism. We have already encountered it on at least one occasion (Chapter 4), when Gramsci regards Louis-Napoleon's idea of a state newspaper as a typical instance of "illiberalism," namely undue interference by the state into the civil society (Q 734). And there are more explicit indications, such as when Gramsci states that "in regard to the limits of state activity, one should examine the discussion which has taken place in the last few years; it is the most important discussion in political philosophy and serves to separate liberals from nonliberals" (Q 399).[15] Nor is it, perhaps, surprising that Gramsci should find such liberalism objectionable. However, the objections he raises are interesting, important, and puzzling.

The main objections are contained in a passage which is one of the best-known and most widely quoted remarks ever made by Gramsci but which is, in fact, one of the least understood:

> The doctrine of the free-trade movement is based on a theoretical error whose practical origin is not difficult to identify—that is, on the fact that the distinction between political society and civil society is turned from a methodological distinction into an organic distinction and presented as such. Thus, people claim that economic activity belongs exclusively to civil society and the state must not intervene to regulate it. However, since in actuality state and civil society are identical, one must declare that laissez-faire is also a form of state "regulation," which is introduced and maintained by legislative and coercive means; it represents a deliberate act aware of its own goals, and not the spontaneous and automatic expression of economic activity. Therefore, laissez-faire is a political program; insofar as it succeeds, it is destined to change the leading personnel of a state and the economic policy of a state—namely, to change the distribution of the national income. [Q 1589–90]

Some things are very clear in this passage, others are less clear, and still others are quite obscure.

It is clear that by laissez-faire liberalism Gramsci means the idea that economic activity belongs exclusively to civil society and that the state ought not to intervene in it. It is also clear that he is saying that laissez-faire is both a political and an economic program. Equally clear is the concept of politics presupposed in this claim. That is, the reason laissez-faire is a political institution is that it affects the relationship between leaders and led, the assumption being that politics is whatever pertains to this distinction, which is a further confirmation of Gramsci's general elitism in the sense elaborated earlier (Chapter 4).

Less clear is the underlying concept of economics; for the reason laissez-faire is said to be an economic institution is that it affects the distribution of wealth. On this last point, it is unclear whether Gramsci means "distribution" literally and as contrasted with production, in which case his concept of the economic might be susceptible to some obvious criticism; but perhaps he is not limiting himself exclusively to distribution, since he speaks of the distribution of income rather than of goods, and income cannot be distributed or redistributed without the production process being affected. Another question concerns the relation between the state and political society on the one hand, and the economy and civil society on the other. I believe that here Gramsci is treating state and political society as synonymous, although elsewhere he takes the state to include also civil society.[16] That is, here we have one of a series of instances in which he gives to "state" a narrow meaning equating it with the domain of politics, while on other occasions he uses "state" in a broad meaning which equates it to all of society. On the other hand, the economy is simply a part of civil society.

Next, what exactly is the error committed by laissez-faire liberalism? One of its difficulties is that it involves a type of self-contradiction: it claims to be against state interference in the economy, and yet it favors the particular kind of intervention needed to create and uphold laissez-faire practices. We may agree with Gramsci that some kind of political intervention is presupposed by laissez-faire, so that to that extent it cannot consistently be against *all* state intervention.

However, Gramsci also claims that ultimately the error of laissez-faire stems from an inadequate understanding of the relation between political and civil society. And here obscurities abound. What is a methodological distinction, what is an organic distinction, and what is the difference between the two? And what does it mean to say that state and civil society are in one sense identical (in actuality), and in another sense distinct (methodologically)?[17]

One thing he is saying is that political and civil society are not "organically" distinct, but rather identical in actuality. In an earlier version of this note, Gramsci states that "in concrete historical life, political and civil society are the same thing" (Q 460). Thus, he seems to have in mind that they are two different aspects of the same thing (human society) rather than two different things; and the organic identity of which he speaks[18] is an ontological or empirical identity. Hence, also, part of what he means by a methodological distinction is a difference which is not an ontological separation but reflects different ways of looking at the same thing.

What then defines these two aspects? The answer is given in the context of his account of an expanded notion of intellectuals, according to which the experts in both domains in question are regarded as intellectuals; but that context need not concern us here. The important thing is that

one can establish two great superstructural "levels": one which can be called that of civil society (namely, the series of institutions which are popularly called private), and a level of the "state or political society"; they correspond to the function of the "hegemony" which the dominating group exercises in the whole society, and the function of "direct domination," or domination which expresses itself in the state and in the "legal" government; . . . that is, (1) of the "spontaneous" consent given by the great masses of the population to the direction impressed on social life by the fundamental dominating group, . . . and (2) of the apparatus of state coercion which ensures "legally" the discipline of those groups which do not "consent" either actively or passively. [Q 1518–19]

That is, civil society is the aspect of human society pertaining to persuasion, leadership relations, hegemony, and the private sphere; while political society is the aspect involving coercion, domination, and public law.

Now, when Gramsci calls the distinction between civil and political society a methodological one, he may be taken to mean also that the distinction involves a difference between two methods of operating within human society, the method of private persuasion and the method of public legislation and coercion. With this clarification we can now make some sense of his objection that laissez-faire philosophy misconceives the distinction between political and civil society; given that political and civil society are ontologically the same thing (human society), and given that they represent different methods of changing society, the issue is not whether the state or government should intervene, but rather how and when to intervene, whether by methods of persuasion or by methods of coercion.

In fact, Gramsci's criticism of laissez-faire cannot be equated to a plea for its opposite, statism. For example, he has misgivings about protectionism, "for it is undeniable that protectionism, especially in countries with a poor and restricted market, limits the freedom of industrial initiative and favors in a morbid manner the growth of monopolies" (Q 1590). This is no isolated criticism. Elsewhere he objects to it for a different reason—that "state intervention with its customs tariffs . . . 'selects' among citizens those who are to be protected even if they are not 'meritorious,' etc." (Q 781). We thus have a pluralist and a meritocratic objection to protectionism. Particularly interesting and important here is that such grounds appeal to characteristically Moschian principles; moreover, it should be noted that Mosca too was basically against protectionism.[19]

More generally, Gramsci has misgivings also about "statolatry," which may be regarded as his label for statism. This emerges clearly in the following note:

The analysis would not be exact unless one took into account the two forms in which the state appears in the language and the culture of various epochs, namely as civil society and as political society, as "self-government" and as "government of the officials." The name "statolatry" is given to a particular attitude toward the "government of the officials" or political society, which in common language is the form of state life which is called the state and which is popularly understood as the whole state.

Consider the claim that the state is identical with the individuals (with the individuals of a social group), and that it is an element of active culture, namely an institution meant to create a new civilization and a new type of man and citizen; this claim must serve to strengthen the willingness to build within the envelope of political society a complex and well-articulated civil society in which a single individual governs himself, without this self-government's thereby coming into conflict with political society, but instead by becoming its normal continuation and organic complement. There are social groups which, before rising to autonomous state life, have not had a long period of independent cultural and moral development of their own (which even in medieval society and under an absolute government was rendered possible by the legal existence of privileged estates or orders); for such social groups, a period of statolatry is necessary and indeed appropriate; such "statolatry" is nothing but the normal form of "state life," of initiation into autonomous state life and into the creation of a "civil society" which historically could not be created before rising to independent state life. Nevertheless, such "statolatry" must not be abandoned to itself; in particular, it must not turn into theoretical fanaticism and be regarded as "perpetual"; it must be criticized, precisely in order for it to develop and to produce new forms of state life in which individual and group initiative has a "state" character, even if it does not stem from the "government of the officials" (one must make state life become "spontaneous"). [Q 8,130/Q 1020–21]

That is, state intervention is not an end in itself, but rather it is normally a means to promote the autonomy and the cultural and moral development of individuals and groups; to phrase it differently, methods of coercion are normally a means of protecting and encouraging methods of persuasion. An emphasis on state intervention and methods of coercion may be occasionally justified; but such an emphasis ("statolatry") is an exception to the norm, and in any case its justification is based on ideals pertaining to civil society.

This criticism of statism corresponds to Gramsci's idea of the night-watchman state, which we discussed earlier (Chapter 4, section 4). In that context, he argued that a night-watchman state is best conceived as a stage of political development in which the primary function of governmental institutions is the defense and promotion of individual liberty. However, the same note makes it clear that it would be unrealistic and utopian to expect that the state could ever wither away or that a completely self-regulated society could ever be actually reached (as opposed to approached), or (to use the language of the note just quoted) that self-government could ever completely replace the government of the officials.

Such explicitly anti-statist sentiments are reinforced by Gramsci with explicitly pro-individualist ones; but, just as his anti-statism is, as we have seen and as we would expect, judiciously balanced, the same applies to his individualist pronouncements. In fact, the thought started in the above quoted note (Q 8,130) is continued in a nearby note (Q 8,142) as follows:

> *Individual Initiative.* . . . Elements for formulating the problem: identity-distinction between civil and political society; hence, organic identification between individuals (of a particular group) and the state; therefore, "every individual is an official," not insofar as he is a salaried state employee and subject to the "hierarchical" control of the bureaucracy, but insofar as, when he "acts spontaneously," his action is identified with the aims of the state (namely, the particular social group of civil society). Thus individual initiative is not a hypothesis of "good intentions" but a necessary presupposition. Now, "individual initiative" is usually understood as individual economic initiative, and it is understood precisely in the sense of an initiative of an immediately "utilitarian" and strictly personal kind. However, this is not the only form of "economic" initiative which has emerged historically (see the list of the great individual initiatives which have ended in disaster in the last few decades . . .). And there are examples of such initiatives which are not "immediately interested," that is, which are "interested" in a higher sense, in the sense of the interest of the state or group which makes up the civil society. [Q 1028–29]

Here Gramsci is in part drawing two important corollaries from the principle he laid down earlier, and in part clarifying the concept of individual initiative. One corollary is that in a certain sense each individual is also a state official; this follows from Gramsci's claim that civil and political society are ontologically identical but methodologically distinct, and from his claim that (ontologically speaking) individual persons and political society are the same. This view in turn presupposes that, ontologically speaking, one is identifying civil society with its individuals.[20] A second, even more important corollary is that individual initiative is necessary and inescapable (just as *some kind* of government intervention is); the reason is that, given that both political and civil society are ontologically identified with the individuals in them, initiative on the part of the constituent elements of human society is unavoidable. But it is important to distinguish different kinds of individual initiative: some is economic, but some is not; and within individual economic initiative, some is economically profitable and some is not; finally, some individual initiative is selfish, but some is not.

Thus, Gramsci's criticism of laissez-faire liberalism should not be confused with a plea for statism, any more than it should be regarded as a denial that political and civil society are "methodologically" distinct. Since such a distinction means that political and civil society are merely different aspects of human society or different methods of operating within human society, since *some* intervention of the state into the economy is unavoidable, and since some individual initiative is equally unavoidable, it follows that the real issues are how and when to initiate what type of intervention, and how and when the state should intervene.

That these are the real issues for Gramsci emerges in another way, which involves the clarification of another criticism he advances against laissez-faire, and which is found in a number of otherwise extremely puzzling passages.[21] The criticism is that laissez-faire is a form of "economism," where that term is defined as a one-sided and excessive emphasis on economic factors, to the exclusion of mental, psychological, and intellectual factors. To understand the argument and the connections, we must begin with one of Gramsci's most fundamental principles, which he calls a basic principle of historical methodology: "In the study of a structure one must distinguish what is permanent from what is occasional. What is occasional gives rise to political criticism, while what is permanent gives rise to sociohistorical criticism; what is occasional is useful in judging political groups and personalities, while what is permanent is useful in judging the great social groupings. In the study of a historical period, this distinction has great importance" (Q 455).[22] Here Gramsci is laying down a fundamental principle for the interpretation of historical and social events.

Next, he calls attention to a fundamental misapplication of this principle: "An error which is often committed in historical analysis consists of being unable to find the relation between what is 'permanent' and what is 'occasional'; thus one ends up either presenting remote causes as if they were immediate causes or claiming that immediate causes are the only effective causes. In one case we have an excess of 'economism,' in the other an excess of 'ideologism'; on the one hand, one overestimates mechanical causes, on the other hand, one overestimates the 'volitional' and individual element" (Q 456). Gramsci is defining two opposite extremes: economism overestimates economic conditions which operate indirectly through the intermediation of mental or psychological factors; whereas ideologism does the opposite—namely, it overestimates mental factors, which are indeed the immediate causes of historical developments, and it disregards the economic conditions which give rise to these mental ones.

Now comes the passage in which Gramsci charges laissez-faire liberalism with the error of economism as just defined, although he simultaneously charges with the same error a twin position which he calls theoretical syndicalism:

> Tied to this general question is the question of so-called economism, which takes different forms and has different concrete manifestations. The category of economism subsumes both the theoretical movement of free trade and theoretical syndicalism. The meaning of these two tendencies is very different. The first is characteristic of a dominant grouping, the second of a subaltern grouping. . . . In the case of the theory of laissez-faire liberalism we have an example of a segment of the dominant grouping which wants to modify political society, and which wants to reform existing legislation in regard to commercial and, indirectly, industrial policy. . . . In the case of theoretical syndicalism the matter is more complicated: it is undeniable that, although it claims to express the independence and autonomy of the subaltern grouping, these are instead sacrificed to the intellectual hegemony of the dominant grouping, since theoretical syndicalism is an aspect of economic liberalism justified through some statement of historical materialism. How and why does this "sacrifice" come about? Because one excludes the transformation of the subordinate grouping into a dominant one, either by not facing the problem at all (Fabianism, De Man, a significant portion of the Labour Party), or by formulating it in an incoherent and ineffective manner (social democracy), or by advocating an immediate jump from the regime of groupings to that of perfect equality (theoretical syndicalism in a strict sense). [Q 460–61]

Here Gramsci is obviously presupposing the elitist distinction between ruling class and ruled class, and then he is attributing the attitude of economism to each group in turn. That is, from an elitist viewpoint, to say that the government ought not to intervene in the economy means that the ruling politicians ought not do so, as if the economy could operate without the mediation of political factors. And to say, as the theoretical syndicalists do, that labor unions ought not to interfere in politics but ought to restrict themselves to economic issues, means that the ruled class should behave as if economic activity can directly produce results without the mediation of noneconomic factors.

Once again, we are led to the conclusion that the real issue is how and when to intervene. For economism is the extreme position, according to which economic causes are all-important; and to say that they are all-important may be taken to mean that they can be effective without the cooperation of any other factors; and if all other factors are indeed excluded, then economic causes do not need to be regulated by the state. Thus in a sense economism implies laissez-faire liberalism; hence, the latter can be deprived of a possible justification if we expose economism for what it is (an overestimation of remote, ultimate, mechanical causes); but to expose economism in this manner is another way of saying that remote, economic causes normally need to operate through intermediate, mental causes; and to appreciate the second kind of cause is to claim that the most important thing is to determine when and how to intervene in human society.

In summary, one of Gramsci's notions of liberalism is that of laissez-faire, namely the doctrine that the state ought not to intervene in economic activity. He seems to have at least three objections to laissez-faire: that it is internally inconsistent (insofar as it favors the intervention needed to promote laissez-faire); that it misconceives the relation between civil and political society (insofar as it regards these as ontologically separate, whereas they are merely distinct methods of affecting human society); and that it is a species of economism (namely, overemphasis on structural or economic causes). While critical of laissez-faire, Gramsci is also critical and wary of statism, which may be regarded as its opposite. The Gramscian position appears once again to be one of balanced pluralism, as we have come to expect from the many cases previously examined.

5. State Versus Society in Mosca

So far, Gramsci's critique of laissez-faire seems to have the general Moschian character of balanced pluralism. However, in regard to specific content it might seem that it is anti-Moschian, insofar as Mosca is supposed to have been a liberal in the sense of the separation of powers—

namely, insofar as he is supposed to have been a laissez-faire liberal. However, when we examine the details of Mosca's reflections on this topic,[23] the results are surprising and the similarities with Gramsci very revealing.

First, the internal incoherence of laissez-faire had been apparent to Mosca ever since his first book, *Theory of Governments* of 1884. In the last section of the last chapter of this work Mosca discusses the so-called social question and, among other things, advances the following argument:

> Those who reject governmental action because they think it perturbs the natural order of things forget that, in the present social conditions, this distribution of wealth which they regard as natural and spontaneous would not be possible without governmental action. If in present-day society the accumulation of large amounts of capital and of land property in the hands of single persons can come about peacefully and can last, the credit belongs entirely to the governmental institutions which protect them with all the forces at their disposal. Therefore, to want to exclude governmental action from the activity of the distribution of wealth, when the present distribution exists precisely because of it, seems to us a desire which may be labeled incoherent.[24]

This corresponds exactly to one of the objections advanced by Gramsci. Thus, at the very least we have a theoretical convergence. However, given Gramsci's acquaintance with this book by Mosca, a certain degree of influence or historical connection is likely.

Moreover, just as in Gramsci, this criticism is also tied to another pertaining to the proper relation between state and civil society. In *Elements of Political Science,* Mosca tackles the problem of this relation very explicitly: "A question that is vigorously debated among writers on the social sciences is the extent to which the state should interfere in the various departments of social life, specifically in business. . . . Still very widespread is the feeling that society and the state are two separate and distinct entities, and people often go so far as to consider them antagonistic. Now, it is necessary, first of all, to decide very clearly what is meant by 'society' and what is meant by 'state.'"[25] Mosca then goes on to summarize rather cryptically his views on the relations between state and society. However, these views are stated more clearly and revealingly in Mosca's *Notes on Constitutional Law,* another book with which Gramsci was acquainted.[26] There, Mosca advances the following view:

Among all the definitions of the state, the best seems to me to be the one according to which it consists of the political and legal organization of a people within a particular territory; but this needs explanations and comments.

In fact, when one speaks of the political organization of a people, one means the organization of all the elements which lead or manage[27] a people politically—namely, which exercise state functions. Therefore, in a modern state are included not only all public officials (counting among these even those who are not public employees), but also members of parliament and provincial and city commissioners; indeed, even voters in national and local elections, during the process of campaigning and balloting, exercise state functions and are part of the state.

However, although in a democratic state organization the state may include most of society (at least legally, for de facto, things are otherwise), the latter never becomes completely confused with the state. For, even in countries which have universal suffrage and in which it is extended to women, there are many individuals (such as minors and convicts who are excluded from the suffrage) who are part of social interaction but who in no way participate in political or state functions.

However, if the state is not society, since it consists of the network of all elements which participate in the political leadership or administration[28] of society, it certainly is not outside society. The brain is not the whole human body but part of it, and without the brain the human body could not live. One must not forget, however, that any parallelism of this kind should be taken with caution because the life of the social body is analogous but not identical to the life of the individual human body.[29]

Although Mosca does not go so far as Gramsci in identifying political and civil society ontologically, the overlap for him is very great. And this enables Mosca to assert that all citizens, or at least all voters, in a society are in a sense political officials; that is, by voting they are performing a political function. And this view shows an uncanny correspondence with Gramsci's assertion, examined earlier, that in one sense "every individual is an official" (Q 1028). The large overlap, however, does not lead Mosca, any more than it leads Gramsci, to a conflation of state and society; for Mosca too, the difference is functional. He describes the political function as being that of giving organization and leadership to all of society; and this description is analogous, though not identical, to the function elaborated by Gramsci.

We are now ready to resume Mosca's main argument addressing the issue of state intervention in civil society, and to see his resolution: "Therefore, according to our view, there cannot be antagonism between state and society since the state may be regarded as the part of society which discharges the political function and all questions about the interference or noninterference of the state acquire a new formulation; that is, rather than studying what should be the limits of state action, one must search for the best type of political organization."[30] Here we have, more explicitly expressed, the same conclusion which Gramsci suggests. Nor should this be surprising, since such a conclusion is a consequence of their essentially common view on the relation between civil and political society and on the nature of the political function.

Also more explicit but not essentially different is Mosca's criticism of both extreme laissez-faire and extreme statism, that is:

> In general, those who insist on limiting the activities of the state should take as their guide the very simple and very practical principle that in every branch of social activity—in education, religion, poor relief, military organization or the administration of justice—management[31] is always necessary, and that managerial functions have to be entrusted to a special class that has the abilities required for performing them.
>
> Now when one sets out to withdraw one of the above-mentioned functions in whole or in part from bureaucratic management, or from control by elective bodies, it must be borne in mind that there has to be present within the society a class of persons who possess the capacities, in other words have the moral and intellectual training and—let us not forget—the economic resources required for performing the new task which is to be turned over to them. . . .
>
> On the other hand, those who favor broader activities on the part of the state ought to consider the practical and positive significance of the term "state," stripping it of everything about it that in common parlance is vague, indeterminate or, we might almost say, magical or supernatural. Often in our day state ownership or control is invoked as a remedy for all the evils of private competition. . . . How much of its confidence this soaring trust would lose if, instead of thinking of the state as an abstract entity, as something foreign to the real world, one were to bear clearly in mind that in reality the state is just the concrete organization of a large number of the elements that rule in a given society, that when we speak of the state's influence we mean the influence that is to be exerted by government officials and government clerks! They are all very fine fel-

lows, to be sure, but however much they may have been improved or chastened by their sense of responsibility, by discipline or pride of office, they nevertheless possess all human capacities and all human frailties.[32]

It seems clear that Mosca is not an unqualified laissez-faire liberal any more than Gramsci is, just as the latter is not an advocate of statism any more than Mosca. One might say that Mosca is a judicious laissez-faire liberal, and that Gramsci is a judicious statist; here the emphasis would be on judiciousness, which would imply that the two positions are either indistinguishable or very close.

In the case of Mosca, we find both more evidence that this is so and a fundamental reason it is so. The fundamental reason [33] is that Mosca's laissez-faire liberalism is a special case of his principle of the separation of powers, the other main instance of this principle being the separation of church and state; moreover, the separation of powers is for him a consequence of the balanced pluralism of social forces, and so his commitment to such separation is not absolute. There is a beautiful illustration of this point, which brings us to the additional evidence just mentioned. It is the following.

In 1897 Mosca published a letter [34] to the editor of the *Journal of the Economists* to answer this clerical challenge to liberals: that, to be consistent, liberals who oppose state interference in the economy should also oppose the state monopoly on public education, and support giving Catholics the freedom to run their own schools. Mosca began his reply with a definition of political liberty which is now familiar to us: political liberty exists in a system where both rulers and ruled are subject to the laws and where both participate in its creation. He then argued that political liberty so defined depends on the separation of powers, and that the latter depends on the existence of a balanced pluralism of social forces and of leading groups. From such balanced pluralism would follow the rejection of the nationalization of the economy favored by socialists, on the grounds that it would give the same group control of both political and economic power; from balanced pluralism would also follow the separation of church and state. Mosca then answers the clerical challenge by pointing out that the situation in Italy at the time was such that if the state had relinquished its monopoly on education, then the totalitarianism of Catholic and of socialist doctrines would have endangered freedom of both thought and research, individual freedom, and indeed political liberty in general; that is, the educational system would have been monopolized by Catholics or socialists. In short, a liberal could oppose state interference in the economy but favor state intervention in religious education, and do so without inconsistency, because both the former nonintervention and the latter intervention were aimed at preventing the excessive concentration and abuse of power.

6. Difficulties: Pluralism, Separation, and the Modern Prince

This account of the Gramscian and Moschian notions of liberty and liberalism has yielded results I find even more surprising than those involving elitism and democracy. My account has shown that there are several notions of liberty and liberalism which both thinkers apply, though there is nothing surprising about this particular result. It has also been shown that both have a significant appreciation of liberty in the sense of civil liberties, and while this is relatively easy to see in Mosca, Gramsci's position on the matter has usually been overlooked. The significance of this is that therefore to some extent this pair can be regarded as an exception to the norm in Italian political tradition, which has tended to neglect such a discussion in favor of theories of Machiavellian reasons of state and theories of the Hegelian ideal of the ethical state.[35] I have also shown that Gramsci has a concept of liberty in the peculiar Moschian anti-autocratic sense of authority flowing from the bottom up; this not only establishes another tie between the two thinkers but also shows another type of commitment to democracy on their part, one to democracy not in the official Moschian sense but in the Platonic sense. Gramsci also advances a critique of a type of liberalism he usually attributes to Croce, but the liberalism which is the target of this criticism turns out to be what would more properly be called undemocratic elitism. In regard to laissez-faire liberalism, it is useful to bear in mind that Gramsci's criticism is advanced in the context of a simultaneous criticism of statism, and that Mosca expresses surprisingly similar reflections.

It is now time to face some difficulties with the account developed thus far. These are not really difficulties internal to my interpretation, but rather external to it in the sense that they stem from the existence of other Gramscian passages which cannot be easily ignored, deciphered, or incorporated into my interpretation. The situation is analogous to the previous accounts of elitism and of democracy; however, it is not at all clear that the present difficulties can be resolved as easily as the earlier problems of the withering away of the state and of transformism, both of which turned out to be more apparent than real.

One difficulty is that there is a passage where Gramsci seems to reject explicitly the principle of pluralistic liberalism. It appears in his critique of Croce, where Gramsci claims (correctly) that one of Croce's most fundamental principles is "the affirmation that the liberal form of the state is 'vital' and inalterable—that is, the form which guarantees to every political force the possibility of operating and struggling freely" (Q 1327). Then Gramsci immediately advances this objection:

> But how can one confuse this empirical fact with the concept of liberty, namely the concept of history? How can one ask that the forces engaged in a struggle should "moderate" the struggle within certain limits (the limits required for the conservation of the liberal state) without falling into arbitrariness and into a preconceived plan? In a fight, "blows are not given subject to mutual agreement"; every antithesis must necessarily act as a radical antagonist of the thesis, with the goal of completely destroying it and completely replacing it. To interpret historical development as a sport, with its referee and its pre-established rules which must be loyally respected, is a type of preconceived history in which the ideology has no political content but consists in a method of struggle. It is an ideology which tends to enervate the antithesis, to break it up into a long series of stages—namely, to reduce the dialectic to a process of reformistic evolution. [Q 1327-28]

It is obvious that the principle which Gramsci is attributing to Croce is also Mosca's most fundamental normative principle, as well as one common meaning for the notion of liberalism. Without question, Gramsci is criticizing the principle. This critique represents a difficulty for my interpretation because Gramsci's criticism would imply that he is not a "liberal" in the most fundamental sense, even though he may be one in the senses specified in my account thus far.

One possible misunderstanding of Gramsci's criticism should be avoided. That is, when he calls the liberal form of the state an empirical fact, it might seem that he is confusing empirical and normative issues by failing to perceive that pluralistic liberalism is a normative principle. However, here Gramsci is contrasting the empirical to the philosophical or metaphysical rather than to the normative; in other words, here he is making a distinction between philosophical and political liberty (along the lines mentioned above) and saying that the pluralism of political liberalism cannot be equated with metaphysical liberty. So far, so good; one may indeed agree with Gramsci that political liberalism is not a metaphysical principle.

However, the distinction between the normative and the descriptive emerges in another way. Gramsci states explicitly at the beginning of this note (Q 10,II,41,XVI) that he is questioning Crocean historicism, and that he intends to question liberalism as a form of historicism. And in the passage quoted above, one of Gramsci's misgivings is that it is incorrect "to interpret historical development" (Q 1328) in accordance with political liberalism, and that the error lies in narrating a "preconceived history" (Q 1328). Thus, Gramsci's objection seems to be that, from the point of view of historical inquiry, namely in the context of interpreting past history, it would be incorrect to prejudge the role that political pluralism has played in history; one cannot assume in advance that political liberalism has always had a certain role or function. Even if historical investigation has revealed that many historical developments are characterized by the feature of being steps toward political liberalism, we cannot be sure that the same feature is present in all historical events. One might want to consider the possibility that the next episode to be investigated has that feature, but one must be open to the possibility of a disconfirmation. In short, part of Gramsci's criticism is a reminder that historical inquiry is an empirical enterprise and cannot adopt an a priori method of investigation. Again, when so interpreted, this Gramscian point is unobjectionable.

Nevertheless, part of Gramsci's criticism explicitly addresses the normative issue and is clearly directed at the idea that the pluralism of the liberal state ought to be preserved at all costs. He seems to thinks that this is wrong because he seems to hold that each side of a struggle must act as a radical antagonist with the aim of completely annihilating the other side, so that some future winning side would have every right to abolish pluralistic liberalism. Gramsci's intent here seems clear, although one might wonder why one should accept the principle of radical antagonism. His talk of thesis, antithesis, and dialectic suggests that his justification of radical antagonism would be based on some such principle as the following: that the nature of the dialectic is such that thesis and antithesis must sharpen their clash by trying to annihilate each other.

The resolution of this difficulty may be sketched as follows. A clue in this regard is given by Gramsci, when he ends this short (one-page) note with this remark: "On the other hand, one could say that such a reform-istic attitude is an instance of the 'cunning of Providence,' in order to pro-duce a faster maturation of the internal forces kept under restrain by the reformistic practice" (Q 1328). This qualification to the previous analysis indicates that that analysis is just one side of the story. The other side per-tains to a valuable function performed by pluralistic liberalism, which in this context may be taken as synonymous with reformism: liberalism is valuable insofar as it enables each of the struggling sides to develop itself to the fullest. Gramsci presents this effect as an unintended consequence of liberalism—unintended, that is, at the conscious level. However, a further consequence not drawn by Gramsci is that even from the one-sided standpoint of developing a particular position to the fullest, the best means is not necessarily to strive for it directly in the absence of any actual opposition, but rather indirectly, by letting the view or position coexist with a multiplicity of others. In such a liberal environment, that particular alternative will not have the whole field to itself, but even so it may well flourish better than in an illiberal, one-dimensional context.

All this can, I believe, be plausibly read into Gramsci's concluding re-mark in the note and so may be taken as a development of Gramsci's own position. This interpretation is further supported by the fact that the ten-sion just defined exists throughout the Prison Notebooks and that it can be resolved in an analogous manner.[36] The tension has to do with how the dialectic should be conceived. Gramsci has two conceptions, monis-tic and pluralistic, and it can be argued that the pluralistic one is more fundamental and prevails over the monistic. The monistic concept de-fines the dialectic as a process of historical development in which a thesis and an antithesis clash without compromise; and the pluralistic concept defines the dialectic as a manner of thinking in which the aim is to avoid one-sidedness and extremes and to overcome oppositions and distinc-tions by creating a synthesis. While Gramsci pays some lip service to the monistic concept, his actual practice of thinking normally conforms to the principle of pluralistic dialectic. This is illustrated even in the note (Q 10,II,41,XVI) just quoted and discussed, where Gramsci starts by ap-pealing to monistic dialectic to justify his criticism of liberalism but then in his usual judicious fashion exhibits his pluralistic and dialectical way of thinking by developing the other side of the situation.

A second difficulty of a different sort comes to light in a passage where Gramsci expresses a more positive view of liberalism than one would expect:

The failure to consider the immediate element of the "relations of forces" is connected with the residues of the popular liberal conception, of which syndicalism is a manifestation that claimed to be more advanced, whereas in reality it took a step backward. In fact, the popular liberal conception attached some importance to the relationship of political forces organized into the various forms of party (newspaper readers, local and parliamentary elections, mass organizations of unions and parties in a strict sense); hence, that popular conception was more advanced than syndicalism, which attached primary importance to fundamental socioeconomic relations and only to these. The popular liberal conception implicitly took into account these relations as well (as is obvious from many signs), but it insisted more on the interrelation of political forces, which were an expression of the others and in reality contained them. These residues of the popular liberal conception can be detected in a whole series of discussions which are said to be connected with the philosophy of praxis and which have given rise to childish forms of optimism and stupidity. [Q 1581]

It is not clear what exactly Gramsci means by "popular liberal conception," whether it is another species of liberalism besides those already examined, or whether it is merely a terminological variation on laissez-faire liberalism. The variation interpretation is suggested by the elaboration in the passage of a critical comparison and contrast between this kind of liberalism and syndicalism. However, it is obvious that this kind of liberalism is not an instance of economism, as laissez-faire presumably is; moreover, the "popular liberal conception" is being evaluated much more favorably than syndicalism, whereas we saw earlier that laissez-faire liberalism was being evaluated as on a par with syndicalism; so this interpretation is problematic.

Nor does the talk of residues add clarity. It is conceivable that "residues" is an implicit reference to Pareto's system,[37] in which it is a technical term; but I find no evidence for this, and the obscurity of Pareto's own notion makes the possibility unattractive. The word is probably being used in its ordinary sense. It should be noted, then, that it is not the popular liberal conception that is being charged with childish optimism and stupidity, but its residues, and that one of the residues is syndicalism; this evaluation of syndicalism corresponds to that given in the other passage discussed earlier, where Gramsci objects to the utopia of "advocating an immediate jump from the regime of groupings to that of perfect equality (theoretical syndicalism in a strict sense)" (Q 461).

The quoted passage comes just after Gramsci has defined economism as the excessive emphasis on causes (economic factors) which act only through the intermediation of other factors (beliefs and politics). Hence, in speaking of "the failure to consider the immediate element of 'relations of forces,'" Gramsci is referring to economism, so that the connection he is pointing out is that between economism and syndicalism.[38] And this is relatively clear.

The main question remaining is then how syndicalism can be a residue of popular liberalism. If liberalism means laissez-faire, I do not see how syndicalism could possibly derive from it. The same would apply if by liberalism we mean any of the other notions we have examined, such as civil libertarianism, the anti-autocratic principle, pluralism, or Gramsci's own favorite target, undemocratic elitism. One notion, however, if inserted into the claim would render it plausible, namely the separation of powers (economics and politics)—if we do not equate it simply with laissez-faire liberalism. The connection would be that, once one separates the economic and political aspects of society, it becomes possible to emphasize and overemphasize economic factors, as syndicalists presumably do. Moreover, once the separation is made, as Gramsci suggests in one of his objections to laissez-faire, laissez-faire liberalism is another possible attitude to adopt. For these connections to hold, the separation in question must be a dichotomy that fails to interrelate political and civil society, and not a conceptual or methodological distinction (which merely declines to conflate them). This interpretation would also help make sense of two other claims, which Gramsci advances in the succeeding note and which would otherwise be quite puzzling; there he reiterates that syndicalism may have originated in liberalism, and suggests that economism probably has the same origin (Q 13,18/Q 1589). Thus, to the previously catalogued meanings of liberalism, we can add this one, namely the dichotomy or (undialectical) separation between politics and economics. The only other thing to add here is that, in this sense of the term "liberalism," Gramsci is not the only one who is not a liberal; as we saw above, Mosca is no liberal either.

A third and final difficulty deserves discussion. It shows up in an important passage where Gramsci seems to explicitly reject liberalism, at least in the sense of the doctrine of civil liberties and perhaps in any other sense as well. This is the famous passage where Gramsci seems to compare the Communist Party to God and the categorical imperative: "As it develops, the modern Prince upsets the whole system of intellectual and moral relationships, to the extent that its development means precisely that every action is conceived as useful or harmful, virtuous or vicious, only insofar as it is referred to the modern Prince itself and contributes to increasing or opposing its power. The Prince takes the place of the divinity or the categorical imperative in one's conscience, and it becomes the basis for a modern laicism and for a complete laicization of all life and all moral relationships" (Q 1561). To quote just one of the most authoritative interpreters, it is hard to disagree with Norberto Bobbio when, referring to the issue of Gramsci's liberalism, he describes these remarks as "the crucial passage in this controversy, a veritable cape of storms, where everyone who tries to traverse it risks being shipwrecked."[39] And to quote one of the most eloquent critics, it is not easy to devise an interpretation different from the following one advanced by Luciano Pellicani: "No theorization of the totalitarian and exclusionary party could be more complete and integral. Not even Lukács in *History and Class Consciousness* managed to formulate the thesis of the hierocratic nature of the revolutionary party with such candor. . . . The duty of man is to blend in with it by destroying and parting with his own liberty. Thus the supreme virtue of the communist militant is 'partisanship,' or the acceptance of the party's will as the only rule of conduct and unquestioned application of his revolutionary being to the party's will."[40]

To begin with, let us immediately agree that Gramsci was not a consistent and simple liberal. This passage is just one more reminder of that. Even if we can formulate an interpretation of this passage which is not anti-liberal, thus explaining it away (so to speak), we should not forget the complexities of the situation and the tensions within Gramsci's thought. But can we come up with a different interpretation? I would suggest one along the following lines.[41]

Let us focus on the last sentence of this Gramscian passage. Its last clause claims that the modern Prince is the basis for a complete secularization of life; thus, it is clear that Gramsci's aim is secularization or laicism. Moreover, in the first clause of that sentence, the modern Prince is contrasted not only with God but also with the categorical imperative; and this contrast suggests that Gramsci's "laicism" involves versions of humanism as well as relativism. Now, secularization, laicism, humanism, and relativism are all things unquestionably associated with liberalism. Further, this aspect of this passage is completely in accordance with a very consistent theme in all of Gramsci's writings. In this regard, here we have merely another expression of his "laicism."

Another important feature of the passage is that Gramsci speaks of the

modern Prince as "taking the place" of God and the categorical imperative. That is, Gramsci is really drawing a contrast rather than a positive
comparison. As Dante Germino and Meindert Fennema have expressed
it, "This taking the place emphatically did not imply an equivalence. . . .
So, for him, the party is a very unmystical, unromantic, almost humdrum
substitute for what had been the exalted but empty Kantian categorical
imperative and religious dogma and superstition."[42]

It is also important to note that Gramsci is talking about what happens "in one's conscience." This reference implies that it would be up
to the individual to judge what the modern Prince requires. Thus, an irreducibly liberal element remains in the passage, even if Gramsci were
trying to replace one absolute with another (which he is not) and even if
this replacement involved an exchange of equivalents (which it does not).

A final point that calls for discussion is the denotation of the term
"modern Prince." The traditional interpretation uncritically assumes that
the only referent is the revolutionary Communist Party. However, another referent is suggested by the several paragraphs preceding the quoted
passage: Gramsci is also referring to a philosophical-political work entitled "The Modern Prince" which he envisaged writing. For example,
he is referring to that work when, earlier in the same note (Q 13,1), he
says that "the modern Prince must have a part dealing with Jacobinism,
in the integral meaning which this notion has had historically and must
have conceptually" (Q 1559), that "one of its first parts should be dedicated precisely to the notion of 'collective will'" (Q 1559), and that "an
important part of the modern Prince must be devoted to the problem of
an intellectual and moral reform" (Q 1560). So the question arises which
of the two meanings is the relevant one in the crucial passage quoted.

I believe that Gramsci is in fact equivocating in that passage.[43] But
the ambiguities can be resolved as follows. The first sentence in the passage means that the work "The Modern Prince" defines utility and harm,
good and evil in terms of the interests of the party-as-modern-Prince.
The second sentence would then mean that the party-as-modern-Prince
becomes the substitute for God and the categorical imperative, and that
the work "The Modern Prince" becomes the basis of a modern laicism.
Formally speaking, the work "The Modern Prince" would do what every
philosophical theory tries to do, namely articulate and systematize moral
and political intuitions. The content of such a work would not necessarily
be anti-liberal. In fact, given Gramsci's talk of laicism, substitution, and
conscience, this passage suggests the contrary.

7. Epilogue

In this chapter I have undertaken a critical examination of the Gramscian and Moschian notions of liberty and liberalism. It was first pointed out that there are several notions of liberty and liberalism which both thinkers apply. Both have a significant appreciation of liberty in the sense of civil liberties, and while that is relatively easy to see in Mosca, Gramsci's position on the matter has been usually overlooked. It was also shown that Gramsci has a concept of liberty that conforms to the peculiar Moschian anti-autocratic sense of authority as flowing from the bottom up. Gramsci also advances a critique of a type of liberalism he usually attributes to Benedetto Croce, but the liberalism which is the target of this criticism turns out to be what would more properly be called *undemocratic* elitism. In regard to laissez-faire liberalism, it is noteworthy that Gramsci's criticism is advanced in the context of a simultaneous criticism of statism, and Mosca expresses surprisingly similar reflections. Finally, I offer a resolution of three difficulties stemming from some key Gramscian claims which do not seem to fit the previous analysis: Gramsci's apparent rejection of pluralistic liberalism; his apparent preference for liberalism over syndicalism; and his comparison of the Communist Party to God and the categorical imperative.

SEVEN

MOSCA AND GRAMSCI ON FREEMASONRY AND FASCISM: AN EMBLEMATIC CASE

THE ANALYSIS SO FAR has been relatively abstract in that it has dealt exclusively with the political theory of Mosca and Gramsci. In the Introduction I explained this limitation as being intrinsic to the nature of the present investigation. Nevertheless, it would be desirable if the theoretical rapprochement between these two figures could be tested or supplemented by an analysis at a level closer to political practice. Moreover, aside from such a motivation, there happens to be a case of practical political convergence which is sufficiently emblematic to merit being studied in its own right, for other reasons as well. The episode regards the speeches each of the two men made in 1925 in Parliament against a bill presented by the Fascist government and designed to disempower the Freemasons. These speeches offer a revealing glimpse of Mosca's and Gramsci's views not only on Freemasonry and Fascism but also on more general sociopolitical issues.

1. The Fascist Bill Against Freemasonry

On 18 November 1925, Mosca delivered at the Italian Senate a speech in opposition to a Fascist bill intended to regulate secret organizations in general and Freemasonry in particular. This speech has attracted little attention from Mosca scholars and none from Gramsci scholars, who seldom read Mosca. However, no Gramsci scholar could read this speech without recalling the one on the same subject delivered by Gramsci in the Chamber of Deputies of the Italian Parliament on 16 May of the same year.[1] In fact, Gramsci's speech is well known as his only parliamentary speech during the two and a half years he served there, although it is regarded as something of a biographical curiosity. I believe this speech by Gramsci to be an extremely important document.[2] Since it was Gramsci's first speech in Parliament, it must be regarded as the result of a serious and emblematic reflection, certainly more serious than the bulk of his pre-prison writings, in regard to which Gramsci himself stated that his journalistic articles "were written on a day-to-day basis and deserved, in my opinion, to perish in the same way."[3]

Thus, there are two reasons a comparative analysis of the two speeches is extremely important. One reason has purely to do with Gramsci: his speech is intrinsically a precious document. The other reason derives from the fact that both legislators declare their opposition to the law proposed by the Fascist government, and so we have here a case in which they are both on the same side, from the point of view of practical politics.

Naturally, one might think at this point that their respective justifications for their common opposition might be very different and express very different points of view, philosophies, and orientations. Certainly I do not deny that it is abstractly possible to arrive at the same conclusion from different and even opposite premises, just as it is possible to arrive at opposite conclusions on the basis of partially common premises. These points are immediate consequences of the most elementary principles of logic. The issue here is whether this is in fact the situation in the case at hand. In fact, Gramsci's and Mosca's speeches reveal many similarities, the number and depth of which make the convergence nothing less than astonishing.

On the other hand, one must not misunderstand or exaggerate the importance of this special case. After all, a parliamentary speech is a document of a circumstantial nature and subsists in a rhetorical context very different from that of scientific research. The value of this case is then primarily emblematic and supplementary; it supplements what has been unearthed in an integrated reading of Mosca's *Elements of Political Science* and Gramsci's Prison Notebooks.

It should be added that, besides the two speeches, another short essay by Mosca is directly pertinent—it is the answer Mosca gave to a survey on Freemasonry sponsored by the newspaper *L'Idea nazionale* and published there in 1913.[4] In his speech, Mosca refers to this answer, and so in the present context we may regard the brief essay as an integral part of the speech.[5]

The proposed law did not explicitly mention Freemasonry but rather secret organizations; however, it was commonly labeled the anti-Masonic law. The bill was presented in Parliament on 12 January 1925 by Mussolini as prime minister and was entitled "Regulation of the Activities of Associations, Organizations, and Institutions and of the Membership therein by Employees of the State, of Provincial and Municipal Governments, and of Public Service Institutions."[6] The first article of the law obliged all organizations to provide various kinds of information to the police, whenever the latter requested it; this was information about by-laws, the identity of officials, and membership lists; moreover, the article gave the chief of police the authority to disband an organization in case of failure to comply with the request. The second article prohibited all public employees from belonging to organizations which were formed and operated in a secret manner and whose members were bound to secrecy; the penalty for violation was dismissal. Before receiving final approval, the bill's second article was amended to include a retroactive clause to the effect that all public employees had to declare their past as well as current membership in such organizations, whenever requested to do so.[7]

2. Gramsci's Speech in Parliament

Gramsci's speech exhibits certain anomalies. The most obvious is the number and frequency of the interruptions by various Fascist members of Parliament, especially Prime Minister Mussolini, who was present in the chamber. These interruptions take the form of interjected objections to what Gramsci is saying. There are scores of them, but they can be classified into about a dozen groups.

One can also readily note that the inexperienced deputy usually responds to these interruptions, which a more practiced parliamentarian would have probably ignored. As a result, the text of the speech, as read by someone today, appears more like a dialogue than a speech and is naturally much longer than the speaker intended—another anomaly by comparison with a typical speech by a member of Parliament. Moreover, the interjections and responses often constitute digressions from the main thread of the argument. Gramsci himself confessed in a letter to his wife that, by responding to the Fascists' interjections, he had played into their hands, and that the constant distractions had prevented him from presenting the speech the way he had planned.[8]

In fact, with regard to its intellectual content, the speech-dialogue is apparently incoherent, in a way which is not easy to eliminate. The incoherence is due in part to the lack of logical or inferential connections among its parts; also, the theses contained in the different parts seem to contradict each other. A summary will give some idea of these incoherences.

The speaker begins by saying that he wants to explore the reasons for which the Fascist government has proposed the law regulating secret associations and the reasons it has been introduced as a law against Freemasonry. After a sort of historical introduction in which Gramsci boasts of having taken Fascism seriously from the very beginning and having predicted the Fascist rise to power, he makes the first of many declarations to the effect that "we know we represent the interests of the great majority of the Italian people, laborers and peasants."[9]

Following this introductory section, the speaker goes on to give an interpretation of Freemasonry and an analysis of other political and social forces. Summarily dismissing the intellectual content of Masonic doctrines, Gramsci expresses an original and important interpretation when he says that "Freemasonry has been the only real and efficient party which the bourgeois class has had for a long time."[10] The traditional opponent of Freemasonry was the clerical party, which represented not only the Vatican but also a large part of the rural elements in both northern and southern Italy.

Then the speech goes on to interpret Fascism as a rural reactionary force which was antibourgeois as well as anticlerical: "The rural classes which in the past were represented by the Vatican today are represented primarily by Fascism; hence it is logical that Fascism should have replaced the Vatican and the Jesuits in the historical task of enabling the more backward classes of the population to subjugate a class which has been more progressive in the history of civilization."[11] The last clause of this quotation expresses also a relatively positive appreciation of the bourgeoisie, and so I would say that the positive evaluation refers indirectly also to Freemasonry.

He then examines the law from the point of view of the prospects that it will be able to deal with the problems of Italian society. The first of these problems is the lack of raw materials; the second is the lack of colonies and hence of a labor aristocracy; the third is the Southern Question, together with the problem of emigration. Mussolini interrupts this list of problems with a comment aimed to justify emigration; it elicits Gramsci's first digression, on the issue of emigration and the nature of imperialism.

Without going back to that list of Italian problems, the speaker goes on to discuss the attempts on the part of the bourgeoisie to face the problems.[12] One was Giovanni Giolitti's attempt, characterized as "the attempt to establish an alliance between the industrial bourgeoisie and a type of labor aristocracy in the North in order to oppress and to subject to this bourgeois-proletarian formation the mass of Italian peasants, especially in the South."[13] The other he labels as the program of the Milanese newspaper *Corriere della sera,* a program he defines as "an alliance between northern industrialists and some vague southern rural democratic forces in regard to free trade."[14] Once again, Gramsci is sufficiently objective to give a somewhat positive appreciation from a viewpoint which can be regarded as generally democratic; that is, he says that "both solutions essentially tended to give to the Italian state a basis larger than the original one—namely, they tended to develop the 'gains' of the Risorgimento."[15]

Then Gramsci resumes the examination of Fascism with regard to these problems and solutions. Thus the Fascist bill becomes merely an attempt to replace Masonic with Fascist officials. By giving a perhaps excessive importance to the law in the context of Fascist proposals, by repeating his interpretation of Freemasonry as a bourgeois party, and by assuming the classic definition of revolution as the replacement of one ruling class by another, the speaker draws the conclusion that the so-called Fascist revolution is not a real revolution. When Mussolini protests, Gramsci reinforces this argument by reiterating the thesis that "Fascism is not based on any class which was not already in power."[16] Mussolini disputes this thesis, but the disagreement is obviously not resolved.

At this point, we must note a contradiction (at least apparent) between the bourgeois interpretation of Fascism and the "rural" interpretation advanced earlier in the speech. It is possible that this contradiction is more apparent than real, but the difficulty cannot be resolved here.[17]

Gramsci continues by stating for the first time his main thesis, according to which "in reality the law against Freemasonry is not primarily against Freemasonry."[18] Presumably this is due to the fact that, for Gramsci, "Fascism will easily come to a compromise with the Freemasons."[19] Gramsci does not justify this important thesis, and it is disputed by Mussolini; this gives rise to another dialogue at cross-purposes. Without this disagreement's being resolved, another emerges in regard to the Fascist persecution of the Communists.

This exchange in turn produces another one on the nature and role of violence in politics. The speaker charges the Fascists with regressive violence, whereas he regards the violence of the Communists as progressive. The basis of this distinction is justified by Gramsci in part "with the difference that you represent a minority of the population, whereas we represent the majority." [20] This, of course, is an expression of a democratic sentiment, in one common meaning of the notion of democracy; but Gramsci elaborates on it with some elements of the dynamics of and interaction between majorities and minorities, and here we find a general formulation of a fundamental elitist principle: "It is certainly very difficult for a class to be able to arrive at the solution of its problems and the achievement of the goals inherent in its existence and in the general social reality without a vanguard's forming itself and guiding this class to the achievement of these goals." [21]

After someone requests him to return to the subject of Freemasonry, Gramsci answers that the formal title and wording of the proposed law do not speak of Freemasonry but of organizations in general. Thus, he feels he has the right to go on and discuss the organization of capitalism in Italy. In this regard, he develops the thesis that southern Italy has been exploited by the state by means of the regular collection of taxes greater in amount than what it spends there. This occasions other interruptions about the situation in Russia in regard to taxation. And here it should be noted that the comparison with the Russian situation is one of the main pretexts for Mussolini's interruptions.

The thread of the argument is resumed when Gramsci claims that the Fascists are unable to solve the problems of Italian society and that the proposed law is useless for that purpose; he discusses whether they will remain in power. There follows another digression on violence. Then Gramsci attempts to conclude with a recapitulation, but he is again interrupted. After a few more exchanges, the speech ends without Gramsci's having been able even to complete his recapitulation.

3. A Reconstruction of Gramsci's Argument

As is apparent, it is not easy to follow the thread of Gramsci's argument. There is no doubt that he is against the bill; that he regards it as actually aimed at the Communists rather than at the Freemasons; that he gives an interesting interpretation of Freemasonry, namely as an effective bourgeois and anticlerical party; that he predicts a settlement between Fascism and Freemasonry; that he gives an inconsistent interpretation of Fascism, first as an antibourgeois and anticlerical reaction and then as a new exponent of the bourgeois class; that he expresses a democratic attitude, in the sense of one favorable to the majority; that he also expresses an elitist attitude, in the sense that he recognizes the need for the majority to be led by a minority; and that he advances an interpretation of the Southern Question according to which the South has been savagely exploited by the state to benefit the industrialization of the North.

Thus, we have a pile of reflections which are individually interesting, but whose connections are not easily discernible and whose tensions are more or less evident. The importance of this document by Gramsci cannot therefore lie in the power of its eloquence, the persuasiveness of its rhetoric, or the logical strength of the reasoning. We will see presently where, in my opinion, its importance lies. However, before turning to that, I want to explore whether a thread of argument is directed at the anti-Masonic law, and whether the speech is really as incoherent as it appears at first sight. After all, a scholar has the duty to understand and not merely to collect data, to reconstruct the available material, and to search for an order underlying the appearances.

In fact, Gramsci's speech can be reconstructed as advancing the following argument. Naturally, in this reconstruction I have tried to eliminate the contradictions, to overlook claims which cannot be integrated with the rest, and to render explicit assumptions which are only implicit in the text. Nevertheless, this reconstruction aims to be faithful to most of the essential points and most of the explicit connections.

Gramsci is opposed to the proposed law because it would not contribute to the solution of the deep problems of Italian society but would instead be an obstacle to their resolution. For he thinks that the historical difficulties of the Italian nation are at least three: (1) the lack of raw materials, (2) the lack of colonies, and (3) the Southern Question, together with the problem of emigration. And he acknowledges two types of solutions which have been tried: the first was Giolitti's program, which Gramsci reduces to an alliance between the bourgeoisie and the laborers of the North, at the expense of the South; the second was the program advocated by the *Corriere della sera,* which he reduces to an alliance between northern industrialists and southern rural elements that is focused on free trade. He thinks that these attempts have not succeeded and have now been exhausted. He believes that the correct solution lies in an alliance between northern laborers and southern peasants—the policy proposed by the political party he headed. In regard to a Fascist solution, he feels the Fascists do not have any essentially new ideas, since they represent the old ruling class, the bourgeoisie.

In particular, according to Gramsci, the Fascist law against Freemasonry will have two principal consequences. First, it will make possible what he calls "the replacement of one type of administrative personnel by another."[22] The old administrative personnel is, generally speaking, Masonic, since for Gramsci Freemasonry is "the only efficiently organized force which the bourgeoisie has in Italy."[23] This is a curious interpretation of Freemasonry, but he expresses it more than once; in fact, Gramsci advances it at the beginning of the speech, when he asks, "What is Freemasonry?"[24] and answers: "Freemasonry has been the only real and efficient party which the bourgeois class has had for a long time."[25] Since the new law forbids all public officials to belong to secret organizations like the order of Freemasons, Gramsci makes the prediction that the law would be used by the Fascists for "taking over the jobs which the state gives to its officials."[26] To this interpretation of Freemasonry as a bourgeois party, Gramsci adds two other important theses: one is the interpretation of Fascism as being itself also based on the old bourgeois class; the other is the thesis that, to the extent that there are differences between Freemasonry and Fascism, they are relatively minor and the two will work out a settlement. These three premises justify in Gramsci's mind the conclusion that the anti-Masonic law does not represent a deep structural change sufficiently novel to deal in a serious way with the traditional problems of Italian society.

Indeed, he thinks that, besides not facilitating their solution, the law will be a hindrance. And here we come to the second consequence which Gramsci fears and repeats many times during the speech. That is, the new law will sanction the persecution of proletarian organizations, such as the party he heads, which advocates an alliance between northern laborers and southern peasants. In fact, Gramsci relates that the persecution has already begun, and the police "arrests our comrades whenever it finds them meeting in groups of at least three."[27] Since for Gramsci the alliance is the only promising way of solving those problems, the new law will in effect be an obstacle to their solution. That is why the speaker never tires of warning of the hidden but real purpose of the law, a point which at the end of his speech he expresses as follows: "To conclude, Freemasonry is the small flag used to smuggle in the antiproletarian goods. It is not Freemasonry you care about! . . . The law must be useful for the laborers and the peasants, who will understand this very well from the way it will be applied."[28]

4. Mosca's Senate Speech

At the Senate the anti-Masonic bill was considered some months after the Chamber of Deputies discussion. Mosca regarded the question as sufficiently important to give a speech on 18 November 1925, expressing his opposition.[29] The old senator had already made another speech the day before, on the question of women's suffrage, and so he began the new one by apologizing for making speeches two days in a row and promised that he would be briefer than usual.

For Mosca the bill is an attempt to regulate the right of association, which he considers to be an extremely important and delicate task for a representative government. He thinks that on the one hand the executive branch of government should not have the power to disband any organization which criticizes and opposes its policies, but that on the other hand the unlimited freedom of association could produce associations whose power might endanger the sovereignty of the state. He bemoans the fact that, unlike other countries, Italy has not been willing or able to adopt a special law which would explicitly regulate this right; instead the regulation has been done by means of "some parliamentary customs"[30] and of the application of some articles of the penal code.

These considerations can be interpreted as a partial praise of the government for its willingness to deal with the issue. However, Mosca's praise ends here, because he goes on the express his dissent from both of the bill's articles.

In regard to the first, the speaker confesses his disappointment at the fact that the law is too vague and does not define exactly "how far this right may be legally exercised and at what point illegal activity or crime begins."[31] Moreover, the bill gives to the executive branch (namely, to the provincial prefects) rather than to the judicial branch (namely, to the judges) "the authority to disband associations or to prevent them from being formed when they neglect certain formalities."[32] It follows, in Mosca's view, that a strong government could de facto suppress this right, whereas a weak government would be incapable of controlling the most dangerous organizations.

In regard to the second article, Mosca thinks it is "deliberately framed to hit Freemasonry."[33] Here he refers to his previous statements against Freemasonry, especially to his answer to a survey carried out by *L'Idea nazionale* in 1913. The speaker summarizes and repeats what he said then, and so it is useful here to analyze that brief essay.

The survey asked three questions, the first of which was: "Do you think that the continued existence of a secret association like the Freemasons is compatible with the conditions of modern public life?"[34] Mosca answers that, empirically speaking, Freemasonry is "most compatible"[35] with Italian public life since this association seems to flourish vigorously. Thus, the more important question becomes that of the reasons for this fact. Mosca mentions a secondary cause, namely "a certain preference for occult and indirect ways and for wily and cunning procedures which is unfortunately still common in the character of Italians."[36] However, the main reason is that Freemasonry performs a necessary political function in Italian public life which has not yet been performed by political organizations such as appropriately organized parties: "A widely extended suffrage, and especially universal suffrage, presuppose the organization of minorities consisting of intelligent persons who guide their response; where there are no open organizations of intelligent minorities, secret organizations substitute for them. Hence, in Italy the *raison d'être* of Freemasonry would vanish if the two great parts of the liberal party (the liberal-conservative and the liberal-democratic) were openly organized, as is the case in England and to some extent with us for the Catholic and the socialist parties."[37] This passage contains an elitist interpretation of Freemasonry, as well as a rather general statement of the fundamental elitist principle.[38]

The second question in the survey was: "Do you think that the materialistic rationalism and the humanitarian and internationalist ideology which appear to inspire Freemasonry correspond to the liveliest tendencies of contemporary thought?"[39] Mosca's second answer contains an additional elaboration of the Masonic philosophy, together with a a summary and contemptuous rejection. For Mosca, the Masonic philosophy derives from eighteenth-century French Encyclopedism and asserts that humanity is capable of constant and indefinite progress, that progress has in the past been hindered by ignorance and religious superstitions, and that to fight these and promote progress one should try "to spread the light of science."[40] Mosca's judgment is a paradigm of curtness: These ideas are "simplistic . . . outdated"[41] and not even deserving of refutation.

Here it is important to note that this anti-Masonic criticism expresses an attitude which can be definitely labeled antipositivistic. To be sure, Mosca also makes a qualification of his criticism, adding that "many human institutions have for centuries retained a vigorous vitality despite the fact that the progress of the human spirit has undermined their intellectual foundations."[42] However, this qualification also embodies an antipositivistic attitude, since in it Mosca denies that there is any simple parallelism between the evolution of the human mind and that of human society, that of ideas and that of institutions. Such an attitude can also be characterized as antiformalist or realist. Finally, it should be noted that these characteristics are also found in Gramsci.

The survey's third question asked: "Do you believe that the open and the secret activities of Freemasonry in Italian life (especially in the military establishment, in the judicial system, in the schools, and in public administration) are beneficial or harmful for the country?"[43] Mosca answers that the results of Masonic secrecy are no doubt harmful, but he adds two considerations pointing in a different direction. The first is another indication of his elitist approach, on the basis of which he arrives at a partially positive evaluation of Freemasonry: "When suffrage is very wide or universal and manipulated by a secret association, it can produce a government of sectarians; but when universal suffrage is not guided by any association of intelligent persons (either secret or public), it may lead to bureaucratic despotism or to something similar to anarchy. Thus, I believe that in the present circumstances Freemasonry may be regarded as a moderating force and even a conservative force."[44] The second consideration is that, to the extent that the Masonic influence is harmful, it extends to Parliament as well; hence, if its influence is combated in regard to the above mentioned institutions, it should also be combated in regard to Parliament; now, if this is to be done, it is necessary to have a more explicit organization of political parties in general, and of the above-mentioned "liberal" ones in particular; this is no easy matter.[45]

Let us now go back to Mosca's Senate speech. He continues by discussing the content of the second article of the proposed law, which prohibited military men, judges, policemen, and other public administrators from belonging to Freemasonry. Because of his generally negative judgment on Masonic secrecy, he would have been predisposed to accept this article. However, one aspect of the article obliges him to a negative vote. The proposed prohibition was in a sense retroactive; that is, the law obliged public officials to reveal not only whether they were Freemasons at the time but also whether they had been in the past. Mosca predicts that this part of the law would be abused because it would encourage the compilation of lists in the interest of those "who would like to take over the positions occupied by the ex-Masonic officials,"[46] and to the disadvantage of those who in an earlier period had violated no law. In Mosca's words, which produced considerable amusement in his listeners, the article would harm the many "employees who had become Freemasons because the department secretary or undersecretary was a Freemason."[47] This prediction corresponds to one of Gramsci's, although Mosca justifies it in a completely different manner.

5. Similarities Between the Two Speeches

The preceding analysis will enable us to appreciate the significant coincidences between Mosca's and Gramsci's speeches. A correspondence which can be labeled practical-political is that both legislators are opposed to the anti-Masonic bill. As we have seen, their shared parliamentary stance could have derived from very different premises and arguments, but this is not so; indeed, the theoretical similarities are undoubtedly surprising. It is now time to examine these similarities in a complete, detailed, and systematic fashion.

First of all, one should underscore a similarity which I would call methodological; the method in question is realism or anti-formalism.[48] Here realism means an approach such that historical facts, social and political phenomena, and human affairs are studied primarily from the viewpoint of their effective reality, and only secondarily from the viewpoint of the legal forms, ideological constructs, and institutional mechanisms which formally define them, or from that of how things ought to be. In other words, the real which this kind of realism stresses is contrasted to normative ideals and to superficial appearances.[49]

Both thinkers display this realistic attitude toward Freemasonry when they refuse to take seriously the intellectual content of its doctrines. Gramsci does it with his typical bite. Addressing his Fascist listeners, he declares: "What is Freemasonry? You have said many things on the spiritual meaning and the ideological movements it represents, etc.; but all this is a form of expression you use only to knowingly deceive one another." [50] I should say parenthetically that here Gramsci exaggerates somewhat, but I should like to stress his realism and his agreement with Mosca. The latter's speech declares analogously that "if we examine its theoretical principles, we must agree that it is all stuff which has been superseded: they say . . . but let us set aside the philosophical part of this organization, to which I think even Freemasons no longer pay any attention." [51]

Such realism is also spontaneously applied to the Fascist bill, more explicitly and anxiously by Gramsci, and more indirectly and calmly by Mosca. In fact, the key point of Gramsci's argument is the thesis that the real purpose of the Fascist proposal is not to strike at Freemasonry, but to hinder proletarian unions and parties. I am not saying that he succeeds in persuasively demonstrating this thesis, but that its content and its role in his speech make it a clear example of realism in the sense in question here. This Gramscian realism is also expressed when he asks, "Will this law against associations be a force, or is it destined to be completely ineffectual and vacuous?" [52] And in regard to Mosca, the main reason he opposes the retroactive application of the law is that it would invite the abuse of blacklisting or replacing ex-Masonic officials; and the discernment of such an implicit consequence involves indirectly the search for the realities underlying the appearances which defines the realistic tendency.

Another correspondence which is of some significance and much more explicit involves the formulation of a general theoretical principle for the analysis of sociopolitical reality. It is what I have called the fundamental elitist principle, which maintains that elites and leaders are necessary even from the viewpoint of the masses and the followers. This is not the same as other principles which might claim the priority of elites, whether the priority is logical, methodological, epistemological, political, or moral; nor should it be confused with the principle which asserts the universality of minority rule. The fundamental principle in question here asserts only the inseparable reciprocity of two social groups. Gramsci's formulation is explicit and admirably clear: "A class cannot permanently remain such and develop until [its] takeover of power without having a party and organization which would represent its best and most reflective part." [53] He is not only explicit but also repetitious for he adds that "certainly it is very difficult for a class to arrive at the solution of its problems and the achievement of the goals inherent in its existence and in the general social context without a vanguard's forming and leading this class to the achievement of these goals."[54] Mosca's formulation is less explicit and found not in the Senate speech but in the answer to the survey. At any rate, there is no need here to elaborate this feature of his thought.

It should perhaps be stressed that this similarity between their speeches is not necessarily an indication of intellectual influence in the (more or less chronological) direction Mosca-Gramsci. For the convergence could be based on different sources or the result of a common source. In this regard, it should be mentioned that Gramsci thinks that the elitist principle is a Marxist one.[55] Now, if this were true in an exclusive manner, then we would have a common source, although the Marx-Mosca part of the connection would have to exist at the level of effectual reality, since at the level of awareness Mosca regards himself as a critic of Marxism. Other comparisons between Mosca and Marx might be attempted in regard to other principles and approaches adopted by Mosca, and then all such comparisons might be regarded as one way of elaborating the Gramsci-Mosca connection. However, this approach (by way of Marx) to the Mosca-Gramsci connection would presuppose a Marxist interpretation of the Prison Notebooks, which in the present context could not be uncritically accepted.[56] At any rate, for now, the point is that both Gramsci and Mosca accept the elitist principle, and that this overlap is discernible in their speeches on Freemasonry.

It should also be noted that the elitist principle is independent of the above-mentioned realistic approach, and so we have two distinct theoretical similarities. The same applies in the case of another similarity which is no less important but perhaps more striking, namely the elitist interpretation of Freemasonry. Obviously, both could have accepted the elitist principle in general, without agreeing on the character of Freemasonry. The almost identical interpretation of Freemasonry is in this context a crucial clue extremely suggestive for the entire case. Let us examine their words on this particular issue.

From the very beginning of his speech, Gramsci declares explicitly that "given the way in which Italy became unified, and given the initial weakness of the capitalist bourgeoisie in Italy, Freemasonry has been the only real and effective party which the bourgeois class has had for a long time";[57] then he repeats this thesis many times in the rest of the speech. Mosca is less direct, but there can be no doubt that he is referring to Freemasonry when he speaks of an "organization of minorities consisting of intelligent persons who guide"[58] the response of the mass of voters; he explicitly calls it a "force"[59] which can be regarded as "necessary"[60] in view of the Italian situation, in which there are no other properly organized political forces.

In addition to this common interpretation, the two thinkers give an analogous positive evaluation of Freemasonry. The evaluation is only partly positive, but even this feature is common to both. Gramsci's evaluation is stated at the end of his reply to the question, "How have the bourgeois parties and Freemasonry tried to solve these problems?"[61] referring to the traditional problems of the Italian nation such as the lack of raw materials or colonies and the Southern Question. Gramsci thinks that, despite the failures of the attempts on the part of Giolitti and of the *Corriere della sera*, "both solutions had essentially the tendency to give to the Italian state a wider basis that the original one, the tendency to develop the 'gains' of the Risorgimento."[62] On the other hand, Mosca expresses his appreciation when he admits to being of the opinion "that in the present circumstances Freemasonry may be regarded as a moderating force and even a conservative force."[63]

These evaluations must not be misunderstood. Gramsci seems to appreciate Freemasonry for its role as a progressive and democratic force, whereas Mosca seems to appreciate its conservative and moderating function. Thus their reasons seem to be different and perhaps opposite. This is not a difficulty for my analysis because it is not my intention to show the complete identity of their thought. This may be taken as one of their differences, and no one can seriously deny the existence of differences. However, precisely because they are commonly known for their differences, it is important to uncover their similarities.

More of these can be uncovered by focusing on their reflections on the bill, dividing the reflections again into evaluations and interpretations. It is clear that their evaluation of the proposed law is negative, but this has already been mentioned. Now I want to add only that what earlier was called a practical coincidence of parliamentary opposition can also be regarded as an evaluative similarity, and hence in a sense a theoretical similarity, if we regard evaluation as a particular type of theoretical and intellectual activity. However, it is the interpretation of the law which is more important here. I have already mentioned the "realistic" nature of their interpretations. Now I want to analyze their content. The content turns out to be one of the most surprising things.

In fact, Gramsci's interpretation is that the proposed law will be used partly to replace the Masonic administrative personnel with Fascists, and partly to hinder or destroy proletarian parties and labor unions. It is certainly curious that these two predictions are essentially the same as Mosca's.

The first prediction is expressed by Gramsci in these words: "In reality,[64] Fascism is fighting against the only effectively organized force[65] which the bourgeoisie has in Italy to replace it in regard to the jobs given to state officials. The Fascist 'revolution' is merely the replacement of one kind of administrative personnel by another."[66] In a very different style, Mosca expresses the same idea: "Honorable Mr. Secretary . . . let us not forget that, when some officials declare that they have belonged to Freemasonry, one could begin to suspect (perhaps incorrectly, but still one could begin to suspect) that one wants to compile lists of exclusion; now, there would exist persons with an interest in the compilation of such lists, namely those persons who would like to obtain the positions occupied by the ex-Masonic officials."[67] This similarity is one of those which strike the reader in a very powerful way.

In regard to the other prediction, the similarity is more difficult to perceive because Gramsci is disturbed by a particular alleged consequence involving his own party and the proletarian class, whereas Mosca is perturbed by an anticipated general result. However, granting this difference, the similarity becomes clear. Gramsci objects that "the fact of the matter is that the law against Freemasonry is not primarily against Freemasonry,"[68] and that "in reality the law is aimed especially against labor organizations."[69] Mosca's perspective is wider and his analysis more detailed. Examining the issue from the viewpoint of the right of association, the senator notes that the bill's first article does not define exactly "how far this right may be legally exercised, and at what point the violation of the law begins";[70] he also notes that the law gives the power to take preventive measures to the provincial prefects rather than to the judges. In his mind, the danger is crystal clear: "A government which preferred strong measures . . . could suppress the right of association"[71]—not just the rights of labor unions, but those of any dissident.

To all these similarities one can add a last one, which can be called logical in the sense of reasoning; that is, the arguments in the two speeches have some essential points in common. These can be exhibited by giving a partial reconstruction of the two arguments.

Let us summarize the reconstruction of the Gramscian argument expounded earlier. Gramsci is opposed to the Fascist bill because he thinks it would facilitate the replacement of Masonic by Fascist officials; this would not constitute a new and serious attempt to solve the traditional

Italian problems, since Freemasonry has historically been a bourgeois political force and Fascism too is a bourgeois political force. Moreover, he thinks that the real purpose of the law is the persecution of labor organizations.

Mosca is also opposed to this bill because he thinks that the retroactive application of its articles would facilitate the Fascist takeover of administrative positions; this would happen because the Freemasons have traditionally been the main political organization in Italy. Moreover, he thinks that the law would facilitate governmental persecution of the opposition in general, since the law is very vague and gives the executive branch new powers.

6. The Problem of the Generality of the Gramsci-Mosca Convergence

At this point the following problem emerges. Granted that Gramsci and Mosca have advanced such similar analyses of Freemasonry and of the Fascist law, how common were such analyses at that time?[72] Did the two legislators express principles, interpretations, and ideas which at that time were in the minds of all or at least many? If so, then the similarities we have elaborated would lose much of their importance.

I would say that the similarities are so many and of such a kind as to render the convergence of ideas rare and significant in the historical context; Mosca's and Gramsci's analyses seem to me rather original. However, this is an intuition or judgment. Two kinds of documents can be examined to test it: one consists of the other parliamentary speeches on the Fascist bill, the other consists of the other replies to the survey on Freemasonry done by *L'Idea nazionale* in 1913.

In regard to the parliamentary debate, it should be mentioned that very few speeches were made opposing or questioning the bill; hence, the common opposition of Gramsci and Mosca is already an unusual circumstance. However, for logical-theoretical reasons analogous to those mentioned earlier, it could happen that different conclusions are partially based on common premises. Thus it is desirable to make a concrete examination.

A good example is the favorable speech by a deputy named Egilberto Martire, which immediately preceded Gramsci's and to which the latter refers.[73] Martire claimed that the bill was an indication of the maturity of the Italian nation, of the fact that the country no longer needed "parasitic" sects like Freemasonry. He rejects the comparison made by another deputy (named Rocca) between Freemasons and Jesuits, and clarifies that Jesuits wear a uniform and are named in a publicly accessible list of members, whereas Freemasons practice deception in a systematic manner. Martire concludes his speech by saying that the fundamental agreement against Freemasonry should not be upset by objections pertaining to matters of detail or wording. As we have seen, this final plea was not accepted by Mosca, who objected precisely over questions of detail. Another legislator who did not favor the bill, for similar reasons, was Senator Benedetto Croce.

Croce felt it necessary to speak in order to justify his abstention. In his very brief speech, Croce recalls that he has always been a critic of Freemasonry because of the harm done to the intellect and to culture by its simplistic, superficial, and outdated doctrines (a judgment similar to Mosca's) and because of the harm caused to civil society by its secrecy. However, he does not approve of the anti-liberal context of the Fascist proposal and so does not want to vote with the government.[74] He thinks that an abstention will enable him to express both his agreement with the anti-Masonic struggle and his disagreement with the Fascist government.

Let us now examine the 1913 survey. Let us recall that L'Idea nazionale asked three questions: whether Masonic secrecy was compatible with modern life, whether Masonic doctrines corresponded to the liveliest contemporary thinking, and whether Masonic infiltration of the public administration was harming the country. The questions were addressed to almost all of the most authoritative persons in the various sectors of Italian society: culture, academia, politics, the armed forces, religion, economy, art, and the literary establishment.

The results were later published in a book[75] which contains more than two hundred replies, some consisting of just a few words, others (like Mosca's) containing an elaboration. Almost everyone answered No to the first question, No to the second, and Yes to the third.[76] Among those who elaborated on their answers were Giovanni Amendola, Ivanoe Bonomi, Luigi Cadorna, Luigi Capuana, Benedetto Croce, Luigi Einaudi, Giovanni Gentile, Giuseppe Lombardo Radice, Achille Loria, Mario Missiroli, Vilfredo Pareto, Bernardino Varisco, Giovanni Verga, Pasquale Villari, and Nicola Zingarelli.

With one exception, none of their answers contain traces of an analytically elitist interpretation of Freemasonry or other important similarities with the Moschian-Gramscian analysis. The exception is Pareto, whose essay thus deserves a detailed examination. However, besides such traces, his essay contains interesting traces of many other different things, such as skepticism, relativism, positivism, and evasiveness.

Pareto begins his essay with the clarification that he is not a Freemason and hence has no direct knowledge of Masonic activities and doctrines; his only information is of the sort available to an outsider.

In his answer to the first question he points out that many associations are de facto secret, although not formally so, and that such associations have always existed and continue to flourish. He mentions, for example, various associations of industrialists aimed at gaining tariff protections, groups of politicians, and what he calls university gangs.[77] He judges such associations to be partly harmful and partly beneficial. He concludes: "Thus, I feel the issue to resolve is the comparison of Freemasonry with many other associations. I do not have sufficient data to resolve it."[78]

In his answer to the second question, Pareto maintains that the materialistic, humanitarian, and internationalist rationalism of the Freemasons is not as widespread as it once was. In fact, history shows an oscillation between such points of view, and he thinks that at that moment the pendulum is beginning to move in the opposite direction. With characteristic and emblematic language, he concludes: "It seems very probable that when an oscillation arrives at an extreme limit, there is harm. With a probability which is still great, but smaller that the preceding one, I believe that to be the case for the materialistic-humanitarian oscillation of last century."[79]

In his answer to the third question he claims that the advisability of abolishing Freemasonry depends on whether it will be replaced by other, similar organizations. If the replacement takes place, then the problem reduces to the first one of relative comparison. He then repeats, with illustrations, that all associations do sometimes good and sometimes evil. One example he gives is that of unions of state employees. These organizations would appear prima facie to be harmful; however, in a context (such as the Italian one) where the state is plagued with parliamentarism,[80] they provide a beneficial force to counterbalance the injustices committed by politicians.

Pareto ends his answer with a favorable evaluation of the anti-Masonic campaign of the nationalists in 1913 and gives the following justification: this campaign "has the precise effect of guiding the pendulum from one extremity to another position, which, owing to its being less extreme, can almost certainly be regarded as more useful."[81] Then he apologizes for his evasive tone by saying: "My answers will seem to be primarily expressions of doubts; but this fault will be excused by those who know how complex and difficult to understand social phenomena are." [82]

Are there any similarities between Pareto's remarks and Gramsci's and Mosca's accounts? The most striking characteristic of Pareto's remarks seems to be a version of positivism or scientism, which can be detected in the passages I have quoted, especially in such locutions as "I do not have sufficient data," "with a probability which is still great, but smaller than the preceding one," and "those who know how complex and difficult to understand social phenomena are." This feature has no counterpart in either Gramsci of Mosca.

Also striking is the formulation and the application of Pareto's principle of the oscillation of tendencies and of the advisability of avoiding extremes and excessive positions. This, of course, is reminiscent of Mosca's balanced pluralism, and it would be interesting to explore more extensively the connection between Mosca and Pareto in regard to this principle.

Moreover, one cannot deny the presence of a realistic approach. This is revealed by Pareto's interest in stressing whether a given association is de facto secret, rather than formally secret; the comparison of Freemasonry to other de facto secret associations is, thus, an indication of realism.

Furthermore, I would say there is an elitist tone in the analysis of the Masonic Order as comparable to such other associations as those of industrialists, politicians, and laborers. To be sure, we do not find an explicit interpretation of the order as an organization (indeed a political party) which has played an effective leadership role in Italian history; however, indirectly this is the interpretation, since it is being compared to other organizations which play such roles.

Finally, Pareto's evaluation of Freemasonry is also partially positive, although his justification is different from both Gramsci's and Mosca's: Pareto maintains in part that there are empirical instances of benefits; moreover, given the human condition, in which no association is completely beneficial, he also claims that often the only choices are between the greater and the lesser evil, after one tendency has been counterbalanced against another.

The result of our test is that analysis along the lines of Gramsci's and Mosca's is neither idiosyncratically original nor widespread. [83] It overlaps with Pareto's view. I am not sure to what extent these three figures belong to a single tradition of thought or research. I know that in this regard some would speak of an "elitist school." I would hesitate to use this label because I prefer to focus on the "democratic-elitist" school and I am not sure whether Pareto can be fitted into it.[84] However, there is no question that the tradition of democratic elitism deserves further articulation, and that part of such an inquiry would be to determine whether other thinkers like Pareto belong to it. In this book I have been concerned with exploring only Gramsci's and Mosca's democratic elitism.

7. Epilogue

This chapter has examined the case of the opposition which both Gramsci and Mosca expressed against the Fascist anti-Masonic bill in their respective speeches in Parliament in 1925. Gramsci's speech is rather anomalous and strikes the reader as somewhat incoherent, but it is possible though not easy to reconstruct his line of reasoning. Mosca's speech is per se very brief, but it must be considered together with a brief essay on Freemasonry, written in 1913. The similarities between the two speeches have to do with methodological procedure, theoretical principle, historical interpretation, and evaluative judgment. These similarities are historically significant because they were not often shared at the time, and they are interesting and important in regard to this particular episode involving Freemasonry and Fascism. Moreover, the quantity and quality of these ties are extremely suggestive for the whole question of the Gramsci-Mosca connection.

The convergences between Mosca and Gramsci are as follows. First, both follow a realist or antiformalist approach in the analysis of social and political phenomena—that is, they stress effective reality vis-à-vis both utopian ideals and superficial appearances. Second, both accept the fundamental elitist principle, according to which political leadership by organized minorities is indispensable for the masses and for majorities; however neither Mosca nor Gramsci is thereby necessarily favoring the role of minorities in an illegitimate manner. Third, the Freemasons are interpreted as an effective political organization which has played and continues to play an important role in Italian history. Fourth, both give a partially favorable evaluation of Freemasonry, because of its progressive and democratic contribution, according to Gramsci, and as a moderating and conservative force, according to Mosca. Fifth, they pose a common objection to the Fascist bill insofar as both predict that the new law will be used

by the Fascist government to replace with Fascists officials and employees who are or have been Freemasons. Sixth, both object also, on the basis
of the prediction, that the Fascists will abuse the new law—in Gramsci's
eyes specifically in order to persecute proletarian organizations, and in
Mosca's to destroy the right of free association among dissidents.

Seventh, as a consequence of these convergences, Mosca's and Gramsci's respective arguments against the proposed law coincide in some
essential points and thus can both be reduced to the following: the bill is
unacceptable for two reasons; first, the new law would enable the Fascist
government to replace with Fascists the state administrative personnel,
since historically Freemasons have been the best organized political force
in Italy; second, the new law would result in the persecution and sup-
pression of opponents because its wording does not define a precise limit
to the right of association and gives the government excessive powers of
repression.

Last but not least, of course, both Gramsci and Mosca are, practically
speaking, on the same side, in parliamentary opposition to the bill.

CONCLUSION

BEYOND RIGHT AND LEFT

THE PRECEDING CHAPTERS suggest three main conclusions. In increasing order of generality and theoreticity, they are as follows. The most historical and specific thesis asserts that Gramsci's political theory is a critical elaboration or constructive critique of Mosca's. The intermediate conclusion involves the notions of democracy and elitism and makes the claim that there exists a tradition of thought which aims to combine these two apparently incompatible concepts; that this tradition has considerable viability; and that Mosca's and Gramsci's political theories belong to this tradition. The most general thesis pertains to the concepts of political Left and Right; it holds that this distinction is relatively unimportant and that Mosca's and Gramsci's democratic elitism helps us to see its unimportance.

1. The Argument for the Gramsci-Mosca Connection

A recapitulation of the preceding chapters will make clear how the Gramsci-Mosca connection adumbrated in Chapter 1 has been documented and substantiated. Chapter 2 contains an interpretation and an evaluation of Mosca's political philosophy. It begins with an examination of the principle which Mosca regarded as a universally true generalization capable of providing the key foundational law of political science: that in every society political power is not equally distributed but rather concentrated in the hands of elites which rule over the masses. It then offers an evaluation of this fundamental principle from the point of view of theoretical fruitfulness and predictive power and suggests that the principle has considerable scientific and methodological merit, when judged according to these criteria. Next, a number of objections to Mosca's law are discussed, raising such issues as whether it has any empirical content, whether it is empirically accurate, whether it is normatively desirable, whether it is causally explicable, whether it will be forever valid, whether it is essentially a myth, whether it is sufficiently free of ideological or class bias, and whether the concept of elite is sufficiently clear; the main result here is that Mosca's law needs to be understood and evaluated in the context of other analytical and normative principles which make up his theoretical system. These are his conception of democracy in terms of open elites, his conception of liberty in terms of authority flowing from the bottom up, his distinction between feudalistic and bureaucratic tendencies, his ideal of mixed government, his ideal of the separation of powers, his ideal of governmental checks and balances, his ideal of the balance of different social forces, his counterrevolutionary principle, and his ideal of meritocracy; the systemic thrust of this cluster of principles can be appreciated by relating them to the basic principle of balanced pluralism. The chapter ends with a discussion of the tension between Mosca's fundamental elitist principle and his principle of balanced pluralism.

Chapter 3 provides a systematic examination of Gramsci's explicit critiques of Mosca, found in the Prison Notebooks. It discusses a group of charges impugning Mosca's scientific objectivity, philosophical sophistication, and historical awareness; another group suggesting the replacement or supplementation of various parts of Mosca's system by Gramsci's own ideas on relations of force, on intellectuals, and on the importance of the political party; and a third cluster taxing Mosca with political irresponsibility, extremism, and a legalist approach. I argue that such criticisms are partly methodological and partly substantive; that the methodological objections are largely incorrect and thus reveal significant methodological similarities between the two; and that the substantive criticisms can be seen as interesting and viable developments of the Moschian research program. The ironical result is that Gramsci's critique of Mosca shows how both their political theories are committed to normative evaluation as well as analytical description, to the importance of philosophical and historical sophistication, to balanced pluralism, to moderation, to antilegalist realism, and to the fundamental elitist principle.

Chapter 4 carries out a systematic examination of a series of related and relevant passages in the Prison Notebooks with the aim of determining both the character of Gramsci's elitism as a theoretical orientation in political theory and its historical relation to Mosca's. It emerges that, like Mosca, Gramsci also adopts the fundamental elitist principle as the most basic principle in the scientific study of politics. However, in many ways, Gramsci's elitist disposition goes deeper than Mosca's. For example, Gramsci extends the scope of the elitist distinction to cover relationships of moral, intellectual, and civil leadership besides those of governmental, military, and political domination. And it goes deeper insofar as he formulates and applies a number of corollary principles which seem to have little or no counterpart in Mosca: for example, the principle that the responsibility of groups of leaders (especially for failures) is primary, vis-à-vis the responsibility of both the masses and of an individual supreme head or commander. Few topics reveal Gramsci's elitism as clearly and authentically as the topic of the history of subaltern classes; when we examine the methodological criteria he advances in describing his approach to the topic, we find him saying that to study the history of subaltern classes, one must also study the history of elites, so that the real focus becomes the interrelationship between elites and masses. Finally, a recognition of Gramsci's commitment to elitism emerges reinforced from an examination of the apparent counterevidence, consisting of his remarks on the ethical state, the regulated society, and the absorption of political by civil society; one reason is that his own extension of Mosca's elitism implies the ubiquity of the elitist distinction, and thus its presence even under those conditions; another is that Gramsci's realism ends up reasserting itself and leads him to reject certain parts or aspects of those conditions as utopian.

In Chapter 5 a systematic examination is carried out of Gramsci's remarks on democracy in the Notebooks. The first point to emerge is that Gramsci claims clearly and explicitly that the most realistic and concrete definition is that democracy is a relationship between elites and masses such that the elites are open to renewal through the influx of elements from the masses; though Gramsci does not mention Mosca, the Moschian origin and character of the definition is unmistakable. The other relevant passages are those embodying the Gramscian notions of national-popular literature, democratic philosophy, and democratic centralism (namely, democratic administration or management). In each case, Gramsci advocates mutual contact, interaction, and exchange between the leaders and the led, whether the leaders be philosophers, writers, or administrators, and whether the led be laymen, readers, or rank-and-file subordinates in a hierarchy or bureaucracy. These claims by Gramsci are shown to involve an application of the Moschian conception of democracy, insofar as the connections between leaders and led are instances of democracy as defined by Mosca. In the course of the discussion, I analyze Gramsci's critique of alternative theories of democracy, especially the egalitarian one, so that the elitist character of Gramsci's democracy acquires reinforcement. This chapter ends with a resolution of an apparent contradiction: that Gramsci also has a notion of transformism such that both democracy and transformism seem to refer to the transition of individuals from the ruled to the ruling class, yet he seems to approve democracy but disapprove transformism.

Chapter 6 is a critical examination of the Gramscian and Moschian notions of liberty and liberalism, in regard to which it must be first pointed out that there are several notions of liberty and liberalism which both thinkers use. Both have a significant appreciation of liberty in the sense of civil liberties, and while this is relatively easy to see in Mosca, Gramsci's position on the subject has been usually overlooked. I also show that Gramsci has a concept of liberty in the peculiar Moschian anti-autocratic sense of authority flowing from the bottom up. Gramsci also advances a critique of a type of liberalism that he usually attributes to Benedetto Croce, but the liberalism which is the target of this criticism turns out to be what could more properly be called *undemocratic* elitism. In regard to laissez-faire liberalism in economic affairs, the important fact to remember is that Gramsci's criticism is advanced in the context of a simultaneous criticism of statism, and that Mosca expresses surprisingly similar reflections. This chapter ends with the statement and resolution of three difficulties stemming from some key claims of Gramsci which do not seem to fit the previous analysis: one in which he seems to reject pluralistic liberalism; another in which he seems to prefer liberalism to syndicalism; and a third in which he seems to compare the Communist Party to God and the categorical imperative.

Chapter 7 examines what is probably the most curious, emblematic, and provocative example of Mosca and Gramsci's political convergence. The particular material examined consists of the speeches they made in Parliament in 1925 opposing the Fascist bill against Freemasonry, a bill which was, however, overwhelmingly approved. Besides their identical practical stance in opposition, the similarities between the two speeches are these: both thinkers practice a realistic method of analysis and accept the fundamental principle of analytical elitism; both interpret Freemasonry as an effective and important political force and give a partly positive evaluation of it; and both predict that the anti-Masonic law would enable the Fascists to get rid of a largely Masonic civil service and to persecute dissenters.

In light of this documentation and evidence, the political-theoretical connection between Gramsci and Mosca which was advanced as a working hypothesis in Chapter 1 must be regarded as firmly established. However, it may be useful to repeat here some of the caveats mentioned there. One is that this thesis applies to only a part of Gramsci's thought, his political theory, as distinct from his philosophical doctrines and his historical interpretations. Another limitation is that the thesis is not meant to apply in an exclusive and one-sided manner, and so I am not denying that Gramsci's political theory originates in part also from the ideas of such thinkers as Marx, Lenin, Croce, Gentile, and Machiavelli. Similarly, the thesis is not meant to deny that Gramsci's political theory originates to some degree in his political practice as a syndicalist and party leader and organizer. Finally, another clarification needs to be reiterated and elaborated; it is the most important one and will lead to a more general and theoretical implication of the present study.

2. The Tradition of Democratic Elitism

As stated, the argument advanced here leaves little doubt that Gramsci's political theory is a critical elaboration or constructive critique of Mosca's. Now, because Mosca's political theory is traditionally interpreted as right-wing, some will draw the further conclusion that my interpretation advances a right-wing interpretation of Gramsci. However, such a further conclusion would be unjustified, in part because of difficulties with the distinction between right and left, as I will discuss in the next section. Moreover, this conclusion would be a misunderstanding, since it is clear that, although I view Gramsci's ideas in the context of Mosca's, I have also articulated a reinterpretation of Mosca. Therefore, the more correct lesson to draw is that I have shown that Gramsci and Mosca belong to the same tradition of political theory.

What is this tradition? The tradition in question is that of democratic elitism. By elitism here I mean a theoretical orientation which takes the most fundamental principle to be the distinction between elites and masses (or rulers and ruled, or leaders and led) and undertakes to interpret all political phenomena in terms of various relationships between the two groups. By democracy, I mean the special relationship between elites and masses such that elites are open to renewal through the influx of elements from the masses; this definition offered by Mosca forms the basis for an original and distinctive theory of democracy. The democratic elitism of Mosca and Gramsci also includes a conception of political liberty as a relationship such that authority flows from the masses to the elites; this second definition is a feature of their approach which can also be called democratic in the ordinary sense of the term, though not in the technical Moschian sense.

In speaking of a "tradition" of democratic elitism, I am suggesting that Mosca and Gramsci are neither the first nor the last thinkers with such a theoretical orientation. Indeed, it would be fruitful to elaborate such a tradition further both through more conceptual analysis and more historical reconstructions. It is obvious that in doing so, one should not be misled by words and labels, so that one would have to find democratic elitism (as I have defined it) among authors and concepts that may not be explicitly associated with such a label. Indeed, we have seen that Mosca himself did not use this particular label to describe his system.

For example, my hunch is that, historically speaking, we could insert into the tradition of democratic elitism the political theory of *The Federalist Papers,* especially the thought of James Madison. In fact, one of Madison's most fundamental principles is the famous claim that "the accumulation of all powers, legislative, executive, and judiciary, in the same hands, whether of one, a few, or many, and whether hereditary, self-appointed, or elective, may justly be pronounced the very definition of tyranny."[1] This clearly bears an uncanny resemblance to Mosca's principle of balanced pluralism: "The absolute preponderance of a single political force, the predominance of any over-simplified concept in the organization of a state, the strictly logical application of any single principle in all public law are the essential elements in any type of despotism, whether it be a despotism based upon divine right or a despotism based ostensibly on popular sovereignty."[2]

Conceptually and theoretically speaking, one of the most valuable elements of democratic elitism is that it problematizes the notion of democracy. It stresses the fact that there is a problem in regard to what democracy is; that we cannot uncritically equate democracy with something like majority rule. Of course, this is the kind of question raised and investigated in that field of study known as democratic theory. From this point of view, we can say that democratic elitism makes a distinctive contribution to democratic theory.

The elaboration of such details is beyond the scope of the present inquiry. However, I believe I can illustrate my key points by means of two examples, the problem of term limits and the democratic theory of Robert Dahl.

The question of term limits is one of the most controversial political issues in the United States today. The issue is whether a limit should be set on the number of times someone can be elected to and serve in a given office.

One argument against term limits is that they are undemocratic because they go against the will of the people, in the sense that at the end of the stipulated number of terms an official could not be re-elected even if the people so desired. This argument obviously presupposes a particular conception of democracy, which can be labeled populistic.[3] Once this presupposition is revealed, the focus of the discussion can shift to the nature of democracy.

The opponents of term limits are the only ones who have connected the issue with the concept of democracy. However, it is possible to formulate an argument in favor of term limits on the basis of a different conception. In fact, Mosca's definition of democracy seems tailor-made for the purpose, although he formulated it about a century ago in a very different context. As we have seen, according to Mosca, "The term 'democratic' seems more suitable for the tendency which aims to replenish the ruling class with elements deriving from the lower classes, and which is always at work, openly or latently and with greater or lesser intensity, in all political organisms."[4]

Starting from this definition, one could point out that term limits are one mechanism to enhance the degree of democracy in Mosca's sense because term limits make the class of government officials more open to the influx of citizens from the outside and decrease the insulation of those officials.

I am not sure that the application of Mosca's conception of democracy to the case of term limits would ultimately be an easy and uncontroversial matter. Here all I want to say is that it has an obvious prima facie application to the case in favor of term limits; a deeper analysis would be needed to determine whether this prima facie appearance corresponds to reality. However, in this regard the situation is similar to that of the application of the populistic conception to formulate the argument against term limits; there the prima facie implication is an obvious initial objection to make, but then a more careful exploration could yield different results. Nevertheless, the problem of term limits brings home that perhaps democracy depends not only on the will of the people but also on such factors as the openness of the ruling classes; and the latter idea involves the democratic elitism of thinkers such as Mosca.

Now, since the field known as democratic theory has been systematically investigating the nature of democracy for at least fifty years, let us examine it by reference to the work of someone who can be regarded as a founder of this field as well as the dean of democratic theorists, Robert Dahl.

Dahl began his pioneering *Preface to Democratic Theory* with the following revealing definition: "Democratic theory is concerned with processes by which ordinary citizens exert a relatively high degree of control over leaders."[5] If we replace "ordinary citizens" with the word "masses," and "leaders" with "elites," we see that democratic theory concerns the interaction between elites and masses; and this formulation is essentially identical to Mosca's research program as I have interpreted it. Dahl himself implicitly admits this when he adds that his definition "can be easily translated into a variety of more or less equivalent statements, should the reader not care for the particular language I choose to use."[6]

Then Dahl undertakes a critical examination of the main available theories of democracy, primarily the Madisonian and the populistic conceptions. He proposes to accept their insights and avoid their errors. He also makes use of relevant available empirical data. A principal result of his investigation is the following claim: "Elections and political competitions do not make for government by majorities in any very significant way, but they vastly increase the size, number, and variety of minorities whose preferences must be taken into account by leaders in making policy choices. I am inclined to think it is in this characteristic of elections —not minority rule but minorities rule—that we must look for some of the essential differences between dictatorships and democracies."[7] This is an interesting and original formulation of the principle of minority rule. However, its Moschian and democratic-elitist character is unmistakable.[8]

In his latest and most mature work, *Democracy and Its Critics*, among many important insights, Dahl manages to provide a new elaboration of the Moschian theme of balanced pluralism. This happens despite the fact

that he interprets Mosca as a critic of democracy rather than as a democratic theorist; but this interpretation of Mosca need not be accepted. Let
us look at some details.

Dahl describes at least five attitudes toward democracy.[9] First, there
are the adversarial critics who hold that democracy is undesirable; examples would be anarchists, and proponents, like Plato, of some form
of guardianship. Second, there are the adversarial critics who hold that
democracy is impossible; Dahl labels his main cluster of examples theories of minority domination, and he mentions Mosca, Michels, and Pareto. Third, there are the sympathetic critics, of whom Dahl does not
explicitly give any example; he defines them generally as "those sympathetic to democracy and wishing to maintain it but nonetheless critical of
it in some important respect";[10] from other parts of Dahl's work one can
gather that Tocqueville might be an instance.

Dahl also speaks (fourth) of "uncritical advocates" of democracy,
namely those who favor democracy but make a number of assumptions
which they are unwilling to explore or perhaps even to acknowledge.
Dahl does not give any examples, but I would assign to that category
most people who oppose term limits on democratic grounds.

Finally, Dahl goes on to elaborate a fifth methodological ideal type,
namely democratic theorists. They seek to understand what democracy
is; how it relates to such other concepts as equality, liberty, participation, autonomy, and self-government; how it relates to institutions such
as representative government, universal suffrage, and majority rule; how
it relates to historical and empirical conditions, such as those that characterize modern, dynamic, pluralist societies; and what the good and the
bad aspects, the advantages and the disadvantages of these things are. It is
important to stress that Dahl's conception of democratic theory is such
as to include not only description, analysis, and interpretation, but also
prescription, norms, and evaluation, and not only favorable and positive
evaluation but also unfavorable and negative criticism. In short, for Dahl,
theorizing includes conceptual analysis, empirical investigation, and normative evaluation. By and large, I would regard Dahl's own work as an
outstanding example of democratic theory in this sense.

For completeness' sake, one might mention (although Dahl does not)
a sixth category, namely that of critical advocate; this would be someone
who favors democracy and is aware that he is presupposing a particular
conception of democracy, that there are alternate meanings, that his own

theory (while it may be the most tenable) is not self-evident but needs elaboration and justification, and that the alternative theories (while they may be less adequate that his) are not absurd and worthless.

I do not wish to magnify the importance of such classifications, but they are useful in formulating and criticizing Dahl's interpretation of Mosca. I claim that Mosca was a theorist of democracy and not an adversarial critic, in Dahl's sense of these terms. However, since Dahl claims that Mosca was an adversarial critic, I have to reject Dahl's interpretation of Mosca. There are two main difficulties with Dahl's account of Mosca: he offers a questionable interpretation of Mosca's principle of minority rule, and he takes it out of context.

The first difficulty is that Dahl prejudices the issue by speaking of minority *domination* rather than *rule*.[11] Moreover, to make the idea of minority rule yield a criticism of democracy, one must assume a democratic theory which Mosca rejects. That is, the principle of minority rule yields for Mosca, as it did in Dahl's earlier work, either an *interpretation* of democracy or a criticism of *majority rule*, not a criticism of democracy.

As we have seen, "minority rule" is a way of formulating one of Mosca's two most fundamental principles. It can be summarized by saying that in all societies organized minorities rule over disorganized majorities. Consequently, what distinguishes one political system from another is the nature, structure, and origin of the ruling classes (elites) and their relationship with the ruled classes (masses). Insofar as the word "domination" connotes arbitrary or dictatorial rule without the consent of the governed, it is important to note that for Mosca not all *rule* by minorities is *domination* by minorities.

However, here someone might interject that, even if we allow for different kinds of minority *rule*, the principle of minority rule still implies that there is no such thing as democracy. Obviously, for this implication to hold, one must define democracy in terms of majority *rule*. In his interpretation of Mosca, Dahl is thinking of this definition, and that is why he thinks that the principle of minority *rule* makes democracy impossible. However, for someone like Mosca (and the earlier Dahl), who is not committed to the majoritarian definition, a different conclusion follows. For him, the principle of minority rule implies (as a special case) that even representative systems with universal suffrage have minority rule. Then, equating democracies and representative systems with universal suffrage, one could conclude that even democracies have minority rule. The further consequence to draw from this is that the majoritarian theory of democracy is incorrect. This is a criticism of a particular *theory* of democracy, not of *democracy* per se.

Mosca was aware of this logic of the situation. He explicitly clarified it on at least two occasions. After the publication of his first essay advancing his formal definition of democracy, he was interviewed by a journalist. In the exchange he pointed out: "My theory of political forces undoubtedly implies a condemnation of theorists of democracy, since it shows that a majority government is really and properly impossible, and that there will always be political minorities confronting apolitical majorities. However, to say that the abstract theory of democracy is wrong does not mean that the practice of democracy is completely wrong. In practice, democracy has substituted a method of selecting the political class for another method of selection; and one cannot say that the substitution has been bad, especially whenever the new criterion is not applied in a manner which is too exclusive and uniform but is supplemented by others."[12] This is a criticism of the majoritarian theory of democracy combined with an endorsement of democratic practice, as well as a qualification of the endorsement. This qualification is a cryptic reference to the principle of balanced pluralism.

The second occasion was in 1912, when Mosca[13] published a long and favorable review of Robert Michels's book on *The Sociology of the Political Party*. There Mosca begins by explaining that Michels follows the same approach as Mosca. However, he objects to the label "anti-democratic." He says that it would be more proper to call their approach the *a-democratic* school. This clarification stresses that the principle of minority rule is not really a normative principle, which would directly imply some thesis about the undesirability of democratic majority rule. Someone like Mosca who believes that majority rule is impossible does not even bother to argue explicitly that it is undesirable.

This point provides another reason Mosca's principle of minority rule does not constitute adversarial criticism: it is not criticism of democratic practice at all, because it is not a normative evaluation at all; it is rather an interpretation of democratic practice. As we have seen, it *is* a criticism of the majoritarian theory of democracy. In short, we might say that with regard to democracy per se, namely democratic practice, Mosca's principle is not adversarial criticism because it is neither adversarial nor critical; rather, it is neutral and interpretive.

Finally, the key parallel between Dahl and Mosca has to do with the structure of the main argument in Dahl's latest theory. First, Dahl formulates a definition of democratic process: a process of decision making in an organization is democratic insofar as (1) all adult members have adequate and equal opportunity for (2) effective participation by (3) controlling the agenda and by (4) voting based on (5) enlightened understanding. These five criteria are meant to be individually necessary and jointly sufficient conditions for democracy.[14]

Then Dahl clarifies that democracy so defined is an ideal which can only be approximated to a greater or lesser extent by existing systems. The word that he uses to describe actually existing systems is "polyarchy." The numbers of such polyarchies have increased in recent times. Dozens of them exist now, and they have the following seven features in common: elected officials, free and fair elections, inclusive suffrage, right to run for office, freedom of expression, alternative sources of information, and right of association.[15]

Part of Dahl's democratic theory involves the exploration of the relation between empirically real polyarchies and the abstractly defined democratic process.[16] For example, for each of the seven identifying characteristics of polyarchies, one can ask to which of the five necessary conditions for democracy it corresponds. Some relationships are obvious, some are not so obvious.

Another part of Dahl's theory consists of further analysis of polyarchies to explore such questions as how and why polyarchies developed in some times and places and not in others.[17] To a large extent this involves studying what empirical variables are correlated with polyarchal political institutions. Dahl finds that the most important of these are what he calls modernity, dynamism, and pluralism.[18] By pluralism, Dahl here means the existence of many autonomous organizations, especially in the economic sphere. He also finds these three sufficiently correlated with one another that he coins the acronym "MDP" to talk about societies that are modern, dynamic, and pluralistic. He is clear that "polyarchal" and "MDP" do not mean the same thing and that, strictly speaking, MDP is neither a sufficient nor a necessary condition for polyarchy. However, he is equally clear that there is a high empirical correlation between the two, and that this correlation is no accident but rather is based on a good reason. In Dahl's own words: "What is crucial about an MDP society is that on the one hand it inhibits the concentration of power in any single unified set of actors, and on the other hand it disperses power among a number of relatively independent actors."[19]

This explanation brings us back to Mosca, although to Mosca as interpreted by me in this work rather than as interpreted by Dahl. I believe this key line of reasoning in Dahl is in effect a powerful new argument in support of Mosca's fundamental principle of balanced pluralism. For what Dahl does in essence is first to assume that democracy is equivalent to polyarchy, then to correlate polyarchy with MDP, and finally to reduce MDP to balanced pluralism in the Moschian sense. Albeit indirectly and unwittingly, Dahl has shown that Mosca's balanced pluralism is the key feature of democracy.

3. The Distinction Between Right and Left

As already stated, the preceding investigation leaves little doubt that Gramsci's political theory is a critical elaboration or constructive critique of Mosca's, and that their political theories belong to the tradition of democratic elitism. And I have already noted that, because Mosca's political theory is traditionally interpreted as right-wing, some will draw the further conclusion that my interpretation advances a right-wing interpretation of Gramsci. Others, however, starting with the interpretation that Gramsci's thought is left-wing, will draw the conclusion that I am advancing a left-wing interpretation of Mosca. Both conclusions would reveal a failure to appreciate that the Mosca in whose terms I have interpreted Gramsci is himself a reinterpreted Mosca, and that democracy and elitism are not necessarily opposites but that in one tradition of thought they are not only compatible but interdependent. Such a misunderstanding is probably the result of the dichotomy between right and left. Thus, it is important to discuss this underlying issue more directly. Is democratic elitism a rightist or a leftist view? And are Gramsci and Mosca, so interpreted, right-wingers or left-wingers?

I have already suggested in the Introduction that the left-right distinction is not an exhaustive one. I did this when I argued that, although Gramsci has been usually approached from the Left, and although lately he has also been approached from the Right, it is best to approach him from a classic point of view. In the classic view of Gramsci it is recognized that he can be approached from both the Left and the Right, but the further consequence is drawn that this twofold possibility implies that he is both partially a rightist and partially a leftist; this in turn means that he is neither totally a right-winger nor totally a left-winger. Thus, he is in a sense both, and in a sense neither. In short, the classic approach is one that transcends the usual distinction between right and left.

To say this is not equivalent to saying that the left-right distinction is meaningless, but rather that it is unimportant. In other words, the left-right distinction is a key part of a certain approach to political theory. If one does not subscribe to such an approach but develops an alternative one, then one's view will be beyond right and left. As stated, I have already implicitly suggested this in the Introduction, but now I want to discuss it more explicitly.

I should begin by pointing out that the "beyond right and left" approach is now itself part of a developing tradition of thought.[20] For example, Anthony Giddens has argued that the current geopolitical and sociohistorical scene shows that conservatives have turned radical and socialists have become conservatives; that the most important features of contemporary life are characterized by such things as globalization, the erosion of tradition, and manufactured uncertainty; that to deal with these conditions, we need to reconceptualize our social and political theory; that the ecological or "Green" movement or philosophy is a good example of an attempt to deal with new problems in a way that transcends right and left. Whatever shortcomings Giddens's view may contain,[21] I believe that the transcendent element is plausible and necessary, and I mention his view here only to substantiate the existence of a developing tradition beyond right and left.

Next, what I want to do is examine some attempts to reiterate the left-right distinction and how they affect my interpretation of Mosca and Gramsci as democratic elitists.

In a wide-ranging study, J. A. Laponce has argued that although the distinction between political Left and Right is relatively recent in human history (since it stems from the French Revolution), it has very deep roots in human nature and human evolution; that the terminology has now spread and been adopted throughout the world; and that the distinction is such that it refers to two contrasts, that between the sacred and the secular and that between hierarchy and equality. One of his main conclusions is that the right pertains to a favorable attitude toward the sacred and hierarchy, and the left pertains to a favorable attitude toward the secular and equality.[22]

Adapting some of his ideas, one could argue that, because of the psychobiological basis of the left-right distinction, we would expect that sooner or later the "left-right" terminology would have been applied to politics to refer to a significant distinction. For example, it is a well-established sociohistorical fact that the overwhelming majority of humans (about 90 percent) are right-handed. This probably stems, at least in part, from some process such as the following. Because the human heart is located at the left side of the chest, being right-handed became an advantage in hunting and battle as compared to being left-handed; the reason is that a right-handed person could use the right hand to hold a weapon and the left hand to shield the heart. During the millennia of human evolution, this asymmetry gave right-handed persons a survival advantage over left-handed ones. Thus, even if originally there had been an equal disposition to use the right and the left hands, eventually only people with a disposition toward right-handedness would remain.

Although we may agree with Laponce that such biological considerations are not decisive, we may also agree that they cannot be dismissed. At any rate, whatever the neurological or physical cause, right-handedness is the norm in human societies. From this, one can easily understand the emergence of the association between power and right, and between weakness and left. Then, in turn, from the contrast between power and weakness, one can easily understand the application to the relationship between man and God (yielding the contrast of sacred and secular), and between one person and another (yielding the contrast between hierarchy and equality).

For our purpose here, one main difficulty stems from the fact that the meaning of the left-right distinction is defined in terms of two dimensions, for there is no guarantee that the two will go together to form the pair hierarchy and the sacred on the one (right) "hand", and the pair equality and the secular on the other (the left). In this regard, Gramsci and Mosca are good examples of this difficulty. Although they are respectful of religion, both are clearly secular-minded thinkers; thus, in regard to this dimension, they should be labeled leftists. However, as we have seen, the fundamental elitist principle which they share involves a tendency to see hierarchy as unavoidable and egalitarianism as utopian; so, according to this dimension, they are "rightists." Thus, it would appear that by Laponce's definition, they are both rightists and leftists. Or to be more exact, both are right-wingers in one sense, and left-wingers in another.

Another main difficulty stems from the fact that, by Laponce's own admission, there is another distinction which is even more deeply rooted than the left-right one, namely the distinction between up and down. Just as the left-right asymmetry leads humans to view the world, including the domain of politics, in terms of a horizontal dimension, the up-down distinction leads us to classify both physical and social reality in terms of a vertical dimension. Now, it so happens that the contrast along the vertical axis is more fundamental than the contrast along the horizontal axis, because the vertical distinction stems not only from the physiological difference in the position of head and feet, but also from the purely physical conditions relating to the gravitational field at the surface of the earth. Therefore, by the same type of argument we would expect that the up-down distinction would prevail over the right-left one. Now, in this type of argument, the up-down distinction leads to such ideas as the distinction between elites and masses, between democracy and aristocracy, and between liberty and autocracy in Mosca's sense. Thus, that Mosca and Gramsci share such "vertical" concepts is more significant than whether they share a "horizontal" position of left or right. Therefore, it follows also that the concepts related to up and down are more important than those related to left and right.

Suppose we take a different, historical approach and trace the history of the political distinction between left and right, for example, along the lines suggested by Marcel Gauchet.[23] As is well known, that history now goes back two hundred years. From this point of view, certain individuals, groups, parties, and movements have been associated empirically with one side, and others with the other side. One need not formulate a generalization about what the entities on the left side have in common and what the common features of the things on the right side are. This is part of Laponce's exploration, and we have seen the results. Instead, now the aim would be to work at the level of purely historical and empirical connections.

As it applies to our case, we would then be led to focus on such matters as Gramsci's involvement with socialist politics in 1914–1918, with labor union activity in 1919–1920, and with the Italian Communist Party in 1921–1926; perhaps we could also focus on the Gramsci myth created and exploited by Togliatti, by the Italian Communist party, and by the geopolitical Left since World War II. In regard to Mosca, we would then be led to stress such things as his alleged antiparliamentarism, his opposition to universal suffrage, his connection with various Italian right-wing prime ministers and governments, and his involvement with the conservative Italian "Liberal" Party.

It is undeniable that such historical connections establish that in one sense Gramsci is an important example of the Left and Mosca an important example of the Right. In other words, there are prima facie reasons for assuming that Gramsci belongs to the Left and Mosca to the Right.

However, I have already admitted (for example, in Chapter 1) that this assumption is not a gratuitous one. Then the rest of my investigation may be regarded as an exploration of the intellectual and conceptual content of their political theories, and a demonstration that their political doctrines are both in the tradition of democratic elitism. In short, I have shown that, *if* Mosca if a rightist and Gramsci a leftist, *then* the left-right distinction is not a viable one. But this is just another way of expressing precisely what is claimed by the proponents of the idea of transcending both right and left.

Another, and perhaps the most eloquent defender of the left-right distinction, is Norberto Bobbio. In contrast to Laponce's sociological approach and Gauchet's historical one, Bobbio follows what can be called an analytical-conceptual approach. His recent booklet on the subject became a best-seller in Italy and generated wide discussion and controversy. Moreover, when he undertook his effort, he was aware of both Laponce's and Gauchet's works.

Bobbio argues convincingly that the language of left and right continues to be very common in political discourse, both among politicians and among political theorists, and so the concepts must have some meaning. Bobbio makes clear that to claim that the distinction is meaningless can only be regarded as an indirect way of expressing an idiosyncratic and untenable theory of meaning; in fact, these terms are meaningful if any are.

He then sees his task to be primarily that of determining what the meaning of the terms is. After a criticism of some alternative analyses, he arrives at his own. For Bobbio, the distinction between left and right involves the concepts of equality and inequality: at the descriptive level, the Left believes that human beings are more equal than unequal, whereas the Right believes that human beings are more unequal than equal;[24] and at the evaluative level, leftists believe that most social inequalities are not based on nature and should be eliminated, whereas rightists believe that most social inequalities are natural and cannot be eliminated.[25]

Bobbio's definition is a sophisticated one, insofar as it is advanced in the context of a distinction between what he calls the concept of equality or the egalitarian principle on the one hand and the ideal of egalitarianism or the egalitarianist principle on the other:

> The concept of equality is relative, not absolute. It is relative to at least three variables, which must be taken into account whenever we discuss

the greater or lesser desirability and/or the greater or lesser actualizability of the idea of equality: (a) the subjects among whom goods or burdens are to be distributed; (b) the goods or burdens to be distributed; and (c) the criterion on the basis of which they are to be distributed. . . . The subjects may be all, many, or a few individuals, or even a single individual; the goods to be distributed may be rights, economic advantages or assistance, positions of power; the criteria may be need, merit, ability, rank, effort, and others; at the limit, we could have the absence of any criterion, which characterizes the maximally egalitarian principle that I shall label egalitarianist, namely "the same thing to all."[26]

And again: "It is one thing to believe in an egalitarian doctrine or movement which tends to reduce social inequalities and to alleviate natural inequalities; it is another to believe in egalitarianism when it is understood as 'equality of all in everything.'"[27] Besides presupposing this distinction between equality and egalitarianism, Bobbio's definition of the distinction between left and right is based on the factual assumption that "men are both equal and unequal among themselves; they are equal in certain respects, and unequal in others."[28]

Given these two assumptions, Bobbio's definition makes clear that the distinction between left and right is a matter of degree: "When one says that the Left is egalitarian and the Right anti-egalitarian, one is not saying in the least that to be a leftist one must proclaim the principle that all men must be equal in everything, independently of any criterion, because this would be not only a utopian vision . . . but, worse, a mere declaration of intention to which it is impossible to assign a reasonable meaning."[29] And "when one attributes to the Left a greater commitment to diminish inequalities, one is not saying that it tries to eliminate all inequalities and that the Right wants to retain them all, but at most that the former is more egalitarian and the latter less so."[30]

Bobbio's distinction is clear, plausible, and sophisticated. However, this clarity, plausibility, and sophistication are achieved at great cost. His definition implies that the difference between left and right is no longer a matter of principle. In that sense, such a difference is relatively unimportant.

In particular, in regard to Gramsci and Mosca, I am not sure that Gramsci would turn out to be a leftist by Bobbio's definition. For I am not sure it is correct to attribute to Gramsci a disposition to exalt human equalities more than inequalities. Instead his ideal seems to have been to foster an appreciation of both, as is apparent from our discussion in Chapters 4, 5, and 6. More simply and emblematically, his appreciation of both can be seen from his remark that "the most delicate, misunderstood, and yet essential endowment of the critic of ideas and of the historian of historical developments is to find the real identity underlying the apparent differentiation and contradiction, and to find the substantial diversity underlying the apparent diversity." [31]

In any case, even if there is a difference of degree between Gramsci and Mosca in regard to their sensitivity to equalities and inequalities, it is unclear that it would be a more important difference between them than the fact they both reject utopian egalitarianism. For, as we saw in Chapters 4 and 5, they are critical of what Bobbio here calls the egalitarianist principle.

It should be mentioned that Bobbio's distinction between left and right in terms of more or less equality is also made in the context of two other important distinctions which crisscross it and are not reducible to it. One is the distinction between extremism and moderatism. [32] For Bobbio, extremists tend to be antidemocratic and anti-enlightenment, and favorably inclined toward discontinuity, revolution, and the martial and heroic virtues; whereas moderates tend to be favorably inclined toward democracy, enlightenment, prudence, tolerance, mediation, and compromise. And he makes clear that there are both left-wing and right-wing extremists, as well as left-wing moderates and right-wing moderates.

Exploiting Bobbio's explicit distinction between extremism and moderatism, we can say that his other explicit definition of the distinction between left and right regards both leftists and rightists as moderates by definition. However, there is no good reason to do this, and it would seem more proper to allow four possibilities: extreme egalitarianism, extreme anti-egalitarianism, moderate egalitarianism, and moderate anti-egalitarianism. Once we allow these four possibilities, we can say that Bobbio is equating the Left with moderate egalitarianism and the Right with moderate anti-egalitarianism. Then another way of formulating the above-mentioned difficulty is to say that it is not obvious that what divides the Left and the Right so defined (degrees of egalitarianism) is more important than what unites them (moderatism).

The other distinction Bobbio makes is between liberty and authority. Here, the logic of his position is to combine this pair of opposites with the opposition between equality and inequality to yield four possible systems and points of view, and he does mention them explicitly: egalitarian and authoritarian; egalitarian and libertarian; anti-egalitarian and libertarian; and anti-egalitarian and authoritarian. However, in discussing and illustrating these possibilities, Bobbio ends up conflating the four combinations of pairs with the distinction between extremism and moderatism. He thus labels the first of these combinations as left-wing extremism, the second as center left, the third as center right, and the fourth as right-wing extremism.[33] This conflation is unjustified, and we should really have eight possibilities, since it is obvious that one's commitment to liberty may be moderate or extreme, just as is the case with the commitment to equality.

Finally, Bobbio is clear about the relationship between equality and liberty but fails to exploit it to formulate a more principled definition of the distinction between left and right than the one he gives. He makes it clear that in some situations equality and liberty are compatible, in others they are incompatible, and in still others the problem is to balance the requirements of the two ideals. In cases of conflict between equality and liberty, one is faced with the choice of whether to attach more importance to the one or to the other. I believe it might be fruitful to define the Left in terms of a tendency to give priority to equality over liberty, and the Right in terms of giving priority to liberty over equality.

If so defined, the difference between right and left would be a difference of principle, and not merely a matter of degree. However, I am not sure that a such difference would really be fundamental. For on the one hand, when this distinction is applied to Mosca and Gramsci, it is probably true that in cases of conflict between the ideals of equality and liberty, Gramsci tends to show a preference for equality, and Mosca for liberty. In this modest sense and to this limited extent, Gramsci would be a leftist and Mosca a rightist. On the other hand, given Bobbio's own conceptual framework adopted here, we would have to say that the preceding chapters have shown that the democratic elitism of Mosca and Gramsci conforms to moderatism and not to extremism, and that by contrast to extreme egalitarianism, they are both moderate anti-egalitarians. Moreover, we could now add that by contrast to extreme anti-egalitarianism, they are both moderate egalitarians; and that in regard to the dimension of liberty versus authority, they are also moderates and centrists. Therefore, their left-right difference, while real, would be a minor one because it would subsist in the context of their more fundamental agreement over moderatism, balanced pluralism, and democratic elitism.

My conclusion remains that the distinction between political left and right is neither meaningless nor fictional, but that insofar as it makes sense and is real, it is relatively minor and unimportant. Or at least it is so from the point of view of that distinctive tradition which I have called democratic elitism.

APPENDIX

CONCORDANCE OF THE CRITICAL EDITION AND ENGLISH TRANSLATIONS

All of my quotations from Gramsci's writings have been taken from the original Italian and translated into English by me. This was a natural procedure to follow, given that my aim was to develop my own interpretation of his thought, and given that no complete translation of his works (or even of the Notebooks) exists in English. However, there do exist several English translations of various selections from the Notebooks; although their scope varies greatly, they all have some usefulness.

Therefore, to facilitate the consultation of Gramsci's text for readers with no access to the original Italian, I·have compiled the following table, which gives the location in the critical edition (*Quaderni del carcere,* Gramsci 1975b) of all passages from the Notebooks in these volumes of translations. I have listed the pages of the critical edition first, so that when the readers want to consult the passages from which my quotations are taken, they can easily look up the number and get the corresponding page for the English. There is some overlap among these volumes of translations, and so I have included references to Gramsci (1957) and to Gramsci (1988a) only for passages not translated elsewhere; this explains why the table includes so few references to them. No specific correspondences are given for Gramsci (1992b) and Gramsci (1996b), because they are complete translations of Notebooks 1-2 and 3-5, respectively, and so the page correspondences are easily ascertained; nevertheless, the collective correspondences for these volumes is given for completeness' sake.

Note that the frequent gaps in the pagination from the critical edition indicate that many passages are not included in the available translations. Some pages of these translations have no Italian counterpart because they contain commentary by the translators and editors. Note also that the correspondence is precise only to the extent of indicating which Gramscian note in the original corresponds to which page(s) in translation; for notes of less than one page, this approximation makes no difference; however, for longer notes the reader will need to do additional work to find the exact passage. Finally, the titles of the volumes of translations, have been abbreviated, respectively, as follows:

MP   *The Modern Prince and Other Writings* (Gramsci 1957)
PN   *Selections from the Prison Notebooks* (Gramsci 1971b)
CW   *Selections from Cultural Writings* (Gramsci 1985)
GR   *An Antonio Gramsci Reader* (Gramsci 1988a)
CEI   *Prison Notebooks*, vol. 1 (Gramsci 1992b)
FS   *Further Selections from the Prison Notebooks* (Gramsci 1995)
CEII   *Prison Notebooks*, vol. 2 (Gramsci 1996b)

Quaderni	Translations
5–280	CEI99–361
281–682	CEII5–402
12–13	FS148–50
26 (no. 34)	FS258 (no. 48)
56–57	PN259–60
65–66	FS11
66–67	FS12
84–85	FS42–43
90–91	CW316–17
95–96	CW327–28
97	FS258 (no. 49)
98	FS116–17
103–10	CW390–99
114	FS139–40
116–17	FS10
120–22	PN231–33
122–23	PN229–31
131–32	FS240–41
137 (no. 154)	FS9–10
154–56	FS264–65
166–72	FS201–7
168–69	FS213–14
169	FS261 (no. 53)
173–74	FS199–200
175	FS108–9
181	FS195 (no. 2)

Quaderni   Translations

Quaderni	Translations
186–88	FS210–13
189–90	FS200
193–94	FS195 (no. 1)
195–96	FS197–98
200–1	FS262
210–12	FS209–10
242 (no. 78)	FS196 (no. 3)
244 (no. 86)	FS120–21
245	FS154–55
246–48	FS132–34
251 (no. 97)	FS196–97
262–63	FS230–31
266–68	FS231–33
269–70	FS49–50
271	FS115–16
272–74	FS235–37
274–75	FS254–55
284–86	CW260–62
288–89	CW262–64
290–91	FS207–8
293	CW273
294–95	CW326–27
305–6	FS40–42
307	FS254
310–11	FS417
311–12	PN275–76
319–21	PN223–26
323–27	PN272–75
328–32	PN196–200
332–33	CW389–90
332–33	FS155–56
333	FS59
334–35	CW345–46
336	FS208–9
337	FS16–17
351–52	CW173–75
353–57	CW167–71
361–63	CW255–57
357	FS12–13
371	CW216–17
386–88	PN227–28
398–99	FS74–75
401–2	FS147–48
406–7	CW131–32
412 (no. 160)	FS231
415	FS113–14

Quaderni	Translations
415	FS117–18
506–7	FS293–94
515	FS24–25
515–16	FS259
516	FS153
516–18	CW150–53
519	CW153–54
519–20	CW154
520	CW155
520–21	CW155–56
522–26	CW156–61
526–27	CW161–62
527	CW162
529–30	CW162–63
533–36	CW282–85
546–47	FS45–46
547	FS196 (no. 4)
547–48	FS107 (no. 67)
553 (no. 15)	FS107 (no. 68)
553–54	FS113
554–55	FS46–47
556–57	FS109
562–64	FS124–26
566	CW332
569	CW250–51
571	CW276
571–72	PN374–75
572–73	FS144–45
578–79	FS42
579–82	FS129–32
582–84	FS127–28
584–85	FS22–23
586–87	CW346–48
591	FS110
592	FS109–110
599–602	CW306–09
604–5	FS72–73
605–6	FS59–60
614–15	FS19–20
615–16	FS262–63
620–21	FS118
621–23	FS134–36
626	CW276–77
632–33	CW235–36
633–35	CW278–79
640–53	CW222–34

Quaderni	Translations
656–62	PN247–53
665–66	FS47–48
666–67	FS114
678	CW178
679	CW333
679–80	CW195
690–92	PN270–72
692	FS274–75
693	PN257–58
700–701	CW175–76
701–2	CW281–82
703–4	FS75–76
704–5	CW137–38
705–6	CW330
706–8	CW273–75
709	FS122
713–14	FS198–99
714–15	FS267–68
715–16	FS8–9
716–19	CW269–71
719–21	CW265–66
722	CW334–35
723	CW279–80
729–32	CW119–21
732–34	CW107–08
737–39	CW176–78
739–40	CW348–49
743	FS217–18
748–49	FS119–20
749–51	CW399–401
751–52	PN245–46
752–56	FS435–39
756–58	PN195–96
760–62	PN173–75
762–63	FS17–18
763–64	PN262–63
767–68	FS218
779–80	FS379–80
780–81	FS247–48
782–83	FS444–45
788	PN239
790–91	CW401–2
792–93	FS215–17
794	CW103–4
797	FS182
798	CW110

Quaderni / Translations

Quaderni	Translations
799	CW349–50
799–800	FS256
800–801	PN264–65
801	PN260–61
801–2	PN238–39
802	FS18 (no. 13)
806–7	CW362–63
809 (no. 151)	FS21 (no. 17)
809 (no. 152)	FS20–21
810–11	PN239
811	FS319–20
811–12	CW237
816	FS100–1
816–17	FS104–5
817	FS282–83
820–21	CW363–64
824–25	FS121
825–26	FS143–44
826–27	FS281–82
828–29	FS35–36
831–32	FS110–12
832–33	FS37–38
834	FS116
836–37	FS94–96
840–41	CW338–39
843–44	FS150–51
844–45	CW350–51
845–46	CW352–53
847 (no. 211)	FS147
855	PN409–10
860–61	FS443
861–63	FS275–77
865–67	PN236–38
868	PN402–03
868–69	PN376–77
869	PN377
870	FS542n11
870–71	FS185–86
871–73	PN407–09
876 (no. 27)	FS186
876 (no. 28)	FS522n21
877–79	FS187–89
880–81	FS448–49
881–82	PN382–83
883–86	PN354–57
887	FS574n32

Quaderni	Translations
887–88	PN362
889	FS244
892–93	FS270–71
893–94	PN346
895–97	CW291–93
901 (no. 62)	FS123–24
902	FS242–43
907 (no. 69)	FS112
908	FS122–23
911	FS4849
911–12	FS442–43
912–13	PN228–29
917–18	FS101–2
919	FS73–74
919–20	PN267–68
922–23	FS112–13
923–24	FS321–22
925–26	FS38–39
930	FS19
930–31	CW332–33
937	PN260
937–38	CW249–50
942–43	CW115–16
944	FS39–40
947	FS443–44
969	CW377–78
969–70	FS214–15
972–73	FS272
975–76	CW402–03
978–79	FS272–73
982–83	FS246–47
986	FS241–42
992	FS132
993	CW280–81
993	FS259–60
994–95	FS320–21
996 (no. 92)	FS245
998	FS18 (no. 12)
999	CW311[iii]
1002	CW339–40
1002–3	CW311–12
1007 (no. 111)	FS13–14
1019	FS107–8
1020–21	PN268–69
1021–22 (no. 131.2)	FS115
1022	PN139–40

APPENDIX

Quaderni	Translations
1028	PN264
1030	CW275
1034	FS14
1037	CW312–13
1038–39	FS163–64
1040	CW251
1040–41	FS186–87
1041 (no. 168)	FS539n13
1049–50	PN258–59
1051–52	PN366
1053–54	PN263–64
1054–55	FS152–53
1055–56	FS557–58n19
1056	PN261
1057 (no. 193)	FS234–35
1057–58	PN194–95
1068	FS378
1069–70	FS184
1076–78	FS180–81
1088–89	FS277
1088–89	GR264–65
1097–98	CW333–34
1105	CW194–95
1110–11	FS269–70
1115–16	FS233–34
1131 (no. 59)	FS283
1131–32	FS268–69
1133–34	PN200–1
1136–37	CW378–79
1137–38	PN201–2
1150–51	CW285–86
1183–85	FS140–43
1195–97	CW138–40
1207–38	FS328–61
1222–25	CW104–7
1227–29	PN118–20
1234–35	GR195
1239	FS366–67
1240–41	FS369–70
1241–42	FS382–83
1242–43	FS371–72
1243–44	FS373
1244	PN366–67
1244–45 (no. 6.II)	FS306 (no. 22)
1244–45 (no. 6.III)	FS402–3
1244–45 (no. 6.IV)	FS306 (no. 21)

Quaderni	Translations
1245 (no. 7)	FS439
1245–46	FS179–80
1246–48	PN399–402
1248–49	PN402
1249	FS417–18
1249–50	PN365–66
1250	PN370–71
1250–53	FS464–67
1253–54	FS166–67
1254	FS420–21
1255–56	PN344–45
1256	FS421–22
1257–59	FS182–84
1259–61	FS467–69
1261–62	FS168–70
1263	PN343–44
1263–64	FS164–65
1264–65	FS447–48
1265	FS167–68
1265–66	FS99
1266–67	PN369–70
1267 (no. 29.I)	FS377
1267–68 (no. 29.II)	FS367
1268–69	FS170–71
1269–75	FS383–89
1275–76	FS424–25
1276–78	FS171–73
1278–79	FS428–30
1280	FS415–16
1280–81	PN362–63
1281–84	FS430–33
1284–85	FS165–66
1285–87	FS176–79
1287–88	FS425–26
1288–89 (no. 38.II)	FS368
1289–90	FS422–23
1290–91	PN368
1291–92	FS403–4
1292–1301	FS406–15
1300	GR193–94
1301–2	FS405–6
1302	FS372–73
1302–3	FS469–70
1303–5	FS470–72
1305–7	FS473–75
1307–10	FS389–92

APPENDIX

Quaderni	Translations
1310–11	FS426–28
1312–13	FS433–35
1313–14	FS419–20
1315	FS379
1315–17	FS399–401
11318	FS418
1318–23	FS394–99
1318–23	GR196–99
1323–24	FS404–5
1324–27	FS373–76
1327	FS445–46
1327–28	FS376–77
1328–29	FS402
1330–32	PN348–51
1331	FS156–57
1333	PN367–68
1333–34	FS470
1334	FS472–73
1334–35	PN348
1335–38	PN357–60
1340–41	PN363–64
1341–42	FS569n38
1342–43	PN347
1343	FS229
1343–46	PN351–54
1347–49	FS226–29
1349–50	FS392
1350–51	FS189–90
1351–52	FS393–94
1352–53	FS462–64
1354	FS416
1354–55 (no. 59.III)	FS370–71
1355–56	FS446–47
1356–57	FS318–19
1358–62	PN114–18
1366–68	FS157–59
1370	FS160
1370–71	FS441
1375–78	PN323–25
1378	PN325–26
1378–96	PN326–43
1396–1401	PN419–25
1401–3	PN436–37
1403–6	PN437–40
1406–11	PN452–57
1411–16	PN440–46

APPENDIX

Quaderni	Translations
1416–17	PN448–49
1417–18	PN471–72
1418–20	PN446–48
1420–22	PN457–58
1422	PN431–32
1422–24	PN432–33
1424	PN433–34
1424–26	PN434–36
1426–28	PN450–52
1428–30	MP94–96
1431–34	PN425–30
1434–37	PN462–65
1438–39	PN449–50
1439–42	PN458–61
1442–45	PN465–68
1445	PN437
1446–47	PN468–70
1447–48	PN431
1448–49	PN446
1449	PN448
1450	PN470–71
1451–55	FS286–90
1455–57	FS290–92
1457–58	FS293
1458–59	FS294–95
1459–60	FS295–97
1461 (no. 41)	FS297–98
1461 (no. 42)	FS298 (no. 15)
1462	FS298 (no. 16)
1462–66	FS298–303
1466–67	FS303–4
1468 (no. 46)	FS306 (no. 23)
1468 (no. 47)	FS307
1468–70	FS307–9
1471–73	FS310–13
1473–76	FS315–18
1476–77	PN371
1477–81	PN410–14
1480–91	PN375–76
1481–82	PN370
1482	PN364
1484–85	PN373–74
1485–86	PN345–46
1486 (no. 61)	FS285 (no. 7)
1487–90	PN404–7
1491–92	PN371–72

Quaderni	Translations
1492–93	PN403–4
1494–1500	FS454–60
1500–1505	FS449–54
1505–6	PN418–19
1506	FS555n7
1506–7	FS460–61
1507–9	PN386–88
1513–20	PN5–14
1520–30	PN14–23
1530–38	PN26–33
1538–40	FS145–47
1540–50	PN33–43
1550–51	MP121–22
1555–61	PN125–33
1561–63	PN175–77
1565–67	PN242–43
1567–68	PN138–39
1568–70	PN136–38
1570–71	PN246–47
1572–73	PN140–41
1573	PN141
1573–76	PN141–43
1576	PN169–70
1577–78	PN171–73
1578–85	PN177–85
1589–97	PN158–67
1598–1601	PN133–36
1601–2	PN147–48
1602–5	PN210–11
1605–10	PN211–17
1610–11	PN217–18
1611–13	PN167–68
1613–16	PN233–36
1619–22	PN219–22
1622–23	FS323–24
1623–24	PN202–04
1624–26	PN192–94
1626–28	PN190–92
1629–30	PN150–51
1632–35	PN185–90
1636–42	GR260–62
1649–50	FS92–94
1650	FS94
1651–52	FS441–42
1655–56	CW129
1656	CW128

Quaderni	Translations
1659	CW134–35
1659	FS284–85
1668–69	PN265–66
1670–74	CW140–44
1675	CW377
1675–76	PN204–5
1676–77	CW379–80
1677–78	FS99–100
1678–79	CW144–45
1680–81	PN222–23
1682	FS303
1682–85	FS25–28
1685–87	CW111–12
1691–92	PN155
1692–93	CW340–41
1693	FS285 (no. 6)
1694–95 (no. 38.I)	FS439–40
1696	CW294
1696 (no. 38.3)	FS440–41
1697–99	CW257–59
1701–3	CW294–96
1707–8	PN253–54
1711–12	FS97–99
1713–14	FS43–44
1714–15	FS153–54
1715–17	FS223–25
1718	CW132
1718–19	CW403–4
1719–21	CW124–25
1721–22	CW404–5
1723–24	CW132–33
1724–25	CW129–31
1726–28	CW125–27
1728–30	PN240–41
1732–35	PN151–55
1736–37	CW405–6
1737–40	CW203–6
1740–42	CW406–8
1742–43	PN254–56
1744	PN256–57
1746	CW408
1749–50	FS243–44
1750–51	PN155–57
1751	PN269
1752–55	PN144–47
1755–59	FS219–23

Quaderni	Translations
1759–61	PN157–58
1762–64	FSlxxxiv–lxxxvii
1765–66	PN243–45
1766–69	PN108–11
1769–71	FS14–16
1769–71	GR243–45
1771–72	CW266–67
1772–74	PN111–13
1774	FS181–82
1774–75	PN106–08
1775–76	PN269–70
1777–79	CW117–19
1780	PN364–65
1781–82	PN113–14
1782–83	FS225–26
1784–85	PN361
1785–86	FS256–57
1787–88	FS323
1790–92	FS380–82
1792–93	CW296–97
1793–94	CW108–10
1798–1800	FS105–6
1800–1801	FS102–4
1801–2	CW236–37
1802–4	FS174–75
1804–5	FS245–46
1805–6	FS176
1806–7	FS151–52
1810–11	PN170–71
1816–17	FS257–58
1820–22	CW99–102
1822–24	PN104–6
1825–27	PN416–18
1827	PN114
1828–29	FS314–15
1833–34	FS273–74
1837–40	FS55–58
1840–44	PN382–86
1844–46	PN414–15
1847	FS137
1849–50	FS266–67
1854–64	PN388–99
1864	FS58–59
1865–66	FS60–61
1866–74	FS61–70
1882–84	FS70–71

Quaderni	Translations
1879–82	CW355–59
1884–85	PN415–16
1889–93	CW380–85
1898–99	FS461–62
1907	CW217
1908–10	CW217–20
1912–14	CW220–22
1914–15	CW247–49
1917	FS423–24
1917–18	CW313–14
1919	FS21–22
1920	CW314[vii]
1922 (no. 18.III)	FS313–14
1925–26	PN372–73
1926 (no. 23)	FS283–84
1926 (no. 23)	PN461–62
1926 (no. 24)	CW314[viii]
1933–34	CW375–77
1938–39	FS324–25
1939–40	PN148–50
1944–45	CW272–73
1947–48	PN266–67
1948–49	FS305
1949	FS261 (no. 52)
1979–80	CW245
1987–89	CW246–47
1988–89	FS253–54
1991–96	FS248–53
1998–99	CW244
1989–91	FS237–39
2004–06	CW241–44
2010–34	PN55–84
2035–46	PN90–102
2046–48	PN102–4
2048–54	PN84–90
2081–86	FS28–33
2086–87	FS33–34
2087–88	FS34–35
2088–92	FS76–80
2092–98	FS80–88
2098–99	FS88
2099–2100	FS96–97
2100–2103	FS88–92
2107–10	CW199–201
2110–12	CW353–55
2112	CW293–94

APPENDIX

Quaderni	Translations
2113	CW264–65
2113–20	CW206–12
2120–23	CW359–62
2123–24	CW364–65
2124–25	CW365–67
2126–27	CW367–69
2128–29	CW369–70
2129–33	CW370–74
2133–35	CW374–75
2139–40	PN279–80
2140–47	PN280–87
2147–50	PN294–97
2150–52	PN287–89
2152–53	PN306–7
2153–58	PN289–94
2158–59	PN307–8
2160	PN297–98
2160–64	PN298–301
2164–69	PN301–6
2169–71	PN308–10
2171–75	PN310–13
2175–78	PN313–16
2178–80	PN316–18
2185–86	CW91–93
2186	CW146
2187–90	CW93–98
2191–92	CW133–34
2192–93	CW98
2193–95	CW122–23
2195–98	CW212–16
2198–2202	CW301–6
2202	CW306
2203	CW321–22
2203–5	CW318–20
2205	CW310–11
2206–8	CW335–37
2209	CW99
2210	CW320
2210–11	CW323–24
2211–12	CW317
2212–13	CW324–26
2214–15	CW322–23
2216 (no. 29)	CW328–29
2216 (no. 30)	CW329
2216–18	CW315–16
2228–29	CW330–31

Quaderni	Translations
2229–30	CW337
2230–32	CW112–15
2233 (no. 37)	CW311[ii]
2233–36	CW267–69
2236–37	CW171–73
2238	CW364
2238–39	CW321
2239–40	CW271–72
2241–42	CW102–03
2242–43	CW277–78
2243–44	CW309–10
2244–47	CW288–91
2250–53	CW252–55
2259–60	CW408–09
2260–62	CW410–12
2263–69	CW412–19
2265–66	FS268
2270–71	CW419–21
2271–72	CW421
2272	CW422[16]
2272–73	CW422[17]
2273–74	CW422–23
2274–75	CW424–25
2279–83	FS50–55
2283–84	PN54–55
2287–89	PN52–54
2290–93	CW238–41
2302–3	PN261–62
2306–7	FS23–24
2311–14	CW188–91
2314–17	CW192–94
2341–42	CW179–80
2342–45	CW180–82
2345–46	CW183–84
2346–47	CW184
2347–48	CW184–85
2348–50	CW185–87
2350	CW187–88

NOTES

Introduction

1. Clark (1975).

2. Limbaugh (1994), pp. 97–98.

3. Joll (1977), p. 24.

4. Limbaugh (1994), pp. 97–98.

5. Ibid., pp. 97–98.

6. Ibid., p. 98.

7. One of the best examples of this type of analysis appears in Del Noce (1978).

8. Novak (1989), p. 54.

9. Gramsci (1975b), pp. 2137–82; cf. Gramsci (1971b), pp. 277–320.

10. Quoted in Novak (1989), p. 54.

11. Gramsci (1958), p. 126, from a newspaper article in *Il grido del popolo*, 18 August 1917. All translations from Gramsci are my own unless otherwise noted.

12. See the essays and lectures collected in Togliatti (1972, 1979).

13. My account is based on such works as Davidson (1977), G. Fiori (1966, 1970, 1991), Germino (1990), Gramsci (1975b, pp. xliii–lxviii), Paulesu Quercioli (1977), and Zucaro (1954, 1961).

14. Joll (1977), p. 24.

15. Ibid., p. 148.

16. G. Fiori (1966), p. 29.

17. Gramsci (1965), p. 38. To express this point, he used the German expression *für ewig*, although he was of course writing in Italian.

18. See the chronology in Gramsci (1975b), p. lxvii.

19. Zucaro (1954), p. 87.

20. Gramsci (1975b), p. 866; cf. Gramsci (1988a), p. 229.

21. Gramsci (1958), p. 149; cf. Gramsci (1988a), p. 32.

22. Gramsci (1975b), p. 1300; cf. Gramsci (1988a), p. 193.
23. Gramsci (1965), p. 38.

Chapter 1: Gramsci as a Political Theorist

1. See Adamson (1980b) and Germino (1990), to mention only some of the best accounts.

2. See the works of mine listed in the Bibliography, especially Finocchiaro (1988a).

3. See especially Femia (1981a, 1981b).

4. Golding (1992).

5. For some new sparks of life, see Caprioglio (1991), De Domenico (1991), Fontana (1993), Holub (1992), and Vacca (1991). Especially original and noteworthy is Holub (1992), which I would describe as a critical interpretation of Gramsci's literary and cultural criticism with an emphasis on the approach (as distinct from the particular theses) implicit in his critical practice.

6. For example, Meisel (1964, 1965a).

7. For example, Gregor (1969).

8. See the interesting work of Nye (1977).

9. Losurdo (1986) speaks of *doppiezza*, which has the connotation of "ambivalence" as well as hypocrisy.

10. For example, Albertoni (1989a); Bachrach (1967); De Mas (1981), pp. 21-34; Mongardini (1980b), pp. 62-63; Ripepe (1983), p. 172; and Sola (1982c), pp. 58-59.

11. As I myself have argued in Finocchiaro (1988b), pp. 220-21, and less explicitly in Finocchiaro (1988a). In the present context, it is also important to note that Gramsci's elitism derives partly from Marx, at least in the sense that traditional Marxism is a version of elitism; hence Gramsci's Marxist background made him predisposed to accept the more theoretically explicit and thoroughgoing elitism he found in Mosca.

12. Here and elsewhere in this book, references to the critical edition of Gramsci's Prison Notebooks will be given in parenthesis in the text; thus, "Q 1766" corresponds to Gramsci (1975b), p. 1766.

13. See the Introduction.

14. Cf. Gramsci's own judgment, expressed in a letter from prison: "In ten years of journalism I have written so many lines as to be able to compile fifteen or twenty volumes of four hundred pages, but they were written on a daily basis and should, in my opinion, be allowed to perish in the same manner. I have always refused to compile such collections, even if selected" (Gramsci 1965), p. 480. The prisoner goes on to mention three particular cases of refusal (in 1918, 1920, and 1924); in one of these (1920) he changed his mind after the volume had gone to press, and had to pay the costs of stopping the publication.

15. Togliatti (1972), pp. 218-19; this passage was originally published in *Paese sera*, 19 June 1964.

16. Cammett (1991); Cammett and Righi (1995).

17. Bobbio (1988), Cerroni (1990), Cofrancesco (1968), Finocchiaro (1990), Galli (1969), Mastellone (1991), Medici (1990a, 1990b), Sgambati (1979), Sochor (1967), and Zarone (1990). To these one could add Asor Rosa (1975a); Bellamy and Schecter

(1993), pp. 147–48 and 153; Bingen (unpublished); Finocchiaro (1988b), pp. 110–28; and Gobetti (1924).

18. See, for example, Albertoni (1978), pp. 92–93; Delle Piane (1952), pp. 265, 271, 290, 312–14, and 319; Lombardo (1971a), p. 23; Meisel (1958), pp. 270, 279, and 315; and Ripepe (1974), pp. 83–84. However, Asor Rosa (1975a) gives a more explicit and appreciative discussion, as was originally done by Gobetti (1924).

19. See Gramsci (1975b), p. 1565. The most generous among the Mosca scholars, Ripepe (1974), p. 83, n. 184, asserts that the Gramscian criticism "represents, paradoxically, the most precise analysis of Mosca's concept that has been provided so far"; the same judgment has been repeated more recently by Ripepe (1983). Meisel (1958), pp. 315–16, also advances a favorable judgment.

20. This does not mean that the available studies do not have their own merits, as may be seen from the critical appreciation undertaken in Finocchiaro (1988b), pp. 111–12 or Finocchiaro (1990).

21. See, for example, Burnham (1943).

22. Gramsci (1965), p. 390.

23. Bobbio (1969b), p. 191.

24. Frascani (1969).

25. Ripepe (1983), pp. 166, 170, and 172.

26. For a valuable discussion of this general issue, see Germino (1967).

Chapter 2: Mosca's Political Science

1. Mosca (1884); see the bibliography for later editions and reprints.

2. Mosca (1982), p. 203.

3. Ibid., p. 608; cf. (1939), p. 50. In quoting from Mosca's writings, I have sometimes (1) translated the passage myself, if no published translation exists or I was dissatisfied with the existing one; at other times I have (2) used an existing translation, if I found it adequate; and at still other times I have (3) made a few emendations to an existing translation, if I thought it was salvageable. Whenever possible, I give references to both the Italian edition and the English translation. For case (1), I follow the convention of first giving the Italian reference and then cross-referencing (by means of cf.) the English translation. For case (2), I do the reverse (reference to the English first and cross-referencing to the Italian second). Thus, for the quotation being referenced in this note, I have translated it from the Italian in Mosca (1982), and I also indicate where Kahn's translation is found in Mosca (1939); whereas, for example, for the passage being referenced in note 61, I am quoting directly from Kahn's translation, and I also indicate where the original Italian text is found in Mosca (1982).

4. Mosca (1982), p. 609; cf. (1939), p. 50.

5. Mosca (1982), p. 195; "of the classes of their leaders" is my translation for delle loro classi dirigenti, which means literally "of their directing classes."

6. For example, Sartori (1978), pp. 46–48.

7. For example, Meisel (1958).

8. One of the best examples is Dorso (1949), for which a very readable and accessible account is provided in Germino (1967), chapter 6.

9. See Pareto (1902, 1964, 1935, 1950), Mosca (1907), and Meisel (1965a).

10. See, for example, Sartori (1961).

11. Mosca (1982), pp. 202–3.

12. Aristotle, *Politics*, III, 7, 1279a–b.

13. Montesquieu, *Spirit of Laws*, books 2 and 3.

14. Mosca (1982), p. 610; cf. (1939), p. 52.

15. Cf. Mosca (1982), pp. 710–13, 859–70, 984–89; (1958), pp. 566–69; (1937), pp. 195–206.

16. A classic statement of this theory is found in *The Communist Manifesto;* cf. Marx (1988).

17. For Mosca's criticism of Marxism, socialism, and communism, see Mosca (1982), pp. 859–922, 1053–65, 1105–9; (1964), pp. 257–71; and (1958), pp. 649–56.

18. Mosca (1982, pp. 582–84; 1949, pp. 14–15); cf. Nye (1977).

19. This principle is receiving increasing general recognition among philosophers of science, as may be seen from McMullin (1976), and it has been specifically discussed in relation to Mosca and elite studies by Zuckerman (1977).

20. The similarities between the two thinkers are discussed in such works as Bobbio (1969b), Bottomore (1964), and Parry (1969); I am nevertheless inclined to agree with Meisel (1964, 1965a) that the pairing of Mosca and Pareto—an almost universal practice—is unfortunate, though more for the former than for the latter.

21. See Michels (1911, 1912, and 1962), and cf. Mosca (1949), pp. 26–36.

22. See Mills (1956; 1959, pp. 203–4; 1965), and cf. Bottomore (1964), Mosca (1971, pp. 445–53), Parry (1969), and Tilman (1984).

23. See Bachrach (1971a, 1971b), Bottomore (1964), Lasswell and Kaplan (1950), Lasswell et al. (1965), Parry (1969), Putnam (1976), and Zuckerman (1977).

24. Lasswell, Lerner, and Rothwell (1971), p. 15.

25. Ibid., p. 15.

26. Ibid., p. 16.

27. Mosca (1982), p. 610.

28. Ibid., p. 940; see also pp. 1121–22.

29. Ibid., pp. 875–76 (which corresponds to Mosca 1939, pp. 283–84), and Mosca (1949), p. 309.

30. Mosca (1939), pp. 285–86; I have made a few emendations to Kahn's translation; cf. Mosca (1982), p. 878. One should read this entire section (Mosca 1982, pp. 873–78, which corresponds to Mosca 1939, pp. 281–86), as well as the analogous prediction and description in the second volume of *Elements* (Mosca 1982), pp. 1105–9. See also Mosca (1971), pp. 154–55.

31. Mosca (1982), p. 1107.

32. Mosca (1949), p. 325. This prediction appears in a newspaper article originally published as "Le forze sindacali e gl'interessi sociali," *La Stampa* (Turin), 8 May 1926, pp. 1–2.

33. Lenski (1980) is one scholar who deserves credit for having stressed this aspect of Mosca's theorizing; my own account is adapted from his.

34. See Dahl (1956, 1958, 1961, 1966, 1989), and cf. Bachrach and Baratz (1962), Bachrach (1967, 1971a), Sartori (1987, pp. 145–48), Walker (1966), and Zuckerman (1977).

35. This criticism is adapted from Friedrich (1965).

36. Meisel (1958), p. 4.

37. Zuckerman (1977) is one scholar who deserves credit for having stressed this

point, though his own context is slightly different. Moreover, I would argue that the situation is analogous in the physical sciences. For example, the first law of motion (inertia) cannot be really tested except in conjunction with the second and third laws as well as such other hypotheses as the principle of universal gravitation, Hooke's law, and so on.

38. See, for example, Sartori (1987), p. 147.

39. Mosca (1982), pp. 608-10.

40. For one such perspective on definition, see Putnam (1962), Quine (1963), and Scriven (1958).

41. See, for example, Ellis (1965) and Hanson (1965).

42. Mosca (1982), p. 940; cf. Mosca (1982), pp. 610-11, 1121-22.

43. See Hook (1939, 1959). Gramsci (e.g., 1975b, pp. 1752-53) seems to echo this objection, but his attitude is rather complex, as will be shown below. This objection is also present, at least implicitly, in Mills (1956); cf. Tilman (1984), pp. 30-60, and Tilman (1987).

44. This type of analysis, which I am attributing implicitly to Mosca, is explicit in Gramsci, as will become evident shortly. However, since, as mentioned in a previous note, Gramsci also seems to express a criticism of the elitist principle based on an ideal society without the distinction between rulers and ruled, there is an apparent inconsistency in Gramsci; I believe that this inconsistency should be resolved by upholding the distinction between utopian dreams and realistic ideals, which is more pervasive and fundamental than that criticism.

45. Hook (1959), p. 55; see also Hook (1939).

46. See Mosca (1949), pp. 26-36.

47. See, for example, Gramsci (1975b), pp. 1565, 972, and 956; Meisel (1958), pp. 315-16; and Ripepe (1974), p. 83, n. 184.

48. Meisel (1958).

49. Mosca (1939), p. 493; I have made a few emendations to Kahn's translation to make it more faithful to the original, the main one being the insertion of the justificative connective "the reason is that," which corresponds to Mosca's *perchè;* cf. Mosca (1982), p. 1116. This strengthens even further my present point, that Mosca is justifying the "elitist" appeal.

50. Meisel (1958), pp. 220-21; see also pp. 234-35.

51. I do not mean to be cavalier about the interpretation of Pareto, an issue that emerges again in Chapter 7, section 6; nevertheless, this is my interpretive hunch. For an alternative interpretation, see Femia (1995).

52. Frascani (1969); of some relevance is also Frascani (1967). Parry more properly speaks of "ideology . . . for the middle class" (1969, p. 42).

53. Ripepe (1983), pp. 166, 170, 172.

54. See, for example, Parry (1969), p. 41; cf. Bobbio (1956, 1961, 1966, 1969b) and Hughes (1954).

55. For helpful accounts of the problem of value judgments in science, see for example Finocchiaro (1986) and Laudan (1984).

56. Mosca (1982), pp. 1015-19. Frascani (1969) has elaborated on this, with the aim of showing how Mosca's thinking became increasingly ideological—a purpose almost opposite to mine.

57. Mosca (1958), p. 529.

58. Ripepe (1983), p. 180.

59. Bobbio (1969b), p. 191.

60. Meisel (1965a), p. 3.

61. Mosca (1939), pp. 428-29; cf. Mosca (1982), pp. 1040-42.

62. Mosca (1939), p. 395; cf. Mosca (1982), p. 1005.

63. Mosca (1949), p. 22.

64. Mosca (1982), pp. 1026-27; the Kahn translation (Mosca 1939, p. 415) does not do justice to Mosca's statement.

65. Mosca (1982), p. 1027; cf. (1939), p. 416.

66. Mosca (1939), p. 419; cf. (1982), p. 1030.

67. Mosca (1982), p. 1004; cf. Plato, *Republic*, VII, 555b-558c.

68. Mosca (1982), p. 684, note m; Mosca (1949), pp. 61-86; cf. Francesco Guicciardini, *Opere inedite* (3 vols. Florence, 1857-59), vol. 2, p. 269.

69. Mosca (1982), pp. 1003-4.

70. Meisel (1958), pp. 198-201.

71. Mosca (1982), p. 1020; (1939), pp. 409-10.

72. Mosca (1939), p. 398; cf. Mosca (1982), p. 1008.

73. Mosca (1982), p. 645; (1939), p. 80.

74. Mosca (1939), pp. 81-83; cf. (1982), p. 646-48.

75. Mosca (1939), p. 83; cf. (1982), p. 648.

76. Mosca (1939), p. 83; cf. (1982), p. 648.

77. Mosca (1939), pp. 80-81; cf. (1982), p. 645-46.

78. Mosca (1939), pp. 85-86; cf. (1982), pp. 651-52. For more details on the idea that the social effects of applying any principle are nonmonotonic, see Finocchiaro (1993).

79. Cf. Mosca (1982), pp. 1036-37.

80. Bobbio (1983) offers an extremely illuminating analysis of this topic, as well as of the question how mixed government is related to separation of powers and to checks and balances (to be discussed later).

81. Mosca (1939), p. 428; cf. (1982), p. 1040, and (1964), p. 305.

82. Mosca (1939), p. 429; cf. (1982), p. 1041.

83. Ibid.

84. Mosca (1982), p. 694; cf. (1939), p. 139. "Juridical defense" is a phrase used by Mosca to mean a measure of the moral-political perfection of a society; the principle just quoted could be called Mosca's principle of juridical defense, or at least one of his special principles of juridical defense; a more general one is the anti-absolutist principle of balanced pluralism, to be quoted later. I regard this phrase an infelicitous expression, and so I shall try to avoid it.

85. Mosca (1939), p. 143-44; cf. (1982), p. 699.

86. Mosca (1939), p. 134; cf. (1982), p. 689.

87. Mosca (1982), pp. 692-93, 1040; (1939), pp. 138, 428.

88. Mosca (1982), pp. 491-94, 847; (1958), p. 337-52.

89. Mosca (1958), pp. 470-73, 487-90.

90. Ibid., pp. 490-96; (1982), pp. 448-53.

91. Mosca (1939), p. 144; cf. (1982), p. 700.

92. Mosca (1939), pp. 291-92; cf. (1982), p. 885.

93. Mosca (1949), pp. 267-76.

94. Mosca (1958), pp. 353-60.

95. Mosca (1939), p. 475; cf. (1982), pp. 1094-95. Cf. also (1939), pp. 389-90, 473-77, 487-89; and (1982), pp. 998, 1093-95, and 1109-11.

96. Mosca (1939), pp. 474-75; cf. (1982), p. 1093-94. A little later in his final chapter, Mosca (1982, pp. 1109-10; 1939, pp. 487-88) interprets this balance between elected and nonelected officials in terms of the balance between liberalism and autocracy; he thereby regards elected officials as a "liberal" component of the system, namely a component through which power flows from the bottom up, and he considers the civil service an "autocratic" component—namely, one whereby power flows in the opposite direction. This view would reduce the present case of balanced pluralism to one previously discussed.

97. Mosca (1939), pp. 428-29; Mosca (1923a), pp. 436-37.

98. Mosca (1982), p. 537.

99. Authors have called attention in various contexts to this feature of Mosca's thinking—for example, De Mattei (1968, p. x), Fotia (1966), Greer (1969, pp. 157, 220n), and Zarone (1990). However, I am not sure that it has been properly appreciated; for example, I believe that it implies that Mosca is not a positivist, despite claims to the contrary by such luminaries and insightful interpreters as Bobbio (1966, 1969b) and Croce (1923). For some details, see Finocchiaro (forthcoming a).

100. Mosca (1939), p. 406; cf. (1982), p. 1017.

101. Ibid.

102. Mosca (1982), p. 1017; cf. (1939), p. 407.

103. Mosca (1939), pp. 407-8; cf. (1982), p. 1018.

104. Mosca (1982), pp. 1017, 1027, 1070-71; (1939), pp. 406, 416, 453; cf. (1964), pp. 217-24. For Saint-Simon, Sola (in Mosca 1982, p. 1071, n. 48) refers to *Oeuvres de Saint-Simon et d'Enfantin* (47 vols. Paris: Dentu, 1865-1876), 22:17, n. 1.

105. Mosca (1982), pp. 1027-31; (1939), pp. 416-19.

106. Mosca (1982), pp. 1065-75); (1939), pp. 448-57.

107. Mosca (1939), p. 449; I have amended the Kahn translation by replacing "to outstrip one's fellows" with "to excel over one's fellows," which is a more accurate translation of Mosca's *primeggiare sui propri simili* (1982, p. 1066).

108. Mosca (1939), p. 456; cf. (1982), p. 1074.

109. Mosca (1939), p. 450; cf. (1982), p. 1067.

110. Mosca (1982, pp. 770, 1066), and Mosca (1939, pp. 193, 450); cf. Machiavelli, *Istorie fiorentine*, VII, 6. Despite his endorsement of this Machiavellian dictum, Mosca was generally unimpressed by Machiavelli, as can be seen from Mosca (1958), pp. 673-720, and from Mosca (1964), pp. 97-123.

111. Mosca (1982), pp. 1068-70; (1939), pp. 451-53; cf. Plato, *Laws*, (XII, 964b-969d), and *Republic* (V, 473b-474d; VI, 499b).

112. Mosca (1982), p. 1069; cf. (1939), p. 452.

113. Mosca (1939), pp. 450-51; cf. (1982), pp. 1067-68.

114. Mosca (1939), p. 450; cf. (1982), p. 1067.

115. Mosca (1939), p. 193; cf. (1982), p. 770, note c.

116. Mosca (1982), p. 1070; (1939), p. 452.

117. See, for example, *Theory of Governments*, Mosca (1982), p. 203; *Elements*, Mosca (1982), pp. 608, 828, corresponding to (1939), pp. 50, 244.

118. Mosca (1939), pp. 70-71; cf. (1982), pp. 633-35.

119. Mosca (1982), p. 609; (1939), p. 50.

120. For example, Aron (1950, p. 9), Bottomore (1964, pp. 1-15), Burnham (1943, p. 88), Field and Higley (1989a), Putnam (1976), Zarone (1990, p. 158).

121. Mosca (1949), p. 5.

122. Mosca (1982), pp. 1089-90, 1096-1100; (1939), pp. 47-73, 477-78.

123. Mosca (1982), p. 521.

124. Ibid., p. 195.

125. Ibid., pp. 611-13.

126. Ripepe (1974), pp. 195-97.

127. Mosca (1939), p. 53; cf. (1982), p. 612.

Chapter 3: Gramsci on Mosca

1. For the account in this paragraph, see Gramsci (1975b), pp. 1154, 1975-76, and 2847; and Mosca (1982), p. 487, note f, and p. 469, note n.

2. Gramsci (1975b), pp. 963-64, and Mosca (1982), pp. 907-9, note f; the translation in Mosca (1939), pp. 312-13 is incomplete and inadequate, and so I have provided my own. Mosca gives the following reference: Guglielmo Ferrero, *Reazione* (Turin: Roux, 1895), pp. 54ff. Ferrero is an important figure in his own right, as well as in relation to Mosca; on their relationship, see Mongardini (1980a, 1980b).

3. Q 2433; Gramsci's bibliographical information is not exact, as may be seen from Q 3066 and Mosca (1908). For the relevant letters, see Gramsci (1965), pp. 259-60 and 263-66.

4. See Mosca (1958), pp. 556-59.

5. For an interpretation and evaluation of these, see Finocchiaro (1988a, 1988b).

6. For ease of reference, the following notational conventions are adapted from Francioni (1984): the symbol "Q" refers to Gramsci (1975b), the critical edition of *Quaderni del carcere;* the "Q" followed by a numeral between 1 and 28 refers to the corresponding notebook as numbered in this critical edition; if the notebook number is followed by a comma and then by another numeral as high as the 200s, the numeral after the comma denotes the number of the section, paragraph, or note, again as numbered in the critical edition. Moreover, if the "Q" is followed by large numerals, going up to 3369, without commas but possibly hyphenated, these denote page numbers in the critical edition, which goes up to p. 3369; and the slash symbol (/) is used when references are given both by notebook and note number and by page number. Now that these abbreviations have been explained, the Moschian passages in question are the following: Q 8,24/Q 956; Q 8,36/Q 963; Q 8,37/Q 964, later revised into Q 13,2/Q 1562; Q 8,52/Q 972, later revised into Q 13,6/Q 1565; Q 9,89/Q 1155-56, later revised into Q 19,5/Q 1978-79; and Q 13,23/Q 1607.

7. The phenomenon is notorious in the history of philosophy but occurs also in the history of (natural) science; for a discussion of the latter case, see Finocchiaro (1980b), pp. 68-73. I believe it to be no less true in the domain of political and social theory.

8. For more information and the textual references to these Gramscian conceptions, see Finocchiaro (1988a), pp. 76-78, 90-91, 102-3, 135-36, and 239-40.

9. For example, Bellamy (1987), Bellamy and Schecter (1993, pp. 142-48), Bob-

bio (1966, 1969b), Croce (1923), and Sola (1982d, p. 169). For a criticism of this interpretation, see Finocchiaro (forthcoming a).

10. Such an attitude was expressed by people as diverse as Croce (1948) and Capucci (1978).

11. See Mosca (1982), pp. 873–78 and 1105–9 (which corresponds to Mosca 1939, pp. 281–86 and 484–87), and Mosca (1949), p. 309. See also Chapter 2.

12. See Mosca (1982), pp. 1017, 1027, 1070–71; (1939), pp. 406, 416, 453. Again, see Chapter 2.

13. See, for example, Q 1255–56, 1330–32, 1342–43, 1375–95, and 1513–51.

14. However, see also Holub (1992) for a philosophical appreciation.

15. Q 1396–1450; cf. Finocchiaro (1988a), pp. 76–86.

16. See, for example, Finocchiaro (1977), Laudan (1977), and McMullin (1976).

17. For a discussion of some of these issues, see Finocchiaro (1980b), pp. 68–73.

18. Mosca (1982), p. 191.

19. Mosca (1982), pp. 929–34.

20. Mosca (1964), pp. 257–71.

21. See, for example, Finocchiaro (1988a), pp. 123–46.

22. Gramsci (1971b), pp. 175–76. I have emended the translation by Hoare and Nowell-Smith by replacing their 'command structure' by 'the organics' as a rendering of Gramsci's *organica;* cf. Gramsci (1975b), pp. 1561–62.

23. See in Q 13 paragraphs 7.2, 14, 15, 17, 18, 19, 21, 23, 24, 26, 27, 28, 32, 34, 35, 37, and 39.

24. Gramsci (1971b), p. 176; cf. Q 1562.

25. Gramsci makes an analogous remark in a discussion of bureaucratic officials, in which he states that "the problem of bureaucratic officials partly coincides with the problem of intellectuals" (Q 1632), and the context is such that bureaucratic officials correspond in large measure to Mosca's political class.

26. Eugenio Ripepe (1974, pp. 83–84, n. 184; 1983) has suggested that the chronology of the two notes just quoted is such that while Gramsci first thought that Mosca's notion of political class was a groping toward Gramsci's own idea of intellectuals, he later found the Moschian concept too problematic to be useful and, displaying a more negative and destructive attitude, rejected it entirely. Ripepe's case is based simply on the fact that the destructive comment was written some time after the constructive one. Therefore, he seems to be assuming that chronology is logic, as it were. However, it seems to me that the logical relationship of the two comments is simply one of being different but not incompatible; that is, the negative comment states that Mosca's concept of political class is full of ambiguities, whereas the positive one asserts that this concept really corresponds to the class of intellectuals. Aside from the fact that it remains to be seen whether Gramsci's notion of intellectuals is not perhaps also full of analogous ambiguities (in which case the two concepts and comments would approach each other by default), it seems to make perfect sense to say (and to attribute to Gramsci the claim) that Mosca's "political class" is to be reinterpreted in terms of the class of "intellectuals" *because* the Moschian notion is too ambiguous and all-inclusive. Finally, even from a chronological point of view the situation is not clear-cut. Ripepe was writing before a more exact chronology was worked out by Francioni (1984). According to the latter, the later version of Gramsci's destructive comment (Q 13, 6/Q 1565) was written between May 1932 and early 1934; but the

earlier version of the same comment (Q 8, 52/Q 972) was written in February 1932, and Gramsci's constructive interpretation was written in January or February 1932. Now, if we give proper weight to the earlier version of the destructive comment, then we would have to say that the destructive and the constructive comments are essentially contemporaneous, and so there is not even a chronological reason for regarding one as superseding the other. This is a good example both of the potential payoff of chronology, and of the fact that mere chronology is not so significant. This is not to deny the unquestionable value of Francioni's work, but it is to say that the interpretive and critical consequences of chronological facts are neither simple nor immediate nor easy to work out. This point is also illustrated by Francioni's own examples — his critique of Anderson (1977) in Francioni (1984, pp. 147-228) and his account of Gramsci's critique of Bukharin in Francioni (1987). Thus, I fail to see how the intellectual content of Gramsci's critique of Bukharin (as elaborated in Finocchiaro 1988a, pp. 68-93) and the evaluative weaknesses of Gramsci's criticism (elaborated in Finocchiaro 1988a, pp. 94-122), are in any way affected by the account in Francioni (1987).

27. Mosca (1982), pp. 738-76; Mosca (1939), pp. 163-98. For a serious and important contribution to the reconstruction of Mosca's theory of the party, see Sola (1983).

28. Gramsci's notes on the topic could be organized into four groups. The first is a criticism of alternative views: Q 1,47; 2,75; 8,132; 13,1 and 6 and 8. The second is a discussion of fundamental principles: Q 4,10; 7,90; 8,52 and 131.2 and 195; 13,21 and 33; 14,34; 15,4 and 6 and 47 and 48.II; 17,37. The third is an analysis of the internal structure of parties: Q 3,42; 13,31; 14,18 and 70. The fourth is an examination of particular examples: Q 3, 119; 13, 29 and 37; 14,3 and 53; 15,2.

29. The first edition was really published in 1884. Gramsci thinks the year was 1883 probably because the 1925 edition reprints the original preface, which does bear the date of 1883.

30. See Mosca (1925d).

31. There is no point here in compiling a list of references, which would have to mention a large number of the more than ten thousand entries in Cammett (1991) and Cammett and Righi (1995). However, a good example of this type of interpretation would be Pellicani (1975, 1976, 1981). An exceptionally insightful interpretation of Gramsci's revolutionism may be found in Gerratana (1977).

32. Finocchiaro (1988a, 1988b).

33. De Mattei (1968), p. x. This is only the key example of Mosca's judiciousness, but his book contains many others, such as his argument on the issue of republic versus monarchy; cf. Mosca (1982), pp. 506-17.

34. See, for example, Mosca (1908; 1958, pp. 551-56 and 593-605); cf. Bobbio (1966, 1969b) and Sola (1984).

35. Mosca (1982), pp. 472-73.

36. Mosca (1982), p. 493.

Chapter 4: Gramsci's Elitism

1. As previously mentioned (Chapter 1, note 11), traditional Marxism was not averse to the elitist principle: its interpretation of history in terms of class struggle is a kind of descriptive elitism; its view that revolutions are made by vanguards is a strain of explanatory elitism; and Leninism seems committed to normative elitism.

Thus, there is little question that Gramsci's exposure to Marxism made him receptive to theoretical elitism in the science of politics. In the present context, this may be taken as strengthening my interpretation that Gramsci's political theory is Moschian insofar as it accepts, extends, and deepens the most fundamental principle of Mosca's science of politics.

2. For the details of Gramsci's critique of Machiavelli, see Finocchiaro (1988a, pp. 123–46), and Fontana (1993).

3. Mosca (1982), p. 608; cf. Mosca (1939), p. 50.

4. Mosca (1982), pp. 1015–16.

5. For more details, see Finocchiaro (1988a), pp. 139–40.

6. Q 19,16 and 29 and 38; Q 2,121/Q 262.

7. See Q 2,121/Q 259–62; Q 3,82/Q 361–63; Q 6,69/Q 736–37; and Q 6,74/Q 740–42.

8. Da Silva (1932).

9. Mosca (1958), pp. 353–75; cf. Mosca (1912a, 1923b, 1925a, 1925b) and Mosca (1982), pp. 710–15, 859–70, and 1047–53.

10. However, Gramsci's lack of appreciation was by no means total, because he too was somewhat concerned with the problem of demagoguery, which lies at the root of Mosca's criticism.

11. See, for example, Meisel (1958, p. 4) and Bachrach (1967, p. 2).

12. See, for example, Q 12,1/Q 1515–16.

13. See Q 5,127/Q 661–62; Q 6,12/Q 693; Q 6,65/Q 734–35; Q 6,82/Q 752–56; Q 6,88/Q 763–64; Q 7,33/Q 881–82; Q 8,2/Q 937; Q 8,179/Q 1049–50; Q 11,1/Q 1366–68; Q 11,62/Q 1487–90; and Q 15,4/Q 1752–55.

14. For some of the best and latest accounts see Adamson (1980b), Femia (1981a, 1981b), and Morera (1990b); cf. Finocchiaro (1988a), pp. 47–50, 88–89, and 172.

15. Q 764. It is unfortunate that the critical edition of the Notebooks contains two typographical errors in this crucial passage. The original manuscript (which may be consulted at the Gramsci Institute in Rome) shows that in the first sentence of this quotation *possibile* (possible) should read *passibile* (liable), and *della* (of the) should read *nella* (to). As it stands, this sentence in the critical edition does not make sense, and the careful reader will wonder about the possibility of misprints, which indeed is the case. Moreover, in the last sentence of the quotation, I have translated *da una fase* freely as "between a phase" rather than literally as "from a phase" in order to improve the sense; in other words, I have assumed that Gramsci himself made a slip of the pen and wrote *da* (from) instead of *tra* (between).

16. Q 1049–50. A more literal translation of the first sentence of this passage would reveal a secondary connection with Mosca. The more literal translation would read: "Every state is ethical insofar as one of its most important functions is to lift the great mass of the population to a particular cultural and moral level, a level (*or type*) which corresponds to what is required for the development of the productive forces and hence for the interests of the dominant classes" (Q 1049, italics mine). I see no way of making sense of the italicized words in this passage unless we take it to have the Moschian meaning of "social type," in regard to which see, for example, Mosca (1982), pp. 633–72.

17. This is, of course, a traditional Marxian idea, and Gramsci may have flirted with it on various occasions. But in the present inquiry I do not want to prejudge the

case; I am trying merely to determine the import of this particular passage. For more details about Gramsci's relationship to Marxism, see Finocchiaro (1988a).

18. See Francioni (1984), pp. 140–46.

19. See Spirito (1929, 1930a, 1930b, 1930c, 1932).

20. Q 756. Here Gramsci makes a pun involving Spirito's name, which means "spirit" or "mind."

21. For more details about the meaning of the dialectic, see Finocchiaro (1988a).

22. Is this not, after all, the meaning of "regulated" in Gramsci's notion of a regulated society?

Chapter 5: Gramsci's Democracy

1. For some of the most insightful and instructive work on the theory of democracy, see Dahl (1956, 1966, 1989), Femia (1985, 1993a), and Sartori (1959, 1962a, 1987).

2. See, for example, Mosca (1901; 1949, pp. 1–25, 331–36; 1982, pp. 710–13, 1004).

3. Not to mention the rest of Gramsci's writings. For example, there is no question that his writings and activities during the Red Years of 1919-1920 exhibit a tendency toward a kind of democracy which might be labeled industrial; see Bellamy and Schecter (1993, pp. 27–58), Salvadori (1977), and Schecter (1991). On this basis, it is tempting to read into the Prison Notebooks a radical, participatory, and egalitarian theory of democracy (Bellamy and Schecter 1993, pp. 157–63). However, I am reluctant to do so, for a number of reasons: partly because I attach primary importance to the Notebooks; partly because of the methodological questionableness of the practice of first attributing a given view to an author on weak textual grounds and then showing its theoretical untenability; and partly because I would argue that the notion of industrial democracy is not unrelated to the elitist democracy which in the Notebooks Gramsci adapts from Mosca.

4. The passage is not included, as far as I know, in the available selected English translations of the Notebooks, namely Gramsci (1971b, 1985, 1995), as the concordance reveals (see the Appendix); on the other hand, in the new English translation of the critical edition (Gramsci 1992b; Gramsci 1996b) only the first through the fifth notebooks have so far been published. In regard to the secondary literature, I still find it puzzling that this passage could have been entirely neglected in the discussion on Gramsci, hegemony, and democracy which flared up in Italy in 1976–1977—see De Giovanni, Gerratana, and Paggi (1977), Diaz et al. (1977), and Sassoli (1977). Salvadori (1977, pp. 5–71) and Prestipino (1987) also offer typical examples of such neglect. The neglect is in turn related to the general lack of interest in the subject of democracy among students of Gramsci, as one can see from the listing of a mere forty-nine entries under "democracy" in the subject index of the Gramscian bibliography, which numbers more than ten thousand works (Cammett 1991, p. 440; Cammett and Righi 1995, p. 221). Important exceptions to this generalization are Femia (1981a, 1993b), Golding (1992), Laclau and Mouffe (1985), Morera (1990a), and Vacca (1991). The latter (Vacca 1991, p. 38), claims that Gramsci saw no contradiction between hegemony and democracy; this assertion is correct, although one could cavil and say that Vacca's admission came only after a delay of about fifteen years; moreover, Vacca says nothing about the Moschian character of Gramsci's definition. Golding's account in some ways parallels

mine; for example, referring to the passage quoted here, she attributes to Gramsci the view that "what was at stake in creating a democracy was making sure that the political system itself reflected an ongoing—that is to say, fluid—'organic unity' between the intellectuals and the people-nation, between leaders and led, between 'theory and practice,' and so forth" (Golding 1992, p. 77); however, insights like these are embedded in a conceptual and terminological framework of such density and obscurity that one cannot be sure of their import. A more readable exception is Morera (1990a).

5. As before, references to Gramsci's Prison Notebooks will be given in parenthesis in the text, and the translation will be my own unless otherwise noted; for example, the notation given here means: Gramsci (1975b, Notebook 8, paragraph no. 191), which is equivalent to Gramsci (1975b, p. 1056).

6. See Q 8,36/Q 962-64 for further evidence of this interpretation of Gramsci's "molecular" terminology.

7. Mosca (1939), p. 395; cf. Mosca (1982), p. 1005. It is important to note that what the English translation (Mosca 1939) renders as "ruling class" and "lower classes," in the original read, respectively, *classe dirigente* and *classi dirette*, which more literally should be translated as "leading class" and "led classes." In view of the issue whether elitism in general, and Mosca's in particular, entails a reprehensible manipulation of the masses, the importance of this point is difficult to overestimate. An original and important articulation of these concepts may be found in Dorso (1949), and a lucid interpretation of the latter is available in Germino (1967).

8. Mosca (1939), p. 395; cf. Mosca (1982), p. 1005. Again, the available English translation has "social control" for *direzione sociale*, which is more accurately rendered as "social leadership."

9. Mosca (1982), pp. 1003-4; (1939), pp. 394-95.

10. Mosca (1939), p. 415, italics mine; cf. Mosca (1982), p. 1026.

11. See for example, Entwistle (1979) and Manacorda (1970).

12. In Gramsci (1971b), pp. 40-41, Hoare and Nowell-Smith translate this passage in such a way that the word "tendency" disappears.

13. Chapter 4, section 2.

14. Chapter 4, section 5; Q 734.

15. See for example, Burnham (1943), p. 105.

16. See, for example, Bates (1978), Forgacs (1984), Nowell-Smith (1977), Portantiero (1981a, 1988), Premoli (1982), Spinazzola (1987), and Tomiolo (1979).

17. Gramsci advances the same concept of elitist, Moschian democracy, with the same qualification about abstract democracy, and with a similar meaning for the latter notion, in his theory of intellectuals in Notebook 12 (Q 1518).

18. Cf. Mosca (1982, p. 1027; 1939, p. 416).

19. From another standpoint there is also something extremely revealing about the passage—namely, Gramsci's conception of the dialectic as a manner of thinking; see Finocchiaro (1988a), pp. 155-58 and 162-63. This conception is not unrelated to the present discussion, but the complexities involved are such that it is advisable to leave consideration of it for another context.

20. Today, a nonspecialist may be easily overwhelmed by the controversy, but the following works may be useful. For an interpretation and criticism of inductivism, see Agassi (1963), and Popper (1959, 1979), but cf. Finocchiaro (1973); for what I

regard as the most original, plausible, and sophisticated view of induction, see Cohen (1970, 1977, 1986, 1989); for more traditional accounts, see Katz (1962), Salmon (1984a, 1984b), and Skyrms (1975).

21. See Chapter 4, section 5.

22. For a very explicit and relevant statement of this caveat, see Q23,51/Q 2247; for Croce's view, see Croce (1950a, 1953, 1981, 1992); for an interpretive and evaluative account of the connection between Gramsci and Croce, see Finocchiaro (1988a).

23. Q 7,50/Q 895–97; Q 8,9/Q 942–43; Q 14,39/Q 1696; Q 14,72/Q 1737–40; Q 21,1/Q 2107–10; Q 23,51/Q 2244–47; Q 23,56/Q 2249–50.

24. An insightful analysis of Gramsci's view of Manzoni is given by Holub (1992), who calls attention to the Gramscian notion of the "popular creative spirit" (pp. 49–60) and occasionally connects the discussion with the notion of democracy (pp. 66, 69). However, she is not explicit about this democratic connection and says nothing about Mosca, but is instead interested in a comparison and contrast with Lukács; moreover, I find unjustified her statement that "Gramsci appears to be determined to eliminate him [Manzoni] from the cultural literacy list" (Holub 1992, p. 59).

25. Gramsci (Q 2246–47) refers to Leo N. Tolstoy, *Shakespeare, eine kritische Studie* (Hannover, 1906), which also contains an article by Ernest Crosby on Shakespeare's attitude toward the working classes, and a letter by George Bernard Shaw on Shakespeare's philosophy. The prisoner is taking this information from Adolfo Faggi, "Tolstoi e Shakespeare," *Il Marzocco*, vol. 33, no. 37 (8 September 1928).

26. Q 4,45/Q 472–73; Q 6,82/Q 756; Q 7,38/Q 887–88; and Q 10,II,35/Q 1280–81. Gramsci quotes this idea from Croce (1926), p. 45, where it is clear that Croce is appropriating it from what he calls an "old German dissertation," his purpose being to justify and explain his own democratic commitment (cf. Q 2649, n. 4).

27. An equally eloquent statement of the pedagogic conception of philosophy is given in what Gramsci calls Note IV to the above-mentioned long essay (Q 11,12): "To create a new culture does not mean only to make individually some 'original' discoveries; it means also and especially to critically disseminate some truths already discovered, to 'socialize' them (so to speak), and thus to make them the basis of vital actions and an element of coordination and of intellectual and moral order. That a mass of men is led to think coherently and in a unified manner about present reality is a 'philosophical' fact of much greater importance and 'originality' than the discovery by a philosophical 'genius' of a new truth which remains the property of small intellectual groups" (Q 1377–78). Elsewhere in the course of this essay Gramsci asks rhetorically: "Is a philosophical movement such only insofar as it strives to develop a specialized culture for various restricted groups of intellectuals, or is it instead such only insofar as, in its work of elaborating a system of thought superior to common belief and scientifically coherent, it never forgets to stay in touch with the 'simple ones' and indeed in this contact finds the source of the problems to be studied and solved?" (Q 1382).

28. For more concrete evidence that Gramsci is not at all committed to a consensus theory of truth, one can examine his remarks on scientific method in the context of his criticism of Bukharin; cf. Q 1396–1450 and Finocchiaro (1988a), pp. 76–88.

29. I owe my discovery of this note (Q 10,II,44) to Prestipino (1987), although other scholars (e.g., Femia) had discussed it earlier. However, Prestipino misses the conception of democracy inherent in it when he interprets Gramsci as saying that a democratic philosopher is a philosopher of praxis and that the philosophy of praxis is

"philosophy which gets involved in politics, or rather which becomes politics" (Prestipino 1987, p. 96).

30. I am translating Gramsci's *buon senso* (which means literally "good sense") as "common sense" and his *senso comune* (which literally means "common sense") as "common belief." That is, by *senso comune* he does not mean what "common sense" connotes in English, but rather what is commonly believed, whether it makes sense or not; hence it would be misleading to translate his *senso comune* literally as "common sense"; this is what Hoare and Nowell-Smith do (Gramsci 1971b, p. 323), even though they are aware of the problem. My point is that it is not enough to have a footnote clarification, or to use quotation marks, or to rely merely on Gramsci's contrast between *senso comune* and *buon senso.* I think my more radical translation suggestion bypasses all these confusions.

31. I am here paraphrasing Gramsci, when he makes a similar move in regard to politics. In a discussion of the connection between science and politics he points out that even science has a political dimension, but then goes one to add: "If everything is 'political' one must, in order not to lapse into a tautological and boring phraseology, distinguish by means of new concepts the politics which corresponds to that science which is traditionally called philosophy from the politics which is called political science in a strict sense" (Q 1766). Similarly, in a discussion of practice, the theory-practice nexus, and its connection with politics, Gramsci makes the same methodological move: "What is politics? . . . Where everything is practice, in a philosophy of praxis, the distinction will not be made among moments of the Absolute Spirit, but between the structure and the superstructures; one will have to fix the dialectical position of political activity as a distinction within the superstructures" (Q 977). Analogous moves are made in discussions of the relationship and distinction between philosophy and ideology (Q 10,I,10/Q 1231) and between artistic form and content (Q 14,72/Q 1737). This technique corresponds in turn to the "dialectical" approach, when the latter is interpreted along the lines of Finocchiaro (1988a), pp. 147-230.

32. See Finocchiaro (1988a).

33. I am referring to a method stemming from classical Greek mathematics and widely discussed during the Renaissance and early modern science and philosophy; it involves, first, starting with a problem (e.g., an effect to be explained), then analyzing it to try to find some hypothesis which entails it, then trying to find independent support for this hypothesis to ensure that it is not ad hoc, and then synthesizing the effect by deriving it from this now-confirmed hypothesis; cf. Hintikka and Remes (1974), Otte and Panza (1997), and Wallace (1992).

34. See "Trasformismo," *Vocabolario Illustrato della Lingua Italiana* (New York: Funk & Wagnalls, 1967); and "Parlamento," *Enciclopedia Italiana*, vol. 26, p. 375.

35. See also Q 2011, in which the passage quoted just before this one continues: "In this sense, political leadership has become an aspect of the domination process, insofar as the absorption of the elites of the enemy groups implies their decapitation and their annihilation for a probably very long period."

36. On the other hand, from the point of view of the Mosca-Gramsci connection, which is certainly a central theme of this investigation, it is important to note that Mosca was also generally critical of Giolitti; I do not think such a joint opposition can be entirely an accident, any more than their common opposition to the Fascist law against freemasonry (discussed in Chapter 7) was. However, a full ex-

amination of this point would require an identification and analysis of the reasons for Mosca's opposition and a fuller account of the character of their respective anti-Giolittian stances; in the process one would probably have to admit that their stance was not entirely negative in any case, but that too could turn out to be another similarity. For an example of a favorable judgment on Giolitti, see Q 13,5/Q 1563–64, where Gramsci sees him in terms of "great" as distinct from "petty" politics and distinguishes Giolitti himself from his uncritical followers and imitators; on this point, cf. also Finocchiaro (1988a), pp. 138–39.

37. For details see Finocchiaro (1988a), pp. 166–76.

38. See Chapter 2, section 4, above, and Mosca (1982), p. 1027.

Chapter 6: Liberalism and Anti-Liberalism in Mosca and Gramsci

1. Mosca (1939), pp. 409–10; cf. Mosca (1982), p. 1020. See also Mosca (1949), pp. 37–60, 61–115, 289, 302–15, and 331–7; (1958), pp. 379–99; (1971), pp. 149–55; and (1982), pp. 964, 1003–5, and 1084–88, which correspond respectively to (1939), pp. 358–59, 394–96, and 466–70.

2. Mosca (1982), p. 1004; (1939), pp. 394–95.

3. Mosca (1949), pp. 61–86, especially p. 68.

4. Mosca (1982), pp. 699, 841, which correspond to (1939), pp. 144, 254.

5. Mosca (1949), p. 35.

6. Mosca (1949), pp. 285–91, especially p. 289.

7. Mosca (1982), p. 1004; cf. Mosca (1939), pp. 394–95; cf. Plato, *Republic*, VII, 555b–558c.

8. An extremely valuable and insightful historical and critical account of various doctrines of liberalism is provided by Bellamy (1992). In this work he does not discuss Mosca or Gramsci, but it is interesting that he sketches and defends a version which he contrasts to liberal democracy and labels democratic liberalism; by this he means "a political theory, in which the central place is occupied, not by liberal values, but by institutions or procedures capable of giving expression to a plurality of points of view and arranging agreements between them" (Bellamy 1992, pp. 7–8; cf. pp. 254, 256, 258, 261). This strikes me as corresponding to Mosca's separation of powers and balanced pluralism, although Bellamy seems to arrive at such a position by a route independent of Mosca's, and although I am uncertain whether he would admit the correspondence.

9. Cf. Q 15,4/Q 1752–55.

10. In the penultimate sentence of this quotation, I have translated *da una fase* freely as "between a phase" rather than literally as "from a phase," in order to improve the sense; in other words, I have assumed that Gramsci himself made a slip of the pen and wrote *da* ("from") instead of *tra* ("between").

11. Q 8,112/Q 1007; Q 10,I,10/Q 1229–32; Q 1293; and Gramsci (1965), pp. 220–21.

12. The Prison Notebooks contain many other critiques of Croce's ideas, although these critiques reveal Gramsci's acceptance of certain aspects of Croce's system; for details, see Finocchiaro (1988a). The ideas being criticized here may be found in such works as Croce (1929, 1946, 1963a, 1965, 1966c, 1967b, 1970a); the original Italian edition of Croce (1966c) is dated 1938, after Gramsci's death, but many parts

of this book had already been published as essays, and so Gramsci was acquainted with them.

13. See also Q 1293, 1381–85.

14. This interpretation is reinforced by Bellamy's judgment that "Italian liberalism became associated with the narrow economic interests of privileged classes who cynically exploited the political system to manipulate and coerce the population into acceptance of their dominance" (Bellamy 1992, p. 6); for this would mean that the notion of liberalism as undemocratic elitism (which notion seems semantically and theoretically gratuitous) was not one of Gramsci's idiosyncrasies but rather was a common usage in Italian political discussions.

15. See also Q 6,81/Q 751–52.

16. Q 763–64, 801, 810–11, 1020–21.

17. For a good example of the traditional interpretation of Gramsci's views on state and civil society, see Bellamy and Schecter (1993), pp. 118–28.

18. Implicitly in Q 1590, and explicitly in Q 8,142/Q 1028.

19. See, for example, Mosca (1982), pp. 895–96; (1939), pp. 301–2.

20. It could be objected that, when Gramsci proclaims the ontological identity of society and individuals, he means this in the anti-liberal sense that the individual is nothing outside society, rather than in the liberal sense that society is nothing but an aggregation of individuals. I am not sure, but I suspect that Gramsci means it in neither of those senses.

21. Q 4,38, especially 456–61; Q 13,17, especially 1580–81; and Q 13,18, especially 1589–91.

22. In this discussion I am using the text of Gramsci's earlier account of these issues in Q 4,38 rather that his later one in Q 13,17–18. The reason is that the earlier note is more coherent than the later ones. Some of the puzzles in the later notes will be discussed as difficulties later.

23. Mosca (1958), pp. 534–36, 556–59; (1982), pp. 522–24, 716–20; the last passage corresponds to (1939), pp. 158–62.

24. Mosca (1982), pp. 522–23.

25. Mosca (1939), p. 158; cf. (1982), p. 716.

26. Though he did not have access to it in prison—see Chapter 3, section 1.

27. Here I am translating the Italian *dirigono* as "lead or manage." There exists no English translation of the *Notes on Constitutional Law* (Mosca 1908).

28. Again, here I am translating the Italian *direzione* as "leadership or administration."

29. Mosca (1958), pp. 556–57.

30. Mosca (1982), pp. 716–17; cf. Mosca (1939), p. 159.

31. Here Kahn's translation (Mosca 1939) renders the Italian *funzione direttiva* as "management" and "managerial functions," although it could be translated as "leadership function."

32. Mosca (1939), pp. 161–62; cf. (1982), pp. 718–20.

33. Mosca (1982), pp. 689–700; (1939), pp. 134–44. See also Chapter 2.

34. Mosca (1949), pp. 61–86.

35. For accounts of such a tradition, see Bobbio (1978, 1988).

36. For a detailed discussion of this issue and the relevant textual references, see

Finocchiaro (1988a), chapter 6, especially pp. 166–80. Another author who seems to have developed a pluralistic interpretation of Gramsci is Golding (1992); if I understand this difficult book correctly, it attributes to Gramsci what is labeled a post-liberal theory of democracy which is "founded upon a radical notion of social diversity or pluralism" (Golding 1992, p. 123; cf. pp. 125, 130, 131).

37. For accounts of Pareto's notion of residue, see, for example, Meisel (1965b), pp. 27–28, 59–60.

38. For a different interpretation, see Gramsci (1981), p. 92, n. 6, where the editor of the book (C. Donzelli) arbitrarily interprets the immediate element to refer to economic factors.

39. Bobbio (1977), p. 55.

40. Pellicani (1981), pp. 79–81.

41. Cf. Finocchiaro (1984), pp. 136–39; (1988b), pp. 149–51.

42. Germino and Fennema (forthcoming).

43. However, the situation is not as bad as the 1975 critical edition makes it look. Although, generally speaking, the philological rigor and accuracy of that edition is beyond question, in this note (Q 13,1) its printing of the word "Principe" introduces some confusions not found in Gramsci's manuscript. Gramsci writes the word in quotation marks or in italics to refer to Machiavelli's book; and he merely capitalizes the initial *P* to refer to either the work "The Modern Prince" or the party-as-modern-Prince; whereas the critical edition neither faithfully follows nor consistently amends Gramsci's writing of the word.

Chapter 7: Mosca and Gramsci on Freemasonry and Fascism

1. The text of Gramsci's speech can be found in the *Atti Parlamentari* (Gramsci 1925a); Gramsci published it a few days after (May 23, 1925) in *L'Unità;* the text was then reprinted under the same title in Gramsci (1971a), pp. 75–85. It should be noted that the version in *L'Unità* does not correspond exactly to that of the *Atti Parlamentari*, although the differences seem relatively insignificant.

2. A historian of Freemasonry has praised its seriousness and open-mindedness, claiming that Gramsci's remarks "are significant because of the many elements they contain (which are not reducible to ideological clichés) and because of the consequent openness to a critical analysis which would be more elaborate and historically more inclusive" (Mola 1976, p. 481).

3. Gramsci (1965), p. 480.

4. Mosca (1913), now in *Inchiesta sulla massoneria*, pp. 162–66.

5. Mosca also mentions having criticized the Masonic doctrines in his scholarly works; indeed such criticism can be found in Mosca (1982), pp. 774–75 (*Elements*, part 1, chapter 7, section 12). Here we should also mention the various notes in Gramsci's Notebooks on the topic of Freemasonry; there are about a dozen such passages: Q 65, 98, 138, 541–43, 545, 579, 593–94, 834–35, 959–60, 1356, 1385, 2075–76, 2140, and 2146. In one of these (Q 2075–76), Gramsci repeats the "elitist" interpretation of Freemasonry, which we will soon see he advances in his 1925 speech, and he also attributes to it an interesting democratic aspect. In another passage, he discusses the connection between Freemasonry and positivism, in regard to which he asserts that "positivism has been an aspect of the Masonic attitude" (Q 545); if this thesis

holds true, Mosca's criticism of Freemasonry would express an antipositivistic attitude, which is an interpretive hypothesis of great novelty and may be confirmed by what will emerge when (later in this chapter) I analyze the content of Mosca's criticism of Masonic "ideology."

6. Mussolini (1925), p. 1.

7. "Legge 26 novembre 1926, n. 2029," p. 9120.

8. Gramsci (1925b). I thank Valentino Gerratana for having given me this reference. Gramsci's confession also confirms that he did not have a prior written text of the speech, which would be a very important document if it did exist.

9. Gramsci (1971a), p. 75.

10. Ibid., p. 76.

11. Ibid., p. 77.

12. This interpretive framework is elaborated in his essay on the Southern Question (Gramsci 1971a, p. 146) and in Notebook 19 on the Italian Risorgimento (Q 2035–46).

13. Gramsci (1971a), p. 79.

14. Ibid., p. 79.

15. Ibid.

16. Ibid., p. 80.

17. Perhaps the contradiction could be resolved by saying that Gramsci's previous interpretation of Fascism as a rural force refers to the rural bourgeoisie, and that hence both interpretations portray Fascism as a bourgeois force. This resolution has some plausibility, but I do not see how it could be harmonized with the assertion Gramsci makes in the context of his previous interpretation—namely, that "Fascism has replaced the Vatican and the Jesuits in the historical task whereby the more backward classes of the population place under their control a class which has been progressive in the history of civilization" (1971a, p. 77). The progressive class mentioned here can only be the bourgeoisie, and so this assertion clearly indicates that according to Gramsci's previous interpretation Fascism is a rural and antibourgeois force.

18. Gramsci (1971a), p. 80.

19. Ibid., p. 80.

20. Ibid., p. 82.

21. Ibid.

22. Ibid., p. 80.

23. Ibid.

24. Ibid., p. 75.

25. Ibid., p. 76.

26. Ibid., p. 80.

27. Ibid., p. 84.

28. Ibid.

29. Mosca (1925c). For reasons which I do not know, when the actual vote came up, Mosca abstained, instead of casting a vote against; see Mola (1982). For other interesting details, see Mola (1976), pp. 463–530.

30. Mosca (1925c), p. 3661.

31. Ibid. p. 3661.

32. Ibid.

33. Ibid., p. 3662.

34. *Inchiesta,* p. xxxi.

35. Mosca (1913), p. 163.

36. Ibid.

37. Ibid.

38. One should also note Mosca's sympathy for the English political system, which is a constant characteristic of his thought.

39. *Inchiesta,* p. xxxi.

40. Mosca (1913), p. 164.

41. Ibid., p. 163.

42. Ibid., p. 164.

43. *Inchiesta,* p. xxxi.

44. Mosca (1913), p. 165.

45. Ibid., pp. 165-66.

46. Mosca (1925c), p. 3662.

47. Ibid.

48. It should be noted that such realism also characterizes Marx's thought, and so this similarity may be qualified in the same way as the similarity involving the elitist principle. That is, here Gramsci's connection with Mosca is nonexclusive and can be regarded as strengthened by Gramsci's Marxist background. However, in the present case the Machiavellian influence and background would be another important element of the situation.

49. See, for example, Bobbio (1966, p. xi), Burnham (1943, p. 87), Sola (1982a; 1982b, p. 98), and Zarone (1990).

50. Gramsci (1971a), p. 75.

51. Mosca (1925c), p. 3662.

52. Gramsci (1971a), p. 77.

53. Ibid., p. 82.

54. Ibid.

55. Here are Gramsci's words (1971a), p. 82: "Some Fascists still remember vaguely the teachings of their old masters, when they were revolutionaries and socialists, and they believe that a class cannot permanently remain such and develop until its takeover of power without its having a party and an organization which would express its best and most self-conscious part. There is some truth in this confused reactionary perversion of Marxist teachings."

56. For some theoretically oriented, rather than historically oriented, analyses, see Aron (1950) and Bottomore (1964), pp. 18-41. See also Hobsbawm (1979), p. 91. Oddo (1982) has also discussed this problem, but with mixed results. For, on the one hand, in a context reminiscent of "vulgar Marxism" and of a vulgarly elitist Mosca (in the pejorative sense of elitism), Oddo claims that "for Mosca as well as for Marx, the state and the law (which is the normal externalization of the state) can only be instruments whereby the ruling class maintains and increases its own power" (Oddo 1982, p. 485); on the other hand, he also advances a profound and penetrating analysis when he says that "for Marx as well as for Mosca, a new class never emerges unless all the creative and conservative power of the preceding class has been exhausted" (Oddo 1982), p. 486; and for this he refers to Mosca (1884), p. 37, which corresponds to *Theory of Governments,* chapter 1, section 5.

57. Gramsci (1971a), pp. 25-26.

58. Mosca (1913), p. 163.
59. Ibid., p. 165.
60. Ibid.
61. Gramsci (1971a), p. 79.
62. Ibid.
63. Mosca (1913), p. 165.
64. Note Gramsci's "realism."
65. Note the "elitist" interpretation of Freemasonry.
66. Gramsci (1971a), p. 80.
67. Mosca (1925c), p. 3662.
68. Gramsci (1971a), p. 80.
69. Ibid., p. 81.
70. Mosca (1925c), p. 3661.
71. Ibid.
72. I am here referring to the historical question, although there is also an evaluative issue, namely whether the elitist interpretation of Freemasonry is de facto correct. It appears to receive confirmation from Ragionieri (1976, p. 1935), who asserts: "In reality, the true and authentic party of the Italian bourgeoisie remained Freemasonry, which under the leadership of Adriano Lemmi had once supported Crispi, and now under the leadership of the Grand Master Ernesto Nathan was supporting the policies of the Giolitti government and of the new King, even though the relation between Freemasonry and Giolitti's politics was not one of simple and automatic identity." One might think, however, that this judgment is essentially (though not totally) an elaboration of Gramsci's own earlier judgment; but obviously the resolution of the issue lies outside the scope of this investigation. As indicated earlier, another positive evaluation of Gramsci's judgment is found in Mola (1976, p. 481).
73. Martire (1925); cf. Gramsci (1971a), p. 76.
74. Croce (1925, p. 165) declares that "the current bill is presented to us not only while the conditions of public liberty in Italy are very precarious, but also at a time when one sees many advocate with wild joy the destruction of the liberal system and regard this bill as an integral part of a whole series of anti-liberal laws." These Crocean comments were interrupted and received with extremely agitated comments and protests.
75. *Inchiesta* (1925).
76. It is interesting to note that Achille Loria was perhaps the only one who answered Yes to the second question (*Inchiesta*, pp. 140–41).
77. Pareto (1913), p. 183.
78. Ibid.
79. Ibid., pp. 183–84.
80. Here Pareto speaks of parliamentarism, not of the parliamentary system; parliamentarism is presumably an abuse of the system itself, namely an excessive development of the flaws and worst tendencies of the latter. I believe this is an extremely important distinction if one is to understand Mosca's own "antiparliamentarism"; cf. Mosca (1982), pp. 841–49, which corresponds to Mosca (1939), pp. 453–65. One could object that in *Theory of Governments* Mosca seems to use the terms *parlamentarismo* and *governo parlamentare* as synonyms, as Albertoni (1983b, p. xiv) claims; the reference he gives is Mosca (1884), p. 174, which corresponds to Mosca (1982), p. 356, and

to *Theory of Governments,* chapter 4, section 6; one could also refer to the passage in Mosca (1982), pp. 489–90, namely *Theory of Governments,* chapter 6, section 5. I would answer this objection by arguing that the identification is more semantic than conceptual or substantive; moreover, *Elements* is a more important work than *Theory of Governments,* and the reference I just gave (Mosca 1982), pp. 841–49, leaves no doubt about Mosca's distinction; finally, even *Theory of Governments* contains traces of a distinction (Mosca 1982), p. 495. See also Chapter 2, section 4.

81. Pareto (1913), p. 185.

82. Ibid.

83. Another proponent of what I have called the elitist interpretation of Freemasonry was Brodero, a Fascist deputy who strongly supported the anti-Masonic bill and who consequently in 1925 collected into a volume (*Inchiesta*) the various answers to the 1913 survey and wrote a preface to it. In this Preface, he interprets Freemasonry as a "powerful organization" (Brodero 1925, p. xiv) and "a focal point of all spiritual vulgarities in national life; it aimed to undertake the task of coordinating all those tendencies, facilitating transactions, securing support, and formulating theoretical presuppositions sufficiently wide so that everyone would feel comfortable with them, as long as one preserved the unquestionable premises of the immortal principles" (p. xv); the principles referred to are the ideals of liberty, equality, and fraternity of the French Revolution. Brodero's evaluation was, of course, highly and completely negative, but at the interpretive level his thesis is analogous to the interpretation of Gramsci and Mosca; nor are there any other common points between Brodero's analysis and theirs.

84. As mentioned in note 51 to Chapter 2, the interpretation of Pareto's thought is a serious and complicated business. While I remain doubtful about the democratic aspects of his thought, one may wish to consult Femia (1995) for an alternative interpretation.

Conclusion

1. Hamilton, Jay, and Madison (1961), p. 301.

2. Mosca (1939), p. 134; cf. (1982), p. 689; cf. also Chapter 2, section 4.

3. Cf. Dahl (1956), pp. 34–60.

4. Mosca (1939), p. 395; cf. Mosca (1982), p. 1005; cf. Chapter 2.

5. Dahl (1956), p. 3.

6. Ibid.

7. Ibid., p. 132.

8. See Chapter 2, section 1.

9. Dahl (1989), pp. 2–8.

10. Ibid., p. 2.

11. Dahl (1989), pp. 264–79.

12. Mosca (1949), p. 334. The interview was originally published in 1904.

13. Ibid., pp. 26–36.

14. Dahl (1989), pp. 106–31.

15. Ibid., p. 221.

16. Ibid., pp. 221–31.

17. Ibid., pp. 232–64.

18. Ibid., p. 251.

19. Ibid., p. 252.

20. Besides Giddens (1994), see also Bouvier (1951), Chickering (1993), Fickert (1987), and Sternhell (1986).

21. See, for example, Fuller (1996).

22. See, for example, Laponce (1981), pp. 10–11 and 138.

23. Gauchet (1992).

24. Bobbio (1995), p. 109.

25. Ibid., pp. 109 and 111.

26. Ibid., pp. 100–101.

27. Ibid., p. 104.

28. Ibid., pp. 107–8.

29. Ibid., p. 103.

30. Ibid., p. 107.

31. Gramsci (1975b), p. 2268; cf. also his definition of democratic centralism, at Q 1635, discussed in Chapter 5.

32. Bobbio (1995), pp. 51–62.

33. Ibid., p. 123.

BIBLIOGRAPHY

Abbondanti, W. 1978. "La fortuna nel mondo anglofono." In Albertoni (1978), pp. 429–518.

Adamson, W. L. 1980a. "Gramsci's Interpretation of Fascism." *Journal of the History of Ideas* 41:615–34.

Adamson, W. L. 1980b. *Hegemony and Revolution: Antonio Gramsci's Political and Cultural Theory.* Berkeley: University of California Press.

Adamson, W. L. 1990. "Modernism and Fascism: The Politics of Culture in Italy, 1903–1922." *American Historical Review* 95:359–90.

Agassi, J. 1963. *Towards an Historiography of Science. History and Theory,* supplement 2. The Hague: Mouton.

Agazzi, E. 1976. "Filosofia della prassi e filosofia dello spirito." In Caracciolo and Scalia (1976), pp. 93–175.

Agger, R., D. Goldrich, and B. Swanson. 1964. *The Rulers and the Ruled.* New York: Wiley.

Albertoni, E. A. 1978. *Gaetano Mosca: Storia di una dottrina politica.* Milan: Giuffrè.

Albertoni, E. A., ed. 1982a. *La dottrina della classe politica ed i suoi sviluppi internazionali: Primo seminario internazionale Gaetano Mosca, Palermo, 27–29 Novembre 1980.* Archivio internazionale Gaetano Mosca per lo studio della classe politica, serie italiana, vol. 1. Palermo: Società Siciliana per la Storia Patria.

Albertoni, E. A. 1982b. "Gaetano Mosca's Thought and Its Place in Italian Political Studies (1879–1980)." In Albertoni (1982c), pp. 19–73.

Albertoni, E. A., ed. 1982c. *Studies on the Political Thought of Gaetano Mosca.* Archivio internazionale Gaetano Mosca per lo studio della classe politica, serie internazionale, vol. 1. Milan: Giuffrè.

Albertoni, E. A., ed. 1983a. *Governo e governabilità nel sistema politico e giuridico di Gaetano Mosca.* Archivio internazionale Gaetano Mosca per lo studio della classe politica, serie italiana, vol. 2. Milan: Giuffrè.

Albertoni, E. A. 1983b. "Introduzione." In Albertoni (1983a), pp. vii–xxxvi.

Albertoni, E. A., ed. 1984. *Etudes sur la pensée politique de Gaetano Mosca: Classe politique et gouvernement.* Milan: Giuffrè.

Albertoni, E. A. 1985. *Dottrina della classe politica e teoria delle elites.* Milan: Giuffrè.

Albertoni, E. A. 1986–87. "Ruling Class, Elites and Leadership Interpreted by Mosca, Pareto, Ostrogorskij and Michels." *History of Sociology* 6(2), 7(1), and 7(2):131–50.

Albertoni, E. A. 1989a. "Democrazia, scelta d'elite." *Il sole 24 ore,* 5 February.

Albertoni, E. A., ed. 1989b. *Elitismo e democrazia nella cultura politica del Nord-America (Stati Uniti–Canada–Messico).* 2 vols. Milan: Giuffrè.

Albertoni, E. A. 1989c. "Introduzione: Alle origini della conoscenza critica dell'elitismo dei classici italiani negli USA: Arthur Livingston e James H. Meisel." In Albertoni (1989b), vol. 2, pp. ix–xxxv.

Albertoni, E. A. 1989d. "Prefazione: Fonti e sviluppo dell'elitismo politico." In Albertoni (1989b), vol. 1, pp. ix–lxxii.

Albertoni, E. A. 1990. "Un benemerito 'italianisant' statunitense: Arthur Livingston." *Nuova Antologia,* no. 2173:298–313.

Albertoni, E. A. 1991. "Per un bilancio dell'elitismo politico." In *Studi e ricerche sulla classe politica in Italia, Argentina e Messico,* pp. 76–81. Padua: CEDAM.

Alderisio, F. 1949–50. "Ripresa machiavelliana: Considerazioni critiche sulle idee di A. Gramsci, di B. Croce e di L. Russo intorno a Machiavelli." *Annali dell'Istituto universitario di Magistero* (Salerno) 1:205–66.

Amendola, G. 1967. *Comunismo, antifascismo, Resistenza.* Rome: Editori Riuniti.

Amendola, G. 1978. *Antonio Gramsci nella vita culturale e politica italiana.* Naples: Guida Editori.

Anderson, P. 1977. "The Antinomies of Antonio Gramsci." *New Left Review,* no. 100 (November 1976–January 1977):5–78.

Archer, M. S., and S. Giner. 1971. "Social Stratification in Europe." In *Contemporary Europe: Class, Status and Power,* ed. M. S. Archer and S. Giner, pp. 1–59. London: Weidenfeld and Nicolson.

Aron, R. 1950. "Social Structure and the Ruling Class." *British Journal of Sociology* 1:1–16, 126–43.

Aron, R. 1960. "Classe sociale, classe politique, classe dirigeante." *European Journal of Sociology* 1:260–81.

Asaro Mazzola, G. 1980. *Gramsci fuori dal mito.* Rome: Laterza.

Asor Rosa, A. 1975a. "La politica come scienza." In Asor Rosa (1975b), pp. 1042–60.

Asor Rosa, A. 1975b. *Storia d'Italia,* vol. 4: *Dall' Unità ad oggi,* book 2: *La cultura.* Turin: Einaudi.

Augelli, E., and C. Murphy. 1988. *America's Quest for Supremacy and the Third World: A Gramscian Analysis.* London: Pinter.

Bachrach, P. 1967. *The Theory of Democratic Elitism: A Critique.* Boston: Little, Brown. (Reprint. Lanham, Md.: University Press of America, 1980.)

Bachrach, P. 1971a. Introduction. In Bachrach (1971b), pp. 1–12.

Bachrach, P., ed. 1971b. *Political Elites in a Democracy.* New York: Atherton.

Bachrach, P., and M. S. Baratz. 1962. "Two Faces of Power." *American Political Science Review* 56:947–52.

Badaloni, N. 1975. *Il marxismo di Gramsci.* Turin: Einaudi.

Badaloni, N. 1981. "Gramsci: La filosofia della prassi come previsione." In *Storia del marxismo,* vol. 3, book 2, pp. 251–340. Turin: Einaudi.

Baldan, A. 1978. *Gramsci come storico: Studio sulle fonti dei "Quaderni del carcere."* Bari, Italy: Dedalo.

Baratta, G. 1989. "Per concludere aprendo un discorso." In Baratta and Catone (1989), pp. 474–77.

Baratta, G., and A. Catone, eds. 1989. *Tempi moderni: Gramsci e la critica dell'americanismo.* Rome: Edizioni Associate.

Barbano, F., and G. Sola. 1985. "Sociologia e scienze sociali in Italia, 1861–1890: Introduzioni critiche e repertorio bibliografico." *Archivio Italiano di Sociologia,* no. 4. Milan: Franco Angeli.

Barber, B. R. 1992. *An Aristocracy of Everyone: The Politics of Education and the Future of America.* New York: Ballantine.

Bates, T. R. 1978. "Il concetto di 'cultura nazional popolare' in Gramsci." *Storia contemporanea* 3:531–47.

Bellamy, R. 1987. *Modern Italian Social Theory.* Stanford, Calif.: Stanford University Press.

Bellamy, R. 1990. "Gramsci, Croce and the Italian Political Tradition." *History of Political Thought* 11:313–38.

Bellamy, R. 1991. Review of E. Morera, *Gramsci's Historicism. History of the Human Sciences* 4:310–12.

Bellamy, R. 1992. *Liberalism and Modern Society: A Historical Argument.* University Park: Pennsylvania State University Press.

Bellamy, R. 1994a. Introduction. In Bellamy (1994b).

Bellamy, R., ed. 1994b. *Pre-Prison Writings.* Cambridge: Cambridge University Press. [Same as Gramsci (1994).]

Bellamy, R., and D. Schecter. 1993. *Gramsci and the Italian State.* Manchester: Manchester University Press.

Berelson, B., P. Lazarsfeld, and W. McPhee. 1954. *Voting: A Study of Opinion Formation in a Presidential Campaign.* Chicago: University of Chicago Press.

Berelson, B., P. Lazarsfeld, and W. McPhee. 1971. "Democratic Practice and Democratic Theory." In Bachrach (1971b), pp. 27–48.

Bergami, G. 1981. *Gramsci comunista critico: Il politico e il pensatore.* Milan: Franco Angeli.

Bermani, C., ed. 1987. *Gramsci raccontato.* Rome: Edizioni Associate.

Bingen, J. n.d. [1984]. "La classe politica, l'intellecttuale collettivo, la politica e la mediazione." Unpublished paper.

Biondi, M. 1977. *Guida bibliografica a Gramsci.* Cesena, Italy: Bettini.

Biscione, F. M. 1990. "Gramsci e la 'questione meridionale': Introduzione all'edizione critica del saggio del 1926." *Critica marxista* 28(3):39–50.

Bobbio, N. 1956. "Liberalism Old and New." *Confluence* (Cambridge, Mass.), 5(3):239–351.

Bobbio, N. 1958. "Nota sulla dialettica in Gramsci." In Istituto Gramsci (1958), pp. 73–86.

Bobbio, N. 1961. "La teoria della classe politica negli scrittori democratici in Italia." In Treves (1961), pp. 54–58.

Bobbio, N. 1966. "Introduzione." In Mosca (1966), pp. vii–xxxiii.

Bobbio, N. 1969a. "Gramsci e la concezione della società civile." In Pietro Rossi (1969), vol. 1, pp. 75–100.

Bobbio, N. 1969b. *Saggi sulla scienza politica in Italia.* Bari, Italy: Laterza.

Bobbio, N. 1977. "Gramsci e il PCI." In Diaz (1977), pp. 55–62.

Bobbio, N. 1978. "Gramsci e la cultura politica italiana." *Belfagor* 33:593–99.

Bobbio, N. 1979. "Gramsci and the Conception of Civil Society." In Mouffe (1979), pp. 21–47. [Translation of Bobbio (1969a).]

Bobbio, N. 1983. "Mosca e il governo misto." In Albertoni (1983a), pp. 19–38.

Bobbio, N. 1984. *Il futuro della democrazia.* Turin: Einaudi.

Bobbio, N. 1987. *The Future of Democracy.* Trans. R. Griffin. Ed. R. Bellamy. Minneapolis: University of Minnesota Press. [Translation of Bobbio (1984).]

Bobbio, N. 1988. "Gramsci e la teoria politica." In Sbarberi (1988), pp. 27–40.

Bobbio, N. 1990. *Saggi su Gramsci.* Milan: Feltrinelli.

Bobbio, N. 1995. *Destra e sinistra: Ragioni e significati di una distinzione politica.* New revised edition. Rome: Donzelli.

Boggs, C. 1976. *Gramsci's Marxism.* New York: Urizen.

Boggs, C. 1984. *The Two Revolutions: Gramsci and the Dilemmas of Western Marxism.* Boston: South End.

Bollati, F. 1988. *Gramsci: Quale rivoluzione?* Rome: Nuova Galassia.

Bollati, F., and G. Mura. 1980. *Gramsci di fronte al fascismo.* Naples and Rome: Edizioni Dehoniane.

Bonetti, P. 1980. *Gramsci e la società liberal democratica.* Rome: Laterza.

Boothman, D., trans. and ed. 1995. *Further Selections from the Prison Notebooks.* Minneapolis: University of Minnesota Press. [Same as Gramsci (1995).]

Bottomore, T. B. 1964. *Elites and Society.* London: Penguin.

Bouvier, E. 1951. *Neither Right nor Left in Labor Relations.* Montreal: Industrial Relations Section, University of Montreal.

Bovero, M. 1988. "Gramsci e il realismo." In Sbarberi (1988), pp. 55–69.

Bracco, F., ed. 1980. *Gramsci e la crisi del mondo liberale.* Perugia: Quaderni della Regione dell'Umbria, Serie Studi Storici, no. 3.

Brodero, E. 1925. "Prefazione." In *Inchiesta sulla massoneria* (1925), pp. vii–xxvii.

Buci-Glucksmann, C. 1975. *Gramsci et l'état: Pour une théorie matérialiste de la philosophie.* Paris: Fayard.

Buci-Glucksmann, C. 1976. *Gramsci e lo Stato.* Rome: Editori Riuniti. [Translation of Buci-Glucksmann (1975).]

Buci-Glucksmann, C. 1977. "Sui problemi della transizione: Classe operaia e rivoluzione passiva." In Ferri (1977), vol. 1, pp. 99–125.

Buci-Glucksmann, C. 1980. *Gramsci and the State.* London: Lawrence and Wishart. [Translation of Buci-Glucksmann (1975).]

Bukharin, N. I. 1969. *Historical Materialism: A System of Sociology.* Ann Arbor: University of Michigan Press.

Bulferetti, L. 1951. *Le idee socialistiche in Italia nell'età del positivismo evoluzionistico (1870–1892).* Florence: Le Monnier.

Bulferetti, L. 1975. *Cesare Lombroso.* Turin: UTET.

Burnham, J. 1942. *The Managerial Revolution.* New York: Putnam.

Burnham, J. 1943. *The Machiavellians.* New York: John Day.

Burzio, F. 1945. *Essenza e attualità del liberalismo.* Turin: UTET.

Buttà, G. 1974. "Sul concetto di classe politica." *Rivista di sociologia* 12(1):147–56.

Buttigieg, J. A. 1992a. Introduction. In Gramsci (1992b), pp. 1–64.

Buttigieg, J. A., ed. and trans. 1992b. *Prison Notebooks.* Vol. 1. New York: Columbia University Press. [Same as Gramsci (1992b).]

Buttigieg, J. A., ed. and trans. 1996. *Prison Notebooks.* Vol. 2. New York: Columbia University Press. [Same as Gramsci (1996b).]

Buzzi, A. R. 1967. *La théorie politique d'Antonio Gramsci.* Louvain: Nauwelaerts.

Calabrò, G. P. 1981. *Antonio Gramsci: La "transizione" politica.* Naples: Edizioni Scientifiche Italiane.

Calzolario, V., ed. 1991. *Gramsci e la modernità: Letteratura e politica tra ottocento e novecento.* Naples: CUEN.

Cammett, J. M. 1967. *Antonio Gramsci and the Origins of Italian Communism.* Stanford, Calif.: Stanford University Press.

Cammett, J. M., ed. 1991. *Bibliografia gramsciana: 1922–1988.* Rome: Editori Riuniti.

Cammett, J. M., and M. L. Righi, eds. 1995. *Bibliografia gramsciana: Supplement Updated to 1993.* Rome: Fondazione Istituto Gramsci.

Canfora, L. 1989. *Togliatti e i dilemmi della politica.* Bari, Italy: Laterza.

Caprioglio, S. 1986. "La conquista dello stato per Gramsci e Malaparte." *Belfagor* 41:256–60.

Caprioglio, S. 1991. "Gramsci e L'URSS: Tre note nei *Quaderni del Carcere.*" *Belfagor* 46:65–75.

Capucci, F. 1978. *Antonio Gramsci: Il materialismo storico e la filosofia di Benedetto Croce.* L'Aquila, Italy: Japadre.

Caracciolo, A., and G. Scalia, eds. 1976. *La città futura* (1959). 2nd ed. Milan: Feltrinelli.

Cardia, U., ed. 1976. *Gramsci e la svolta degli anni trenta.* Cagliari, Italy: Editrice democratica sarda.

Catone, A. 1989. "Introduzione." In Baratta and Catone (1989), pp. 9–15.

Cavalli, L. 1970. *Il mutamento sociale.* Bologna: Il Mulino.

Cerroni, U. 1978. *Lessico gramsciano.* Rome: Editori Riuniti.

Cerroni, U. 1990. "Elite e democrazia di massa: Sviluppi teorici dopo Gramsci." In Tega (1990), pp. 113–22.

Chickering, A. L. 1993. *Beyond Left and Right: Breaking the Political Stalemate.* San Francisco: ICS Press, Institute for Contemporary Studies.

Clark, M. 1975. "The Patron Saint of the Left." *Times Literary Supplement* (London), 31 October, no. 3842, p. 1280.

Clark, M. 1977. *Antonio Gramsci and the Revolution That Failed.* New Haven, Conn.: Yale University Press.

Cofrancesco, D. 1968. "Appunti su Gramsci e la teoria dell'elite." *Mondoperaio* 21(August-September):28–34.

Cohen, L. J. 1970. *The Implications of Induction.* London: Methuen.

Cohen, L. J. 1977. *The Probable and the Provable.* Oxford: Clarendon Press.

Cohen, L. J. 1986. *The Dialogue of Reason: An Analysis of Analytical Philosophy.* Oxford: Clarendon Press.

Cohen, L. J. 1989. *An Introduction to the Philosophy of Induction and Probability.* Oxford: Clarendon Press.

Colletti, L. 1975. "Marxism and the Dialectic: Contradiction and Contrariety." *New Left Review* no. 93(September-October):3–29.

Colletti, L. 1979a. *Marxism and Hegel.* London: Verso.

Colletti, L. 1979b. "Marxismo." In *Enciclopedia del novecento* 4:1–18. Rome: Istituto della Enciclopedia Italiana.

Cozens, P. 1977. *Twenty Years of Antonio Gramsci: A Bibliography of Gramsci Studies, 1957-1977.* London: Lawrence and Wishart.

Croce, B. 1913. "Risposta ad un'inchiesta sulla massoneria." Reprinted in *Inchiesta sulla massoneria* (1925), pp. 75–76.

Croce, B. 1923. Review of G. Mosca, *Elementi. La Critica* 21:374–78.

Croce, B. 1925. "Intervento al Senato sulla massoneria (20 novembre 1925)." Reprinted in Croce (1966a), pp. 164–66.

Croce, B. 1926. *Cultura e vita morale.* Bari, Italy: Laterza.

Croce, B. 1929. *A History of Italy.* Trans. C. M. Ady. Oxford: Clarendon Press.

Croce, B. 1931. "L'economia filosofata e attualizzata." *La Critica* 29(1):76–80.

Croce, B. 1944. *Storia del regno di Napoli* (1925). 3rd ed. Bari, Italy: Laterza.

Croce, B. 1946. *Storia dell'età barocca in Italia* (1919). 2nd ed. Bari, Italy: Laterza.

Croce, B. 1947. "Antonio Gramsci, *Lettere dal carcere.*" *Quaderni della critica* 3(8):86–88.

Croce, B. 1948. "Antonio Gramsci, *Il materialismo storico e la filosofia di Benedetto Croce.*" *Quaderni della critica* 4(10):78–79.

Croce, B. 1950a. *Estetica come scienza dell'espressione e linguistica generale* (1902). 9th ed. Bari, Italy: Laterza.

Croce, B. 1950b. "Un gioco che ormai dura troppo." *Quaderni della critica* 6(17–18):231–32.

Croce, B. 1953. *La poesia* (1936). 5th ed. Bari, Italy: Laterza.

Croce, B. 1963a. *History of Europe in the Nineteenth Century.* Trans. H. Furst. New York: Harcourt, Brace and World.

Croce, B. 1963b. *Scritti e discorsi politici.* 3rd. ed. 2 vols. Bari, Italy: Laterza.

Croce, B. 1964. *Storia della storiografia italiana nel secolo decimonono* (1921). 5th ed. 2 vols. Bari, Italy: Laterza.

Croce, B. 1965. *Storia d'Europa nel secolo decimonono* (1932). Economical edition. Bari, Italy: Laterza.

Croce, B. 1966a. *Discorsi parlamentari.* Rome: Bardi.

Croce, B. 1966b. *Historical Materialism and the Economics of Karl Marx.* Trans. C. M. Meredith, 1914. Reprint. New York: Russell & Russell.

Croce, B. 1966c. *La storia come pensiero e come azione* (1938). Economical edition. Bari, Italy: Laterza.

Croce, B. 1967a. *Saggio sullo Hegel* (1913). 5th ed. Bari, Itali: Laterza.

Croce, B. 1967b. *Storia d'Italia dal 1871 al 1915* (1928). Economical edition. Bari, Italy: Laterza.

Croce, B. 1968. *Materialismo storico ed economia marxistica* (1900). Economical edition. Bari, Italy: Laterza.

Croce, B. 1970a. *History as the Story of Liberty.* Trans. S. Sprigge. London: Allen & Unwin, 1941. Reprint. Chicago: Regnery, Gateway Edition.

Croce, B. 1970b. *History of the Kingdom of Naples.* Trans. F. Frenaye. Chicago: University of Chicago Press.

Croce, B. 1981. *Poetry and Literature: Introduction to Its Criticism and History.* Trans. G. Gullace. Carbondale: Southern Illinois University Press.

Croce, B. 1992. *The Aesthetic as the Science of Expression and of the Linguistic in General.* Trans. C. Lyan. Cambridge: Cambridge University Press.

Cunningham, F. 1987. *Democratic Theory and Socialism.* Cambridge: Cambridge University Press.

Czudnowski, M. M. 1989. "Per una valutazione critica delle tesi neo-elitiste di Field e Higley." In Albertoni (1989b), vol. 1, pp. 115–41.

Dahl, R. A. 1956. *A Preface to Democratic Theory.* Chicago: University of Chicago Press.

Dahl, R. A. 1958. "A Critique of the Ruling Elite Model." *American Political Science Review* 52:463–69.

Dahl, R. A. 1961. *Who Governs?* New Haven, Conn.: Yale University Press.

Dahl, R. A. 1966. "Further Reflections on the Elitist Theory of Democracy." *American Political Science Review* 60:296–305. [Reprinted in Bachrach (1971), pp. 93–115.]

Dahl, R. A. 1985. *A Preface to Economic Democracy.* Berkeley: University of California Press.

Dahl, R. A. 1986. *Democracy, Liberty, and Equality.* Oslo: Norwegian University Press.

Dahl, R. A. 1989. *Democracy and Its Critics.* New Haven, Conn.: Yale University Press.

Da Silva, M. 1932. "Sipario su Weimar." *Critica fascista* 10:303-4.

Davidson, A. 1977. *Antonio Gramsci: Towards an Intellectual Biography.* London: Merlin Press.

Davis, J. A., ed. 1979. *Gramsci and Italy's Passive Revolution.* London: Croom Helm.

De Caprariis, V. 1962. "Le elites e la democrazia." *Nord e Sud* (Naples), 9(25):22-34.

De Domenico, N. 1991. "Una fonte trascurata dei *Quaderni del carcere* di Antonio Gramsci: Il 'Labour Monthly' del 1931." *Atti dell'Accademia Peloritana dei Pericolanti* (Messina), vol. 67, pp. 1-65. "Pre-print."

De Felice, F. 1971. *Serrati, Bordiga, Gramsci e il problema della rivoluzione in Italia, 1919-1920.* Bari, Italy: De Donato.

De Giovanni, B., V. Gerratana, and L. Paggi. 1977. *Egemonia, Stato, partito in Gramsci.* Rome: Editori Riuniti.

De Grazia, A. 1952. *Political Organization.* New York: Free Press.

Delle Piane, M. 1949. *Bibiografia di Gaetano Mosca.* Florence: La Nuova Italia.

Delle Piane, M. 1952. *Gaetano Mosca: Classe politica e liberalismo.* Naples: Edizioni Scientifiche Italiane.

Delle Piane, M. 1988. "Gaetano Mosca: Una voce di enciclopedia." *Studi senesi,* supplement, pp. 796-805.

Del Noce, A. 1978. *Il suicidio della rivoluzione.* Milan: Rusconi.

Delzell, C. F. 1980. Review of A. J. Gregor, *Young Mussolini and the Intellectual Origins of Fascism* and *Italian Fascism and Developmental Dictatorship. American Political Science Review* 74:1114-15.

De Mas, E. 1981. *L'Italia tra ottocento e novecento e le origini della scienza politica.* Lecce, Italy: Milella.

De Mattei, R. 1968. "Presentazione." In *Teorica dei governi e governo parlamentare,* by G. Mosca, pp. iii-xvii. Milan: Giuffrè.

Dialettica e filosofia della prassi. 1979. Milan: Franco Angeli Editore.

Diaz, F., et al. 1977. *Egemonia e democrazia.* Rome: Edizioni Avanti!

Di Giorgi, P. L. 1981. *Fondazione "marxista" dell'analisi socio-economica nei Quaderni del carcere.* Poggibonsi, Italy: Lalli Editore.

Di Palma, G. 1970. *Apathy and Participation: Mass Politics in Western Societies.* New York: Free Press.

Dombroski, R. S. 1989. *Antonio Gramsci.* Boston: G. K. Hall.

Dorso, G. 1949. *Dittatura, classe politica e classe dirigente.* Turin: Einaudi.

Drake, R. 1980. *Byzantium for Rome: The Politics of Nostalgia in Umbertian Italy (1878–1900)*. Chapel Hill: University of North Carolina Press.

Drake, R. 1981. "The Theory and Practice of Italian Nationalism, 1900–1906." *Journal of Modern History* 53:213–41.

Drake, R. 1989. *The Revolutionary Mystique and Terrorism in Contemporary Italy*. Bloomington: Indiana University Press.

Drake, R. 1991. "Mosca, Gaetano." In *Great Historians of the Modern Age*, ed. Lucian Boia, pp. 416–17. New York: Greenwood.

Dubla, F. 1986. *Gramsci e la fabbrica*. Rome: Piero Lacaita Editore.

Duncan, G., ed. 1983. *Democratic Theory and Practice*. Cambridge: Cambridge University Press.

Ehrenhalt, A. 1991. *The United States of Ambition: Politicians, Power, and the Pursuit of Office*. New York: Times Books.

Einaudi, L. 1913. "Risposta ad un inchiesta sulla massoneria." Reprinted in *Inchiesta sulla massoneria* (1925), pp. 111–12.

Einaudi, L. 1923. "Parlamenti e classe politica." (Review of G. Mosca, *Elementi*, 2nd ed.). *Corriere della sera*, 2 June. [Reprinted in Einaudi (1965), vol. 7, pp. 264–68.]

Einaudi, L. 1925. "La costituzione nella vita nazionale." (Review of G. Mosca, *Teorica*, 2nd ed.). *Corriere della sera*, 10 February. [Reprinted in Einaudi (1965), vol. 8, pp. 65–67.]

Einaudi, L. 1965. *Cronache economiche e politiche di un trentennio*. Turin: Einaudi.

Eley, G. 1984. "Reading Gramsci in English: Observations on the Reception of Antonio Gramsci in the English-speaking World 1957–1982." *European History Quarterly* 4:441–78.

Ellis, B. 1965. "The Origin and Nature of Newton's Laws of Motion." In *Beyond the Edge of Certainty*, ed. R. Colodny, pp. 29–68. Pittsburgh, Pa.: University of Pittsburgh Press.

Entwistle, H. 1979. *Antonio Gramsci: Conservative Schooling for Radical Politics*. Boston: Routledge.

Fagone, V. 1983. *Il marxismo fra democrazia e totalitarismo*. Rome: Edizioni La Civiltà Cattolica.

Femia, J. V. 1981a. *Gramsci's Political Thought: Hegemony, Consciousness, and the Revolutionary Process*. Oxford: Clarendon Press.

Femia, J. V. 1981b. "An Historicist Critique of 'Revisionist' Methods for Studying the History of Ideas." *History and Theory* 20:113–34.

Femia, J. V. 1985. "Marxism and Radical Democracy." *Inquiry* (Oslo) 28:293–319.

Femia, J. V. 1993a. *Marxism and Democracy*. Oxford: Clarendon Press.

Femia, J. V. 1993b. "Mosca Revisited." *European Journal of Political Research* 23:145–61.

Femia, J. V. 1995. "Pareto's Concept of Demagogic Plutocracy." *Government and Opposition* 30:370–92.

Femia, J. V. 1996. "Complexity and Deliberative Democracy." *Inquiry* (Oslo) 39:359-97.

Femia, J. V. Forthcoming. "The Machiavellian Legacy." London: Macmillan.

Fergnani, F. n.d. [1976]. *La filosofia della prassi nei "Quaderni del carcere".* [Milan:] Unicopli.

Ferrarotti, F. 1965. "The Italian Context: Pareto and Mosca." In Meisel (1965b), pp. 129-34.

Ferrata, G., and N. Gallo, eds. 1964. *2000 Pagine di Gramsci.* 2 vols. Milan: Il Saggiatore.

Ferrero, G. 1899. "Lo Stato e la libertà secondo uno scrittore italiano." *Nuova antologia* (Rome), 16 July, vol. 166 (4th series, vol. 82), no. 666, pp. 280-96.

Ferrero, G. 1923. "La democrazia nel pensiero di Gaetano Mosca." *Studi politici* (Rome), 1(6-7):158-60.

Ferri, F., ed. 1977. *Politica e storia in Gramsci.* 2 vols. Rome: Editori Riuniti and Istituto Gramsci.

Fickert, K. J. 1987. *Neither Left Nor Right: The Politics of Individualism in Uwe Johnson's Work.* New York: Lang.

Field, G. L., and J. Higley. 1980. *Elitism.* London: Routledge.

Field, G. L., and J. Higley. 1989a. "La dialettica tra elitismo e liberalismo." In Albertoni (1989b), vol. 1, pp. 91-114.

Field, G. L., and J. Higley. 1989b. "Racconto di un itinerario personale al neo-elitismo." In Albertoni (1989b), vol. 1, pp. 75-90.

Finocchiaro, M. A. 1973. *History of Science as Explanation.* Detroit: Wayne State University Press.

Finocchiaro, M. A. 1975. Review of G. Gentile, *La filosofia di Marx. The Thomist* 39:423-26.

Finocchiaro, M. A. 1977. "The Uses of History in the Interpretation of Science." *Review of Metaphysics* 31(1977-78):93-107.

Finocchiaro, M. A. 1979a. "Gramsci's Crocean Marxism." *Telos,* no. 41(Fall):17-32.

Finocchiaro, M. A. 1979b. "Methodological Criticism and Critical Methodology: An Analysis of Popper's Critique of Marxian Social Seience." *Zeitschrift für allgemeine Wissenschaftstheorie* 10:363-74.

Finocchiaro, M. A. 1980a. "Croce and Marxism: A Bibliographical Prolegomenon." *Rivista di studi crociani* 17:157-63.

Finocchiaro, M. A. 1980b. *Galileo and the Art of Reasoning: Rhetorical Foundations of Logic and Scientific Method.* Boston: Reidel [Kluwer].

Finocchiaro, M. A. 1980c. "Sztompka's Philosophy of Social Science." *Inquiry* (Oslo) 23:357-71.

Finocchiaro, M. A. 1984. "Gramsci: An Alternative Communism?" *Studies in Soviet Thought* 27:123-46.

Finocchiaro, M. A. 1985-86. "Marxism, Science, and Religion in Gramsci: Recent Trends in Italian Scholarship." *The Philosophical Forum* 17:127-55.

Finocchiaro, M. A. 1986. "Judgment and Reasoning in the Evaluation of Theories." In *PSA 1986: Proceedings of the 1986 Biennial Meeting of the Philosophy of Science Association*, ed. A. Fine and P. Machamer, vol. 1, pp. 227-35. East Lansing, Mich: Philosophy of Science Association.

Finocchiaro, M. A. 1988a. *Gramsci and the History of Dialectical Thought.* Cambridge: Cambridge University Press.

Finocchiaro, M. A. 1988b. *Gramsci critico e la critica.* Rome: Armando.

Finocchiaro, M. A. 1989. Review of E. A. Albertoni, *Mosca and the Theory of Elitism. Differentia: Review of Italian Thought*, nos. 3-4 (Spring-Autumn):383-86.

Finocchiaro, M. A. 1990. "Mosca, Gramsci, and Democratic Elitism." In *Italian Echoes in the Rocky Mountains*, ed. S. Matteo, C. D. Noble, and M. U. Sowell, pp. 135-50. Provo, Utah: David M. Kennedy Center for International Studies at Brigham Young University Press.

Finocchiaro, M. A. 1991a. "The Hermeneutics of Negative Evaluation, or, A Hunt for the Red October." *History of the Human Sciences* 4:161-67.

Finocchiaro, M. A. 1991b. "Logica e politica in Gramsci." *Mondoperaio* 44(3):76-83.

Finocchiaro, M. A. 1992. "Logic, Politics, and Gramsci." In *Logic and Political Culture*, ed. E. M. Barth and E. C. W. Krabbe, pp. 25-43. Amsterdam: Royal Netherlands Academy of Arts and Sciences.

Finocchiaro, M. A. 1993a. "Gramsci, Mosca, e la Massoneria." *Teoria politica* (Turin), 9(2):135-61.

Finocchiaro, M. A. 1993b. "Logic, Democracy, and Mosca." In *Empirical Logic and Public Debate*, ed. E. C. W. Krabbe, R. J. Dalitz, and P. A. Smit, pp. 227-38. Amsterdam and Atlanta: Rodopi.

Finocchiaro, M. A. 1994. "Gramsci e Gaetano Mosca." In Giacomini, Losurdo, and Martelli (1994), pp. 115-64.

Finocchiaro, M. A. 1995a. "Gramsci, Antonio." In *The Cambridge Dictionary of Philosophy*, ed. R. Audi, p. 304. New York: Cambridge University Press.

Finocchiaro, M. A. 1995b. "Mosca, Gaetano." In *The Cambridge Dictionary of Philosophy*, ed. R. Audi, p. 514. New York: Cambridge University Press.

Finocchiaro, M. A. Forthcoming a. "Croce and Mosca: Pluralistic Elitism and Philosophical Science." In *Benedetto Croce: Essays on What is Living in His Legacy*, ed. D. Trafton, J. D'Amico, and M. Verdicchio. Toronto: University of Toronto Press.

Finocchiaro, M. A. Forthcoming b. "Democracy, Philosophy, and Gramsci." *The Philosophical Forum.*

Finocchiaro, M. A. Forthcoming c. "Gramsci, Antonio." In *Censorship: An International Encyclopedia*, ed. D. Jones. London: Fitzroy Dearborn.

Fiori, G. 1966. *Vita di Antonio Gramsci.* Bari, Italy: Laterza. Rpt. 1981.

Fiori, G. 1970. *Antonio Gramsci: Life of a Revolutionary.* London: New Left.

Fiori, G. 1977. "Prefazione." In Paulesu Quercioli (1977), pp. 5-16.

Fiori, G. 1991. *Gramsci Togliatti Stalin.* Rome: Laterza.

Fiori, S. 1991. "Gramsci sbarca a New York." *La Repubblica* (Rome) 2 November, p. 37.

Fiorot, D., and G. Sola. 1986. "Positivismo e politica tra '800 e '900." *Schema* 8(2), appendix.

Fontana, B. 1993. *Hegemony and Power: On the Relation Between Gramsci and Machiavelli.* Minneapolis: University of Minnesota Press.

Fontana, B. 1996. "The Concept of Nature in Gramsci." *The Philosophical Forum* 27(1995-96):220-43.

Forgacs, D. 1984. "National-Popular: Genealogy of a Concept." In *Formations of Nation and People,* pp. 83-98. London: Routledge and Kegan Paul.

Forgacs, D., ed. 1988. *An Antonio Gramsci Reader: Selected Writings, 1916-1935.* New York: Schocken. [Same as Gramsci (1988a).]

Forgacs, D., and G. Nowell-Smith, eds. 1985. *Selections from Cultural Writings.* Cambridge, Mass.: Harvard University Press. [Same as Gramsci (1985).]

Fotia, M. 1964a. "Intellettuali e classe politica in Gaetano Mosca." *Stato sociale* 8(3):286-98.

Fotia, M. 1964b. "Per una revisione critica del concetto di classe politica." *Storia e politica* 3(3):380-429.

Fotia, M. 1966. "Classe politica, liberalismo, e democrazia in Gaetano Mosca." *Rivista di sociologia* 4(11):5-68.

Franceschini, F. 1989. *Cultura popolare e intelletuali: Appunti su Carducci, Gramsci, De Martino.* Pisa: Giardini Editori e Stampatori.

Francioni, G. 1984. *L'Officina Gramsciana. Ipotesi sulla struttura dei "Quaderni del carcere."* Naples: Bibliopolis.

Francioni, G. 1987. "Gramsci tra Croce e Bucharin: Sulla struttura dei *Quaderni* 10 e 11." *Critica marxista* 25(6):19-45.

Francioni, G. n.d. [1992]. *Tre studi su Gramsci.* Naples: Bibliopolis.

Frascani, P. 1967. "Croce e Gaetano Mosca: Significato di una recensione." *Rivista di studi crociani* 4:470-75.

Frascani, P. 1969. "Gaetano Mosca e il mito della 'middle class.'" *Critica storica* 8(1):78-108.

Friedrich, C. J. 1950. *The New Belief in the Common Man.* Boston: Little Brown.

Friedrich, C. J. 1963. *Man and His Government.* New York: McGraw-Hill.

Friedrich, C. J. 1965. "The Political Elite and Bureaucracy." In Meisel (1965b), pp. 171-79.

Fuller, T. 1996. Review of A. Giddens, *Beyond Left and Right. American Political Science Review* 90:174-75.

Galasso, G. 1977. "I cattolici nella società e nella storia dell'Italia contemporanea." In Ferri (1977), vol. 1, pp. 283-319.

Galasso, G. 1978. *Croce, Gramsci e altri storici.* 2nd ed. Milan: Il Saggiatore.

Galli, G. 1969. "Gramsci e la teoria delle elites politiche." In Pietro Rossi (1969), vol. 2, pp. 201-16.

Gallino, L. 1969. "Gramsci e le scienze sociali." In Pietro Rossi (1969), vol. 2, pp. 81–108.

Garin, E. 1958. "Gramsci nella cultura italiana." In Istituto Gramsci (1958), pp. 395–418.

Garin, E. 1967. "La formazione di Gramsci e Croce." In *Prassi rivoluzionaria e storicismo in Gramsci,* supplement no. 3 of *Critica marxista,* pp. 119–33. Rome: Editori Riuniti.

Garin, E. 1969. "Politica e cultura in Gramsci: Il problema degli intellettuali." In Pietro Rossi (1977), vol. 1, pp. 37–74.

Gauchet, M. 1992. *La droite et la gauche.* Paris: Gallimard.

Gentile, G. 1913. "Risposta ad un'inchiesta sulla massoneria." Reprinted in *Inchiesta sulla massoneria* (1925), pp. 128–29.

Gentile, G. 1974. *La filosofia di Marx* (1899). 5th ed. Florence: Sansoni.

Germino, D. 1967. *Beyond Ideology.* Chicago: University of Chicago Press.

Germino, D. 1982. *Political Philosophy and the Open Society.* Baton Rouge: Louisiana State University Press.

Germino, D. 1990. *Antonio Gramsci: Architect of a New Politics.* Baton Rouge: Louisiana State University Press.

Germino, D., and M. Fennema. Forthcoming. "Antonio Gramsci on the Culture of Violence and Its Overturning." *The Philosophical Forum.*

Gerratana, V. 1975a. "La ricerca e il metodo." *Rinascita* 32(30):11–13.

Gerratana, V. 1975b. "Note di filologia gramsciana." *Studi storici* 16:126–54.

Gerratana, V. 1975c. Preface. In Gramsci (1975b), pp. xi–xlii.

Gerratana, V. 1977. "Gramsci come pensatore rivoluzionario." In Ferri (1977), vol. 2, pp. 69–101.

Gerratana, V. 1991. "Gramsci e Sraffa." In Sraffa (1991), pp. xiii–lv.

Gerratana, V. 1992. "Gramsci." In *Enciclopedia Italiana,* appendix 2, pp. 3177–79. Rome: Istituto della Enciclopedia Italiana.

Ghiringhelli, R. 1982. "A Brief Survey of Other Papers Read by Italian Scholars on the Intellectual, Political and Social Background of Gaetano Mosca." In Albertoni (1982c), pp. 137–52.

Giacomini, R., D. Losurdo, and M. Martelli, eds. 1994. *Gramsci e l'Italia.* Naples: Edizioni La Città del Sole.

Giddens, A. 1994. *Beyond Left and Right: The Future of Radical Politics.* Stanford, Calif.: Stanford University Press.

Gigli, L. 1928. "Napoleone III prigioniero." *I libri del giorno* 11:70–72.

Giraldi, G. 1979. *Gramsci e altri miti.* Milan: Edizioni Pergamena.

Girvetz, H. K. 1967. *Democracy and Elitism.* New York: Scribner.

Gobetti, P. 1924. "Un conservatore galantuomo." *La Rivoluzione liberale,* 29 April, 3(18):71. [Reprinted in Gobetti (1960), pp. 652–57.]

Gobetti, P. 1925. *La rivoluzione liberale.* Bologna-Florence: Luciano Cappelli Editore. [Reprinted in Gobetti (1960), pp. 913–1078.]

Gobetti, P. 1960. *Scritti politici.* Ed. P. Spriano. Turin: Einaudi.

Golding, S. 1992. *Gramsci's Democratic Theory.* Toronto: University of Toronto Press.

Gouldner, A., ed. 1950. *Studies in Leadership.* New York: Harper and Brothers.

Gramsci, Un'eredità contrastata: La nuova sinistra rilegge Gramsci. 1979. Milan: Ottaviano.

Gramsci: Un protagonista del nostro tempo. 1987. Bologna: Festa dell'Unità.

Gramsci, A. 1925a. "Intervento alla Camera dei Deputati, 16 maggio." *Atti Parlamentari,* Camera dei Deputati, Legislatura XXVII, Sessione I, Discussioni, vol. 4, pp. 3658–63. Rome: Tipografia della Camera dei Deputati.

Gramsci, A. 1925b. "Lettera a Iulca, 25 maggio." In Ferrata and Gallo (1964), 2:72–73.

Gramsci, A. 1925c. "Origini e scopi della legge sulle associazioni segrete." *L'Unità* 2(177):2. [Reprinted in Gramsci (1971a), pp. 75–85.]

Gramsci, A. 1948. *Il materialismo storico e la filosofia di Benedetto Croce.* Turin: Einaudi.

Gramsci, A. 1949a. *Gli intellettuali e l'organizzanione della cultura.* Turin: Einaudi.

Gramsci, A. 1949b. *Il Risorgimento.* Turin: Einaudi.

Gramsci, A. 1949c. *Note sul Machiavelli, sulla politica e sullo Stato moderno.* Turin: Einaudi.

Gramsci, A. 1950. *Letteratura e vita nazionale.* Turin: Einaudi.

Gramsci, A. 1951. *Passato e presente.* Turin: Einaudi.

Gramsci, A. 1954. *L'Ordine Nuovo, 1919–1920.* Turin: Einaudi.

Gramsci, A. 1957. *The Modern Prince and Other Writings.* Trans. L. Marks. New York: International Publishers.

Gramsci, A. 1958. *Scritti giovanili, 1914–1918.* Turin: Einaudi.

Gramsci, A. 1960. *Sotto la Mole, 1916–1920.* Turin: Einaudi.

Gramsci, A. 1965. *Lettere dal carcere.* Ed. S. Caprioglio and E. Fubini. Turin: Einaudi.

Gramsci, A. 1966. *Socialismo e fascismo. L'Ordine Nuovo 1921–1922.* Turin: Einaudi.

Gramsci, A. 1971a. *La costruzione del partito comunista.* Turin: Einaudi.

Gramsci, A. 1971b. *Selections from the Prison Notebooks.* Trans. and ed. Q. Hoare and G. Nowell-Smith. New York: International Publishers.

Gramsci, A. 1973. *Letters from Prison.* Trans. and ed. L. Lawner. New York: Harper.

Gramsci, A. 1975a. *History, Philosophy, and Culture in the Young Gramsci.* Trans. and ed. P. Cavalcanti and P. Piccone. St. Louis, Mo.: Telos.

Gramsci, A. 1975b. *Quaderni del carcere.* 4 vols. Critical edition by V. Gerratana under the auspices of the Gramsci Institute. Turin: Einaudi.

Gramsci, A. 1977a. *Quaderno 19: Il Risorgimento italiano.* Ed. C. Vivanti. Turin: Einaudi.

Gramsci, A. 1977b. *Selections from Political Writings (1910–1920).* Ed. Q. Hoare. Trans. J. Mathews. New York: International Publishers.

Gramsci, A. 1978a. *Quaderno 22: Americanismo e fordismo.* Ed. F. De Felice. Turin: Einaudi.

Gramsci, A. 1978b. *Selections from Political Writings (1921–1926).* Trans. and ed. Q. Hoare. New York: International Publishers.

Gramsci, A. 1980. *Cronache torinesi, 1913–1917.* Ed. S. Caprioglio. Turin: Einaudi.

Gramsci, A. 1981. *Quaderno 13: Noterelle sulla politica del Machiavelli.* Ed. C. Donzelli. Turin: Einaudi.

Gramsci, A. 1982. *La città futura, 1917–1918.* Ed. S. Caprioglio. Turin: Einaudi.

Gramsci, A. 1984. *Il nostro Marx, 1918–1919.* Ed. S. Caprioglio. Turin: Einaudi.

Gramsci, A. 1985. *Selections from Cultural Writings.* Ed. D. Forgacs and G. Nowell-Smith. Trans. W. Boelhower. Cambridge, Mass.: Harvard University Press.

Gramsci, A. 1986. *Nuove Lettere.* Ed. A. A. Santucci. Rome: Editori Riuniti.

Gramsci, A. 1987. *L'Ordine Nuovo, 1919–1920.* Ed. V. Gerratana and A. A. Santucci. Turin: Einaudi.

Gramsci, A. 1988a. *An Antonio Gramsci Reader: Selected Writings, 1916–1935.* Ed. D. Forgacs. New York: Schocken.

Gramsci, A. 1988b. *Prison Letters.* Ed., trans., and introduction by H. Henderson. London: Zwan.

Gramsci, A. 1991. *La questione meridionale.* Rome: Editori Riuniti.

Gramsci, A. 1992a. *Lettere, 1908–1926.* Ed. A. A. Santucci. Turin: Einaudi.

Gramsci, A. 1992b. *Prison Notebooks.* Vol. 1. Ed. J. A. Buttigieg. Trans. J. A. Buttigieg and A. Callaro. New York: Columbia University Press.

Gramsci. A. 1994a. *Letters from Prison.* 2 vols. Ed. F. Rosengarten. Trans. R. Rosenthal. New York: Columbia University Press.

Gramsci, A. 1994b. *Pre-Prison Writings.* Ed. R. Bellamy. Trans. V. Cox. Cambridge: Cambridge University Press.

Gramsci, A. 1995. *Further Selections from the Prison Notebooks.* Trans. and ed. D. Boothman. Minneapolis: University of Minnesota Press.

Gramsci, A. 1996a. *Lettere dal carcere, 1926–1937.* 2 vols. Ed. A. A. Santucci. Palermo: Sellerio Editore.

Gramsci, A. 1996b. *Prison Notebooks.* Vol. 2. Ed. and trans. J. A. Buttigieg. New York: Columbia University Press. [Same as Buttigieg (1996).]

Grassi, F. 1978. *Gramsci e la "critica" della diplomazia "tradizionale."* Lecce, Italy: Milella.

Greer, S. 1969. *The Logic of Social Inquiry.* Chicago: Aldine.

Gregor, A. J. 1969. *The Ideology of Fascism.* New York: Free Press.

Gregor, A. J. 1974a. *The Fascist Persuasion in Radical Politics.* Princeton, N.J.: Princeton University Press.

Gregor, A. J. 1974b. *Interpretations of Fascism.* Morristown, N.J.: General Learning.

Gregor, A. J. 1979. *Young Mussolini and the Intellectual Origins of Fascism.* Berkeley: University of California Press.

Gregor, A. J. 1980. *Italian Fascism and Developmental Dictatorship.* Princeton, N.J.: Princeton University Press.

Griffo, M. 1990. "Sistema elettorale e sistema politico in Gaetano Mosca." In Quagliariello (1990), pp. 671-93.

Guccione, E. 1982. "Gaetano Mosca candidato dei cattolici nelle elezioni generali del 1913." In Albertoni (1982a), pp. 405-21.

Guccione, E. 1983. "Gaetano Mosca e i cattolici durante la XXIV Legislatura (1913-1919)." In Albertoni (1983a), pp. 209-23.

Hall, S. 1980. "Popular-Democratic Versus Authoritarian Populism: Two Ways of Taking Democracy Seriously." In *Marxism and Democracy,* ed. A. Hunt, pp. 175-85. London: Lawrence and Wishart.

Hamilton, A., J. Jay, and J. Madison. 1961. *The Federalist Papers.* Ed. C. Rossiter. New York: Penguin

Hanson, N. R. 1965. "Newton's First Law: A Philosopher's Door into Natural Philosophy." In *Beyond the Edge of Certainty,* ed. R. Colodny, pp. 6-28. Pittsburgh, Pa.: University of Pittsburgh Press.

Hintikka, J., and U. Remes. 1974. *The Method of Analysis: Its Geometrical Origin and Its General Significance.* Dordrecht, Netherlands: Reidel [Kluwer].

Hoare, Q., and G. Nowell-Smith. 1971a. Introduction. In Gramsci (1971b), pp. xvii-xcvi.

Hoare, Q., and G. Nowell-Smith, eds. 1971b. *Selections from the Prison Notebooks.* New York: International Publishers. [Same as Gramsci (1971b).]

Hobsbawm, E. J. 1974. "The Great Gramsci." *New York Review of Books,* 4 April, 21(5):39-44.

Hobsbawm, E. J. 1979. "La cultura europea e il marxismo fra Otto e Novecento." In *Storia del marxismo,* vol. 2: *Il marxismo nell'età della Seconda Internazionale,* ed. E. J. Hobsbawm et al., pp. 59-106. Turin: Einaudi.

Hoffman, J. 1984. *The Gramscian Challenge: Coercion and Consent in Marxist Political Theory.* Oxford: Basil Blackwell.

Holub, R. 1992. *Antonio Gramsci: Beyond Marxism and Postmodernism.* New York: Routledge.

Hook, S. 1939. "The Fetishism of Power." *The Nation,* 13 May, 148(20):562-63. [Reprinted in Meisel (1965b), pp. 135-39.]

Hook, S. 1959. *Political Power and Personal Freedom.* New York: Criterion.

Hughes, H. S. 1953. *Consciousness and Society.* New York: Knopf.

Hughes, H. S. 1954. "Gaetano Mosca and the Political Lessons of History." In *Teachers of History,* ed. H. S. Hughes, pp. 146-67. Ithaca, N.Y.: Cornell University Press. [Reprinted in Meisel (1965b), pp. 141-60.]

Hunter, F. 1953. *Community Power Structure: A Study of Decision Makers.* Chapel Hill: University of North Carolina Press.

Inchiesta sulla massoneria. 1925. Preface by E. Brodero. Milan: Mondadori.

"An Italian Political Philosopher." 1950. *Times Literary Supplement* (London), 17 March, p. 172.

Invernici, F. 1983. "Gaetano Mosca nelle interpretazioni del socialismo liberale." In Albertoni (1983a), pp. 249-68.

Istituto Gramsci, ed. 1958. *Studi gramsciani.* Rome: Editori Riuniti.

Jacobitti, E. E. 1981. *Revolutionary Humanism and Historicism in Modern Italy.* New Haven, Conn.: Yale University Press.

Jannaccone, P. 1930. "Scienza, critica e realtà economica." *La Riforma sociale* 27(6):521-28.

Jocteau, G. C. 1975. *Leggere Gramsci.* Milan: Feltrinelli.

Joll, J. 1977. *Antonio Gramsci.* New York: Penguin.

Jones, G. L. 1993. "Elite Culture, Popular Culture and the Politics of Hegemony." *History of European Ideas* 16:235-40.

Kariel, H. S., ed. 1970. *Frontiers of Democratic Theory.* New York: Random House.

Katz, J. J. 1962. *The Problem of Induction and Its Solution.* Chicago: University of Chicago Press.

Kaye, H. J. 1986. "Intellectuals and the Making of History." *Humanity and Society* 10(1):1-9.

Keller, S. 1963. *Beyond the Ruling Class: Strategic Elites in Modern Society.* New York: Random House.

Kilminster, R. 1979. *Praxis and Method: A Sociological Dialogue with Lukács, Gramsci and the Early Frankfurt School.* Boston: Routledge.

Kiros, T. 1985. *Toward the Construction of a Theory of Political Action: Antonio Gramsci.* Lanham, Md.: University Press of America.

Koff, S. P. 1989. "Luci ed ombre sulla diffusione dell'opera di Gaetano Mosca nella vita intellettuale statunitense." In Albertoni (1989b), vol. 1, pp. 3-23.

Koff, S. Z., and S. P. Koff. 1972a. "Gaetano Mosca: The Man and His Times." In Mosca (1972), pp. 259-70.

Koff, S. Z., and S. P. Koff. 1972b. "Preface to the English Translation." In Mosca (1972), pp. v-vii.

Kornhauser, W. 1959. *The Politics of Mass Society.* New York: Free Press.

Laclau, E. 1977. *Politics and Ideology in Marxist Theory.* London: New Left.

Laclau, E., and C. Mouffe. 1985. *Hegemony and Socialist Strategy: Towards a Radical Democratic Politics.* Trans. W. Moore and P. Cammack. London: Verso.

Lagorio, L., and G. Lehner. 1987. *Turati e Gramsci per il socialismo.* Milan: Sugarco.

Lajolo, L. 1980. *Gramsci, un uomo sconfitto.* Milan: Rizzoli.

La Palombara, J. 1982. "The Study of Gaetano Mosca in the United States." In Albertoni (1982c).

La Palombara, J. 1987. *Democracy, Italian Style.* New Haven, Conn.: Yale University Press.

Laponce, J. A. 1981. *Left and Right: The Topography of Political Perceptions.* Toronto: University of Toronto Press.

La Rocca, T. 1991. *Gramsci e la religione* (1981). 2nd ed. Brescia, Italy: Queriniana.

Lasswell, H., and A. Kaplan. 1950. *Power and Society.* New Haven, Conn.: Yale University Press.

Lasswell, H., and D. Lerner. 1952. *The Comparative Study of Elites.* Stanford, Calif.: Hoover Institution.

Lasswell, H., and D. Lerner. 1965. *World Revolutionary Elites.* Cambridge, Mass.: MIT Press.

Lasswell, H., D. Lerner, and C. E. Rothwell. 1965. *The Comparative Study of Elites.* Cambridge, Mass.: MIT Press.

Lasswell, H., D. Lerner, and C. E. Rothwell. 1971. "The Elite Concept." In Bachrach (1971b), pp. 13–26.

Laudan, L. 1977. *Progress and Its Problems.* Berkeley: University of California Press.

Laudan, L. 1984. *Science and Values: The Aims of Science and Their Role in Scientific Debate.* Berkeley: University of California Press.

Lay, G. 1965. "Colloqui con Gramsci nel carcere di Turi." *Rinascita,* 20 February, 22(8):21–22.

"Legge 26 November 1925, no. 2029 [2292]." In *Leggi e decreti del Regno d'Italia,* vol. 9, no. 2292, pp. 9119–21. Rome: Libreria dello Stato.

Leiserson, A. 1958. *Parties and Politics: An Institutional and Behavioral Approach.* New York: Knopf.

Lenski, G. 1980. "In Praise of Mosca and Michels." *Mid-American Review of Sociology* 5(2):1–12.

Lentini, B. 1967. *Croce e Gramsci.* Palermo and Rome: Edizioni Mori.

Lepre, A. 1978. *Gramsci secondo Gramsci.* Naples: Liguori.

Liguori, G. 1996. *Gramsci conteso: Storia di un dibattito, 1922–1996.* Rome: Editori Riuniti.

Limbaugh, R. 1994. *See, I Told You So.* New York: Pocket Star.

Lippmann, W. 1956. Introduction. In Wilson (1956), pp. 7–17.

Lipset, S. M. 1962. Introduction. In Michels (1962), pp. 15–39.

Lisa, A. 1973. *Memorie: In carcere con Gramsci.* Milan: Feltrinelli.

Liseto, D. 1997. "Carlo Rosselli e le elites: Una teoria tra l'elitismo democratico e la democrazia partecipativa." *Scienza e politica,* no. 16, pp. 69–86.

Lively, J. 1975. *Democracy.* Oxford: Basil Blackwell.

Livingston, A. 1939. Introduction. In Mosca (1939), pp. ix–xli.

Lombardo, A. 1971a. "Gaetano Mosca e la classe politica nell'età giolittiana." In Mosca (1971), pp. 19–62.

Lombardo, A. 1971b. "Sociologia e scienza politica in Gaetano Mosca." *Rivista italiana di scienza politica* 1:297–323.

Lombardo, A. 1976. *Teoria del potere politico: Mosca e Pareto.* Bologna: Boni.

Lo Piparo, F. 1979. *Lingua intellettuali egemonia in Gramsci.* Bari, Italy: Laterza.

Losurdo, D. 1982. "Hegel: Grande Enciclopedia, Piccola Logica e 'Zusatze.'" *Il Pensiero* 23:123–39.

Losurdo, D. 1986. "Le catene e i fiori: La critica dell'ideologia tra Marx a Nietzsche." *Hermeneutica* 6:87–143. Urbino: QuattroVenti.

Losurdo, D. 1990. "Gramsci, Gentile, Marx e le filosofie della prassi." In Muscatello (1990), pp. 91–114.

Losurdo, D. 1992. "Lotta culturale e organizzazione delle classi subalterne in Antonio Gramsci." In *Un progresso intellettuale di massa,* ed. G. Baratta and A. Catone. Milan: UNICOPLI.

Lucas, J. R. 1971. "Against Equality." In *Justice and Equality,* ed. H. Bedan, pp. 138–51. Englewood Cliffs, N.J.: Prentice-Hall.

Mack Smith, D. 1978. *Storia di cento anni di vita politica italiana visti attraverso il "Corriere della sera."* Milan: Rizzoli.

McMullin, E. 1976. "The Fertility of Theory and the Unit of Appraisal in Science." In *Essays in Memory of Imre Lakatos,* ed. R. S. Cohen, P. K. Feyerabend, and M. W. Wartofsky, pp. 395–432. Dordrecht, The Netherlands: Reidel [Kluwer].

Maiello, R. 1980. *Vita di Antonio Gramsci.* Turin: ERI/Edizioni RAI.

Maier, B., and P. Semana 1978. *Antonio Gramsci: Introduzione e guida allo studio dell'opera gramsciana.* Florence: Le Monnier.

Manacorda, M. A. 1970. *Il principio educativo in Gramsci: Americanismo e conformismo.* Rome: Armando.

Mancina, C. 1980. "Rapporti di forza e previsione: Il gioco della storia secondo Gramsci." *Critica marxista* 18(5):41–55.

Mandolfo, S. 1980. *La filosofia della prassi: Engels, Labriola, Gramsci.* Rome: Dialogos.

Mandolfo, S. 1982. *Contributi alla lettura di Antonio Gramsci.* Catania, Italy: Bonanno Editore.

Mangini, C., and L. Del Fra. 1979. *Antonio Gramsci, I giorni del carcere: Un film come storia.* Milan: Edizioni Ottaviano.

Mannheim, K. 1950. *Freedom, Power, and Democratic Planning.* New York: Oxford University Press.

Maranini, G. 1967. *Storia del potere in Italia, 1848–1967.* Florence: Vallecchi.

Maraviglia, M. 1925. "Il caso Mosca." *L'Idea nazionale* (Rome), 22 December, 15(303):1. [Reprinted as "Nascita del capo di governo," in *La Stampa nazionalista,* ed. F. Gaeta, pp. 439–41. Bologna: Cappelli, 1965.]

Marini, G. 1990. "Elaborazione di temi hegeliani in Gramsci." *Archivio di storia della cultura* 3:315–38.

Mariotti, A. 1978. *Gramsci e l'architettura e altri scritti.* Bari, Italy: Dedalo.

Marks, L., ed. 1957. *The Modern Prince and Other Writings.* New York: International Publishers. [Same as Gramsci (1957).]

Martinelli, R. 1972. "Il 'Che Fare?' di Gramsci nel 1923." *Studi storici* 12:790-802.

Martinelli, R., ed. 1977. *Antonio Gramsci: Mostra bibliografica-catalogo.* Florence: [Publisher unknown].

Martire, E. 1925. "Intervento alla Camera dei Deputati, 16 maggio." *Atti Parlamentari,* Camera dei Deputati, Sessione 1924-25, Discussioni, vol. 4, pp. 3654-58. Rome: Tipografia della Camera dei Deputati.

Marx, K. 1988. *The Communist Manifesto* (1848). Ed. F. L. Bender. New York: W. W. Norton.

Marxism Today. 1987. Gramsci Supplement, 31 April.

Mastellone, S. 1991. "Una metodologia ermeneutica per studiare Mosca, Croce e Gramsci." *Il Pensiero politico* 24:241-43.

Mastroianni, G. 1979. *Vico e la rivoluzione: Gramsci e il diamat.* Pisa: ETS.

Masutti, E. 1975. *Perché Gramsci ateo?* Udine, Italy: Grillo.

Matteucci, N. 1977. *Antonio Gramsci e la filosofia della prassi* (1951). 2nd ed. Milan: Giuffrè.

Mauro, W. 1981. *Invito alla lettura di Gramsci.* Milan: Mursia.

Medici, R. 1989. *Gramsci: Machiavelli tra storia e metafora.* Bologna: Istituto Gramsci Emilia-Romagna.

Medici, R. 1990a. *La metafora Machiavelli: Mosca Pareto Michels Gramsci.* Modena: Mucchi.

Medici, R. 1990b. "Mosca, Gramsci e la 'metafora Machiavelli.'" In Tega (1990), pp. 241-56.

Meisel, J. H. 1958. *The Myth of the Ruling Class: Gaetano Mosca and the Elite.* Ann Arbor: University of Michigan Press. 2nd ed., 1962. [Reprinted, Westport, Conn.: Greenwood Press, 1980.]

Meisel, J. H. 1961. " 'Loro': Vicissitudini di un'idea. Dalla classe politica alla *elite* del potere." In Treves (1961), pp. 88-93.

Meisel, J. H. 1964. "Mosca 'transatlantico.'" *Cahiers Vilfredo Pareto* 4:109-17.

Meisel, J. H. 1965a. Introduction. In Meisel (1965b), pp. 1-44.

Meisel, J. H., ed. 1965b. *Pareto and Mosca.* Englewood Cliffs, N.J.: Prentice-Hall.

Meisel, J. H. 1965c. "Power Source and Power Flow." In Meisel (1965b), pp. 165-69.

Melchiorre, V., C. Vigna, and G. De Rosa, eds. 1979. *Antonio Gramsci: Il pensiero teorico e politico, la "questione leninista."* 2 vols. Rome: Città Nuova Editrice.

Mengozzi, D. 1981. *Gramsci e il futurismo (1920-1922).* Turin: Quaderni della FIAP/Federazione Italiana delle Associazioni Partigiane.

Merli, S. 1967. "I nostri conti con la teoria della 'rivoluzione senza rivoluzione' di Gramsci." *Giovane critica,* no. 17 (Fall):61-67.

Michels, R. 1911. *Zur Sociologie des Parteiwesens in der modernen Demokratie: Untersuchungen über die oligarchischen Tendenzen des Gruppenlebens.* Leipzig: Klinkhardt.

Michels, R. 1912. *La sociologia del partito politico nella democrazia moderna: Studi sulle tendenze oligarchiche degli aggregati politici.* Turin: UTET.

Michels, R. 1962. *Political Parties: A Sociological Study of the Oligarchical Tendencies of Modern Parties.* Trans. E. Paul and C. Paul. Introduction by S. M. Lipset. New York: Collier.

Mills, C. W. 1956. *The Power Elite.* New York: Oxford University Press.

Mills, C. W. 1959. *The Sociological Imagination.* New York: Oxford University Press.

Mills, C. W. 1965. "Notes on Mosca." In Meisel (1965b), pp. 161–63.

Mioni, F. 1988. "Un teorema del potere unitario: Politica, legittimazione, istituzioni in Gaetano Mosca." *Il Pensiero politico* 21:26–48.

Mirsky, D. S. 1931. "The Philosophical Discussion in the C.P.S.U. in 1930–31." *The Labour Monthly,* October, pp. 649–56.

Missiroli, M. 1929. "Luigi Cadorna." *Nuova antologia,* 64(1367): 43–65.

Misuraca, P. 1980. "Politica, ecomonia, diritto, sociologia come scienze dello Stato." *Critica marxista* 18(5):65–87.

Mola, A. A. 1976. *Storia della massoneria in Italia dall'Unità alla Repubblica.* Milan: Bompiani.

Mola, A. A. 1982. "Gaetano Mosca e la massoneria." In Albertoni (1982a), pp. 435–44.

Monasta, A. 1985. *L'educazione tradita: Criteri per una diversa valutazione complessiva dei "Quaderni del carcere" di Antonio Gramsci.* Pisa: Giardini Editori e Stampatori.

Mongardini, C. 1965. "Mosca, Pareto e Taine." *Cahiers Viefredo Pareto* 5:175–86.

Mongardini, C., ed. 1980a. *Carteggio Mosca-Ferrero, 1896–1934.* Milan: Giuffrè.

Mongardini, C. 1980b. "Mosca e Ferrero: Storia di un'amicizia." In Mongardini (1980a), pp. 1–71.

Mongardini, C. 1982. "Società e politica in Italia alla luce dell'Archivio Mosca." In Albertoni (1982a), pp. 151–62.

Morera, E. 1990a. "Gramsci and Democracy." *Canadian Journal of Political Science* 23:23–37.

Morera, E. 1990b. *Gramsci's Historicism: A Realist Interpretation.* New York: Routledge.

Morpurgo-Tagliabue, G. 1948. "Gramsci tra Croce e Marx." *Il Ponte* 4(5):429–38.

Mosca, G. 1884. *Sulla teorica dei governi e sul governo parlamentare: Studi storici e sociali.* Turin: Loescher. [2nd ed., Milan: Società anonima istituto editoriale scientifico, 1925. Reprints: Mosca (1958), pp. 17–328; 1968; Mosca (1982), pp. 183–542.]

Mosca, G. 1887. *Le costituzioni moderne.* Palermo: Amenta. [Reprinted in Mosca (1958), pp. 445–549.]

Mosca, G. 1896. *Elementi di scienza politica.* Turin: Bocca.

Mosca, G. 1898. *Questioni pratiche di diritto constituzionale.* Turin: Bocca. [Reprinted in Mosca (1958), pp. 337–52.]

Mosca, G. 1901. "Un nuovo libro sulla democrazia americana." Reprinted in Mosca (1971), pp. 445–53.

Mosca, G. 1907. "Piccola polemica." Reprinted in Mosca (1949), pp. 116–20.

Mosca, G. 1908. *Appunti di diritto costituzionale.* Milan: Società Editrice Libraria. [3rd ed., 1921. Reprinted in Mosca (1958), pp. 551–90.]

Mosca, G. 1912a. "Intervento alla Camera dei Deputati, 14 Maggio." *Atti Parlamentari,* Camera dei Deputati, Legislatura XXIII, Sessione I, Discussioni, vol. 16, pp. 19357–59. Rome: Tipografia della Camera dei Deputati.

Mosca, G. 1912b. *Italia e Libia. Considerazioni politiche.* Milan: Treves.

Mosca, G. 1913. "Risposta ad un'inchiesta sulla massoneria." Reprinted in *Inchiesta sulla massoneria* (1925), pp. 162–66.

Mosca, G. 1920. "Feudalismo e sindacalismo: Il pericolo presente." *La Tribuna* (Rome), 1 February, 37(28):1.

Mosca, G. 1921. "Intervento al Senato, 29 Luglio." *Atti Parlamentari,* Senato del Regno, Legislatura XXVI, Sessione I, Discussioni, vol. 1, pp. 208–11. Rome: Tipografia del Senato.

Mosca, G. 1922. "Intervento al Senato, 27 Novembre." *Atti Parlamentari,* Senato del Regno, Legislatura XXVI, Sessione I, Discussioni, vol. 4, pp. 4240–42. Rome: Tipografia del Senato.

Mosca, G. 1923a. *Elementi di scienza politica.* 2nd ed. Turin: Bocca. [3rd ed. Bari, Italy: Laterza, 1939. Reprinted in Mosca (1982), pp. 543–1158.]

Mosca, G. 1923b. "Intervento al Senato, 13 Novembre." *Atti Parlamentari,* Senato del Regno, Legislatura XXVI, Sessione I, Discussioni, vol. 5, pp. 5365–68. Rome: Tipografia del Senato.

Mosca, G. 1923c. "Risposta." In *Dove va il mondo? Inchiesta tra scrittori italiani con una conclusione di A. Ghisleri.* Rome: Libreria politica moderna.

Mosca, G. 1925a. "Intervento al Senato, 13 Febbraio." *Atti Parlamentari,* Senato del Regno, Legislatura XXVII, Sessione I, Discussioni, vol. 2, pp. 1665–68. Rome: Tipografia del Senato.

Mosca, G. 1925b. "Intervento al Senato, 17 Novembre." *Atti Parlamentari,* Senato del Regno, Legislatura XXVII, Sessione I, Discussioni, vol. 4, pp. 3619–21. Rome: Tipografia del Senato.

Mosca, G. 1925c. "Intervento al Senato, 18 Novembre." *Atti Parlamentari,* Senato del Regno, Legislatura XXVII, Sessione I, Discussioni, vol. 4, pp. 3660–62. Rome: Tipografia del Senato.

Mosca, G. 1925d. "Prerogative del capo del governo." (Senate speech, 19 December 1925). Reprinted in Mosca (1949), pp. 277–84.

Mosca, G. 1937. *Storia della dottrine politiche.* Bari, Italy: Laterza.

Mosca, G. 1939. *The Ruling Class.* Trans. H. D. Kahn. Ed. and intro., A. Livingston. New York: McGraw-Hill. [Reprint. Westport, Conn.: Greenwood Press, 1980.]

Mosca, G. 1949. *Partiti e sindacati nella crisi del regime parlamentare.* Bari, Italy: Laterza.

Mosca, G. 1958. *Ciò che la storia potrebbe insegnare. Scritti di scienza politica.* Milan: Giuffrè.

Mosca, G. 1964. *Storia delle dottrine politiche.* "Universale Laterza" edition. Bari, Italy: Laterza.

Mosca, G. 1966. *La classe politica.* Ed. N. Bobbio. Bari, Italy: Laterza.

Mosca, G. 1971. *Il tramonto dello stato liberale.* Ed. A. Lombardo. Preface by G. Spadolini. Catania, Italy: Bonanno.

Mosca, G. 1972. *A Short History of Political Philosophy.* Trans. S. Z. Koff. New York: Thomas Y. Crowell.

Mosca, G. 1974. *Scritti sui sindacati.* Ed. F. Perfetti and M. Ortolani. Rome: Bulzoni.

Mosca, G. 1982. *Scritti politici.* 2 vols. Ed. G. Sola. Turin: UTET.

Mouffe, C., ed. 1979. *Gramsci and Marxist Theory.* Boston: Routledge.

Muscatello, B., ed. 1990. *Gramsci e il marxismo contemporaneo.* Rome: Editori Riuniti.

Mussolini, B. 1925. "Disegno di Legge n. 314, 12 gennaio 1925." *Atti Parlamentari,* Camera del Deputati, Legislatura XXVII, Sessione 1924–25, Documenti, Disegni di Leggi e Relazioni, vol. 9, no. 314. Rome: Tipografia della Camera dei Deputati.

Nardone, G. 1971. *Il pensiero di Gramsci.* Bari, Italy: De Donato.

Natoli, A. 1990. *Antigone e il prigioniero: Tania Schucht lotta per la vita di Gramsci.* Rome: Editori Riuniti.

Nemeth, T. 1980. *Gramsci's Philosophy: A Critical Study.* Atlantic Highlands, N.J.: Humanities.

Nieddu, L. 1990. *L'altro Gramsci.* Cagliari, Italy: GIA Editrice.

Novak, M. 1989. "The Gramscists Are Coming." *Forbes,* 20 March, p. 54.

Nowell-Smith, G. 1977. "Gramsci and the National-Popular." *Screen Education* 22:12–15.

Nun, J. 1987. "Elementos para una teoria de la democracia: Gramsci y el sentido comun." *Revista mexicana de sociología* 49(2):21–54.

Nye, R. A. 1975. *The Origins of Crowd Psychology: Gustave Le Bon and the Crisis of Mass Democracy in the Third Republic.* London: Sage.

Nye, R. A. 1977. *The Anti-Democratic Sources of Elite Theory: Pareto, Mosca, Michels.* London: Sage.

Oddo, F. L. 1982. "Suggestioni marxiane da approfondire nella 'Teorica dei Governi.'" In Albertoni (1982a), pp. 483–87.

Orfei, R. 1965. *Antonio Gramsci, coscienza critica del marxismo.* San Casciano, Italy: Relazioni Sociali.

Ortolani, N. 1974. "Sindacato e conflitto politico in Gaetano Mosca." In Mosca (1974), pp. 29–46.

Otte, M., and M. Panza, eds. 1997. *Analysis and Synthesis in Mathematics: History and Philosophy.* Dordrecht, The Netherlands: Kluwer.

Paggi, L. 1969. "Machiavelli e Gramsci." *Studi storici* 10:833–76.

Paggi, L. 1970. *Antonio Gramsci e il moderno principe.* Rome: Editori Riuniti.

Paggi, L. 1974. "La teoria generale del marxismo in Gramsci." In *Annali Feltrinelli XV (1973),* pp. 1319–70. Milan: Feltrinelli.

Paggi, L. 1977. "Gramsci's General Theory of Marxism." *Telos,* no. 33 (Fall): 27–70. [Reprinted in Mouffe (1979), pp. 113–67.]

Paggi, L. 1984. *Le strategie del potere in Gramsci.* Rome: Editori Riuniti.

Pala, A. 1960. *Il rapporto uomo-natura in Antonio Gramsci.* Sassari, Italy: Palumbo.

Panichi, N. 1985. *Antonio Gramsci, storia della filosofia e filosofia.* Urbino: Università degli Studi di Urbino.

Panunzio, S. 1933. "La fine del parlamentarismo e l'accentramento della responsabilità." *Gerarchia* 11(4):298–305.

Papini, G., and G. Prezzolini. 1914. *Vecchio e nuovo nazionalismo.* Milan: Studio Editoriale Lombardo.

Pareto, V. 1902. *Les systèmes socialistes.* 2 vols. Paris: Marcel Giard.

Pareto, V. 1913. "Risposta ad una inchiesta sulla massoneria." Reprinted in *Inchiesta sulla massoneria* (1925), pp. 182–85.

Pareto, V. 1935. *The Mind and Society.* 4 vols. Ed. A. Livingston. Trans. A. Bongiorno and A. Livingston. New York: Harcourt Brace.

Pareto, V. 1950. *The Ruling Class in Italy Before 1900.* New York: Vanni.

Pareto, V. 1964. *Trattato di sociologia generale* (1923). 2 vols. Ed. N. Bobbio. Milan: Edizioni di Comunità.

Parry, G. 1969. *Political Elites.* New York: Praeger.

Passerin d'Entreves, A. 1961. "Le *elites* politiche." In Treves (1961), pp. 111–16.

Paulesu Quercioli, M., ed. 1977. *Gramsci vivo nelle testimonianze dei suoi contemporanei.* Milan: Feltrinelli Economica.

Paulesu Quercioli, M., ed. 1987. *Forse rimarrai lontana . . . (Lettere a Iulca, 1922–1937).* Rome: Editori Riuniti.

Paulesu Quercioli, M. 1991. *Le donne di casa Gramsci.* Rome: Editori Riuniti.

Pellicani, L. 1974. *Dinamica delle rivoluzioni.* Milan: Sugarco.

Pellicani, L. 1975. *I rivoluzionari di professione.* Florence: Vallecchi.

Pellicani, L. 1976. *Gramsci e la questione comunista.* Florence: Vallecchi.

Pellicani, L. 1981. *Gramsci: An Alternative Communism?* Stanford, Calif.: Hoover Institution.

Pellicani, L. 1990. *Gramsci, Togliatti e il PCI.* Rome: Armando.

Pennati, E. 1961. "Le *elites* politiche nelle teoriche minoritarie." In Treves (1961), pp. 3–53.

Peregalli, A., ed. 1978. *Il comunismo di sinistra e Gramsci.* Bari, Italy: Dedalo Libri.

Perez Miranda, R., ed. 1987. *Clase politica y elites politicas.* (Seminario "Clase Politica, Elites Politicas y Partidos Politicos." Tlaxcala, Mexico, 1984.) [Mexico City]: Plaza y Valdez.

Perfetti, F. 1974. "I sindacati nella scienza politica di Gaetano Mosca." In Mosca (1974), pp. 7–27.

Pergolesi, F. 1957. "Appunti sulla 'scienza politica' di Gaetano Mosca." *Sociologia* 2(3):213–68.

Perlini, T. 1974. *Gramsci e il gramscismo.* Milan: CELUC.

Perrotti, G. 1977. "Gramsci, Ricardo e la filosofia della prassi." *Lavoro critico,* no. 9 (January–March):109–56.

Piccone, P. 1976. "Gramsci's Marxism: Beyond Lenin and Togliatti." *Theory and Society* 3:485–512.

Piccone, P. 1977. "From Spaventa to Gramsci." *Telos,* no. 31 (Spring):35–65.

Piccone, P. 1977-78. "Labriola and the Roots of Eurocommunism." *Berkeley Journal of Sociology* 32:3–44.

Piccone, P. 1983. *Italian Marxism.* Berkeley: University of California Press.

Piccone, P. 1992. "Gramsci's *Prison Notebooks*—The Remake." *Telos,* no. 90 (Winter):178–83.

Pierini, F. 1978. *Gramsci e la storiologia della rivoluzione (1914–1920): Studio storico-semantico.* Rome: Edizioni Paoline.

Piñón, F. 1989. *Gramsci: Prolegómenos, filosofia y politica.* Mexico City: Plaza y Valdes; Centro de Estudios Sociales Antonio Gramsci.

Piovani, P. 1950. "Il liberalismo di Gaetano Mosca." *Rassegna di diritto pubblico* 5(3–4):265–305.

Pistillo, M. 1989. *Gramsci Come Moro?* Rome: Piero Lacaita Editore.

Pizzorno, A. 1969. "Sul metodo di Gramsci: Dalla storiografia alla scienza politica." In Pietro Rossi (1969), vol. 2, pp. 109–26.

Pizzorno, A. 1972. "Sistema sociale e classe politica." In *Storia delle idee politiche, economiche, e sociali,* ed. L. Firpo, vol. 6. Turin: UTET.

Plamenetz, J. 1973. *Democracy and Illusion.* London: Longman.

Poggi, A. 1929. Review of C. A. Biggini, *Il fondamento dei limiti all'attività dello Stato. L'Italia che scrive* 12:295.

Popper, K. R. 1957. *The Poverty of Historicism.* London: Routledge.

Popper, K. R. 1959. *The Logic of Scientific Discovery.* New York: Basic Books.

Popper, K. R. 1963. *Conjectures and Refutations.* New York: Harper.

Popper, K. R. 1966. *The Open Society and Its Enemies* (1945). Vol. 2. 5th ed. Princeton, N.J.: Princeton University Press.

Popper, K. R. 1979. *Objective Knowledge: An Evolutionary Approach.* Rev. ed. Oxford: Clarendon Press.

Portantiero, J. C. 1979. "Gramsci y el analisis de coyuntura (algunas notas)." *Revista mexicana de sociología* 41 (January–March):59–73.

Portantiero, J. C. 1981a. "Lo nacional-popular y la alternativa democratica en America Latina." In *American Latina 80: Democracia y movimiento popular,* pp. 230–50. Lima, Peru: Desco.

Portantiero, J. C. 1981b. *Los Usos de Gramsci.* Mexico City: Folios.

Portantiero, J. C. 1988. "O nacional-popular: Gramsci em chave latino-ameri-cana." In *Gramsci e a America Latina*, ed. C. N. Coutinho and M. A. No-gueira, pp. 47–60. Rio de Janeiro: Paz e Terra.

Portelli, H. 1972. *Gramsci et le bloc historique*. Paris: Presses Universitaires de France.

Portelli, H. 1974. *Gramsci et la question religieuse*. Paris: Anthropos.

Pozzolini, A. 1970. *Antonio Gramsci: An Introduction to His Thought*. London: Pluto.

Premoli, A. 1982. "Gramsci, Luigi Russo e l'indirizzo nazional-popolare." *Belfa-gor* 37:497–512.

Prestipino, G. 1979. *Da Gramsci a Marx*. Rome: Editori Riuniti.

Prestipino, G. 1987. "Filosofo democratico." In Ricchini (1987), pp. 96–97.

Prezzolini, G. 1903. "L'aristocrazia dei briganti." *Il Regno* (Florence) 13 Decem-ber. [Reprinted in Papini and Prezzolini (1914), pp. 37–47.]

Putnam, H. 1962. "The Analytic and the Synthetic." In *Minnesota Studies in the Philosophy of Science*, vol. 3, *Scientific Explanation, Space, and Time*, ed. H. Feigl and G. Maxwell, pp. 358–97. Minneapolis: University of Minnesota Press.

Putnam, R. D. 1976. *The Comparative Study of Political Elites*. Englewood Cliffs, N.J.: Prentice-Hall.

Putnam, R. D. 1992. *Making Democracy Work: Civic Traditions in Modern Italy*. Princeton, N.J.: Princeton University Press.

Quagliariello, G., ed. 1990. *Il partito politico nella belle époque: Il dibattito sulla forma-partito in Italia tra '800 e '900*. Milan: Giuffrè.

Quine, W. V. O. 1963. *From a Logical Point of View*. New York: Harper Torch-books.

Ragazzini, D. 1976. *Società industriale e formazione umana*. Rome: Editori Riu-niti.

Ragazzini, D. 1991. "Consistenza e dinamica delle categorie gramsciane: Un ap-proccio lessicologico di filologia elettronica." Paper presented at the Gramsci Conference, Pavia, 17–19 October.

Ragionieri, E. 1976. *La storia politica e sociale*. In *Storia d'Italia*, vol. 4, book 3. Turin: Einaudi.

Ravera, C. 1973. *Diario di trent'anni, 1913–1943*. Rome: Editori Riuniti.

Razeto Migliaro, L., and P. Misuraca. 1978. *Sociologia e marxismo nella critica di Gramsci*. Bari, Italy: De Donato.

Ricchini, C., E. Manca, and L. Melograni, eds. 1987. *Antonio Gramsci: Le sue idee nel nostro tempo*. Rome: Editrice L'Unità.

Riechers, C. 1970. *Antonio Gramsci: Marxismus in Italien*. Frankfurt: Euro-päische Verlagsanstalt.

Ripepe, E. 1971. *Le origini della teoria della classe politica*. Milan: Giuffrè.

Ripepe, E. 1974. *Gli elitisti italiani*. 2 vols. Pisa: Pacini.

Ripepe, E. 1982. "Due apparenti paradossi nell'opera di Gaetano Mosca: Meritocrazia come democrazia e idealismo come realismo sociologico." *Il pensiero politico* 15:514–24.

Ripepe, E. 1983. "Intellettuali, classe politica e consenso nel pensiero di Gaetano Mosca." In Albertoni (1983a), pp. 157–81.

Romeo, R. 1951. *Risorgimento e capitalismo.* Bari, Italy: Laterza.

Rossi, Paolo. 1976. "Antonio Gramsci sulla scienza moderna." *Critica marxista* 14(2):41–60.

Rossi, Pietro. 1949. "Liberalismo e regime parlamentare in Gaetano Mosca." *Giornale degli economisti* 8(11–12):621–34.

Rossi, Pietro, ed. 1969. *Gramsci e la cultura contemporanea.* 2 vols. Rome: Editori Riuniti and Istituto Gramsci.

Sabetti, F. 1982. "Mosca in Canadian Social Science." In Albertoni (1982c), pp. 165–80.

Salamini, L. 1981. *The Sociology of Political Praxis: An Introduction to Gramsci's Theory.* Boston: Routledge.

Salmon, W. C. 1984a. *Logic.* 3rd ed. Englewood Cliffs, N.J.: Prentice-Hall.

Salmon, W. C. 1984b. *Scientific Explanation and the Causal Structure of the World.* Princeton, N.J.: Princeton University Press.

Salvadori, M. L. 1976. "Gramsci e il PCI: Due concezioni dell'egemonia." *Mondoperaio* 29(11):59–68.

Salvadori, M. L. 1977. *Gramsci e il problema storico della democrazia* (1970). 2nd ed. Turin: Einaudi.

Sanguineti, F. 1982. *Gramsci e Machiavelli.* Bari, Italy: Laterza.

Santarelli, E., ed. 1991. *Gramsci ritrovato, 1937–1947.* Catanzaro, Italy: Abramo Editore.

Sartori, G. 1959. *Democrazia e definizioni.* Bologna: Il Mulino.

Sartori, G. 1961. "I significati del termine elite." In Treves (1961), pp. 94–99.

Sartori, G. 1962a. *Democratic Theory.* Detroit: Wayne State University Press. (Reprint. Westport, Conn.: Greenwood Press, 1973.)

Sartori, G. 1962b. "Preface to the American Edition." In Sartori (1962a), pp. vii–xi.

Sartori, G. 1966. *Stato e politica nel pensiero di Benedetto Croce: Una radiografia critica delle strutture essenziali della dottrina politica crociana.* Naples: Morano.

Sartori, G. 1976. *Parties and Party Systems: A Framework for Analysis.* Cambridge: Cambridge University Press.

Sartori, G. 1977. "Democrazia competitiva e elites politiche." *Rivista italiana di scienza politica* 7(3):327–55.

Sartori, G. 1978. "Anti-Elitism Revisited." *Government and Opposition* 13(1):58–80.

Sartori, G. 1982. *Teoria dei partiti e caso italiano.* Milan: Sugarco.

Sartori, G. 1987. *The Theory of Democracy Revisited.* 2 vols. Chatham, N.J.: Chatham House.

Sasso, G. 1950. "Antonio Gramsci, interprete di Machiavelli." *Lo Spettatore italiano,* April, 3(4):91–93.

Sassoli, D., ed. 1977. *Oltre Gramsci?* Rome: Cinque Lune.

Sassoon, A. S. 1980. "Gramsci: A New Concept of Politics and the Expansion of Democracy." In *Marxism and Democracy,* ed. A. Hunt, pp. 81–99. London: Lawrence and Wishart.

Sassoon, A. S., ed. 1982. *Approaches to Gramsci.* London: Writers and Readers.

Sassoon, A. S. 1987. *Gramsci's Politics* (1980). 2nd ed. Minneapolis: University of Minnesota Press.

Saville, J. 1973. "The Ideology of Labourism." In *Knowledge and Belief in Politics,* ed. R. Benewick, R. N. Berki, and B. Parekh, pp. 213–26. New York: St. Martin's.

Sbarberi, F. 1986. *Gramsci: Un socialismo armonico.* Milan: Franco Angeli.

Sbarberi, F., ed. 1988. *Teoria politica e società industriale: Ripensare Gramsci.* Turin: Bollati Boringhieri.

Schecter, D. 1991. *Gramsci and the Theory of Industrial Democracy.* Brookfield, Vt: Avebury.

Schucht, T. 1991. *Lettere ai familiari.* Preface by G. Gramsci. Ed. and introduction by M. Paulesu Quercioli. Rome: Editori Riuniti.

Schumpeter, J. A. 1950. *Capitalism, Socialism, and Democracy.* New York: Harper.

Scriven, M. 1958. "Definitions, Explanations, and Theories." In *Minnesota Studies in the Philsophy of Science,* vol. 2, *Concepts, Theories, and the Mind-Body Problem,* ed. H. Feigl, M. Scriven, and G. Maxwell, pp. 99–195. Minneapolis: University of Minnesota Press.

Scuderi San Filippo, G. 1980. *Da Vico a Gramsci (Linee italiane dello storicismo pedagogico e didattico).* Catania, Italy: Edigraf.

Segre, S. 1985. *Weber, Mosca, Pareto. La teoria della stratificazione sociale: Un'analisi comparativa.* Milan: Franco Angeli.

Sereno, R. 1962. *The Rulers.* New York: Praeger.

Sgambati, V. 1979. "Per un'analisi del rapporto tra Gramsci e gli elitisti." In Ferri (1977), vol. 2, pp. 606–16.

Sichirollo, L. 1973. *La dialettica.* Milan: ISEDI, Istituto Editoriale Internazionale.

Simon, R. 1982. *Gramsci's Political Thought: An Introduction.* London: Lawrence and Wishart.

Skyrms, B. 1975. *Choice and Chance: An Introduction to Inductive Logic.* 2d ed. Encino, Calif.: Dickenson.

Sochor, L. 1967. "Antonio Gramsci e la questione delle elites politiche." *Praxis* (Zagreb), 3(3):340–45.

Società politica e Stato in Hegel, Marx e Gramsci. 1977. Padua: CLEUP.

Sola, G. 1970. "Per un'analisi della teoria della classe politica nelle opere di Gaetano Mosca." *Annali della facoltà di giurisprudenza della Università di Genova* 9(2):673–744. Milan: Giuffrè.

Sola, G. 1982a. "Elements for a Critical Re-Appraisal of the Works of Gaetano Mosca." In Albertoni (1982c), pp. 91-112.

Sola, G. 1982b. "Gaetano Mosca: Profilo biografico." In Albertoni (1982c), pp. 17-52.

Sola, G. 1982c. Introduction. In Mosca (1982), vol. 1, pp. 9-79.

Sola, G. 1982d. "Una rilettura critica dei pricipali testi di Gaetano Mosca." In Albertoni (1982c), pp. 163-88.

Sola, G. 1983. "L'analisi dei partiti politici in Gaetano Mosca." In Albertoni (1983a), pp. 271-95.

Sola, G. 1984. "Scienza e teoria nei padri fondatori della scienza politica italiana." *Quaderni della Fondazione Giangiacomo Feltrinelli*, nos. 28-29, pp. 407-40.

Sola, G. 1985. "Classe politica ed elite del potere in Mosca e Pareto." *Teoria politica* 1(2):117-52.

Sola, G. 1989. "La democrazia rivisitata da Sartori: Una nota." *Rivista italiana di scienza politica* 19(1):113-36.

Sola, G. 1991. "L'impatto del fascismo sulla scienza politica in Italia." In *Fra scienza e professione: Saggi sullo sviluppo della scienza politica*, ed. L. Graziano, D. Easton, and J. Gunnell, pp. 193-229. Milan: Franco Angeli.

Solari, G. 1930. Review of W. C. Sforza, *"Jus" et "directum."* Leonardo 1:504-5.

Somai, G. 1979. *Gramsci a Vienna: Ricerche e documenti 1922-1924.* Urbino: Argalia.

[Sonnino, S.] 1897. "Torniamo allo Statuto." *Nuova antologia* (Rome), 1 January, vol. 151 (4th series, vol. 67), no. 1, pp. 9-28. [Reprinted in Valeri (1976), pp. 251-69.]

Spadolini, G. 1971. Preface. In Mosca (1971), pp. 7-17.

Spinazzola, V. 1987. "Nazional-popolare." In Ricchini (1987), pp. 113-15.

Spinella, M. 1988. *Sei lezioni su Gramsci (1965).* Pavia, Italy: Fototipolitografia Bizzoni.

Spirito, U. 1929. "Verso l'economia corporativa." *Nuovi studi di diritto, economia e politica* 2(5):233-52.

Spirito, U. 1930a. *La critica della economia liberale.* Milan: Treves.

Spirito, U. 1930b. "La libertà economica." *Nuovi studi di diritto, economia e politica* 3(4):292-301.

Spirito, U. 1930c. "La storia dell'economia e il concetto di Stato." *Nuovi studi di diritto, economia e politica* 3(5):321-24.

Spirito, U. 1932. "Individuo e Stato nella concezione corporativa." *Nuovi studi di diritto, economia e politica* 5(2):84-93.

Spitz, D. 1949. *Patterns of Anti-Democratic Thought.* New York: Free Press.

Spriano, P. 1977. *Gramsci in carcere e il partito.* Rome: Editori Riuniti.

Spriano, P. 1979. *Antonio Gramsci and the Party: The Prison Years.* London: Lawrence and Wishart. [Translation of Spriano (1977).]

Sraffa, P. 1991. *Lettere a Tania per Gramsci.* Ed. V. Gerratana. Rome: Editori Riuniti.

Sternhell, Z. 1986. *Neither Right nor Left: Fascist Ideology in France.* Trans. D. Maisel. Berkeley: University of California Press.

Stölting, E. 1987. "Armer Gramsci: Über Hegemonie, Kultur und politische Gegenwartsstrategien." *Leviathan: Zeitschrift für Sozialwissenschaft* 15:266-84.

Struve, W. 1973. *Elites Against Democracy: Leadership Ideals in Bourgeois Political Thought in Germany, 1890-1933.* Princeton, N.J.: Princeton University Press.

Suppa, S. 1976. *Il primo Gramsci: Gli scritti politici giovanili (1914-1918).* Naples: Editore Jovene.

Suppa, S. 1979. *Consiglio e Stato in Gramsci e Lenin.* Bari, Italy: Dedalo.

Tamburrano, G. 1977. *Antonio Gramsci: Una biografia critica.* 2nd ed. Milan: Sugarco. (1st ed. *Antonio Gramsci: La vita, il pensiero, l'azione.* Manduria, Italy: Lacaita, 1963.)

Tanturri, R. 1973. *Pensiero e significato di Gaetano Mosca ed altri scritti.* Padua: CEDAM.

Tasca, A. 1972. *I primi dieci anni del Partito comunista italiano.* 2nd ed. Bari, Italy: Laterza.

Tega, W., ed. 1990. *Gramsci e l'Occidente: Trasformazioni della società e riforma della politica.* Bologna: Cappelli Editore.

Terracini, U. 1975. *Sulla svolta: Carteggio clandestino dal carcere, 1930-31-32.* Milan: La Pietra.

Texier, J. 1969. "Gramsci, théoricien des superstructures." *La pensée* 139:35-60.

Thellung, F. 1983. *Antonio Gramsci: La strategia rivoluzionaria nei paesi a capitalismo avanzato.* Genoa: Tilgher.

Thoenes, P. 1966. *The Elite in the Welfare State.* Trans. J. E. Bingham. New York: Free Press.

Tilman, R. 1984. *C. Wright Mills: A Native Radical and His American Intellectual Roots.* University Park: Pennsylvania State University Press.

Tilman, R. 1987. "The Neo-Instrumentalist Theory of Democracy." *Journal of Economic Issues* 21(3):1379-1401.

Tilman, R., and M. Clarke. 1988. "C. B. Macpherson's Contribution to Democratic Theory." *Journal of Economic Issues* 22(1):181-96.

Togliatti, P. 1962. *La formazione del gruppo dirigente del Partito comunista italiano nel 1923-1924.* Rome: Editori Riuniti.

Togliatti, P. 1972. *Antonio Gramsci.* Ed. E. Ragionieri. Rome: Editori Riuniti.

Togliatti, P. 1979. *On Gramsci and Other Writings.* London: Lawrence and Wishart.

Tomiolo, A. 1979. "Le note sul 'nazional-popolare.'" In *Gramsci un'eredità contrastata* (1979), pp. 84-90.

Tosin, B. 1976. *Con Gramsci: Ricordi di uno della "vecchia guardia."* Rome: Editori Riuniti.

Treitschke, H. von. 1897-98. *Politik: Vorlesungen gehalten an der Universität zu Berlin.* 2 vols. Leipzig: Hirzel.

Treitschke, H. von. 1916. *Politics*. 2 vols. Trans. B. Dugdale and T. De Bille. New York: Macmillan.

Treves, R., ed. 1961. *Le elites politiche*. Bari, Italy: Laterza.

Vacca, G. 1989. "Americanismo e rivoluzioni passiva—L'Urss staliniana nell'analisi dei Quaderni." In Baratta and Catone (1989), pp. 317–36.

Vacca, G. 1991. *Gramsci e Togliatti*. Rome: Editori Riuniti.

Valeri, N. 1976. *La lotta politica in Italia dall'Unità al 1925*. Florence: Le Monnier.

Van den Berghe, P. L. 1969. "Dialectic and Functionalism: Toward a Theoretical Synthesis." In *Sociological Theory: An Introduction*, ed. W. L. Wallace, pp. 202–13. Chicago: Aldine. [Reprinted from *American Sociological Review* 28(1963):695–705.]

Vasale, C. 1979. *Politica e religione in A. Gramsci: L'ateodicea della secolarizzazione*. Rome: Edizioni di Storia e Letteratura.

Vecchini, F. 1968. *La pensée politique de Gaetano Mosca et ses différentes adaptations au cours du XXe siècle en Italie*. Paris: Editions Cujas.

Viglongo, A., ed. 1977. *Almanacco piemontese*. Turin: Viglongo.

Vigna, C. 1979. "Gramsci e l'egemonia: Una interpretazione metapolitica." In Melchiorre, Vigna, and De Rosa (1979), vol. 1, pp. 11–69.

Vinco, R. 1983. *Una fede senze futuro? Religione e mondo cattolico in Gramsci*. Verona: Mazziana.

Wagner, B. 1991. "La radicale provvisozietà del pensiero." *Il Manifesto*, 6 November.

Walker, J. L. 1966. "A Critique of the Elitist Theory of Democracy." *American Political Science Review* 60(2):285–95. [Reprinted in Bachrach (1971), pp. 69–92.]

Wallace, W. A. 1992. *Galileo's Logic of Discovery and Proof: The Background, Content, and Use of His Appropriated Treatises on Aristotle's* Posterior Analytics. Dordrecht, The Netherlands: Kluwer.

Walzer, M. 1988a. "The Ambiguous Legacy of Antonio Gramsci." *Dissent* 35: 444–56.

Walzer, M. 1988b. *The Company of Critics: Social Criticism and Political Commitment in the Twentieth Century*. New York: Basic Books.

Williams, G. 1975. *Proletarian Order: Antonio Gramsci, Factory Councils, and the Origins of Italian Communism*. London: Pluto.

Wilson, W. 1900. "Preface to the Fifteenth Printing." In Wilson (1956), pp. 19–23.

Wilson, W. 1908. *Constitutional Government in the United States*. New York: Columbia University Press.

Wilson, W. 1956. *Congressional Government: A Study in American Politics* (1885). Reprint. Cleveland, Ohio: Meridian.

Winthrop, N., ed. 1983. *Liberal Democratic Theory and Its Critics*. Beckenham, England: Croom Helm.

Wolin, S. S. 1967. Foreword. In Bachrach (1967), pp. v–x.

Zacheo, E. 1991. *Gramsci, la democrazia, la cultura.* Manduria, Bari, and Rome: Piero Lacaita Editore.

Zannoni, P. 1977. "Il concetto di elite." *Rivista italiana di scienza politica* 7(1):357-91.

Zarone, G. 1990. *Classe politica e ragione scientifica: Mosca Croce Gramsci: Problemi della scienza politica in Italia tra Otto e Novecento.* Naples and Rome: Edizione Scientifiche Italiane.

Zolo, D. 1992a. *Democracy and Complexity: A Realist Approach.* University Park: Pennsylvania State University Press.

Zolo, D. 1992b. *Il principato democratico: Per una teoria realistica della democrazia.* Milan: Feltrinelli.

Zucaro, D. 1952. "Gramsci a San Vittore per l'istruttoria del processone." *Il Movimento di liberazione in Italia* 16:3-16.

Zucaro, D. 1954. *Vita del carcere di Antonio Gramsci.* Milan and Rome: Edizioni Avanti!

Zucaro, D. 1957. "Gramsci all'università di Torino 1911-1915." *Società* 13(6):1091-1111.

Zucaro, D. 1961. *Il processone: Gramsci e i dirigenti comunisti dinanzi al tribunale speciale.* Rome: Editori Riuniti.

Zuckerman, A. 1977. "The Concept of 'Political Elite': Lessons from Mosca and Pareto." *Journal of Politics* 39(2):324-44.

INDEX